POLICE PROFESSIONALISM
The Renaissance of American Law Enforcement

POLICE PROFESSIONALISM
The Renaissance of American Law Enforcement

By

THOMAS J. DEAKIN, J.D.

Special Agent
Federal Bureau of Investigation
Editor, FBI Law Enforcement Bulletin

With a Foreword by
Clarence M. Kelley

CHARLES C THOMAS • PUBLISHER
Springfield • Illinois • U.S.A.

Published and Distributed Throughout the World by

CHARLES C THOMAS • PUBLISHER
2600 South First Street
Springfield, Illinois 62794-9265

© *1988 by* CHARLES C THOMAS • PUBLISHER

ISBN 0-398-05471-1

Library of Congress Catalog Card Number: 88-2143

Printed in the United States of America
SC-R-3

Library of Congress Cataloging-in-Publication Data

Deakin, Thomas J.
    Police professionalism.

    Bibliography: p.
    Includes index.
    1. Police professionalization—United States—
History.   2. Law enforcement—United States—History.
I. Title.
HV8141.D42   1988   363.2′0973   88-2143
ISBN 0-398-05471-1

Dedicated to my sons, Danford and Douglas,
and to my wife, Carol,
who rekindled for me, by example,
the spirit of scholarship

FOREWORD

The principal responsibility for controlling crime in the last century has been with the police. Today, this responsibility remains law enforcement's, but in cooperation with a responsible citizenry who know that this task must include the whole community. How well this responsibility is discharged depends, in part, upon the professionalism that we in law enforcement bring to the task. The police have led the way toward their own professionalism, and today our citizens, realizing this, have joined with police and the entire criminal justice system to make our communities safer.

According to the dictionary, professionalism requires "long and intensive preparation including . . . scientific, historical, or scholarly principles." Professionalism includes a commitment to "a kind of work which has for its prime purpose the rendering of a public service." Today, law enforcement has traveled a long way toward meeting these standards of professionalism. Intensive preparation is achieved through the training now required of police officers, although educational standards still need to be raised.

Over the last fifty years, training toward professionalism has been one of the goals of the FBI. In response to the American people's demand in the 1930s for improved law enforcement, the FBI expanded its service to police function to include training and laboratory services. Of the two missions of the FBI—one, to be the premier investigative arm of the federal government, the other to be the service arm of the entire law enforcement community—both have had great impact on the development of law enforcement professionalism.

Fingerprint identification, uniform crime reporting, scientific crime detection, the FBI National Academy and other police training, and the *FBI Law Enforcement Bulletin* have all been major contributions toward police professionalism that, over the years, have been a source of pride to me and to all the men and women of the FBI.

This book is an effort to outline the historical aspect of law enforcement professionalism that the author has observed at first hand. A veteran FBI Agent, a former police officer with an undergraduate degree in political science and a graduate degree in law from Washington University, and a fellow Missourian, Special Agent Deakin has had a unique perspective on the last 25 years of police history. His editing of the *FBI Law Enforcement Bulletin* for the past decade has represented the best in professionalism. As a long-time student of history and a career peace officer he brings a practical perspective to this study and documentation of the history of police professionalism, along with an academic background. This work will be an asset to police as they progress in professionalism.

One mark of professionalism is an academic tradition—and that includes the history of the calling. This volume tells the history of professionalism in law enforcement which began, of course, before the FBI existed, but which took a giant step forward when the FBI pointed the way. I am proud that the FBI continued this tradition of service to the law enforcement profession during my term as Director and beyond, during Judge William Webster's tenure.

Clarence M. Kelley
Director, FBI, 1973–1978
Chief of Police, Kansas City, Missouri,
1961–1973

PREFACE

J. Edgar Hoover, Director of the Federal Bureau of Investigation for forty-eight years, said that the 1930s brought a "renaissance" to American law enforcement. Hoover's death in 1972 marked the beginning of a second renaissance in American policing.

In a January, 1950, message to all law enforcement officials in the *FBI Law Enforcement Bulletin*, Hoover wrote:

> The first half of the Twentieth Century is now history. The present halfway mark affords an opportunity for critical appraisement of the fifty years of law enforcement just past . . . The reign of public enemies ended; a period which might be termed the Renaissance of law enforcement followed.
>
> Law enforcement as a profession became the goal.

Hoover's assessment of the first half of the century was the genesis of this book, which is an attempt to show law enforcement's progress toward professionalism in our time. The history of policing in America during the past 50 years shows two rebirths, or "periods of vigorous intellectual activity," the definition of renaissance, that must be appreciated in terms of directions to be taken in the next half century.

Unfortunately, Hoover did not compile his thoughts on the philosophy of policing in book form. We have to rely on his articles, speeches, and the overall record of the FBI in the second of its two missions—that of a law enforcement service organization, which began with Hoover's appointment as Director—to understand the first renaissance.

America is a Nation of laws, not men; this is what we teach in our civics courses. But we know that laws are enforced and interpreted by men. Charles Reith (1886–1957), one of the first writers on police history, pointed out that thousands of books on law have been written, but little on how laws, over the years, have been enforced:

> . . . of infinitely greater importance to mankind is the record of the means by which rulers and governments have secured observance of

their laws, because, if they are not observed, the most perfect laws which the wit of man can devise are useless. . . . [1]

This "history is the record not of what happened but of what has mattered." In 1975, George L. Mosse, editor of *Police Forces in History*, wrote that:

> Police history is as yet in its infancy. . . . Historians have analyzed almost every aspect of the men, movements, and states which rule over us; it seems high time to examine in greater depth the prime instrument of power in the modern state.[3]

This work is an attempt to increase the knowledge of the progress toward law enforcement professionalism through an analysis of the development of police professionalism in America, a development of the last century. As Philip John Stead, editor of the British *Police Journal*, said of police history: " . . . knowledge of the way one's profession has developed is itself a mark of professionalism."[2] It is also an attempt to analyze the effect of a federal agency, the FBI, on that development, by an author with over a decade of experience as the editor of the FBI's police professional journal, the *FBI Law Enforcement Bulletin*, and nearly 30 years of service as an FBI Agent.

While police pioneer August Vollmer advocated less political control of policing, he also believed in a social work role for police professionalism. J. Edgar Hoover also advocated ending political control of police, but eclipsed Vollmer on the national scene in the 1930s with his crime fighting professionalism model, an alternative route to professionalization which appealed more to the American public at that time.

Part of the exemplar role of Hoover and the FBI in the 1930s was for professionalism to include scientific crime detection, fingerprint identification, and nationwide police training. This volume examines the law enforcement service role of the FBI, particularly, in historical perspective. This role was seen by J. Edgar Hoover and Attorney General Homer S. Cummings to be the alternative to a national police and it was a rebirth, or renaissance with its intellectual connotations, of professionalism in policing. The crime fighting role of police, along with the military model of organization and organizational efficiency, reached its peak in the 1950s with California-style policing as the national example, as depicted by the new medium of television.

But in the 1960s America's political stance returned to the progressive movement's reform era, although this new revolution did not involve the propertied segment of the population, as the Progressive Movement had before. A redefinition of the role of police resulted on the part of academic students of criminal justice, protesting intellectuals, and representatives of America's ghettos. Academics and intellectuals took up the complaint of the ghetto that policing should return to the social work—now termed community service—mode.

A new academic approach to policing appeared, in part financed by the federal government. Police managers re-evaluated their approaches to policing. The FBI made radical changes in its police training and crime laboratory functions. Another giant of police professionalism appeared, Patrick V. Murphy, the only man to have headed four different large urban police departments, including New York City, and most important, the guiding genius behind the work of the Police Foundation. Patrick Murphy said in his book, *Commissioner*, that the philosophy of the Police Foundation:

> rests not on the proposition that American policing, with minor modifications, is in good shape, but on precisely the opposite.[4]

Murphy, a police executive like Vollmer, provided the intellectual basis for what might be called Renaissance II in police professionalism. This period is marked by the willingness of police executives to experiment and to act on the conclusions thus reached. In this, the last two decades of the 20th century, we can do no more than a preliminary evaluation of Renaissance II in law enforcement, but both periods of renaissance must be considered as we approach policing in the 21st century.

Notes to the Preface

1. Keith, 1952, 13.
2. Stead, 1977, 11.
3. Mosse, 1975, 5.
4. Murphy, 1977, 256.

ACKNOWLEDGMENTS

I would like to thank my family in the preparation of this book. My brother, James Deakin, a professional journalist all his life, my sister, Norah Deakin Davis, an editor, and both published authors, and my wife, a professional historian, have added to my understanding of writing and history. My extended family in the FBI, beginning with Charles P. Monroe, Assistant Director of the FBI's Records Management Division when this project began, furnished wise counsel and invaluable assistance. His help goes back even further, as he was responsible for assigning me to the *FBI Law Enforcement Bulletin* in 1977 and his friendship back to our days together in the FBI's Intelligence Division.

George C. Moore, a professor in the law enforcement program at Northern Virginia Community College and before that an official at FBI Headquarters, was kind enough to review the manuscript. My associates in the FBI's Office of Congressional and Public Affairs of the Director's Office, particularly Research Unit Chief Jack A. French, now retired, and his staff whose historical knowledge of the FBI is unsurpassed, and Special Agent Stephen D. Gladis, who taught writing at the FBI Academy and is now the FBI Director's speech writer, were gracious and helpful to their colleague down the hall. All my friends in the Public Affairs Section were most supportive the entire period of this effort; their encouragement saw this project through.

To those in the FBI Training, Identification, and Laboratory Divisions who gave so much insight, my appreciation. Special Agent Thomas L. Hughes, now retired, and his associate, Robert L. Gleason, of the Laboratory Division Administrative Unit deserve special mention. It was the custom in past years for non-fiction writers to thank librarians for their help. Histories could not be written without the assistance of that profession, so I would like to thank two librarians at the FBI Academy, Sandy Coupe and Melinda Davis, who were unfailingly helpful—and always so cheerful about their assistance.

Today, I appreciate the opportunity to have worked for over a decade for one of the three giants of police professionalism, J. Edgar Hoover, and greatful for the friendship of another, Patrick V. Murphy, past president of the Police Foundation. Their work was the inspirational genesis for this book.

Everyone who has helped deserves my heartfelt thanks, including the contributors to the *FBI Law Enforcement Bulletin* from whom I learned so much more about policing. Again, my thanks to my wife, Carol, a professional historian who added to my understanding of history and professionalism. Her support and love, during the three years this book was in preparation, sustained me, as always.

But none should be held responsible for errors of fact or judgment in this book. As a fellow Missourian once said, "The buck stops here"—with the author.

THOMAS J. DEAKIN

CONTENTS

POLICE PROFESSIONALISM
The Renaissance of American Law Enforcement

Chapter 1

BEFORE PROFESSIONALISM

History has produced two main forms of social control: first, ruler-mandated law and law enforcement and, second, custom or kin-imposed rules of society and appropriate policing of these rules. In modern terms, these two types of social control give us today's centralized and decentralized systems of law and law enforcement. There are elements of each that cross over between the two systems, exemplified by the national police systems of most European nations and the local policing in the United States.

The term "police" is now used to describe a body of men and women organized to maintain civil order and to investigate breaches of the criminal law. In past centuries "police" was used more generally (especially in countries influenced by the Napoleonic Code) in the ancient Greek connotation denoting the internal civil administration of a state or town, including public health, morals, safety, and the prosperity and general comfort of the body politic. This meaning has affected American policing, especially in the 19th century. The word "police" itself is derived from the Greek "politeia" meaning the administration of government.

American law enforcement dates back to 500 A.D. when the Germanic tribes (Anglo-Saxons) of central Europe invaded England and replaced the Roman-inspired law that had governed Britain. British law enforcement became a product of custom, or kin-inspired, social control, not ruler-mandated. Imperial Rome, which had ruled Britain for several hundred years, had ruler-mandated law and also had history's first recorded police department. Similarities between Imperial Rome's policing system and today's mandates a brief examination of the law enforcement system developed by Caesar Augustus, first emperor of Rome.

CAESAR AUGUSTUS AND THE VIGILES

Rome's police department developed from its fire department. Rome was a city of open fires and wooden buildings built close together. A candidate for a local office in 14 B.C., Egnable Rufus, promised the voters that if elected he would maintain a fire brigade to protect their homes. Caesar (emperor) Augustus feared that this proposed fire brigade could become a personal gang of thugs reminiscent of those that plagued Rome in the last days of the Republic.

Augustus immediately organized a fire department of seven thousand men (seven cohorts) for the entire city: the "Vigiles" or night watchers (from which our words "vigil" and "vigilante" come). Made up of former slaves (freedmen) who signed up for twenty years of service, with citizenship being conferred after six years of good service, the Vigiles patrolled at night to identify fires that were out of control. During the day they inspected furnaces, ovens, and other controlled fires to insure compliance with laws about sweeping chimneys regularly and having buckets of water on hand.[1]

During their night patrols, if the Vigiles observed a burglary, mugging, or other crime being committed, they could not be expected to ignore it. Therefore, the fire department was charged with making arrests for crime in addition to fire safety violations. In time, the department was also charged with the capture of runaway slaves and with service as guards at the public baths.

Vigiles were armed with a broad sword and a night stick-type device called a "festus." This weapon symbolized the dual duties of the force; the night stick, for law enforcement, and, for fire control, it had a hook at one end useful in pulling wood apart to search for burning embers. But the Vigiles had no standard or ensign such as army units displayed. The force of Vigiles was not a military body; Augustus did not want it to appear he controlled the city through use of military force, a concept the English and Americans copied 1800 years later. The Vigiles were separate from the Praetorian Guards (which had become the Emperor's personal guards) and the three Urban Cohorts, city troops, which did have some policing duties. The Praetorians and Urban Cohorts were recruited from citizens, not the freed slaves which made up the Vigiles. But officers, including centurions, a title meaning that they controlled a hundred men (a century), could move up from the Vigiles to the Urban Cohorts and eventually to the Praetorian Guards.

The New Centurions by Joseph Wambaugh, a veteran Los Angeles detective, is one of the most thoughtful novels about today's American police. The book's title comes from that of a commissioned officer, a Centurion or captain, in the Vigiles, the police of ancient Rome. Every student of police science should read this 1970 work to understand the stresses that affect today's urban police officer.

Rome, the capital, was an urban center of a million people—at least half of them slaves, or indentured servants, captured in war or otherwise enslaved. Most of the work in Rome was done by these slaves and slave rebellion, such as the uprising by Spartacus in 71 B.C., was a constant concern of the citizens.

Crime was almost as large a problem as fire, as shown by archaeological digs which reveal that first floor windows of buildings were usually barred. A lack of street lighting (not corrected until 220 A.D.), minority problems, and the nearby location of the Pontine Marshes, a hiding place for criminals, plus the absence of an efficient law enforcement agency all contributed to Rome's unrest. The Vigiles ended this unrest. They also prevented insurrection, which eventually came not through violence by slaves, but from the teachings of Jesus Christ.

One writer on police history noted that "in the matter of police service it was not until the beginning of the 19th century that the cities of Europe regained the standards of civilization which had existed in the Roman Empire eighteen hundred years before."[2]

ENGLISH HERITAGE

After the fall of Rome, European civilization lapsed into the Dark Ages and little is recorded about law enforcement or about daily life in general, for that matter. The church was the prime source of social control, but except in the Ten Commandments it had little influence on today's law or law enforcement. When the Anglo-Saxons invaded England in 500 A.D., custom or kin-imposed policing began there. Some of these customs included trial by ordeal; trial by combat, which has evolved into the "combat" of opposing lawyers today, the adversary system; and trial by compurgation, an oath by friends and relatives which has descended today to the custom of character witnesses for defendants.

The number 100 was significant in Anglo-Saxon law enforcement as it was in Rome's police establishment. One of the Anglo-Saxon customs was *teothing* (tything), where inhabitants of London were organized into groups of ten, with a leader responsible for seeing that the other nine discharged the responsibilities prescribed for them. These groups of ten were pyramided into a *hynden* or hundred under a head-man who directed the ten leaders. They caught and punished thieves and reimbursed individual members for property lost through theft. The other two customs of Anglo-Saxon law were the *bohr*, or suretyship, and *gegildan*, or community of guild members who were obliged to assume the responsibilities of kin. This last assured that a man was a member of some kind of group even if he had no relations.

Another government feature of the Anglo-Saxon realm was the division of the territory into shires, each under a ruler of royal lineage. Later enlargement of the shires made necessary subordinate officials who were called *scirgerefa*, which eventually became shire-reeve and then sheriff. The head-men of the hundreds, to whom the tything-men were responsible, were themselves responsible for enforcement of the law to the shire-reeve. This was a highly developed kin-police system without a kin basis.

After the Norman Conquest, the shire-reeve or sheriff gave way to the *vicecomes* in the interest of central government efficiency and eventually central government tyranny. But the tything-man and kin-police survived. From leader of the tything, with responsibility for the behavior of ten men, the tything man became a leader responsible for apprehensions. By the 13th century he was acting alone without the tything. The tything-man, now known as *custodes pacis*, came under the control of the Justices of the Peace, the local gentry who had replaced the sheriffs in holding court. Eventually the *custodes pacis* became the Petty Constable of Queen Elizabeth I's reign and later the Parish Constable. The word constable is of Norman origin.

Each parish had a constable, either elected or appointed by the local court, who was unpaid and served for one year. All able-bodied men in the parish were expected to serve in turn. At this time, the same system in towns developed a variation in the form of the Watch. The Watch evolved from the same Anglo-Saxon source, the *gegildan*, or guilds, which had assumed the craft basis of their Continental equivalents. The Parish Constable lasted until the Industrial Revolution, long enough to be transplanted to the American colonies.[3]

COLONIAL LAW ENFORCEMENT

The prime law enforcement officer in colonial America was the sheriff, part of the English legal system the colonists naturally brought with them. One of the sheriff's duties was the collection of taxes, for which he was paid a fee. Thus law enforcement, which was not based on a fee system, became the less important duty. In towns, the mayor was the chief law enforcement officer, but he only acted in emergency cases, such as riot, and appointed constables and marshals to assist in law enforcement duties.

The constables and marshals had law enforcement responsibilities similar to the sheriffs; they could serve warrants and make arrests. In some towns, the constables and marshals were elected and in some they were paid by fees, making the jobs sought after, as sheriff's positions were. But these were by tradition daytime jobs; to provide protection at night towns added the night watch, inherited from England and Europe. Cities eventually added a day watch to supplement the night watch and Southern towns developed mounted patrols to control the slave population. But in case of serious riot, the militia had to be called out. The colonies had inherited the Riot Act from England; the Riot Act had to be read to any mob before the militia could be activated. This was, of course, a cumbersome and inefficient means of dealing with disorder and riots were fairly common in colonial times. Mobs protested elections, economic conditions, and standards of morality in Philadelphia, Boston, and New York, then the largest towns in the colonies.[4]

Three important and long-lasting developments in American law enforcement marked the colonial period. The first was the continuation of the English system of decentralization of local government functions. Each colony was separately governed under the authority of the king, but with considerable local control which included the means of law enforcement. When the colonies became states of a new nation this system of local control became even more established. Development of law in the main was reserved to the states, not the national government. Law enforcement, too, was a product of state and local government.[5]

This system of local control of law enforcement still controls today. It is partly due to the American preference for responsible local government rather than a strong centralized system. Although today it has lost its sharp earlier definition, the sense of the American body politic is that local control of police has helped prevent the rise of a national, repressive police force such as other nations have experienced.[6]

The second development of colonial times in America important to the whole history of law enforcement was the importation from England and flowering in New England of Puritanism.

Puritanism, which dominated the intellectual life of colonial New England for nearly a century after its founding, has been a major force in shaping the American mind. Puritan ideology rested on the assumption that government was necessary because of the sinfulness of man, hence it was essential that government enforce conformity to law — God's law as the Puritans interpreted it.[7]

Puritanism led on one hand to a comparatively high intellectual and literary level, but it also led to political intolerance and the suppression of dissent. These two developments, local control and Puritanism, have had tremendous influence on all facets of government in America throughout our history and even today influence law, government, and law enforcement.

The third important development of law enforcement in the colonies illustrates the cyclical nature of the history of law enforcement. The "watch" was also an English tradition: every able-bodied citizen helped authorities enforce the law (and discover fires) in towns on a regularized volunteer basis. The watch appeared first in Boston in 1636 as a citizen body and spread to other towns, lasting for almost two hundred years. Eventually day watches supplemented the night watch and, in 1712, Boston voted to pay members of the watch. Consolidation of the day and night watches led to the formation of modern police forces, which today are supplemented by the recent development of neighborhood watches — again, citizen volunteers who assist authorities.[8]

Industrialization in the second half of the 18th century led to the urbanization of England and serious crime problems developed in the new urban areas, especially London. Urbanization also led to urban disorder and the English system of law enforcement was unable to cope with the increase of crime and disorder. Military force had to be used to control urban unrest; in the quaint terms of the English Riot Act, troops had to be called out "in aid of the civil power." The often bloody results were perceived as beyond the British sense of fair play by many and, as demands of Empire allowed, the search for a new means of control of civil unrest and crime began.

Again, as the English system of law enforcement had been wholly imported to the colonies, when the same problems of urbanization affected America almost a century later, it was natural to look to England again for solutions. But America adopted a system only superficially resembling Britain's and when it didn't work as well over here, police reformers late in the 19th century called for a more complete adoption of the way that London's "bobbies" policed their city. Reformers and police themselves realized that American local politics had defeated the American adaptation of the British system of law enforcement; their remedy was to professionalize the police.

PEEL'S INNOVATION

Richard Mayne, the first of a pair of commissioners appointed to guide the London Metropolitan Police, wrote instructions to the rank and file of the "new police" which formed the basis for this service as a preventive, not repressive, agency:

> It should be understood at the outset that the object to be attained is the prevention of crime. [The Constable] will be civil and obliging to all people of every rank and class. He must be particularly cautious not to interfere idly or unnecessarily in order to make a display of his authority; when required to act, he will do so with decision and boldness; on all occasions he may expect to receive the fullest support in the proper exercise of his authority. He must remember that there is no qualification so indispensable to a police-officer as a perfect command of temper, never suffering himself to be moved in the slightest degree by any language or threats that may be used; if he does his duty in a quiet and determined manner, such conduct will probably excite the well-disposed of the bystanders to assist him if he requires them.[9]

A growing realization had come to Britain's governing class that the ancient system of law enforcement needed reform. Constables and the watch could not cope with the unrest and violence, plus increased crime, attendant to urbanization. Soldiers' muskets and cannon were unsuitable for controlling crowds and demonstrations, as England's bloody Peterloo "massacre" of 1818 showed. In this Manchester incident, authorities' attempt to arrest an orator caused a crowd who had come to hear him to riot; troops had to intervene and a regular cavalry charge by the 15th Hussars killed 11 and wounded over 500 of the crowd. Even the Duke of Wellington urged the government to form a police force instead of using troops in future disorders.

But at the same time, there was fear of a full-time corps of professional police on the Continental model as this could endanger traditional British liberties, plus there was concern about the expense involved, which would fall on the governing and mercantile classes. The same need for control of unrest coupled with the fear of despotism and the costs factor would later affect America. America's "new police" superficially resembled the London Metropolitan Police, but there were significant and long lasting differences.

The London Police were virtually created by Sir Robert Peel, later Britain's Prime Minister, with the aid of the two first commissioners of police, a lawyer and a soldier. Robert Peel had the political ability to carry Parliament (London police became known as bobbies) just as he had with the Peace Preservation Act of 1814, which set up the Irish police organization later known as the Royal Irish Constabulary (popularly known as "The Peelers"). After his service as chief secretary for Ireland, Peel accepted the post of Secretary of State for the Home Department (Home Secretary, the British equivalent of the American Attorney General). In the period 1825 to 1830, Peel first met the demands of Whig members of Parliament for radical changes in the criminal law.[10]

Second, when reform of the police followed the reform of the law, Peel was able to benefit from the writing of Patrick Colquhoun, the London magistrate who published *Treatise on the Police of the Metropolis* in 1796. Colquhoun had advocated a preventive police somewhat along the line of Henry Fielding's (another magistrate) Bow Street Runners, an effective, but very limited police and detective force.[11] Peel determined that a new police system could be developed in England by borrowing just enough from Europe to promote professional excellence, while avoiding features that could endanger liberty.

The governing principle of the London Metropolitan Police was to be the prevention of crime, not just the apprehension of wrongdoers, which had been the duty of constables. The watch, which had patrol duties, was also to be supplanted by the "new police." Peel's two commissioners, called justices at first, had virtual carte blanche in setting up the new organization, within Peel's guidelines. Charles Rowan, a lieutenant colonel in the British military who had been wounded at Waterloo, and Richard Mayne, a practicing attorney, together cast the police as a *service* rather than a *force*. The police were to be unarmed, but were to wear a "quiet uniform," so that those wanting assistance could recognize the officers. A military organization was adopted and former military men were sought, at least for supervisory personnel. Lists of retired sergeant majors were used to recruit company commanders. Instead of being called captains, however, these company commanders were designated superintendents in the British service.

At the same time as Peel sought a mild tempered agency that would succeed through public approval rather than a show of force, he knew that under the British system of government the commissioners were responsible to the Home Secretary and through him to Parliament—not directly to the people being policed. This centralization was carried to other British cities as their need for police developed. Police services in England were, and are, partly supported by and answerable to the central government.

Modern-style police departments began in this country between the 1830s and 1870s as a response to urban disorder. While this urban disquiet had many of the same effects that Britain's had had earlier, the disorders had more varied causes than those that had affected Britain. Between the 1830s and 1870s, major civil disorders swept this Nation's cities due to unsettling urbanization and other elements of social change that challenged old and established values. There was conflict between different ethnic groups as a result of massive immigration from Ireland and Germany in the first half of the century. Even before the Civil War, there was racial violence including attacks by whites on abolitionists and non-slave blacks. These two causes of unrest, immigration and racial violence, were unknown in Britain until the latter part of the 20th century.

Economic disorders marked the rise of capitalism and industrialization. This violence included labor attacks on employers' property and attacks on banks by ruined investors. Even the populist Andrew Jackson, who had to use federal troops on three occasions to suppress labor riots, spoke out against mob violence: "this spirit of mob-law is becoming too common and it must be checked. . . . " Boston was affected in the Panic of 1837 when a mob of 15,000 (then a sixth of the population) battled in the streets over unemployment. The militia was called out, backed up by cannon, to restore order and many citizens were injured.[12]

Election day rioting affected many cities—St. Louis in 1844 and 1852; Baltimore in 1834, 1848, and 1856; New York, Philadelphia, and most other large cities experienced the same. Even questions of morality were decided in the streets—medical schools were attacked by those who objected to use of cadavers and brothels were mobbed by moralists who wanted to "clean up" the cities. Abraham Lincoln warned in 1837 of "the growing disposition to substitute the wild and furious passions in lieu of the sober judgment of the courts and the worse than savage mobs for the executive ministers of justice."[13]

The law enforcement establishment then existing—the sheriffs, constables, marshals, and night watches—as was previously the case in England, could not cope with the recurring riots and cities began to organize what were then called "new police." A gradual process began of consolidating day and night watches and the force of constables under one administrative head, which is considered to be the beginning of modern police departments. To an extent, as the English experiment of 1829 became known in this country, these "new police" forces were modeled after London's Metropolitan Police, but America produced no Richard Mayne to establish an overall policy for the guidance of the constable.

The major difference between the British and American police systems has to be remembered; America developed, and still has, the most decentralized law enforcement system in the world. Although local American law enforcement agencies operate under the authority of the state government, agencies of cities and counties within the state are not generally answerable to the state government nor to the central, federal government.

Urban police in the United States, however, were answerable to the local government structure and by today's standards, local government in the 19th century was highly political. Early in the 19th century local government was in an era of increasing democratic participation. American cities were decentralized and real political power lay in the wards or neighborhoods of each city. Mayors were figureheads with little administrative power; the real political powers were the councilmen or aldermen who controlled the wards. They gave out contracts to local businessmen, found and created jobs for recent immigrants, and otherwise traded material benefits for political loyalty.[14]

In line with this municipal structure, police chiefs also had little real power; instead, the captains in each ward or precinct, who were appointed by the ward bosses, had the real power. In 1845, the aldermen in New York City appointed each captain, his assistants, and "as many policemen as the Ward was entitled to. . . . "[15] Men received their appointments as a reward for political service; there was then no concept of a trained, professional police service. Indeed, as soon as an officer received his badge and a few words of guidance from his superior he began walking his beat. This was the standard of training, or lack of training, for most of the rest of the century. Police work was considered simply common sense; it had just become a job and was not yet a career. Turnover in departments was wholesale at time of changes in city administration.

Before the Civil War American policemen did not wear uniforms, only a badge. The uniform was a sign of a distinct occupation and policemen did not think of themselves in those terms. In America's two largest cities, New York and Boston, the police departments had a high percentage of Irish-born men on the forces and uniforms after the English model were not looked on with favor—even the public resisted uniforming police. An attempt to uniform police in New York led to the public attacking police as "liveried lackeys." Policemen realized, too, the advantages in not wearing uniforms; it was relatively easy to remove the badge and melt into a crowd to avoid an unpleasant responsibility. The uniform, finally adopted in New York in 1857, was partly an attempt by supervisors to gain control over their men. The Civil War, three years later, removed the onus from wearing a uniform.[16]

The uniform, too, had implications for the military/civilian orientation of police departments. American police adopted a limited set of military rank titles—captain, lieutenant and sergeant for supervisors. But the lowest rank became a patrolman, not a private. The chief of police was just that, although a few chiefs had, and still have, the rank of major or colonel. The departments did not deliberately recruit their supervisors or patrolmen from former military men as the English did. Nor were the men equipped as soldiers; for forty years American police were armed only with a club. But when criminals began to use firearms, especially handguns, some policemen began to carry concealed small caliber pistols. Boston adopted revolvers for its police in the 1880s, New York in 1895—and then only patrolmen, not detectives.[17]

While at least one writer on policing, Robert M. Fogelson, says that "Americans had a strong conviction that the police should have an essentially civilian orientation," there is little evidence of this sentiment. Instead, it appears that police had a more political orientation, because of who appointed them and how they performed their jobs. The military rank structure did not denote real power in American police departments in the 19th century; political connections did.[18]

Duties of police departments then included a great many community services, in the absence of other specialized public bureaucracies. Municipal authorities were handed a wonderful political tool: an agency that was on duty 24 hours a day, had an ill-defined mission, and could be used for whatever purposes suited the city fathers. Hence, the political powers made the police a catchall agency with health and welfare duties, in addition to law enforcement. The health and welfare duties would help assure the continuation of political power by those in office.

Thus, the police distributed food supplies to the poor, used horse drawn paddy wagons to transport the sick, and accommodated the homeless in most cities. In Philadelphia, the number of overnight lodgers at station houses was estimated at 127,000 annually in the 1880s. The professionalization of police and establishment of social service agencies eventually removed these responsibilities from police, but cost police the public respect and sense of community that these services had generated.[19]

The heavy immigrant staffing of urban police agencies in the 19th century was natural because of the early political purposes of the departments. Policing, because of its ease of entry and its non-career status, was a logical job for America's immigrant population. The first police chief in St. Louis, for example, was the son of Irish-born parents. In New York City, an 1855 police report claimed that 27% of the new police force were Irish-born, which nearly matched the proportion of Irish-born in the city as a whole. (A city council investigation suggested that this figure was actually under reported by 50%.) Cleveland's police department in 1872 was almost equally divided among German-born, Irish-born, and American-born.[20]

The political nature of police departments determined not only the social service roles given to the departments, but also the manner in which they enforced the law. Cities were composed of differing neighborhoods determined by their clusters of immigrant population. American-born neighborhoods had more of the Puritan sense of morality, immigrants the morality they brought from Ireland or Europe. Thus, vice laws, primarily enacted by American-born state legislators, were viewed differently by the different neighborhoods, or wards, in a city. The political nature of policing led to different standards of law enforcement of these laws depending on the views and habits within the different wards.

Thus, the police force was in the position not of controlling "crime" of this type, but tolerating it in certain neighborhoods. This licensing, in effect, of certain vice violations of the law led to corruption, which was not disapproved by the municipal government—in the 19th century corruption throughout the city government was expected. Police were involved in payoffs from violations of the drinking, gambling, and prostitution laws because of the prevailing social and political mores of the community; police then were not oriented toward abstract legal norms and the political machines effectively nullified many vice laws.[21]

The political nature of 19th century police agencies in America, in its many facets, led to the birth of police professionalism in this country. But this professionalism was one of the factors that cost police the limited public respect and sense of community that they had gained through the performance of health and welfare measures.

Notes to Chapter 1

1. Stead, 1977, 15.
2. Kelly, 1973, 50–60
3. Reith, 1975, 25–29
4. Walker, 1980, 20–21
5. Ibid, 18
6. Eastman, 1981, 120
7. Bopp, 1972, 13
8. Ibid, 17–18
9. Critchley, 1972, 52–53
10. Eldefonso, 1982, 291–292
11. Reith, 1975, 135–137
12. Lee, 1971, 53
13. Walker, 1977, 4
14. Fogelson, 1977, 17
15. Walker, 1977, 9
16. Ibid, 12–13
17. Lee, 1971, 53
18. Fogelson, 1977, 15
19. Bopp, 1972, 46; Walker, 1977, 18; Fogelson, 1977, 16
20. Walker, 1977, 11
21. Ibid, 24

PART I

BIRTH OF PROFESSIONALISM—1890-1910

American policing has closely followed the development of the American political philosophy and system. The English pattern was sufficient for the colonies, but as the industrial revolution brought the urbanization of America, answers to accompanying urban unrest had to be found. The use of military force clashed with American philosophy regarding human life, as in England. A civilian alternative to musket and cannon fire had to be found.

As in England, municipal police came into being as part of urban (as opposed to rural) government. In America, though, municipal police quickly became adjuncts of the political machines of the day. But as America progressed out of the immigration era, long-time Americans of the upper and middle classes began to object to political machine control of the cities, where corrupt political machines often catered to an immigrant population.

Police, as the most visible symbol of the political machine, came under attack—ostensibly for not being professional. At the same time, police leadership banded together in the International Association of Chiefs of Police (IACP). Under reform-minded chiefs such as August Vollmer, professionalism was advocated as an alternative to political control. This period, 1890 to 1910, saw the birth of law enforcement professionalism in America.

Chapter 2

THE BIRTH OF PROFESSIONALISM

The origins of police professionalism in America are rooted in class struggle. The first improvement in American policing, beginning in the last decade of the 19th century, was part of the effort by the progressive movement to "reform" America.

The progressive movement sought to wrest control of the cities from the political machines that dominated American municipal politics toward the end of the 19th century. Progressives believed that American value standards were threatened by large-scale immigration of those without the same values. The political machines were supported by immigrants and supported immigrants' aspirations, in turn. Today, we realize that the upper- and middle-class members of the progressive movement sought to recapture their dominance in American life, which they believed threatened by massive immigration at the turn of the century.

Police "reform" was one avenue of attack on political machines by the progressives. In analyzing this movement in terms of today's values, we must remember that these reformers were acting as they thought best for the country and in terms of improvement of urban life. The underlying rationalization, as seen from the historical perspective, helps us understand why professional law enforcement has developed as it has.

Many parts of this progressive movement toward professionalism of police, such as the necessities of entrance requirements, tenure of personnel, and administrative self-control, were all advanced before the turn of the century and still guide law enforcement today. But at least one thrust of the movement, the use of the military model, rebounded against the profession and caused the cyclical redirection of American policing in the late 1960s.

IMMIGRATION'S CONSEQUENCES FOR POLICING

Over the years, immigration had a tremendous effect on policing, as on other facets of American life. From the time of the American Revolu-

19

tion until the 1830s, the number of immigrants coming to America averaged only 10,000 per year. This barely recovered the population lost during the Revolution by the departure of the Loyalists, almost a third of Americans at the outset of the Revolutionary War. This shortage of population, and the excess of land available for agricultural use, delayed the industrial revolution in this country until almost a hundred years after England's.

But in the 1830s immigration climbed to 600,000 and almost tripled in the 1840s to 1,700,000. Immigration increased again in the 1850s to 2,600,000. This was the period now known as "old immigration," which was primarily composed of some 1.5 million Irish immigrants and 4 million Germans, although the latter were spread over a longer period, from the 1840s to the 1880s. These immigrants affected policing in that they formed a majority of the recruits for the "new police" in the cities where these immigrants settled. They also affected policing in this country because of their views of the sumptuary laws, different from those of native-born Americans of English and Puritan background. Sumptuary laws, by this period, were those laws designed to regulate habits on moral or religious grounds—today, known as vice laws.

The "new immigration," which occurred from the late 1800s to the early 1900s, exceeded all the total immigration from colonial times until today, bringing almost 20 million new Americans to these shores, one-fifth of the population then. Compare this figure to today's immigration of some 600,000 Mexicans and 165,000 Vietnamese—less than one two-hundredth of today's population. The era of "new immigration" gave the U.S. the name "Nation of Immigrants," as we have had more immigrants than any other country on earth.

The new immigration consisted of 4.5 million Italians, 6.5 million Eastern Europeans, 1 million Poles, and 1.5 million Scandinavians—all with different cultural backgrounds from the Americans, Irish, and Germans already here. Both immigration periods coincided with the industrialization of America, the half century after the Civil War, when machines replaced hand labor in this country.

The age of industrialization brought the growth of cities; in 1870, 26% of U.S. population was urbanized, some 10 million people. By 1916, this had grown to 49% of 99 million or almost 49 million people in cities—a 500% increase in urbanization. Industrialization was, of course, centered in cities and brought tremendous changes in the American way of life. "The American population kept pace with the growing industrial order

...in one generation the population had more than doubled. ... they were a new people, with different languages, different religions, and *different ways of life.* " [Emphasis added.][1]

This era brought the growth of industries, such as coal mining, petroleum, railroads, and manufacturing; it saw the development of communications: the telegraph, the telephone in 1876, the increase in mail-carrying by railroads, and the increase in railroad trackage from 9,000 miles in 1850 to 200,000 miles in 1900, and the beginning of mass transit in cities.

Called the "Gilded Age" by Mark Twain, this period brought America materialism, pursuit of profit, and corruption in business and government. It also saw great growth of mostly corrupt political machines in the cities, dependent on the urban, mainly immigrant, poor. The political machines catered to the immigrant poor as their votes were needed to maintain the machine in office. A contrast between extreme wealth, caused by the pursuit of profit, and abject poverty, coupled with America's democratic tradition, led to the tentative beginnings of a socialist movement in the U.S. At first, this took the form of a "progressive movement," which addressed the problems of rapid industrialization: crowded city slums, poor working conditions, business monopolies, and dishonest politics.

The progressive movement's campaign for political, social, and economic reform in this country began during the depression of 1893–1897, though the progressives did not call themselves by that name until 1905. This reform movement lasted until America's entry into World War I in 1917. At the national level, the progressive movement was able to effect the federal income tax to counter wealthy citizens' avoidance of property taxes, but the greatest impact of the progressive movement was at state and local levels in campaigns against corruption in municipal government.

The progressive era was marked by the writings of the "muckrakers," such as Lincoln Steffens, Upton Sinclair, and Jacob Riss, the last a police reporter in New York City who advised Theodore Roosevelt, New York's Police Commissioner. This era brought the emergence of the social work profession, which had its own impact on policing, and the establishment of settlement houses in the crowded city slums, such as Jane Addams's Hull House in Chicago. Arthur M. Schlesinger, Sr., described the growth of urbanization in *The Rise of the City, 1878–1898,* noting rural America's historical mistrust of cities—the progressives gained support in their various campaigns from rural America. Schlesinger wrote that the

" . . . heirs of the older American tradition did not yield without a struggle. To them, as to [Thomas] Jefferson, cities were 'ulcers on the body politic.' "

Rise of the City went on to describe the alleged rise in crime in this period, noting that being more centralized in cities, crime was more "conspicuous rather than greater in volume." But crime was "accentuated by lax law enforcement. The official guardians of society only too often were in league with the antisocial elements, passively or actively."[2]

Political power depended on control of the immigrant industrial worker and the political machines allied themselves with this element by creating jobs for their relatives and compatriots in the municipal administration, including the police department. The machines also saw to it that the police enforced their brand of order at the polls—who would vote and how many times. The political machines "spoke for millions of lower- and lower-middle class newcomers whose opposition to reform aspirations formed an imposing obstacle" to the progressive movement and its supporters. Most police officers "were linked to the politicians by strong personal, familial, class, and ethnic bonds" in addition to loyalty and economic dependence on the machines, the source of their jobs.[3]

Thus, the progressive movement's underlying motive for the attempt to "reform" local policing: the progressive reformers believed that the customs and values underlying immigrant life-styles were not proper or appropriate for American culture. The author of *Big City Police* analyzed the reformers' beliefs:

> Their "position reflected the upper-middle-class assumptions about the moral order of urban America, which favored abstinence and respectability, rejected self-indulgence and deviance, and relied on the criminal sanction to distinguish the one from the other. This position also led to the conclusion that the police, courts, schools, and other urban institutions should attempt to impose the conventional morality on ethnic minorities with little or no regard for the long-standing tradition of cultural pluralism. . . . the reformers revealed that their campaign was an attempt not only to improve the quality of the police, but also to retard the mobility, reduce the power, and lower the prestige of the newcomers.[4]

This was class struggle, not in the Marxist sense of the revolt of the proletariat, but a reaction by the upper class to an increase in lower class influence. The progressives were the "heirs of the older American tradition" and reflected upper-middle-class assumptions on morality, differing from lower-class immigrants or second-generation Americans' beliefs and practices. Progressives' attempts to capture control of America's cities challenged the basic assumption of political machines in the 19th century: to improve the social mobility of the immigrant. The reformers insisted, however, that the primary purpose of municipal services should be to provide essential public services as efficiently as possible — not improve social mobility for immigrants. "The reformers' view reflected the upper-middle and upper-class Americans' assumptions about the process of mobility in urban America, which emphasized the importance of individual, economic, and private action."[5]

The progressive movement campaign, a loose alliance of Protestant clergy, lawyers, doctors, bankers, insurance men, businessmen and other established American reformers, set up societies for the suppression of vice and associations for the maintenance of law and order to accomplish the moral regeneration of America. They pressed municipal officials to enforce laws on drinking, gambling, prostitution, and Sunday business. Of course, enacting sumptuary laws is easier than getting people to obey them, but the reformers blamed non-compliance on non-enforcement by the police, rather than on the ill-conceived laws. The progressives believed that removal of political influence on the police would remedy this.

The progressives, who shared characteristics of ethnicity, class, and religion, which set them apart from immigrants and second generation Americans, believed that policing should be a profession committed to public service. As a profession, policing should contribute to the betterment of society. A science of policing depended on formal training, as was required in other professions; though this new profession would not, of course, have the status of the long-established professions of law or medicine. Training was only one of the many ideas advanced by the reformers to professionalize policing. Centralization of administration with special squads assigned to headquarters handling vice was advocated, for example, as was upgrading the quality of personnel through entrance requirements and civil service examinations. Tenure for the chief of police and a narrowing of the police function to crime control matters were sought. But the first requirement was seen to be correction of police internal administration, looking toward managerial efficiency through lessening of the influence of the ward bosses.

THE MILITARY MODEL

Reformers of the progressive movement were attracted to the corporate model for the improvement of schools and other municipal agencies. Reformers were fascinated with corporate scientific management and enthusiastic about corporate organization. According to the reformers, American cities were essentially business corporations: citizens were stockholders, elected officials were the board of directors, and appointed officials were the managers. For policing, "however, most reformers adopted a military analogy instead of a corporate model." But this police historian noted, " . . . the military analogy demonstrated little understanding of the military and even less of the police."[6]

The reasons for adoption of the military model are not entirely clear, even today. While there were superficial similarities to the military, such as uniforms, some of the rank structure, and the fact that police were now armed, there were also fundamental differences. The police officer usually had to operate on his own, away from supervision, while the combat soldier performed in ranks under close discipline. As one writer on police management observed:

> The vast bulk of police operational problems now consist of those that can be handled by one or perhaps two people. What is required is initiative, imagination and a willingness to make decisions — not regimentation.
>
> The military managerial philosophy, which has been used by the police for the past 150 years, probably was inappropriate after the New Police were formed and, at least at the present time, it is completely inconsistent with the American concept of the police function.[7]

The decision to adopt the military model for this country's various urban police departments was not made by one man or even a small group, as policies for the London police had been formulated by Peel, Rowan, and Mayne. It was a philosophy advanced by the whole of the progressive movement, endorsed by a large segment of the American public, and over a period of time adopted by police executives themselves. Probably the underlying argument for adoption of the military model was the need for discipline within large organizations. Modern concepts of management had not yet been developed. The mission of the individual patrol officer in crime control had not yet been studied and analyzed. However, most important at this time, discipline in police departments would enhance control up and down the chain of command in a given department, lessening the influence of the political machine and ward bosses.

Over the next fifty years, the influence of the military model grew, with the perhaps too enthusiastic support of the law enforcement community until, in the late 1960s, it became itself a reason for repudiating the police presence in the inner city ghetto. The police found themselves assailed as an "occupying army." And the intellectual successors of the progressive movement, the academic community, also abandoned what their predecessors had championed for the police establishment. This was confusing to law enforcement and incomprehensible to the American public.

The military model was the only one available at the time the London Metropolitan Police were formed in 1829. It was the only organizational model for controlling a large body of men, but in many ways the London police did not resemble the military units that policed European nations, nor did the American police. But at the time of the reform of the American police, the American military was held in great esteem for its empire-building activities and, even more important to the reformers, for its lack of perceived political influence on operations. This is what the reformers sought for police: a lack of political influence on operations. Changes were advocated and made to militarize the police; military drill was instituted and many former military officers were recruited for the police chief position. "The militarization of the American police would be one of the dubious accomplishments of professionalization," according to one police historian.[8]

St. Louis, a city with a large German immigrant population, was perhaps the first to institute a training program on the military model. The Mayor's Message to the City Council for 1868 recommended that one month's instruction for new officers be afforded in a "school of the policeman:

> The new officer "should also be instructed in the school of the soldier, the positions and movements to qualify him to take rank in the school of the company when placed on full duty, as well as the proper use of the baton on established principles of the broadsword exercises.[9]

Two years later the school of instruction had been established; today this school is a model of cooperation for urban areas with many jurisdictions. The Greater St. Louis Police Academy trains virtually all the police officers serving the City of St. Louis, St. Louis County, and the multiplicity of municipalities within the County.

In Cincinnati, also a city with a heavy German population, a nonpartisan Board of Police Commissioners appointed by the Governor in 1886 selected a new chief, a Bavarian-born former Cincinnati police lieutenant, Philip M. Dietsch, who had served on the force from 1863 to 1873, but had worked for the U.S. Revenue Service for the past 13 years. Some 238 of the 289 patrolmen and 8 of the 16 sergeants were dismissed after a public inspection that revealed the lack of discipline and the inadequate physical condition of the force. Regular military drill and exercise for one hour a week in the new police gymnasium were instituted. At the end of the year, regular physical examinations by a new Board of Medical Examiners were started.

The two-platoon system of policing, where half the men were on patrol or stand-by duty at any one time, was replaced by a three-platoon system in Cincinnati. (Stand-by duty at that time was for the purpose of having men available for emergencies requiring a number of personnel; although the men could rest at the station house they were still on duty, as firemen are today.) The three-platoon system gave the men more time with their families, as industrial workers were beginning to gain at the time.

The most important change toward police professional status was in 1888 when a school of instruction for police was instituted. The commissioners found that the school of instruction had to be centralized to insure uniformity of instruction; new recruits began with four hours of schooling each day during their first seven days on the job, the other four hours were the more traditional on-the-street indoctrination by experienced officers. For the next three months, the recruits spent two hours in a classroom twice a week and at the end of their first six months on the job they had to take mental and physical examinations; failure resulted in suspension from the force.

St. Louis and Cincinnati were years ahead of other American police departments in training. Berkeley, California, did not begin its school for recruits until 1908 and the next year New York City started an academy, an outgrowth of its School of Pistol Practice, which had been in operation since 1895. Detroit established a training school for police in 1911 and Philadelphia followed suit two years later. In 1916, the University of California at Berkeley created the first university police training program.[10]

The Cincinnati department was also in advance of other departments in its single executive control. Various means were advanced and tried by the progressive reformers for administering police departments: bipartisan boards, commission government plans, and single executive control. Prior to this time, popular election, partisan administrative boards, and state control of municipal police had all been used and found wanting.

"The Finest," the New York City Police Department, was far behind the Cincinnati police at this time. In 1895, Theodore Roosevelt had just been appointed a member of the new bipartisan four-man police board. Roosevelt became president of the board and acted as if he was the board—using it as his "bully pulpit." Roosevelt's two-year career as a police commissioner in New York City illustrates the intellectual links between police professionalism and the broader progressive movement. He viewed policing in the abstract, in terms of public duty and respect for law, in spite of not being a lawyer. According to Roosevelt, the question of a more or less liberal Sunday closing law was really a question "as to whether public officials are to be true to their oaths of office, and to see that the law is administered in good faith."[11]

Roosevelt also tried to raise the standards of police performance and relied on the military model:

> In our present highly complicated civilization there are a number of occupations which, even when carried on during a time of profound peace, call for the development in a very high degree of the prime virtues of the soldier—energy, daring, power of obedience, and marked bodily prowess.

However, Walker's *A Critical History of Police Reform* highlights Roosevelt's tenure as police commissioner as one "... of the less attractive aspects of police professionalism: the often jingoistic militarism, the soaring and self-righteous idealism, and implicit but deeply rooted contempt for the mass of humanity, and an excessive emphasis on rhetoric and imagery."[12]

But the progressive movement was not monolithic in its concepts of police reform; some of the reformers sought to change the administrative structure of urban police departments, while others were interested in improvement in the law enforcement role of police. Still others viewed the police as an agency of social reform, but not one contributing to the upward mobility of the immigrant class, as the political machines saw police. Social reform in this progressive case took the viewpoint of crime prevention, mainly through work with juveniles. Since the beginning of this first reform or professionalism period, there had been a tension between the issues of crime fighting and crime prevention. This still exists today, as neither the body politic nor the police themselves in America have agreed on the role and responsibility that the police should have in society.[13]

By the turn of the century, the main elements of professionalism had been introduced as concepts into American policing: training, entrance requirements, administrative self-control (as opposed to political influence), and job tenure (accomplished through civil service which was adopted for police in Brooklyn in 1883, but not widespread until the mid-1890s). Two other elements of professionalism were needed and appeared at this time: a professional literature and a forum for police themselves to exchange and debate ideas. The development of a police forum is the subject of the next chapter, but it was preceeded by the beginnings of a police literature, which marked the beginnings of professional consciousness.

BEGINNINGS OF A POLICE LITERATURE

Histories of various police departments, heavy on individual accomplishments and partisan in presentation, appeared in the late 1800s. First, in 1865, was Edward H. Savage, Boston police chief between 1870 and 1878, who wrote *Police Records and Recollections, or Boston by Daylight and Gaslight for Two Hundred and Forty Years.* While the beginning of this book was a chronicle of the development of the Boston police, the second part was a random selection of essays, such as "Advice to a Young Policeman." Savage was the foremost proponent of the crime prevention concept of policing and eventually he became the first chief probation officer for Boston.

More typical of the police books toward the last of the 19th century was police reporter Augustine E. Costello's detailed 1885 history of the New York City Police, *Our Police Protectors.* This work, which was written to benefit the police pension fund, described the policeman's work: "Night and day, fair weather and foul, when his tour of duty commences, the Policeman, like the trusty sentinel, must go to his post and be prepared to meet all kinds of danger."[14]

Two years after Costello's book, John J. Flinn, another police reporter, published his *History of the Chicago Police,* also for the benefit of the pension fund. By 1890, histories of the Philadelphia, Pittsburgh, Baltimore, and Cincinnati police had been published, marking the beginning of organizational awareness among American police. But these histories were generally anecdotal and heroic, not analytic; they did not mention corruption, either in terms of payoffs for vice protection or bribes for promotions. These histories do, however, balance the volume of words put out on policing by the very articulate progressive movement. In the case of Costello's book, many original documents are woven into the work and by reading between the lines the reader can get an impression of the political controversies that affected the New York City Police Department. The Chicago and Philadelphia police histories offered descriptions of each precinct in the departments, giving a picture of each department as a collection of smaller, precinct units.

Not until 1920, however, do we see the culmination of the beginnings of a police literature. In that year Raymond B. Fosdick followed his 1916 *European Police Systems* with *American Police Systems.* Based on visits by Fosdick to some 70 U.S. police departments between 1915 and 1917 (World War I interrupted his publishing schedule), this work was the first comparative analysis of American police agencies. Until Bruce Smith's *Police Systems in the United States* was published twenty years later, Fosdick's pioneering effort was *the* basic reference for students of police administration.

Fosdick, a young attorney and Princeton graduate, spent 1913 in Europe researching his first book. Both of his books were financed by the Rockefeller Bureau of Social Hygiene, a "think tank" in today's terminology, that sought "reform" of America in the progressive movement mode. Fosdick's book on American police made many of the criticisms of law enforcement first advanced by the progressive movement: political interference with policing, lack of tenure for police executives, lack of proper entrance criteria for police recruits, and inadequate training.

American Police Systems also documents in great detail the problem of "heterogeneity of population" in this country. European police, according to Fosdick, did not have to contend with large foreign-born populations as the American police did. This anti-alien bias surprised the criminal justice professor who wrote the 1969 introduction to the reprinted edition of Fosdick's work. But this kind of bias motivated most of the progressive movement.

Perhaps more surprising is Fosdick's analysis of sumptuary laws; here he breaks with the progressive logic of blaming non-compliance of these laws on non-enforcement by police:

... this presents one of the strange anomalies in American life: with an intolerance for authority and an emphasis upon individual rights, more pronounced, perhaps, than in any other nation, we are, of all people, not even excepting the Germans, pre-eminently addicted to the habit of standardizing by law the lives and morals of our citizens. Nowhere in the world is there so great an anxiety to place the moral regulation of social affairs in the hands of the police, and nowhere are the police so incapable of carrying out such regulation. ... We are less anxious about preventing a man from doing wrong to others than in preventing him from doing what we consider harm to himself. We like to pass laws to compel the individual to do as we think he ought to do for his own good. We attack symptoms rather than causes and in doing so we create a species of moralistic despotism which overrides the private conscience and destroys liberty where liberty is most precious.[15]

Fosdick also made three other recommendations in his book on American police of long lasting significance. He reported the decentralization of American law enforcement agencies, many of them very small, and he urged consolidation of smaller departments to effect efficiency, a recommendation that is still being implemented today. Second, he urged the formation of a national bureau of identification, which occurred just four years after his book was published (as set out in Chapter 5). Third, Fosdick commented on the wastefulness and ineffectiveness of foot patrol. Foot patrol was replaced within a generation by motorized patrol, the effectiveness of which is still being evaluated and debated today by inquiring police executives and by the public.

Lastly, Fosdick's knowing comment that American "hereditary sympathies are for the underdog" often becomes an:

... irrational public attitude which first shrieks for the punishment of the perpetrator and then seeks to find excuses for his act and reasons for his pardon — has done much to vitiate the restraints of the law and weaken its administration.[16]

This, of course, is the complaint that all who wear a police uniform eventually make.

The development of law enforcement professionalism is, of course, still continuing. Considering the profession's beginnings as a tactic to re-gain political control by the progressives, the progress of law enforcement away from the partisan political arena is remarkable. Important as the progressive reformers were in initiating the concept of professional law enforcement, as this chapter shows, the lasting effect of the concept was due to the police themselves, as the next chapter will begin to demonstrate. In spite of the continuing debate on the nature and scope of policing in America, we still have not reached a consensus on the nature and scope of law enforcement that Americans have, or want. Progress in the area of professionalism has been mainly the result of efforts on the part of law enforcement itself.

Notes to Chapter 2

1. Weinstein, 1978, 539
2. Cary, 1975, 71, 81
3. Fogelson, 1977, 67–69
4. Ibid, 91
5. Ibid, 90
6. Ibid, 41–42, 53–54, 88
7. Eliot, 1973, 57
8. Walker, 1977, 42
9. *Mayor's Message to the City Council,* 1868, 45–46
10. Bopp, 1972, 84
11. Walker, 1977, 45
12. Ibid, 44
13. Ibid, 37
14. Ibid, 36
15. Fosdick, 1969, 48
16. Ibid, 44

Chapter 3

THE IACP

In the days when patrolmen still wore high-topped helmets (at a cost of three dollars each in 1910), Marshal Thomas F. Farnan of Baltimore described his 1867 apprenticeship as a policeman to the 1910 annual convention of the International Association of Chiefs of Police:

> I can remember when I was serving what might be styled my apprentice-ship as a policeman forty-three years ago that we did not have a patrol wagon service. The officer who arrested a man or woman sometimes had to literally drag the prisoner to the station, and sometimes the station was a mile or more from the point where the arrest was made. If the prisoners were unruly, and they often were, it was a matter of muscle motor power and physical endurance between the policeman and the man he was "running in."
>
> Sometimes the policeman requisitioned a passing team if the prisoner was very unruly or helplessly intoxicated. I have known prisoners to be taken to stations in wheel-barrows, pushcarts and milk wagons, and on one occasion I knew of a policeman who requisitioned an empty hearse returning from a funeral, and, entering that gruesome vehicle with the prisoner, laid down upon him and held him until a police station was reached.
>
> Then came the horse-drawn patrol wagon ... uncovered ... but they were a vast improvement . . . [1]

Less than a hundred years ago, police operated with the latest advance: the horse-drawn patrol wagon. There was virtually no training for police, no central records system, no system of identification, and virtually no cooperation or even contact between the decentralized American police agencies. This, then, is the story of how police executives in this country built the International Association of Chiefs of Police (now better known as the IACP) and how this organization fostered police professionalism in the 20th century through the advancement of training, records, and identification. This voluntary association of police executives initiated many of the cooperative programs in law enforcement that are now operated or funded by the federal government.[2]

The chiefs of police in this country took the ideas of the progressive movement on police professionalism and made them more, much more, than a political tool to wrest control of the cities from the hands of the machines. The tremendous technological achievements of this century — radio, television, computers, motor vehicles, aircraft, and helicopters — plus the voluntary cooperation among policing's executives in the IACP, has made law enforcement unrecognizable to those of us who came a hundred years later.

The IACP, under the early leadership of men like Omaha, Nebraska, Chief of Police William S. Seavey, first president of the organization; Washington, D.C., Chief of Police Richard Sylvester, president from 1901 to 1915; and Cincinnati Chief Philip M. Deitsch, initiator of the IACP's identification bureau, began practical police professionalism in this country. The chiefs made police professionalism over — from the political device of the reformers to an end in itself.

August Vollmer, often called the "father of modern policing," was elected president of the IACP in 1921, in spite of his representing a small police department in the far West. Vollmer's views, especially those on police training, represented the best in police professionalism; his IACP presidency six years after Sylvester stepped down demonstrated the police association's commitment to professionalism. At this time, the IACP had no professional staff; pertinent issues were addressed by the Executive Committee, led by the president of the association, by specially appointed committees of chiefs (often widely separated geographically) and by the national conventions.

Details on August Vollmer's advancement of police professionalism and career are covered in Chapter 7; the two major contributions of the IACP to professionalism in the period of the first three decades of this century (national identification services and uniform crime reporting) are also covered in detail in Chapters 5 and 11, respectively. But at this point in the story of police professionalism, the IACP's genesis of these two important aspects of professionalism should be recorded. The IACP recognized its financial and governmental limitations and successfully lobbied for the federal government to take on these two programs, which helped establish the Federal Bureau of Investigation as a law enforcement service agency.

In 1934 the IACP began its professional journal, *The Police Chief,* as a training aid, and in 1935 cooperated with the FBI in the establishment of a local police training school. It also began a traffic safety division in that year and twenty years later established its own training division. The late 1950s saw a tremendous increase in the organization's professional staff; more increase in staff services came after Quinn Tamm took over as Executive Director in 1962. Tamm led the IACP during the period during the late 1960s and early 1970s when the law enforcement profession was undergoing yet a new examination and re-evaluation.

FALSE START

Voluntary professional associations were the early driving force for reform of the criminal justice system in the U.S. at the turn of the century, in what has been called the "age of organizations." The IACP, first organized in 1893 and renamed in 1902, spearheaded the drive for police professionalism from then on. Other organizations that impacted on the criminal justice system in this country included the National Prison Association, formed in 1870, and the National Conference of Charities and Corrections, a social work professional group. These were joined by the National Probation Association in 1907 and the American Institute of Criminal Law and Criminology, formed as a result of a 1909 conference at the Northwestern University Law School. This last group began publishing the *Journal of Criminal Law and Criminology* in 1910.[3]

In 1871, the Chief of Police in St. Louis, Missouri, invited fellow chiefs to the first U.S. police convention. In a letter to his police commissioners, St. Louis Police Chief James McDonough proposed that such a convention be held to adopt rules "whereby the whole detective force of the country can act in unison for the prevention and detection of crime." The St. Louis city government appropriated $4,000 to defray the costs of the convention and some 112 police officials from 21 states and territories attended. Several railroads provided free transportation from various parts of the country to the meeting.[4]

The delegates met to discuss mutual concerns, including "improving the condition of neglected and abandoned youth . . . a systematic plan of transferring detective information throughout the several states . . . a perfect system of police telegraphing . . . a regular system of exchanges of photographs" and other matters. While the attendees at the convention, held in St. Louis, called for a second meeting to be held in Washington, D.C., in June, 1872, it did not take place for unknown reasons and no national organization came out of this first meeting of American police officials.[5]

The lack of a national police organization was partially remedied by the National Prison Association, which formed a Standing Committee on the Police soon after its 1870 founding. Naturally enough, this committee defined police professionalism in terms of crime prevention and rehabilitation. One committee member, Charles Felton, who was the superintendent of the Board of Inspectors of the Chicago House of Correction, said: "Of what use are reform schools if crime-creating, recruiting agencies among the children are allowed to exist." His view was that prison reform was dependent upon crime prevention. This was echoed by Reverend Frederick C. Wines, a leading prison reformer of the period, who argued that "we punish too much and do too little in the way of prevention."

This association presaged the progressive movement's view of the political influence on police. The 1874 report of the association's Standing Committee on the Police stated: "The worst aspect of our politics is not its bitterness or onesidedness, but its demoralizing tendency in this respect—that men, chosen to execute the law, will not do their duty because the law has been made by another party." The reformers hoped that civil service would be the means of separating the police from politics. As Charles Felton put it, "the entering wedge of police reform is civil service."

An additional way to improve policing was through training; the National Prison Association's Committee on the Police noted in 1888 that "it is the common belief that any man who is of proper height and weight, and who has fair intelligence, and the physical ability to protect himself and to make arrests, is competent for the duties of a policeman." But the committee argued that "no public police department can claim efficiency, if its members are not schooled in their duty."[6]

THE BEGINNING

Some twenty years after the first police convention in St. Louis, the idea was tried again by Omaha, Nebraska, Chief of Police William S. Seavey and Chicago Police Superintendent Robert McLaughrey. A charter member, then chief of police in Altoona, Pennsylvania, recalled the 1893 organizing efforts of Seavey and McLaughrey to the 1925 IACP convention:

> I received a circular letter jointly signed by Robert McLaughrey . . . and W. S. Seavey . . . in this letter they pointed out at what a disadvantage

the municipal departments were as compared with England and continental Europe. They told us what was perfectly obvious to any policeman in the country; that there was no sort of efficient co-operation between the municipal police departments and the United States.[7]

The letter from McLaughrey and Seavey suggested that chiefs of police meet in Chicago in May while the Columbian Exposition was being held there. Fifty-one chiefs responded, the majority from smaller towns within a hundred miles of Chicago. But outside Illinois and Nebraska, there were representatives from Boston, Newark, Atlanta, Pittsburgh, Washington, D.C., and the states of Colorado, Michigan, and Utah. The police chiefs organized themselves as the National Chiefs of Police Union.

Convention attendees went to the Jefferson Street police station in Chicago where Chief McLaughrey had set up the first Bertillon (scientific identification) bureau in this country. The interests of the new organization may also be judged by the group's first formal resolution: "That we, the members of this organization of Chiefs of Police, hereby agree to assist each other on all occasions, by arresting and detaining any criminal who may be called for, or any person known to have committed a crime in any other city or state."

Topics discussed at the Chicago meeting were practical ones: civil service rules for police; a uniform practice of arresting for felonies committed in other states on telegraphic notification; adoption of a police telegraphic code; adoption of a uniform system of identification and a central bureau of identification. The agenda concentrated on practical police problems capable of solution, not on the theories of law enforcement then being developed and discussed.

Reformers of the progressive movement and chiefs of police alike were agreed on the need for administrative efficiency in police agencies. Both groups also agreed on the need for tenure for the chief executive officer, to wrest control of police agencies from the political machine in the reformers' view, or from the chiefs' perspective, to afford the chiefs job tenure to enhance their professional status. But the chiefs were divided over what came after administrative efficiency: a "crime-fighting" role or a more "social work" role. But this divergence took a secondary position to the more immediate, and practical, problems facing the police executives.

Chief Seavey, elected the first president of the National Chiefs of

Police Union, was not a man who steadily rose through the ranks of the Omaha police department like many of his fellow chiefs, nor was he of the social class of the reformers of the day. Born in Maine in 1841, Seavey went to Wisconsin at age 16 to work as a woodcutter. Two years later, he joined the 1859 Colorado gold rush to make his fortune, but enlisted as a private in the 5th Iowa Cavalry at the outbreak of the Civil War and rose to Captain. From 1866 to 1873, he clerked on a Mississippi River steamboat, then traveled to California to become City Marshal of Santa Barbara from 1874 to 1879, his first law enforcement experience. Before finally being appointed Chief of Police of Omaha in 1887, Seavey spent six years traveling and trading in the "South Sea Islands."

Wary of the idea of reform, Chief Seavey said at the Chicago convention: "To introduce and accomplish reform; to advance and promote the efficiency of the American police system is a grand and noble work," but he doubted the worth of the "alleged 'moral wave' which has swept over our country, having for its object the disruption of the police departments in many instances." Seavey recognized the disruptive approach of the reformers in their quest to wrest control of the police departments from the political machines; the reformers felt it was necessary to tear down the department before rebuilding it in their new image.[8]

As one IACP history notes, "The Chiefs concentrated on improving the tools of their trade."[9] A motion passed that the next meeting would be held in St. Louis the next year, the site of the very first police convention in America. Proceedings of the following year's meeting, 1895, were published under the new title of the National Association of Chiefs of Police of the United States and Canada.

MAJOR RICHARD SYLVESTER

In 1902, the name of the organization took its present form, International Association of Chiefs of Police, under a new president, Major Richard Sylvester, Chief of Police in Washington, D.C. One author, Samuel Walker, noted that: "... the advent of Richard Sylvester [as President of the IACP] in 1901 clearly marked the dawn of a new era in American police administration."[10]

Sylvester studied law in Missouri, but began his working life as a journalist. He then served as an official of the Ute Indian Commission in Utah and when that job ended, he was able to secure a position with the District of Columbia police as chief clerk, not a policeman. In 1894, he authored a history of the Washington police and in 1898, based at least in part on the reputation gained by his book, he was promoted to Major and Superintendent of the District of Columbia police. The political patronage nature of his appointment differed from the political machine appointments of many of his contemporaries, however, as the District of Columbia was then governed by commissioners controlled by a committee of the U.S. Congress. In spite of his political lineage, Sylvester became a reformer and led the IACP in that direction.

Major Sylvester was named president of the organization of police chiefs in 1901 and served in this capacity, and in charge of the District of Columbia police, until 1915. His first IACP convention in 1901 featured, for the first time, serious presentations and debate on topics of importance to policing: crime prevention, the value of probation, and various strategies to control prostitution. Sylvester's annual presidential address was usually a summary of the progress toward professionalism to date. For example, he told the 1911 IACP convention (he had been instrumental in changing the name to the International Association of Chiefs of Police) that technology had changed the nature of society and "The changed conditions have called for readjustments, many new features have had to be systematized and new methods invoked, particularly in the operating of municipal affairs which would meet with the modern situation." Sylvester went on to say that "If there was a realization of what we have accomplished for the benefit of society, there would be in evidence a more liberal spirit to promote recommendations."[11]

Early IACP conventions concentrated on discussions of crime problems in terms of the day: "yeggmen and porch climbers," burglars of the day; detective work, drug abuse, and even the Mafia. Discussions of hobos and tramps were common along with vice problems, or "keeping the city clean." Uniforms, patrol officer qualifications, including Cincinnati Chief of Police Phil Deitsch's views on elementary training in the law, and developments in the technology of policing were also covered.

A 1910 "History of the 'Sweat Box' and 'Third degree'" by Chief Richard Sylvester described the origins of these techniques: the "sweat box" developed during reconstruction after the Civil War. For the "sweat box" a large iron stove was located next to a detention cell. When the stove was stoked up, particularly with pieces of rubber shoes and other noxious fuel, it would "...make a terrible heat, offensive as it was hot...[sufficient] to cause the sickened and perspiring..." suspect to confess.

The "third degree" has as its origin the police and criminal terminology that the arrest is the "first degree" of detention, the temporary confinement is the "second degree" and the interrogation about the crime is the "third degree." Sylvester ended his presentation with a resolution that the IACP go on record condemning the "third degree." After discussion, this resolution was passed unanimously.[12]

Another subject that occupied the chiefs was that of the infant movie industry's treatment of police, specifically Max Senett's Keystone Kops. These comedies, the chiefs felt, degraded their efforts to professionalize the police by the movies' characterization of police as bumbling incompetents. Of course, one of the roles of a professional organization is that of protector of the image of the profession and in 1910 the IACP resolved that: " . . . this association deprecates and condemns the moving picture shows that are making false representations of the police, together with tragedy, burglary, and all immoral displays, as they tend to the encouragement of crime." The progressive reformers also voiced concern over the impact of the film industry on the young; even social worker Jane Addams thought perhaps films were a direct cause of juvenile delinquency.[13]

THE IACP AND THE RENAISSANCE

In the 1930s two major objectives of the IACP were realized that had developed over the organization's first thirty years. The first of these was the establishment of a nationwide system of criminal identification. The second was the development of a system of recording the amount of criminality in the nation, for use in judging police effectiveness. Both of these IACP accomplishments eventually helped establish the FBI as the lead federal law enforcement service agency and led to a close working relationship between the IACP and the FBI.

One of the primary objectives at the IACP's founding was the exchange of criminal identification information among police departments. The IACP was initially unsuccessful in persuading Congress to establish such an identification facility. A committee, chaired by Marshal Jacob Frey of Baltimore and including William Pinkerton of the Chicago detective agency and Chief Philip Deitsch of Cincinnati, was established to explore ways to meet this need. The committee proposed that the chiefs establish their own identification bureau, but progress was slow until 1897 when Chief Phil Deitsch of Cincinnati was appointed as the new chairman.

Chief Deitsch acted with "startling speed," according to the IACP's own history on identification, to establish an identification facility. The IACP began a central clearinghouse in Chicago of Bertillon records, the most scientific form of identification then available. This clearinghouse, called the "National Police Bureau of Identification," later added finger-print records and switched over to fingerprints only as that system replaced Bertillonage in the early 1900s.[14]

The Bureau of Identification was operated under the supervision of a board of governors, with a full-time director, and was financed by assess-ments of $10 to $100 on participating cities. This method of support was a constant problem for the IACP, which lobbied Congress to take over and have the Bureau of Investigation, as the FBI was then known, in the Department of Justice perform this function. This would replace the system of assessing member cities for support and would expand the system to all cities, beyond those that voluntarily chose to participate. The story of Bertillonage and its replacement by fingerprint identifica-tion is detailed in Chapter 5, including the successful effort by the IACP to have the U.S. Department of Justice's Bureau of Investigation take over the IACP's Bureau of Identification.[15]

The second major IACP contribution to police professionalism during this period was the development of the uniform crime reporting system, which is the subject of Chapter 11. In brief, the first 1871 convention of police officials addressed this issue, and resulted in resolutions "to pro-cure and digest statistics for the use of police departments." Even Con-gress was concerned with the lack of crime statistics; in 1870 it passed a statute making it the duty of the Attorney General to collect statistics of crime under the laws of the *various states* plus violations of the laws of the United States. This statute failed for two reasons: (1) lack of support by police departments in reporting statistics, as the federal government could not force the states to collect these records and (2) lack of develop-ment of a uniform method of collecting and tabulating the data.[16]

Between 1894 and 1926, the IACP generated interest among its mem-bers in collecting the necessary statistics. By 1922 the IACP had devised a preliminary uniform method of collecting and tabulating the data. IACP president Richard Sylvester had argued for such a system throughout his tenure, but it wasn't until August Vollmer took over the presidency that a recommended procedure for the classification and recording of crime statistics was issued by the IACP. Study of the subject was continued by a committee under Commissioner William P. Rutledge of the Detroit

Police Department (one of the few chiefs in this period who had risen from the ranks). The committee secured a grant from the Laura Spellman Rockefeller Fund and engaged a staff headed by Bruce Smith, one of the 1920s most respected experts in police administration. In 1930, a revised *Manual on Uniform Crime Reporting* was issued. The IACP was successful in getting Congress to assign the job of recording and reporting these statistics to the Bureau of Investigation under J. Edgar Hoover, who had been a member of the IACP committee for this project. In a 1931 speech, Hoover said that he considered this action by the IACP "one of the most constructive and intelligent contributions to the cause of law enforcement. . . ."[17]

These two accomplishments by the IACP, which recognized the role the federal government would have to play, brought Hoover's FBI and the IACP into a close working relationship. In 1935, when the FBI established the National Academy for training local police officers in the law enforcement professionalism then developing, Hoover sought and received the fullest IACP cooperation in this endeavor. That cooperation lasts to this day; for example, in the 1970s cooperative efforts between the IACP and FBI led to the development of a system of recording statistics on bombings and a record of the numbers of attacks on police officers nationwide.

The IACP did not enter the police training field until 1955, when its Training Division was begun as a result of a contract with the International Cooperation Administration (now Agency for International Development). Hundreds of police officers from various countries cooperating in the Technical Assistance Program came to the U.S. for training. This division was headed by Colonel Russell A. Snook, retired superintendent of the New Jersey State Police. This training effort was later expanded to include specialized courses for U.S. officers.

The third contribution of the IACP towards law enforcement professionalism in the decade of the 1930s was the beginning of a professional journal, which, in turn, led to the creation of a national IACP headquarters office. In 1934, the IACP Executive Committee, through officials of the Public Administration Service and the American Municipal Association, applied for another grant from The Spelman Fund to finance a membership and service program, including funds to publish a monthly Police Chiefs' Newsletter. In January, 1934, an IACP Service and Publications Office was established at 850 East 58th Street in Chicago, a building also occupied by other public associations. William P. Rutledge, then chief of police in Wyandotte, Michigan, was named Executive Vice President to supervise this office. While he made frequent trips to Chicago for this purpose, day-to-day operations were directed by Donald C. Stone, director of the Public Administration Service and Arnold Miles, assistant director of the American Municipal Association.

The Police Chief's Newsletter was the forerunner of today's monthly journal, *The Police Chief.* This journal, along with the *FBI Law Enforcement Bulletin,* has been, and continues to be, the voice of professional policing in this country. The Publications Office was designated IACP Headquarters in 1937 and the functions previously performed by the organization's secretary were transferred to headquarters. In 1935, through the efforts of then President Andrew J. Kavanaugh of Wilmington, Delaware, the IACP received funds from the Automobile Manufacturers' Association to establish a traffic safety and field service division. Franklin M. Kreml, director of the Northwestern University Traffic Institute, who was formerly with the Evanston, Illinois, police department, headed the new safety division for the next 24 years.

In April, 1940, the IACP Executive Committee appointed the first full-time Executive Secretary, Edward J. Kelly, retired police superintendent of Providence, Rhode Island. Kelly had to return to Providence during World War II, but continued to serve as IACP Executive Secretary until returning full-time in 1947. The Executive Secretary has become the day-to-day administrator of the IACP and, in recent years, a spokesman for the police profession. In December, 1940, the IACP offices were moved to Washington, D.C., with the assistance of Major Ernest J. Brown, then President of the IACP and superintendent of the District of Columbia police. The next year the IACP was incorporated as a not-for-profit organization under the laws of the District. 1954 brought the resignation of Executive Secretary Kelly, and Leroy E. Wike, retired Chief of Police in Endicott, New York, was named his successor. In 1962, Secretary Wike's illness brought Quinn Tamm, a former FBI official, to the Executive Secretary position.

The IACP expanded its national offices from 10 to 150 professional employees under Quinn Tamm; its 51 charter members had grown to include over 5,000 law enforcement executives when the causes of the second renaissance in American policing began in the 1960s. During this period the IACP had wrested control of police professionalism from the progressive movement and made it the police executives' own. The formal objectives of this organization of police executives, as set out in the IACP's constitution, are:

> ...to advance the science and art of police services, to develop and disseminate improved administrative, technical, and operational practices and promote their use in police work to foster police cooperation and the exchange of information and experience among police administrators throughout the world, to bring about recruitment and training in the police profession of qualified persons, and to encourage adherence of all police officers to high professional standards of performance and conduct.[18]

Chapter 18 is an examination of the redefinition of police professionalism. In the terminology of the IACP constitution, the first renaissance of law enforcement's professionalism was in the "science" of police services: fingerprint identification, uniform crime reporting, police training, and scientific crime detection; the second renaissance, which continues today, is in the "art of police services."

Notes to Chapter 3

1. Dilworth, 1976, 12.
2. Deakin, 1978, 15.
3. Walker, 1980, 130.
4. IACP, 1964, 10.
5. Dilworth, 1976, 2.
6. Walker, 1977, 38–39.
7. Dilworth, 1976, 3.
8. Ibid, 4–6.
9. Ibid.
10. Walker, 1977, 48.
11. Ibid, 57.
12. Dilworth, 1976, 71–78.
13. Walker, 1977, 58.
14. Dilworth, 1977b, 18.
15. Ibid, 11.
16. Thompson, 1968, 23.
17. Hoover, 1931a, 17.
18. IACP, 1964, 10–14.

Chapter 4

SCIENTIFIC CRIME DETECTION

Today, forensic science—the scientific techniques for examining evidence which is to be introduced in courts of law—is a well established element of police professionalism. Before 1900, it was virtually unknown to police in the U.S., except those few officers who read Sherlock Holmes, Sir Arthur Conan Doyle's fictional creation. This legendary detective had scientific training which he used to help solve his cases.

The end of the 19th century saw the birth of police professionalism in America and the beginnings of forensic science in Europe. Then forensic science developed in England and America, once forensic medicine (legal aspects of medicine) had established itself over the Anglo-American coroner system. Forensic science was a logical extension of forensic medicine and of the scientific technologies that began to develop in this period. Police were already adopting technological advances in transportation and communications, such as the automobile, the telegraph and various signal devices necessary to message patrolmen, and finally the radio.

Adoption of scientific methods to the solution of crimes added to the professional status of police, of course, and helped to eliminate law enforcement's dependency on forced confessions, the "third degree." While most scientific examinations do not develop suspects in a crime by name and thus do not "solve" crimes; scientific examinations are useful in positively linking a suspect to a crime and then proving the suspect's guilt in a court of law. Or, particularly important in the Anglo-American system of justice, scientific evidence can also eliminate suspects in crimes by proving their innocence with scientific certitude.

Developments in this field really began in America after World War I in the 1920s at the instigation of Chief August Vollmer, called the "father of police science in America." But, in this field Europe was far in advance of the U.S. before the 1920s, except in the area of forensic ballistics, where America's Dr. Calvin Goddard was the pioneer. However, both Europe and America had to wait for two developments before

45

forensic science could develop: (1) the establishment of forensic medicine, which grew out of "public medicine," or today's public health medicine, and (2) the discovery and application of necessary scientific techniques in non-medical physical sciences.

It should be remembered that when modern policing began with the establishment of the "new police," first in London and then in America before and after the Civil War, medicine and science overall were in very primitive states by today's standards. Anesthetics and asepsis were unknown, so patients died from the pain and shock of surgery or from the germs introduced by surgeons' bare hands or filthy instruments. Only in the last hundred years have the tremendous advances of modern science and medicine appeared.

Today, with modern psychological techniques casting doubts about the overall reliability of eyewitness testimony, scientific evidence can be increasingly valuable in many criminal cases. The development of forensic science is itself a series of detective stories which show how new a field this is, and there are hints of potentially greater advancements in this field of crime detection and proof.

EUROPEAN ORIGINS OF "PUBLIC MEDICINE"

Forensic science in fact, not Conan Doyle's fiction, began just before the 20th century in Europe, where it was termed "criminalistics." The word "criminalistics" was not used in this country as it was thought to relate to criminology, which in America meant the study of the causes of crime. America's advances in science at this time were oriented toward improvements in the means of production, but Europe was beginning to turn to other uses of science. However, all of law enforcement had to wait for advances in medicine and then in "public" medicine and its subsidiary, forensic medicine, to develop before science could also be harnessed by the new field of criminal justice.

The earliest example of a text for applying what was then scientific knowledge to the solution and proof of crimes was in the medical field. The Chinese *Hsi Yuan Lu*, published in 1248, was a handbook for applying medical knowledge to the solving of crimes. Not until 1507 did a book appear in Europe about the usefulness of physicians in legal cases: *Constitutio Bambergenisis Criminalis.* This work became the basis for the extensive penal code issued by Charles V in 1532.

More than a half century passed before the first practitioners of forensic medicine appeared: Ambroise Pare, the French pioneer of surgery, and two Italians, Palermo's Fortunato Fidelis and Rome's Paolo Zacchia. They all followed the example of Andreas Vesalius, the anatomist of the sixteenth century who, by dissecting cadavers, built a real picture of the human body instead of the fantastic ideas then in circulation. The Frenchman, Pare, looked into the effects of violence on the body organs including the lungs of children smothered by their parents, and he studied the results of sex crimes. Fidelis discovered how an accidental drowning could be distinguished from one deliberately caused. Zacchia wrote on bullet and stab wounds, death by smothering, strangling and choking, and infanticide.

Then, in 1663, the Danish physician Thomas Bartholin made an important contribution to the then common judicial problem of infanticide: whether a dead infant had been born alive or still born? Bartholin reasoned that examination of the infant's lungs would determine whether there was air in them. If there was, it proved that the baby had breathed and had been born alive. A German doctor devised a simple test in 1682 to determine if there was air in the infant's lungs: place them in water to determine if they floated. This was the first standardized procedure in forensic medicine, " . . . crude, but based on experience."

Advances in forensic medicine eventually led, in the early 1800s, to the establishment of "public medicine" in Germany, France, Austria, and Hungary. Physicians trained to combat epidemics occurring in cities and at the same time to serve as consultants to courts of law. At this time, some European universities began offering courses in public medicine. The new Napoleonic code ended the secret judicial processes of preceding centuries so that the testimony of physicians was no longer shrouded in secrecy.

Pathology, the study of disease and death, was founded by an Italian anatomist, Morgagni, at the end of the 17th century. But only by the middle of the 19th century was microscopic anatomy coming into use, which allowed the discovery of the basic unit of the human body, the cell. This allowed the development of microscopic histology (the study of minute structures in the body) and microscopic pathology. This was all before refrigeration and the development of rubber gloves, of course; early pathfinders in pathology had to work on often rotting corpses with bare hands and could seldom free themselves of the smell of decomposing flesh.

The three great pioneers of true forensic medicine, a branch of public medicine, appeared in Berlin and Paris in the mid-19th century: Johann Ludwig Casper; Mathiew Joseph Bonaventure Orfila; and Marie Guillaume Alphonse Devergie. Devergie published his *Theory and Practice of Forensic Medicine* in 1835 and Casper his *Practical Manual of Forensic Medicine* in 1856. These works accepted only one basis for judgment: rigorous observation, based on autopsy, microscopic or chemical examination.

A treatise on the values of tattoos for identification, a result of his army service, was the first forensic medical work of Alexandre Lacassagne, who became the first professor of forensic medicine at Lyons, France. In the area of public medicine, he developed methods for determining death with certainty. This was during the time when doctors had only the mirror or feather test for breathing (breath would fog the mirror or move the feather). Because of this uncertainty, morgues were equipped with bell pulls, intended for use by any corpse who might only be in a coma!

Lacassagne also made useful discoveries about the blotches which appear on dead bodies. These were the result of blood falling to the lowest level of the body, which could be predictably timed. These discolorations began a half hour after death, and, in the period of the first ten to twenty hours after death, pressing on the spot could make the blotch disappear, because the blood in the capillaries yielded to the pressure. Later, though, the blood leaked through the walls of the capillaries and the blotches would not yield to pressure.

A common problem in crime detection at this time was that of suspects in murder cases who claimed that the bloodstains on their persons came from slaughtering an animal or handling meat. Until a scientific test to differentiate between human or animal blood was found, this kind of alibi was irrefutable. In 1901, a paper was published in a German medical journal by Paul Uhlenhuth, of the University of Greifswald:

> ... I have succeeded, taking blood of men, horses and cattle dissolved in physiological NaCl [salt] and dried on a board for four weeks, in identifying the human blood at once by means of my serum—a fact that should be of particular importance for forensic medicine.[1]

Uhlenhuth, a native of Hanover, was barely thirty years old when he published these research results. A pupil of Robert Koch, Director of the Berlin Institute for Infectious Diseases (as well-known in Germany as Pasteur was in France), and of his assistant Friedrich Loffler, Uhlenruth went with Loffler to the University of Greifswald where their search for an immunizing serum against hoof-and-mouth disease put Uhlenhuth on the track of his discovery of the test for human blood differentiation. A serum made from rabbit blood precipitins could be extracted by Uhlenhuth which reacted in different ways with the blood of different animals, including man. The test worked whether the blood was fresh or dried.

This was perhaps the beginning of the differentiation, too, between forensic medicine and forensic science. Another German scientist, Richard Kockel of Leipzig, called for the widening of forensic science to take in non-medical matters of importance to the solution of crimes. Others might ridicule Kochel's elaborate experiments in ballistics or his inspection of traces of dust, but Kockel "could feel fairly sure that the future was his, even if, ultimately, technological methods were carried to such lengths that each became an independent specialty on its own." The study of the effects of bullet wounds and the complementary work on firearms illustrates this diversion of paths between forensic medicine and forensic science, and the necessity of cooperation between these disciplines.[2]

How to differentiate between an entrance wound and an exit wound, determining the distance from which a shot was fired, and under what circumstances is a shot fatal are all questions that the medical profession had to address. By the time of the First World War, forensic medicine had found the answers to most of these questions when black powder was used, but the invention of smokeless powder made new research necessary.

Smokeless powder did not leave the burns on flesh that had characterized black powder and this caused at least one specialist in forensic medicine, Harvey Littlejohn of Scotland, to make an incorrect conclusion in the 1926 case of Donald Merrett, indicted for the murder of his mother. Littlejohn pronounced the mother's death a suicide, but Donald Merrett confessed to the murder 25 years later. Littlejohn, like most older specialists in forensic medicine, had left the study of firearms to gunsmiths. But younger specialists, such as his pupil, Sydney Smith, had begun to study the weapons themselves. Smith, on receiving his medical degree, became Professor of Forensic Medicine at the University of Egypt and the medico-legal expert to the Egyptian Government in 1917.

In the next decade Smith analyzed thousands of murders in Egypt. Returning to Edinburgh in 1926 for a vacation, he found his professor worrying about the Merrett case. Smith suggested to Littlejohn that tests with Merrett's cheap revolver might show what marks would be left on human skin. Using skin from an amputated leg, these tests gave the doctors new evidence in the case. Smith, in his first *Textbook of Forensic Medicine,* assumed that forensic ballistics was a part of forensic medicine, but later other specialists realized that forensic medicine could not include other scientific disciplines: those of physics, chemistry, engineering, toxicology, and other physical sciences. But forensic medicine had to cooperate with these disciplines.[3]

Europe continued to lead in the development of forensic medicine and forensic science. Other disciplines besides medicine began to study the uses of science in solving and/or proving crimes. Edmund Locard, of the University of Lyons developed or inspired many of the techniques of forensic science still used today. His Institute of Criminalistics, which began in 1910 as a small laboratory for the Rhone prefecture of police, grew into a university department. Many of Locard's contributions formed the basis for Hans Gross's book, *Criminal Investigation,* published in 1903 and in English in 1906.

Gross was trained as a lawyer and became an examining justice, a court official responsible for the detection of crime (and later still professor of criminology at the University of Prague). His first book, *Manual for the Examining Magistrate: A System of Criminalistics* became the seminal work for criminal investigators for decades. It stressed the help science could give in the detection of crime. Locard, himself, published his encyclopedic *Traite de Criminalistique* in 1923.

R. A. Reiss, a Swiss-naturalized German who taught forensic photography at the University of Lausanne, founded what became the Lausanne Institute of Police Science, which has awarded degrees from the University of Lausanne since 1909. Forensic laboratories began to appear in other countries in Europe. Robert Heindl, who had worked at Lausanne with Reiss, began one in Dresden, Germany, in 1915. It foundered because of World War I, but became the German national police laboratory in Berlin in 1919. Another laboratory was begun in Vienna in 1923. Smaller countries, including Sweden, Finland, and Holland, had laboratories before 1925; the Swedish laboratory was headed by H. Soderman, a pupil of Locard, who helped the New York City Police Department set up a laboratory in New York some years later. But the coroner system of England and America retarded the development of forensic medicine and forensic science in those countries.[4]

THE CORONER SYSTEM

The office of the coroner, which still exists today, originated in England in the 12th century; the coroner was originally an agent of the crown, hence the name from the Latin word for crown, *corona.* Originally the coroner's duties included tracking down punishable offenses of all kinds and securing the property of convicted persons, or suicides, for the crown. Over the years it evolved into an elected office responsible for the investigation of dubious deaths. And the law required no special knowledge for this office, only honesty and good reputation. When the coroner required medical advice, he simply asked doctors who happened to be at hand.

By the beginning of the 20th century coroners in the larger British cities consulted pathologists for medical advice, but, unlike Europe, there were few specialists in forensic medicine in England. The British Home Office sought the few such specialists for the Scotland Yard cases that required them. The coroner system was carried to America by the colonists, as was much of early English law enforcement practice. As in England, coroners were elected, but there was no Home Office in the U.S. to encourage pathologists at the beginning of this century and certainly no pathologists were elected to the position of coroner.

In the United States, too, the office was responsible for the investigation of suspicious deaths, but one survey found that of the coroners elected in New York City between 1898 and 1915, eight were undertakers, seven professional politicians, six real-estate agents, two barbers, one butcher, one milkman, and two saloon proprietors! The undertakers were presumably the most qualified for the office, but they were "notoriously unwilling to spoil the bodies consigned to them by performing autopsies."[5]

Boston was the first large U.S. city to replace the elected coroner with an appointed medical examiner, who had to be a qualified pathologist. This began in 1877 and the Boston system was a success, judging by the rise in homicide statistics. One of the most prominent of Boston's medical examiners was Dr. George Burgess Magrath, who took office in 1906. Magrath was aware of the anti-scientific attitudes of the period, especially among juries, and set out to impress the populace of Boston. But he also had a clear view of his function and impressing the public was only a means to this end. As he wrote in his journal: "If the law has made you a witness, remain a man of science; you have no victim to avenge, no guilty or innocent person to ruin or save. You must bear testimony within the limits of science," a philosophy first attributed to a French medico-legal specialist, P. C. H. Brouardel.[6]

Three decades later this became the philosophy of the scientists in the FBI Laboratory, and of all those in the various local and state crime laboratories, to "bear testimony within the limits of science."

In New York City, a reform mayor was elected in 1914 and caused a survey of the coroner system which resulted in a scathing report:

> The elected coroner in New York City represents a combination of power, obscurity and irresponsibility which has resulted in inefficiency and malfeasance in administration of the office.... The character of the medical examinations may be judged from the fact that the keeper of the morgue testified that the coroners' physicians often merely looked at the head of a body and that an examination lasting as much as five minutes was an infrequent occurrence.... So far as the activities of the coroner's office in New York City are concerned, infanticide and skillful poisoning can be carried on almost with impunity.[7]

This report provoked action in New York City and in 1918, the city replaced the coroner system with a Chief Medical Examiner, with a number of assistants, all of whom had to be experienced pathologists. This began a wave of reforms in the coroner system in this country with most being replaced with medical examiners or at least with the requirement that the coroner had to be a qualified pathologist.

The use of science in law enforcement was dependent on the overall development of scientific methods in the world as a whole. Forensic medicine was at least the partial impetus to the development of forensic science as many of the doctors involved went beyond today's limits of forensic medicine, but forensic medicine did not develop until the latter part of the 19th century. By the end of World War I, it was apparent that Europe had outstripped the U.S. in development of forensic science. European police organized crime laboratories and used specialized technicians to develop scientific evidence, but American police, except for a few visionaries, were far behind in this area of professionalization.

FORENSIC SCIENCE IN THE U.S.

At first, the use of technology in law enforcement in the U.S. was confined to patrol operations. U.S. police quickly adopted the automobile for patrol use. They also experimented with various signal systems for communicating with patrolmen. Scientific methods of identification, Bertillonage and then fingerprinting, were quickly adopted by U.S. police, however, as set out in the next chapter.

In 1916, it took the vision of August Vollmer, Chief of Police in Berkeley, California, to employ a scientist from the University of California Medical School as a full-time criminologist to operate the first crime detection laboratory in this country.[8] Vollmer also began the Los Angeles police forensic laboratory in 1923, the year that this pioneer was acting chief of police in that city, and the Detroit police laboratory was started when Vollmer was a consultant there in 1926. Today, Vollmer is called the "father of modern police science" for this and his many other innovations in policing. (See Chapter 6 for Vollmer's career.)[9]

But even more important to all of U.S. law enforcement was the 1922 IACP convention in San Francisco, the year that Vollmer was president of this national police professional organization. Vollmer enlisted several scientists from the University of California to address the chiefs about scientific aids for criminal investigation. As Vollmer told the assembly:

> ...we cannot ignore the value of a fully equipped, scientific police laboratory as an aid in the detection and apprehension of criminals and the prevention of crime. A single hair, a blood stain or particles of dust have been the sole clues that finally solved mysterious and perplexing crimes in the past.... We must be prepared to meet the criminal with better tools and better brains than he possesses, if we hope to command the respect of the community that we serve.[10]

At Vollmer's invitation, Professor Albert O. Schneider of the University of California spoke about the use of the microscope in crime detection at this convention and Professor E. O. Heinrich, himself a former chief of police in Alameda, California, addressed the need for police laboratories. Presentations were made on the detection of human blood stains, on searches for poisons, and on forensic photography. Then, the chief of police in Colorado Springs, H. D. Harper, gave a lengthy presentation on a local rape investigation that would not have resulted in a conviction without scientific evidence.

According to Chief Harper, a college girl walking home at dusk was raped by a young black man. Her assailant was tracked to his home by bloodhounds, but he denied any connection to the crime. The Chief called a Dr. A. L. Bennett, a Denver criminologist, to examine the suspect's person. Scrapings from his fingernails revealed a minute piece of fabric which was eventually matched to fabric in the girl's hat under microscopic examination. A golden hair was found in the knot of the suspect's necktie, which he was in the habit of removing by loosening the knot instead of untying it. The victim had blond hair and a sample from her head had an identical appearance under the microscope. A bloody fingerprint on her glasses contained a Negro hair and the suspect's fingernail scrapings contained minute pieces of Caucasian skin; her face had been scratched in the attack. The jury in this case credited these items of circumstantial, but scientific, evidence as aiding in the conviction of the man.[11]

This was a 1919 case. It showed an amazing knowledge of the capabilities of forensic science for the period, not to mention the abilities of the Colorado Springs police in collecting the necessary evidence. As Chief Harper noted, it would have not been solved with a conviction if it had not been for the careful scientific examinations afforded the evidence.

At the same time there were developments in America on the east coast in the field of forensic ballistics. Colonel Calvin H. Goddard has been cited as one of the most notable of the criminalists at this time.[12] Colonel Goddard had received a medical doctorate from Johns Hopkins University in 1915, but developed a consuming interest in ballistics during Army service in World War I. In 1926, Goddard presented a paper on forensic ballistics developments at the annual convention of the IACP. He described his New York Bureau of Forensics Ballistics as:

> an organization of four individuals who have been trying to collect, correlate, tabulate and disseminate to duly constituted authorities information dealing with the broad subject of arms and ammunition as they figure in legal and particularly criminal cases.[13]

Goddard went on to describe the state of forensic ballistic science at that time, starting with the work of Charles E. Waite, begun in 1915 when Waite was assigned to a special inquiry by a governor in a murder case. Waite determined that the murder bullets could not have been fired by the gun owned by the accused, who had already been convicted. The governor pardoned the man and the real killers were later apprehended.

This caused Waite to look into ways to make firearms evidence infallible, which led to the collection of data on all firearms made in this country and then on those made abroad. This data indicated that no two firearms manufacturers cut the spiral grooves inside the barrel with the same specifications. This process is called rifling, which imparts the spinning motion to the bullet thereby improving accuracy. Each gun maker cut the grooves with a different pitch (the rate the grooves turn within the barrel), different widths of grooves, different numbers of grooves, and different depths of grooves. By precise measurement of these different factors, which leave marks on bullets fired from a gun, it is possible to determine exactly which type of gun fired the bullet in question.

Goddard then explained how irregularities of wear inside each barrel leave additional distinctive marks on each bullet fired from an individual gun. Irregularities of manufacture of each barrel in the cutting of the barrel grooves also leave tool marks which are imparted to each bullet that passes through the barrel and may later be identified on the bullet. By 1926 Waite had died, but his associate Philip O. Gravelle, who had recently been awarded a medal by the British Royal Microscopic Society, was able to develop the comparison microscope. This instrument allowed viewing the images of two bullets side by side as a composite image and allowed forensic ballistics to become a reliable science.

Goddard, after he perfected his technique with Gravelle's comparison microscope, in 1927 offered to examine the bullets involved in the Sacco-Vanzetti case, in which two Italian-born anarchists had been convicted of a holdup-murder in Massachusetts. Goddard's careful examination caused two defense firearms witnesses to withdraw and Sacco and Vanzetti's guilt was confirmed.[14]

This was just one of the well-known cases during the decade of the twenties that cried out for forensic science examinations. The Black Tom case, a 1916 explosion of munitions intended for the Allies, resulted in a 1922 commission investigation that focused on a magazine with a coded message spelled out by pin pricks beneath letters on one page. German and American experts disagreed on the age of the magazine in question. The 1921 Sacco-Vanzetti case, subject of controversy for years afterward, saw testimony by "firearms experts" for both sides who used low power magnifying glasses instead of comparison microscopes and had no knowledge of the precision measurements required. Only in 1927 was Goddard able to bring scientific exactitude to the controversy.

The Lindbergh kidnaping case in 1932, the 1929 St. Valentine's Day Massacre in Chicago, and the 1933 Kansas City Massacre, all had forensic science elements, as did an airplane crash in 1933. Some of the evidence in that crash was sent to the National Bureau of Standards laboratory, which had been established in 1901 to develop accurate standard measurements for science, industry and commerce in the United States. In about 1921 this laboratory developed a capability in forensic science for experimental purposes, as opposed to work on individual cases. One of the Bureau of Standards' experts was Dr. Wilmer Souder, an authority on document examination and forensic ballistics. Souder and Calvin Goddard lectured before the chiefs of police at IACP conventions in the early 1930s on the use of science for the detection of crime. These two men had a great deal of influence on the establishment of the FBI's scientific crime laboratory, as set out in Chapter 12, in both their devotion to scientific truth and their application of this truth to forensic examination of evidence.[15]

In 1934, Dr. Souder told the IACP convention that:

> ... the most an unscrupulous counsel can do to counteract scientific testimony is to create confused opinions among the jury. When our scientific experts learn to testify in simple language, explain the details of their tests, and re-explain in similar or greater detail each time opposing counsel attempts to confuse the testimony, we shall see an improvement in the effectiveness of scientific testimony.[16]

Notes to Chapter 4

1. Thorwald, 1964, 124–127, 148.
2. Ibid, 221.
3. Ibid, 150–151, 209–243.
4. Walls, 1974, 2.
5. Thorwald, 1964, 201.
6. Ibid, 202.
7. Ibid, 202–203.
8. Eldefonso, 1982, 298.
9. Douthit, 1975, 340.
10. Dilworth, 1977a, 1–3.
11. Ibid, 6–19.
12. Eldefonso, 1974, 264.
13. Dilworth, 1977a, 68.
14. Thorwald, 1964, 428–453.
15. Miller, 1956, 6–14.
16. Dilworth, 1977a, 108.

Chapter 5

IDENTIFICATION REQUIRED

The question of "who is who" is the business of identification. Through-out history there has been a need in the criminal justice field to identify those who break the law.

Questions of property rights, family relationships, or any claim for recognition depending on identity could only be resolved before the 20th century through the physical appearance and manner of the individual. When social control began, accountability for behavior added another dimension to the question of identification.[1]

Identification is needed to help ascertain guilt or innocence after the commission of a crime. At the time punishment is imposed identification is required to determine the behavioral record of the offender. In most societies, the behavior history is needed to determine the degree of punishment.

Without the ability to positively distinguish one person from another, there is no certain means to establish an arrested person's identity or to determine any previous record of criminality. Urbanization in America— and in Europe and England—highlighted this problem of human identification. The day when every man knew his neighbor had disappeared.

The International Association of Chiefs of Police (IACP), in its history of the development of the American criminal identification system, noted that little could be done by any police department, American or European, in the area of identification until a suitable technology was developed.[2]

The history of scientific identification for law enforcement extends back only to the period just before the U.S. Civil War. The first technology developed was photography, which was widely adopted by newly formed police departments in Europe and in this country. But limits inherent in photography and cases of mistaken eyewitness identification, plus the difficulty in searching large files of photographs, meant the identification problem was not yet solved.

Bertillonage, a scientific system of measurements of parts of the body, held some promise of solution of the problem, but this system lasted only for a generation before its inherent problems led to its abandonment. Discoveries in dactyloscopy (from the Greek word for finger), the science of fingerprint identification, had the added advantage of solving some crimes in addition to being an error-free method of identification. This led to acceptance of this new means of identification by police and judicial authorities.

The breakthrough in fingerprint identification came when classification of fingerprints was developed. This was a means of filing fingerprint records in such a way that a new set of fingerprints, when classified, would lead to the identical previously filed set. This development, which had baffled one of England's best known anthropologists, a cousin of Charles Darwin of evolution fame, was accomplished by a working police official in British India. To the credit of law enforcement, the official understood the need for simplicity in the system so that it could be used by those not scientifically trained.

The need for identification helped lead to the formation of an organization of law enforcement executives in this country, who then started their own identification agency. At their urging, the national government eventually took over and the Division of Identification was established in the then Bureau of Investigation within the Department of Justice.

Later, we will learn how the Federal Bureau of Investigation built the world's largest collection of fingerprints and pioneered humanitarian uses of this collection. Less than a century into the history of fingerprint identification, the development of computer technology by the FBI, in what had been an extremely labor intensive, time-consuming field, held the promise of instant, unquestioned identification, even for the police officer on patrol.

PHOTOGRAPHY

The camera (invented in France in 1822) probably more than humanitarianism, put an end to the ancient and barbaric practice of branding malefactors. Branding had been used since earliest history for identification as well as punishment. Photography provided a new method of identification that was eagerly adopted by law enforcement. By the 1850s, photography in its earliest form of daguerreotypes was being used by police departments in this country, in New York City and San Francisco at first.[3] However, daguerreotypes did not allow copies to be made—a major need of law enforcement in the field of identification.

"Rogues' galleries" were developed by large police departments and private police agencies like the Pinkertons by the late 1800's. Thousands of criminals were included in these collections; developments in photography allowing copies to be made enabled the exchange of photos by the various agencies on an informal basis. The Pinkerton Detective Agency became the only nationwide source of these photograph collections as they built their files.

But it was impossible to catalog these photographs and their attendant physical descriptions in any meaningful way. Photography proved no more than a convenient extension of identification by witnesses who can be, and sometimes are, wrong in their identification. Improper photographic technique, grimacing or resisting subjects, changes in appearance (such as growing or removing beards) often altered physical appearance.

By the 1870s, the Prefecture of Police at Paris, one of the oldest law enforcement agencies in Europe, had compiled enormous archives of photographs and descriptions of criminals. But these had created an equally huge problem, common to all law enforcement agencies: to classify and file these photographs in a way that would permit later efficient use for identification. In 1879, a Frenchman named Bertillon came up with the first scientific method of identification.[4]

ANTHROPOMORPHIC BERTILLONAGE

In the last quarter of the 19th century, European scientists developed a preoccupation with crime and explored ways that new developments in scientific techniques could be brought to bear on problems of crime. The science of criminalistics developed—working back from the fact of the crime to the perpetrator of the crime with the intention of apprehending the author.

Alphonse Bertillon, born in Paris in 1853, was the son of a medical doctor who was also a statistician and an anthropologist. As a young man, Bertillon failed high school and finally, at age 26, became a clerk with the Prefecture of Police of Paris through his father's influence.

He was promoted to records clerk after six months; his job was to transcribe onto files the descriptions of arrested persons. Boredom with the job and his exposure at a young age to new scientific theories of statistics and anthropology led Bertillon to think about identification. Bertillon developed a new theory on identification which rested on three principles:

1. The unchangeable nature of human bone structure after the twentieth year of age.

2. The diversity of dimensions in the human skeleton comparing one individual to another.

3. The ease and precision with which certain dimensions of the human skeleton can be measured in living people.[5]

The identification system developed by Bertillon, which he published in 1893, included what he called "Anthropometric Signalment"—bodily measurements, description, special marks, and photography. Bodily measurements were broken down into three categories: whole body, head, and limbs.[6]

Each of these were subdivided into three or four categories for filing: For the body, the height (of a person standing), the trunk (of a person seated), and the reach (with arms outspread). For the head, the length of the head, the breadth of the head, the length of the right ear and breadth of the right ear. For the limbs, the length of the left foot, length of the left middle finger, length of the left little finger, and length of the left forearm.[7]

This system of eleven measurements, later reduced to nine, permitted division and subdivision of police files on offenders, enabling Bertillon to identify recidivists (repeat offenders) with regularity and with the greatest scientific exactitude then available. After some difficulty with the French police bureaucracy, Bertillon was able to get his identification system adopted in France. It spread to most European nations and then to American police, beginning with Chicago in 1892.[8]

AMERICAN DEVELOPMENTS

With what they believed to be an effective scientific technology available for identification, chiefs of police in Chicago and Omaha, Nebraska, called for a meeting in 1893 to organize the National Chiefs of Police Union. (This organization changed its name in 1902 to the International— to include Canada—Association of Chiefs of Police, today known by its initials, IACP.[9])

This group recognized the need for a national exchange of identification data. This need had been partly fulfilled by the Pinkerton Detective

Agency, a private business, but the wider cooperation of regular law enforcement agencies was sought by the chiefs. Chief Roger O'Mara of Pittsburgh called for the formation of a national identification bureau to use the Bertillon system, as would all of the departments represented at the convention. At the second meeting of this new police organization, the association voted to petition Congress to establish such a bureau in the Department of Justice. But with no action by Congress over the next three years, the IACP voted in 1896 to form its own identification bureau which was established the next year in Chicago.[10]

The Superintendent of the IACP's new National Bureau of Criminal Identification, George M. Porteous, explained the Bertillon system to IACP members at the 1898 convention; he disabused the membership of the general impression that "no two men can register exactly the same in all their measurements." Instead, he said, the purpose of the measurements was to facilitate a search of a collection of pictures. However, he did note that "it is almost a physical impossibility to find two men who measure the same in every particular."[11]

Less than five years later, this "impossibility" was found to be possible in the case of two prisoners at the Federal penitentiary at Leavenworth, Kansas. The Will and William West case also caused discussion of other problems with Bertillonage. The inventor of the system knew that it did not work with anyone under 21 as their physiques were not yet fully developed. Then, as now, a high percentage of offenders are young men under 21. He also knew, as did the American chiefs, that a good deal of exactitude in the measurements was required. The problems of different Bertillon measurements being obtained by different technicians or by the same technician at different times were a recurring defect in the system.

In 1903, a prisoner named Will West was committed to the U.S. Penitentiary at Leavenworth, Kansas. After his Bertillon measurements were taken, the clerk located another record with the same measurements. West denied any previous admission to Leavenworth and the clerk determined that the duplicate measurements belonged to another prisoner, named William West, who was still incarcerated in Leavenworth. The two men were brought together and their appearance was found to be remarkably similar, in addition to the similar measurements.

The two men denied being related, but recent research suggests they might have been twin brothers. Twins or not, this experience undermined American law enforcement's faith in the Bertillon system. Fortunately, a new system of identification—fingerprints—appeared in this country a year later. Later, the FBI would use the West incident to make a case for fingerprint identification, as the Wests' fingerprints differed considerably.[12]

THE HISTORY OF FINGERPRINTING

Pioneers in Policing notes: "In the history of criminology no accomplishment compares in importance with the discovery of a means through which the identification of a human individual could be positively established."[13]

Fingerprints had been used in ancient China by illiterates in lieu of a signature; in the 16th century some contracts for the sale of children had the fingerprints of the young chattels. Other ancient civilizations used fingermarks to sign pottery. But ancient notions of human identity through fingerprints lacked scientific methodology to make these notions a certainty.[14]

The history of the use of fingerprints for identification in our time can be traced to two men who published their findings in 1880 in *Nature,* a British science journal. The first of these "fathers of modern fingerprint science" was Dr. Henry Faulds, a Scottish medical missionary working in a hospital in Tokyo, Japan. He wrote that he had been able to identify culprits from "greasy fingerprints" left at the scene of a crime and had eliminated a suspect in a crime where "sooty finger-marks" had been left on a wall. He collected numerous fingerprints by pressing fingertips on a smooth surface thinly spread with printer's ink and then onto a blank white card—the same method used today![15]

The other "father" of the process was William James Herschel, a British administrative official in Bengal, India. When Faulds's letter to *Nature* was published, Herschel replied (while on home leave in England) that he had been taking fingerprints for more than 20 years for identification purposes to prevent pension fraud and for criminal identification.[16]

These two men had hit upon the dual use of fingerprints: identification of individuals and identification of perpetrators who leave fingerprints at the scene of a crime. But Herschel's recommendation to the Inspector General of prisons in Bengal that fingerprinting be used for prisoner identification was not approved. Neither man had developed a method of classifying fingerprints so that they could be filed in categories in any number for retrieval and comparison.

Just three years after these two men published, the first mention of fingerprinting appeared in American literature; Mark Twain's book *Life on the Mississippi* had a story entitled "A Thumb-Print and What Came Of It," which told the story of how a man traced the murderer of his wife and child through a bloody thumbprint found at the scene of the murders. Twain's character based the procedure on the practice of an old French prison keeper who recorded each convict's thumbprint because "there was one thing about a person which never changed, from the cradle to the grave—the lines in the ball of the thumb; and . . . these lines were never exactly alike in the thumbs of any two human beings."[17]

Some writers in the field of criminal justice have wondered just how Twain acquired knowledge in this area. The answer is that Twain was reared in an atmosphere of faith in palmists. A photograph of his right hand and the story of how he tested palmists appears in a Mark Twain biography.[18]

At this time, the only other American use of fingerprinting was that of an American engineer building railroads in New Mexico. Gilbert Thompson put his thumbprints on wage chits for the railroad workers to verify the payments. A San Francisco photographer had considered registering Chinese immigrants by the aid of fingerprints, but this was apparently never carried out, nor was a Cincinnati proposal to stamp thumbprints on railroad tickets in 1885.[19]

The missing part of the fingerprint puzzle not supplied by Faulds and Herschel was a means of classification of these unique human marks so that large collections of fingerprints could be filed in a logical order and then a new set of prints could be matched with a previously filed set. This needed an approach both scientific and bureaucratic. Scientists as early as 1684 had commented on the ridged patterns at the ends of fingers (Dr. Nehemiah Grew, England) and in 1686, using the newly discovered microscope, an Italian professor of anatomy (Marcello Malpighi, University of Bologna) wrote a treatise which noted the patterns were drawn out into loops or spirals. A century later, a Polish professor of physiology (John Evangelish Penkinje, University of Breslau) defined nine varieties of patterns of fingerprints.[20]

But it took the publication of a book on fingerprints in 1892 by a renowned anthropologist, Sir Francis Galton (a cousin of Charles Darwin), to publicize the value of fingerprints and spur work on classification. Galton had been attracted to Bertillonage as a means of studying heredity and racial traits. With a scientist's thoroughness, he also studied

Herschel's work and found that fingerprints held more promise than anthrometry as a means of identification.

Galton realized that three facts had to be established before finger-printing could be adopted to criminal identification or investigations:

> First it must be proved, not assumed, that the pattern of a fingerprint is constant throughout life. Secondly that the variety of patterns is really very great. Thirdly that they admit of being so classified or "lexiconized" that when a set of them is submitted to an expert, it would be possible for him to tell, by reference to a suitable dictionary, or its equivalent, whether a similar set had already been registered.[21]

In 1891, Galton's research was brought to the attention of Juan Vucetich of the Argentine provincial police. Vucetich, who had been ordered to establish a Bertillonage bureau, instead took Galton's work and devised the first practical system for classifying fingerprints for law enforcement use. By 1896, the Argentine government adopted fingerprints for criminal identification, beating England, Europe, and the United States to the use of this new system.

But Edward Henry, Inspector General of the province of Bengal, India (who was familiar with Herschel's work), independently developed his own system of classification in 1896, again based on Galton's research. The Henry system of classification became the basis of systems of identification in England and the United States within a few years.[22]

Henry was a talented British administrator in Bengal, an Indian province then part of the British Empire. In 1893, Henry introduced Bertillonage in Bengal, but found native police could only make very slow and uncertain identifications because of their lack of education. Henry was aware of Herschel's work on fingerprints in India and after Galton's book, *Finger Prints,* came to his attention he determined to visit Galton while on leave in England. Galton briefed him on the status of the classification effort and gave him notes on the subject.

Henry returned to India and spent the next two years of his free time on the matter of classification. He noted five basic patterns: plain arches, tented arches, radial loops, ulnar loops, and whorls, which he named with the code letters, A, T, R, U, and W. Each of these he broke down into subpatterns based on the number of ridges crossed by a straight line drawn between two easily recognized key points in the print. By arranging the code letters and numbers as a formula, Henry found he could file cards bearing ten fingerprints according to the classification and then locate a certain card with ease and simplicity.

An ingenious solution, but a simple and easily learned one—Henry had made the breakthrough which provided for the cataloguing of millions of prints and quick location of any one record for comparison. Brown and Brock, in their book *Fingerprints* noted:

> Police work demanded simplicity—both because this saved time and because a workable system must be one that could easily be grasped by men with no previous scientific training. Henry's success, where such men as Herschel and Galton had failed, may have been due to the fact that he was not a man of science, but a policeman.[23]

Henry's work was advanced by the solution of a murder case through the identification of a latent fingerprint found at the crime scene. Henry also testified before a committee appointed by the British Home Office to evaluate the comparative worth of Bertillonage and fingerprinting which resulted in the adoption of fingerprinting in England in 1901 as the official police identification system. Henry, later knighted, was appointed to head the Criminal Investigation Department of Scotland Yard.[24]

Europe slowly began to follow; Hungary and Denmark adopted fingerprinting over Bertillonage in 1902. Spain, Norway, and Russia soon abandoned Bertillonage for fingerprinting, too. This could have been viewed as a blow to French prestige, except that Bertillon had begun including some fingerprints, as special marks, in his records as early as 1894. And, in 1902, it fell to Bertillon to be the first to solve a murder case with fingerprints on the Continent, which led to the legend that Bertillon had discovered fingerprints!

Bertillon died in 1914; a few weeks later an international police conference (attended by Bertillon's successor and other French criminal justice specialists) considered the question of how to facilitate the hunt for international criminals. Bertillon's successor proposed a new standard method of identification, fingerprinting. But, by 1914, the new world was ahead of the old in this emerging science.[25]

THE AMERICAN SCENE

In the United States, the Will West case dealt a real blow to Bertillonage, and at the 1904 World's Fair in St. Louis, Missouri, American police officials were introduced to fingerprinting. The annual convention of police chiefs was held in conjunction with the fair and a British police official arrived to set up security for the English crown jewels being exhibited. The official, Detective Sgt. John Kenneth Ferrier of the London Metropolitan Police, actively sought converts to the British system of fingerprinting.[26]

Actually, the first systematic use of fingerprints in the U.S. is credited to the New York City Civil Service Commission for job applicants taking the civil service exam in 1902. The next year, the New York State Prison at Albany took fingerprints of inmates, but fingerprinting was generally unknown to American police officials until the World's Fair. The IACP had moved its National Bureau of Criminal Identification to the Fair in order to publicize the Bertillon system.[27]

But at the IACP meeting held at the Fair, the report of the "Committee to Examine Into the System of Identification by Finger Impressions" was read. This British/Indian report listed the four weak points of Bertillonage:

1. Skilled persons were needed to take the measurements.
2. Delicate instruments were needed to take the measurements.
3. Eighteen measurements had to be taken.
4. Time of search of previous records averaged an hour.

These disadvantages to Bertillonage, plus the problem illustrated by the West case, made a powerful case for fingerprinting. Two incidents in New York in the next few years reinforced the case. Police Commissioner McAdoo of New York City, who had heard of the case at Leavenworth, sent Detective Sgt. Joseph A. Faurot to London to study fingerprinting. Then, in 1906, Faurot arrested a hotel burglar, who denied his identity in a British accent. Faurot sent the burglar's fingerprints to London and in two weeks learned that London had his record: twelve convictions for hotel theft.

In 1908, Faurot solved a murder case through a fingerprint left on a bottle and three years later solved a burglary, which led to the adoption of fingerprint evidence in a court of law. The burglar had alibi witnesses, but Faurot had found a fingerprint at the scene. After the judge insisted on a test demonstration of the ability of fingerprints to identify a suspect, the defendant changed his plea to guilty.[28]

Recognition of the value of fingerprints in courts of law was relatively slow, because of the decentralization of British and American court systems. Generally, fingerprint experts had to prove the certainty of fingerprint identification de novo in each jurisdiction, until the highest court of the jurisdiction recognized the value of fingerprints.

Detective Sgt. Ferrier addressed the 1904 IACP convention on the subject of fingerprints, but more important, he demonstrated the subject for the St. Louis Police Department, which led to the establishment of the first American police department fingerprint bureau. Another student of Ferrier was Edward A. Evans, superintendent of the IACP's Bertillonage National Bureau of Criminal Identification. He was the son of Michael P. Evans, who headed the Chicago Police Identification Bureau. Emmett A. Evans, Edward's brother, later took his father's place in the Chicago bureau.

Mary E. Holland, the wife of Philip Holland, publisher of *The Detective*, took instruction from Ferrier on fingerprints, becoming the first female expert on the subject in this country. In the early years of this century *The Detective* was *the* police publication, predecessor to the IACP's magazine *The Police Chief*, and *The FBI Law Enforcement Bulletin*. Mrs. Holland helped set up fingerprint systems for the Army and Navy and at the invitation of Major Richard Sylvester, District of Columbia chief of police, instructed the head of the Washington police department's identification bureau. Another student of Detective Sgt. Ferrier was Constable Edward Foster of Canada who later became the founder of the Identification Bureau of the Royal Canadian Mounted Police.

The heads of identification bureaus in Cleveland and Indianapolis were also trained in fingerprinting. But Ferrier's most important convert was Robert W. McClaughry, former Chief of Police in Chicago and later warden of the federal penitentiary at Leavenworth, Kansas. McClaughry and Ferrier recorded all the fingerprints of prisoners at Leavenworth during October, 1904. This collection became part of the Justice Department file on all federal prisoners and, later, an initial part of the FBI's fingerprint collection.[29]

ADOPTION OF FINGERPRINTING

In 1905, E. Van Buskirk was hired as Superintendent of the IACP's National Bureau of Criminal Identification to replace Edward Evans, who returned to the Chicago Police Department Identification Bureau. A year later, Van Buskirk urged IACP members to adopt fingerprinting "in connection with Bertillon as it is now practiced," so as to not lose all the work already done. But some agencies, including the New York City Police Department, adopted fingerprints and discarded Bertillonage.

The end of the period that marked the birth of police professionalism saw the gradual adoption of fingerprinting. This highlighted IACP concern for a government-supported collection of identification data once again. The problem of financing the IACP's National Bureau of Identification had been a continuing difficulty since its formation in 1897. The IACP again advanced its proposal that the Department of Justice take over this project. This is what eventually happened, but it took a generation more to come about, while fingerprinting continued to gain adherents in the police community and acceptance in courts of law.

Chief Richard Sylvester of the District of Columbia, having failed at first to get national government support for a Bertillonage identification bureau in the Department of Justice, convinced the District Commissioners to operate the IACP bureau, but the IACP, having persuaded individual cities to support its bureau, felt that the individual cities would have to support this move.[30]

The debate in the IACP over Chief Sylvester's plan to have the District of Columbia take over the organization's identification bureau caused him to abandon this plan in favor of the Justice Department sponsorship of an identification bureau. In the meantime, fingerprinting continued to gain support. The Leavenworth, Kansas, chief of police told the 1911 convention of the IACP of the low cost of taking fingerprints and of the ease of learning to classify them for later retrieval.[31]

The Director of the Bureau of Identification at Leavenworth, A. J. Renoe, published a paper on how to take and classify fingerprints in *The Detective* in 1919. He did not bring up a sore point with law enforcement: the fingerprints at Leavenworth were classified and kept by convicts! Michael P. Evans, now Chief of the Bureau of Criminal Identification of the Chicago Police Department, explained to the IACP convention in 1920 how to demonstrate conclusively (to judges and juries, for example) that no two fingerprints were alike. Evans based this conclusion on a report to the French Academy of Sciences that the chances of two prints being identical was 4^{100} to 1. Four to the one-hundredth power is four with one hundred zeroes (a billion has only nine zeroes).[32]

In 1913, Chief Sylvester pointed out to the IACP that fingerprinting had not yet reached the stage of being a "system" in this country as it had in England, India, Argentina, or France, but it would when (1) each police department established an identification bureau and (2) each department lent its support to a national "clearing house" for fingerprint information. As the chief said:

> In other words, it requires all the units to make a whole, and the whole constitutes a system. We have the methods now, and it is hoped that one of them [fingerprints or Bertillonage] may be adopted within the next

several years by all cities and towns in order that there may exist a system in fact.[33]

Problems continued with the IACP National Bureau of Identification, which was now keeping both Bertillon and fingerprint records. One way of dealing with the difficulties was to improve communications among identification personnel. This had been long sought and in 1914 took place in conjunction with an IACP meeting. It led to the formation of the International Association for Identification (IAI) in that year; A. J. Renoe of Leavenworth Penitentiary was elected Secretary-Treasurer of the new organization. The word "criminal" was dropped from the group's name after only four years as the possibilities for humanitarian uses of fingerprint identification began to be realized.[34]

Police officials had long recognized the necessity for standardization in identification matters, but the decentralized structure of American police departments actually encouraged local experimentation. With the formation of the IAI, experimentation could be encouraged to gain professional recognition and, at the same time, be kept out of the mainstream of procedure until any innovation gained acceptance. This eased the standardization problem, but the financial strain in supporting a national bureau continued.

IACP members observed that their Canadian brethren had achieved a national system, but the Canadians, of course, had the organizational advantage of having law enforcement under federal control. However, in the U.S. there was a long tradition of local control over local policing (which, of course, continues today). In spite of this tradition, IACP members also recognized the need for a nationwide system of criminal identification, in addition to standardization.

The IACP's Van Buskirk, head of the identification bureau, warned that the bureau was in financial difficulty in 1920 and Chief Sylvester, formerly chief in the District of Columbia and now chief of police in Wilmington, Delaware, was named to represent the identification bureau's interests before Congress. Sylvester found himself waging the same battle he had fought twenty years before. The IACP had to wait until the new (Harding) administration took office to deal with the new Attorney General, Harry Daugherty. But by the next year IACP representatives found themselves in discussions with the Attorney General, who assured them that the government did indeed want to establish a national bureau of identification.

Chief Sylvester and other members of the IACP met with a committee formed by the Attorney General on November 30, 1921, and outlined a proposal that the Department of Justice take over the National Bureau of Criminal Identification. The proposal further provided that the Department would enlarge the bureau's functions to the benefit of all cities and towns at the expense of the federal government, provided that a majority of the supporting members of the bureau in the IACP voted to transfer all bureau property to the Department of Justice. A bill for the establishment of a National Bureau of Identification was introduced in Congress to do this; unfortunately it failed to pass in 1922, and in December the Board of Governors of the IACP met again with the Attorney General.[35]

Daugherty's idea was to place the bureau of criminal identification within the Department's Bureau of Investigation, then headed by William J. Burns. Burns, the son of a Columbus, Ohio, police commissioner, founded his own detective agency in 1889 and soon gained the reputation of a pro-management enforcer in labor disputes. But another complication arose at this point, after legislation failed again to pass Congress. A controversy arose between the IACP and Police Commissioner Richard Enright of the New York City Police Department who sponsored a competing bill that would have placed the national bureau of identification within the Interior Department (responsible for the census and population statistics) and located it in New York City.

To support its position the IACP turned to the American Bar Association for help. The chairman of a special committee on law enforcement, a former Governor of New York, promised to lobby the Attorney General for the IACP's position on a national bureau of identification. Donald Dilworth, IACP historian, noted that whether or not the bar association fulfilled its promise, within a month the Attorney General did take extraordinary action. The Comptroller General would not authorize acceptance of the IACP files without enabling legislation and the legislation had failed before Congress. Nonetheless, Attorney General Daugherty issued orders on September 21, 1923, to transfer the IACP bureau and the Leavenworth fingerprint files to the Justice Department in Washington.

The Attorney General acted a few hours after meeting with IACP Governors, along with William J. Burns, Director of the Bureau of Investigation, and J. Edgar Hoover, Burns's Assistant Director. Subsequent Congressional hearings criticized Burns and the Attorney General for this action. An irony of history is that the establishment of a national bureau of criminal identification was probably outside the law.[36]

Notes to Chapter 5

1. Stead, 1977, 159.
2. Dilworth, 1977b, 1.
3. Hoover, 1973, 9.
4. Ibid
5. Stead, 1977, 127.
6. Dilworth, 1977b, 27.
7. Stead, 1977, 134.
8. Dilworth, 1977b, 4.
9. Ibid, 8.
10. Ibid, 8–10.
11. Ibid, 23.
12. Nickell, Joe, 1980, 406.
13. Stead, 1977, 159.
14. Hoover, 1973, 9.
15. Stead, 1977, 160, 167.
16. Hoover, 1973, 11.
17. Ibid,
18. Meltzer, 1960, 151.
19. Walls, 1974, 93.
20. Hoover, 1973, 9.
21. Stead, 1977, 169.
22. Hoover, 1973, 9–14.
23. Stead, 1977, 172–173.
24. Hoover, 1973, 12.
25. Walls, 1974, 81–90.
26. Dilworth, 1977b, 54.
27. Ibid, 64.
28. Walls, 1974, 98–101.
29. Dilworth, 1977b, 64–66, 78–79.
30. Ibid, 86–87.
31. Ibid, 103.
32. Ibid, 100–101.
33. Ibid, 107.
34. Ibid, 109.
35. Ibid, 134–140.
36. Ibid, 150–151.

Chapter 6

THE DETECTION OF CRIME

American poet Edgar Allan Poe (1809–1849) is credited with the invention of the deductive detective story, a genre copied by the creator of the deliberative Sherlock Holmes, Sir Arthur Conan Doyle. The detection of crime, besides its fascination to writers and their readers even today, is, of course, a branch of policing, although it was slow in coming to America's "new police." Detection of crime is sometimes called "real policing" by police officers, who thus contrast their law enforcement role with their police service role.

Except for the very smallest police agencies in this country, American police departments have detective units: police officers in civilian clothes who are responsible for the detection of crime. (Recent studies suggest, however, that these units spend more effort gathering evidence for prosecution after a suspect has been arrested by patrol officers than actually solving crime.) There are, moreover, law enforcement agencies, both public and private, that are composed entirely of detectives with no uniformed officers, such as the FBI. The Pinkertons, oldest of the private detective agencies, was best known for its detection of crime, but also has had a uniformed guard service since Pinkerton's Protective Police Patrol was formed in 1858.

A major part of police professionalism has been the advancement of the means of detecting and proving of crimes. Thus, the development of detective units as part of police agencies, or as separate agencies of detectives entirely, is an element of law enforcement's renaissance. What detectives do and how they do it is an important facet of police professionalism. Historically, today's detectives can trace their origins to English law enforcement. As patrol officers are descended from The Watch, detectives are the descendents of English constables.

The office of constable, traditionally a daytime position often called "thief-taker," was transplanted to the American colonies and was supplemented by the night watch, a patrol force. These two groups were united into the "new police" at the middle of the 19th century in America and the smaller unit of constables later became the detectives of the new police. The Chicago Police Department, for example, did not establish a detective force until 1861, six years after the patrol force was formed. The question of how much protection the state was going to give to private property governed the organization and duties of the various detective units, just as this question had governed various issues in English law enforcement.

Industrialization in America, accompanied by the growth of this country's railroad system, caused profound changes in law enforcement not only in the developing cities but in rural areas where railroad property was subject to criminal attack. The lack of effective law enforcement on a county or state level brought the growth of private policing. Best known of the private policing organizations was the Pinkerton agency, the first modern crime detection agency and, in its nationwide capabilities and pioneering role as a central repository of criminal identification data, the forerunner of today's FBI.

Detectives have traditionally relied on information received from citizens to solve cases. The information usually comes from informants, criminals themselves who inform for monetary reward or to eliminate competitors. The French criminal investigative service was begun by a convicted criminal, who hired other criminals to detect their fellow felons, for example. But English and American constables were not criminals to begin with; they descended from the "thief-takers" of earlier times, but the necessity of association with criminals, coupled with the corruption in government, politics, and law enforcement, often changed their nature.

ENGLISH BACKGROUND

Jonathan Wild "was one of the most remarkable geniuses of modern times. . . . With efficiency of plan and perfection of organization unrivalled by any commodity market controller of modern times . . . Wild . . . planned and achieved the complete cornering of crime industry in London."[1]

Born in 1682 of a poor carpenter, Wild came to London as a young man determined to live by his wits alone. This soon led to a four-year term in prison, where he met every type of criminal, learned of the impact on the capital of the hordes of highwaymen, thieves and swindlers, and of the breakdown of the weak law enforcement system in the capital. The increase in crime was closely followed by the spread of corruption from the constable even to the judges. The crime industry of London was profitable, but not organized. Wild determined to control it.

Trade in receiving stolen goods was becoming one of the most important of London's commercial activities, but receivers of stolen property were suffering from new laws designed to restrict their activities—execution had been decreed for those convicted of receiving property stolen in a theft or burglary, knowing that the goods had been stolen. Wild, posing as a public benefactor, called on victims of theft and explained how he was sometimes able to trace thieves, contact them through a third party, and induce them to return the property for a cash payment. Deploring London's crime conditions, Wild offered to do this without any reward for himself. He claimed that he wanted to serve his fellow citizens and eventually entrap the thieves and secure their prosecution. He only needed to know how much the victim was willing to pay for the return of the property stolen.

Because of the breakdown of the law enforcement system, owners of property took Wild at his word. The efficiency of the services which followed made Wild an indispensable "public benefactor." He soon opened and staffed an office and quit calling on victims. On discovery of a loss, the victim would hurry to Wild's office—as today they would report to their insurance agent and the police. The victims found that the amount necessary to regain their property was almost always less than they had agreed to pay and Wild was always reluctant to accept a reward. This, of course, only enhanced his reputation as a public benefactor.

A system of rewards to anyone who gave information securing the conviction of a thief and pardon for anyone who implicated himself in so doing gave Wild a further means of controlling crime in London. Thieves who rebelled at the meager share of plunder that Wild allowed them found themselves dispatched to the gallows, through clandestine collaboration with corrupt constables and magistrates that Wild had arranged. Wild could, and did, issue orders to London's thieves to steal only on command. Wild's career in crime lasted until 1725, when a judge became an enemy and prosecuted him for receiving a reward for recovering stolen property—another capital crime at that time.[2]

Wild's career set the tone for the close and often corrupt relationships between thieves and "thief-takers" (constables and later detectives) for some time, but the pattern was disrupted by Henry Fielding, a lawyer, who was appointed a magistrate at Bow Street in 1748, a generation after Wild. Magistrates had detective-like staffs. Fielding and his half brother,

John, who succeeded him, were important voices for police reform in 18th century England. The reform was begun by men like the Fieldings who did not plunder the office of magistrate. Fielding began *The Covent-Garden Journal* to publicize thefts, give descriptions of criminals, and interest the public in the criminal law. John Fielding extended this effort and in 1772 the government agreed to finance this publication, now known as the *Quarterly Pursuit of Criminals* and later as the *Police Gazette.*

The Fielding brothers' contribution to the detection of crime was in the form of the "Bow Street Runners." Runners formed the staff of the magistrate and the Fieldings' runners actually pursued criminals, rather than fees. In 1753, Henry Fielding was ordered by the government to prevent the continuation of a series of murders which had been committed in the course of robberies. Fielding assembled a force which accomplished this in a month. Known as "Mr. Fielding's people" the force was maintained by John Fielding when he succeeded his brother and eventually became known as the "Bow Street Runners." These "pursuers," as they were also known, constituted the first professional detective force in England.[3]

The Fieldings were followed in England by another lawyer appointed justice of the peace, who brought "the mind of a man of business" to policing. A Scots magistrate and businessman in 1782, Patrick Colquhoun (pronounced "Cohoon"), moved to London where he was part of the movement to reform the corrupt system of magistrates through the device of paying the magistrates from government funds, on the Bow Street model, rather than from fees. Colquhoun was successful in capturing counterfeiters and embezzlers; magistrates had to be their own detectives then. He wrote three police books which had long-range influence on the development of policing, but is perhaps best known for the establishment of the Thames Police.

The river Thames was the lifeblood of English commerce. Half a million people lived off the river; 120,000 men were employed in Thames commerce. In 1797, some 22,500 vessels moved $150 million worth of goods, triple that of forty years before. Colquhoun described the predators who menaced this commerce, as "river pirates," "night plunderers," and "mud larks," who, he estimated, stole some $2 or $3 million of this property. Based on an idea developed by John Harriott, a widely traveled military and naval person, Colquhoun was able to implement a detailed plan to police the Thames. He established a police magistrate's court in the river area which included a river police. This was so successful that the river pirates vanished within a year and the Thames police were incorporated into the Metropolitan Police some forty years later.[4]

THE SURETÉ

The French department of "criminal police," as detective forces are called in Europe, began in 1810 when Joseph Fouché was Minister of Police under Napoleon. His reputation as a domestic spy master, and the reputation of the founder of the Sureté, Eugene Francois Vidocq, had a negative influence on the development of English and American policing in the early 19th century. What were conceived of as excesses by the Continental police from the English common law viewpoint, especially practices of Fouché's Sureté, contributed to the English and American fear of centralized, militaristic policing. The apocryphal tale, that of three Frenchmen meeting to discuss public affairs, one of them would be Fouché's spy, was taken to heart by Englishmen and Americans who valued their hard-won political freedom.

Fouché, associated with the bloodiest excesses of the "Terror" when appointed to head the French police under the Directory that preceeded Napoleon, stayed on under that new dictator. He is credited with the policing system that includes a high degree of surveillance of the population in France and countries conquered by Napoleon.[5] Vidocq, first head of the Sureté, was a prison breaker. Son of a baker, he worked as a showman, soldier, sailor, and puppetmaster, until he was convicted of beating an officer who had seduced his girl. In 1799, he was successful in his third escape from prison and then lived for ten years as an old-clothes dealer in Paris. But former fellow convicts kept threatening to inform on him. In disgust he finally went to the Paris police headquarters and offered the knowledge of the criminal underworld that he had acquired over the years in return for freedom from the menace of prison that hung over him.

The Paris Prefect of Police, Baron Pasquier, decided to put Vidocq in charge of fighting crime in all of Paris. A sham arrest and yet another escape were arranged for Vidocq, who then set up his headquarters and employed at first four, then twelve, and later twenty, former convicts who were paid from a secret fund. As proof of the saying that it takes a thief to catch a thief, these former convicts arrested 812 murderers, thieves, burglars, robbers, and embezzlers in one year.

Vidocq and members of his organization regularly visited prisons in order to keep up with criminals (forerunner of today's police lineups) and developed an extensive archive of drawings of known criminals, the origin of the material that led Bertillon to develop his system of criminal identification much later. Vidocq resigned in 1833 because of a change in administration and opened a private detective agency, probably the first in the world. But it was another private detective, a Scot, who had the most profound influence on American law enforcement.[6]

THE PINKERTONS

In 1855, 35-year-old deputy sheriff Allan Pinkerton, an immigrant who had fled Scotland to avoid arrest for radical activities, won a contract for $10,000 to establish a railroad police for six midwestern railroads. This contract allowed Pinkerton to build America's largest and most successful private investigative firm, which had a profound impact on American policing and police professionalism.

In that year America was just beginning to adopt the "new police" as an answer to urban unrest. Historic fears of a militaristic police system had been replaced by a concern over disorder in the rapidly growing cities. Between 1820 and 1860 urban population grew eightfold—Boston alone grew from 38,000 to 212,000, Philadelphia from 75,000 to 450,000. Midwestern cities such as St. Louis, Cincinnati, and Chicago grew even faster. This growth was fueled by America's tremendous increase in immigration. The Know Nothing Party gained a considerable following at that time on its anti-Catholic and anti-foreign platform.

This party was even able to elect a Mayor in Chicago in 1855 who dismissed the constable-night watch system of law enforcement and instituted a "new police" staffed by non-immigrants. Citizens, who had historically served on the night watch and who had responded to the constables' "hue and cry" in the daytime, now turned to government to take over these duties. But, in the formation of the "new police" from the old night watch and constable system, most cities disbanded the constables and did not replace them with a detective system for some years. It was six years after the formation of Chicago police before the city hired its first detective, for example. Private detectives, primarily the Pinkertons, filled this investigative gap in the ranks of "thief-takers" and, in effect, became competitors to the public police—but also a model for later public police detectives.

Allan Pinkerton was the son of a Scots policeman. Born in Glasgow in 1819, at age 10 young Pinkerton's father was invalided as a result of injuries suffered in a street riot and the boy had to be appreciated to a cooper (barrel-maker) to support the family. Pinkerton later joined the workers' movement called Chartists and gravitated to the more violent branch of this movement. He had to flee Scotland for Canada to avoid arrest for these activities in 1842. Shipwrecked off Nova Scotia and forced to surrender his new bride's wedding ring to a band of Indians that met the shipwreck (his wife never wore another wedding ring), Pinkerton traveled to Chicago rather than Canada where he established a cooperage in Dundee, a small farming community 38 miles northwest of the city.[7]

His second contact with law enforcement, after his father's service as a policeman, was in Dundee where he discovered some counterfeiters, a widespread American problem at the time. This led to an appointment as a deputy sheriff while he managed his cooperage. But Pinkerton's abolitionist views against slavery made him unpopular in Dundee, so he sold his business and moved back to Chicago where he became a prominent abolitionist and worked for the Secretary of the Treasury on a contractual basis to investigate counterfeiting in Illinois. The Secret Service, the Treasury's investigative arm, was not formed until 1865.

Basic changes in American industry coupled with problems inherent in the American system of federalism came together at this time to create Pinkerton's opportunity. Industrialization posed problems of worker control; a new discipline was needed as large numbers of workers were gathered together in environments vastly different from those in the previously prevalent cottage industries. The work day was no longer governed by the sun; in middle-class business society, time was money and expansion of business enterprises increased the difficulty of control. Before, the craftsman or entrepreneur had worked in close proximity with his workers, which insured close control and no opportunities for thievery.

Two of the businesses that were expanding at this time had these problems of control: the U.S. Post Office and the railroads. In 1851, Illinois had less than a hundred miles of railroad trackage; five years later there were over 2,000 miles of tracks. During this period the constable-night watch system of policing the cities was giving way to the "new police," but the detection duties of the constables were not continued by the patrol-oriented new police at first. Further, rural law enforcement depended on the rural sheriff, but the sheriff could not cope with the criminal depredations that accompanied railroad trackage in the rural environment. State police did not appear until the turn of the century, except for the Texas Rangers which had been begun for military reasons. Thus, law enforcement faced problems in a society enamoured of federalism. When a railroad train left the city it lost all protections of urban society until it reached its destination.[8]

Pinkerton had worked for the railroads before; in 1854 he apprehended a railroad wrecker for the Southern Michigan line. But when he formed the North West Police Agency most of his work involved checking on railroad workers to insure their honesty. Pinkerton had first made a reputation in private investigation for the U.S. Post Office as a special agent. In Chicago, he had arrested postal clerks who were stealing from the mails. Although Pinkerton's was not the first private investigative firm in the United States—two St. Louis police officers had formed an agency in 1846—it quickly became the best known.[9]

Pinkerton's national reputation initially came when he uncovered a plot to assassinate President-elect Abraham Lincoln. Historian Bruce Catton described Allan Pinkerton as one who had a "peculiar combination of energy and imagination" in recounting the supposed plot against the newly elected President that Pinkerton supposedly foiled by changing Lincoln's travel plans to the capital in 1861. Catton's first volume in his Centennial History of the Civil War goes on to note that Pinkerton's service to the Union army in the next year (as chief of McClellan's secret service) was to prove a "decided handicap" to that army.[10]

But the Pinkerton agency went on to forge a considerable reputation by tracking and capturing the gangs that preyed on the railroads after the Civil War, although the Pinkertons infuriated labor unions with their investigation of the Molly Maguires, the Pennsylvania Irish miners' fraternity accused of murdering mine owners in the 1870s. Concern for his firm's public image, and that of private detectives in general, led Pinkerton to publish some 16 detective books in the decade before he died in 1884. Some of these were simply detective stories in the genre begun by Poe, but in some Pinkerton assumed the position of America's expert crime fighter. In this, and in other ways, there are some parallels between Pinkerton, his agency, and the FBI and its long-time director, J. Edgar Hoover.

Pinkerton built up the agency's rogues' gallery of criminal photographs and exchanged the pictures and identifying data with police agencies across the Nation, preceeding the International Association of Chiefs of Police (IACP) in the establishment of a national collection of criminal identification data. The IACP's file eventually became part of the FBI's Division of Identification, as detailed in Chapter 5. In the days when federalism beliefs limited nationwide crime fighting capabilities and local police and sheriffs were limited in their jurisdiction by state and local boundaries, the Pinkertons picked up the slack in law enforcement by operating nationwide without regard to geographic limitations. It would take the federal government nearly a century to develop these same capabilities in the form of the FBI of 1935 and beyond.

Indeed, William Pinkerton, who followed his father as head of the agency, addressed the IACP after World War I and called for a "central government agency force of Federal detectives that will centralize, connect up and weave together data gathered by its representatives North, South, East, and West." This organization, he proposed "would never be used against labor" (a repudiation of much of the work by which his father had gained his reputation) and would become a "centralized clearing house of secret service data for the protection of the people...." This agency, Pinkerton thought, would meet the threat of communist subversion, an echo of his father's 1878 book, *Strikers, Communists, Tramps and Detectives.*[11]

Founder Allan Pinkerton even showed some personal similarities to J. Edgar Hoover beyond the similar capabilities of their respective organizations. They were both innovative, authoritarian, and conservative. As energetic younger men, Pinkerton and Hoover were both innovative in methods of crime fighting with great influence on other law enforcement agencies for years to come. Pinkerton's technique of infiltration of organized criminal groups is reflected today in the FBI after Hoover. Conservative in outlook (in spite of his early association with the English Chartists), Pinkerton insisted on honesty in his operatives (even writing a guidebook for them in 1867), in the way Hoover built the FBI into the most honest law enforcement agency of its day. But towards the end of his life Pinkerton became slightly paranoiac about mysterious "powers" that he thought were fighting his agency.

Even when his sons became active in the business, Allan Pinkerton refused to turn over control to them. The Molly Maguire investigation was the last one to be personally supervised by Allan Pinkerton; in 1877, the agency assisted the U.S. Secret Service in foiling the plot to steal Lincoln's body from its marble sarcophagus in Springfield, Illinois.

Records show that insurance companies, business firms, banks, and even state governments, before state police were established, automatically called in the Pinkertons when they were hit by a major crime. The Pinkertons even filled the role of a national police agency in their cooperation with the principal police organizations of Europe; they maintained liaison with Scotland Yard, the Sureté, and other national police organizations, as the FBI does today.

The Pinkerton Agency's biographer, James Horan, sums up the contribution the father, and the two sons who followed him in the agency, made:

> The Pinkertons fulfilled a need in America at a critical juncture in the nation's history—indeed, their growth was in answer to the strict law of supply and demand. They fulfilled it with fidelity to those who employed them and in accordance with their own moral principles and the ethics of their time.[12]

The motto of today's FBI is fidelity, bravery, and integrity (for the initials F.B.I.). Fidelity—to those who employ FBI Agents, the people of the United States. The Pinkertons, too, demonstrated bravery as they faced the West's outlaws with drawn guns. And the Pinkertons' integrity far outshown that of local police detectives in the last half of the 19th century.

CORRUPTION AND THE "THIRD DEGREE"

Political influence on public law enforcement at this time, which influenced both patrol and detective operations, led to corruption which was exposed time after time by the various crime commissions of the day. This political influence, of course, did not affect the Pinkertons or other private investigative firms. Other unprofessional conduct, such as the use of the "third degree" in interrogation, was addressed not only by the crime commissions but by the police chiefs themselves through the IACP conventions.

When the "new police" were first formed in America as primarily a response to disorder in urban areas, these new agencies were patrol oriented. Regular patrol was thought to be the answer to the problems of order maintenance and crime prevention. The solution of crimes already committed through detection was at first handled by the patrol force, which was not uniformed in the beginning, or by separate agencies such as existed at first in Philadelphia, Washington, D.C., and some other cities.

The movement for police professionalism was broad enough to include both patrol and detective functions of departments. Both functions suffered from ward-level political influence. In the case of the detective branch political factors affected how detectives dealt with enforcement, particularly of the sumptuary laws. Detectives and patrol officers dealt with vice law enforcement, but detectives, having responsibility to investigate criminality, had to deal with those involved with vice on a regular basis, as these persons were the citizens with the best knowledge of crime conditions overall.

As Deputy Chief Stark of the Toronto, Canada, Police Department noted at the 1909 IACP convention:

> Information regarding criminals is not usually picked up in the Sunday School or the prayer meeting, but must be sought for in the haunts of the criminal classes, although goody-goody people, who are usually the most exacting in the matter of police efficiency, have been known to hold up both hands in horror if a policeman or detective is seen within a block of a house of ill-fame, or gambling house, or in conversation with men or women who cannot produce certificates of church membership. . . . Criminal information is generally a purchasable commodity, and the individual possessed of it is usually not averse to parting with it for a consideration.[13]

Detectives soon learned that to insure their regular flow of information about the more serious crime that besides buying the information, they had to allow their sources to participate in less serious criminality, such as violations of vice laws.

Police were faced on the one hand with the reform movement which opposed gambling, drinking, and doing business on Sunday, and on the other hand the immigrants and ethnics whose life-style differed radically from the reformers. Thus, the police and their political patrons, and especially the detectives, had to decide whether to tolerate gambling, prostitution, drinking, and other vices and, if so, in what neighborhoods. As one New Yorker reminded police, they would, no matter what, drink their beer, even "bathe in it, swim in it."[14]

Urban politicians, often completely dependent for their political survival on the immigrant vote, endorsed or even demanded, police toleration of vice. They also used contributions from vice interests to support their political machines. Local politicians, especially in ethnic and slum neighborhoods, financed their organizations through levies on businesses, which were often collected by detectives not only from illegal businesses, houses of prostitution and gambling dens, but also from legitimate businesses.[15]

Detectives, inured to collecting political money for ward bosses, saw that they could also collect from thieves—for themselves. As one deputy commissioner of police in New York City noted at this time, detectives operated out of saloons and dives on the edge of the underworld and the detectives were hard to tell from the criminals. The detectives, in a symbiotic relationship with criminals, allowed con men, pickpockets, burglars, and other thieves to operate in return for a share of their proceeds. They also took a share from pawnbrokers and even from victims, this last in the form of rewards, a practice dating back to England's Jonathan Wild. And the detectives usually split their take with the politicians, who would otherwise use their influence to reduce the detectives to uniform or get them thrown off the force. The police, then, did not eradicate crime; they regulated it.[16]

In Chicago, for example, detectives on the bunco squad, insisted that a newly arrived con man seek out a detective and make a payment of $20 or face arrest. This gave the con man the privilege of operating, but if a victim complained to police the con man was informally "fined;" he was expected to share 10% of the take with the police for operating so ineffectively as to cause a complaint.[17]

Corruption among police at this time reflected the general mores of the times, of course. There was corruption, by today's standards, in municipal government affairs, at the state level and in the national government. And there were segments of the reform movement that were as interested in eliminating this corruption at all levels of government as in wresting control of the political process from the hands of "machine" politics. One target of the reformers interested in "cleaner" government and more professional public service was police use of the so-called "third degree" in interrogation.

Reformers advocated police training to promote professionalism; there was no training while the police were dominated by political machines. For one thing, the politicians wanted their own supporters in police jobs, which often meant a virtual "clean sweep" of the department if a new political faction won at the polls. Training, obviously, would be a waste in this situation. This lack of training meant, too, a complete lack of legal background for police. Coupled with the police patrol necessity to physically establish a police presence in the streets, this lack of legal training contributed to a tradition of police brutality that was evidenced, too, in interrogation.

One of the first chiefs of police to recognize this problem in discussions with his peers was Chief Richard Sylvester of Washington, D.C. In his "History of the 'Sweat Box' and 'Third Degree'" given to the 1910 IACP convention (see Chapter 3), Sylvester offered this resolution:

> That the International Association of Chiefs of Police go on record as stating it is their aim and intention to at all times condemn such practice [the third degree] and to punish those guilty, if possible, and it asks the cooperation of all law-abiding citizens and organizations to that end.[18]

During the considerable discussion that followed, several chiefs noted that their departments did not force confessions or offered the pre-Miranda [Miranda v. Arizona, 348 U.S. 436 (1966)] rights warnings that their investigators used. New Orleans police noted that they included the District Attorney or an assistant in interrogations. Chiefs in Jersey City, New Jersey, and Dayton, Ohio, had instituted formal rights statements as early as 1895.

Chief Sylvester's motion condemning the "third degree" was carried unanimously. Police themselves, very early in the progress toward professionalism, were addressing the unprofessional, and very difficult, aspects of law enforcement that took the Supreme Court of the U.S. another half century to decide.

Notes to Chapter 6

1. Reith, 1952, 34.
2. Ibid, 34–41.
3. Stead, 1977, 33–41.
4. Ibid, 48–58.
5. Ibid, 64, 70.
6. Thorwald, 1964, 3–5.
7. Eldefonso, 1974, 72–73.
8. Stead, 1977, 96–105.
9. Horan, 1967, 25.
10. Catton, 1961, 223.

11. Horan, 1967, 495–496.
12. Ibid, 252–253, 516.
13. Dilworth, 1976, 58–59.
14. Fogelson, 1977, 16, 21.
15. Haller, 1976, 307.
16. Fogelson, 1977, 33.
17. Haller, 1976, 311.
18. Dilworth, 1976, 72.

PART II

CAUSES OF THE RENAISSANCE—1920s

Public perception of a crime wave in the 1920s, aggravated by the impact of Prohibition, is generally cited as the cause of national attention being directed at law enforcement during this period. The influence of two strong personalities in law enforcement and social trends of the period also have to be examined to understand the direction American policing was to take in the 1930s.

August Vollmer, one of the three giants of American police professionalism, was an innovative thinker on the police role, an experimenter with new technologies for policing, an initiator of research on the causes of crime, and an advocate of police education who virtually began the teaching of policing on the college level. Vollmer was the author of the Report on Police of the Wickersham Commission, the first significant national examination of law enforcement in this country. The Wickersham Commission itself was a culmination of the forces unleashed by the Progressive Movement to begin police professionalism.

Vollmer's activities in the first two decades of this century were then followed by J. Edgar Hoover, a brilliant administrator who pioneered needed national elements of professionalism. Hoover had a longer tenure as America's "top cop" and his access to a national forum brought his ideas to virtually every police officer in the country. Both of these leaders were also practical men who had to, and did, run their different agencies with efficiency and results that more than satisfied their constituencies, allowing them the freedom to innovate.

Chapter 7

AUGUST VOLLMER'S INFLUENCE

The "father of modern police science," as August Vollmer came to be called, began his long law enforcement career as the elected marshal of a Western town. But Berkeley, California, was a progressive college town, not a frontier outpost. In spite of his original election, throughout his life Vollmer opposed political influence in policing. Vollmer had only a grade school education, but he pioneered the hiring of college students as police officers; he began one of the first departmental police academies and virtually founded two of the first criminal justice programs at universities.[1]

He began the analysis of the police patrolman's work and developed theories on the police role. His other contributions to police professionalism in his day included the new technologies then being developed: (1) the use of vehicles for patrol work (first, bicycles, then motorcycles, and finally automobiles before World War I); (2) the development of scientific crime laboratories; (3) one of the first workable signal systems for contacting patrol officers; (4) leadership of the IACP in the 1920s after Major Sylvester of Washington, D.C., stepped down; (5) the urging of a nationwide identification bureau in Washington, D.C.; and (6) the writing of the section on policing for the first nationwide study of law enforcement. He also was a realistic thinker in the consideration of the vice problem; he advocated control, not repression of vice, in contrast to much of the Progressive Movement.

Vollmer's view of police professionalism included the element of administrative efficiency, as exemplified by the military example. His view of policing included both crime fighting and elementary community/social work on the part of police. This latter policing role eventually was overshadowed in America by the former, as Vollmer's protege, O. W. Wilson, gained prominence and adopted the crime fighting role of policing over community/social service. J. Edgar Hoover's advocacy of the crime fighting role, along with Hoover's nationwide forum and leadership, helped lead to denigration of the community/social service role and Vollmer, in effect, was carried along.

The second renaissance in policing, beginning in the late 1960s, vindicated this community service/social work view of policing developed by August Vollmer two generations before. The work of the Police Foundation under the leadership of Patrick V. Murphy, chief of four different large city police departments during his career, has proven this. The result could be termed policing's Renaissance II. It has been fostered by Hoover's successor as Director of the FBI, Clarence M. Kelley, who worked closely with Murphy and the Police Foundation while Kelley was Chief of Police in Kansas City, Missouri, before being appointed to head the FBI.

MARSHAL OF BERKELEY

August Vollmer was born March 7, 1876, in New Orleans, the son of John and Phillipine Vollmer, German immigrants. He completed grade school in New Orleans and later went to the New Orleans Academy, a trade school, for two years taking secretarial-type courses. On the death of his father, a grocer, Phillipine Vollmer took the eight-year-old August and his sisters back to Germany for two years. Returning in 1886 to New Orleans, the family then moved to San Francisco in 1888, later moving to nearby Berkeley, California, where August had a number of jobs, plus a year in the U.S. Army during the Spanish-American War, which included some 25 engagements on the gunboat "Laguna de Bay" in the Phillipines.

Returning to Berkeley after the war, Vollmer had five years service as a letter carrier until he was persuaded to stand for election to the post of Town Marshal by several leading citizens, including his employer, the postmaster, and a newspaper publisher, who later became Governor of California. In excellent physical condition, a champion boxer and wrestler with a local reputation for bravery (after he stopped a runaway railroad car from causing a train wreck), Vollmer was elected Town Marshal of Berkeley on April 10, 1905. His department consisted of four deputy marshals at first.[2]

Vollmer established a national reputation as a police leader, in spite of commanding only a small department in the West, by his use of technology, training, and experimentation with new ideas. Berkeley's growth in Vollmer's first two years as marshal increased the size of his force from four deputies to twenty-six. After another two-year term, Berkeley changed its form of government and provided for an appointive chief of police; Vollmer was appointed and held the position for another twenty-three years.[3]

In the early years of the century, before the development of motorized patrol with radio capability, police executives tried to develop signal systems to contact their patrolmen. This was for two reasons: first, in order to improve police response time to reported crimes and second, to better control their patrol forces. In 1906, after reading a newspaper item about a private detective in Los Angeles who had developed a workable signal system, Vollmer examined this recall system and hit upon the idea of having red lights suspended at intersections in Berkeley which could be used to flash code messages to patrolmen. The town's trustees would not approve the $25,000 such a system would cost, but Vollmer persuaded them to submit a bond issue to the citizens, who did approve. Such systems, of course, were outmoded by motor patrols when radio capability developed; the first radio patrol car in the nation was put into service in 1921 by Vollmer.[4]

By 1911, Chief of Police Vollmer, recognizing the advantages of mobility in police work, had placed his entire force on bicycles. With advances in technology, in the next two years half of the force was put on motorcycles and the other half in automobiles (motorcycles, because of their noise and tendency to injure officers, were phased out by 1917). Motorizing the entire department had far-reaching effects on American policing, effects that are only now being challenged in the 1980s.[5]

A chronology of his innovative career, probably compiled by Vollmer himself in the late 1940s, notes that in 1906 he installed the first centralized police record system and the first "modus operandi" system. The latter was a tool to identify repeat offenders through similarities in the ways they carried out their crimes. This system was copied by the Wichita Police Department where Vollmer's protege, O. W. Wilson, had been made chief. After a study of the system seemed to negate its value, Wilson wrote in *Police Administration,* "The technique is of less utility in the United States [than in Britain] because of the indiscriminate nature of street crimes, unpredictable youth-gang criminal patterns, and the prevalence of crime resulting from drug addiction."[6]

But the system was also put into operation in Los Angeles in 1924 when Vollmer served as "reform" police chief there. According to a 1955 study of policing, the Los Angeles "Modus Operandi" files there contained some two million punch cards and had solved a long list of cases.

Of course, the usefulness of any such system depended in large measure on the quality and quantity of data contained in it. Vollmer's early interest in compiling complete records—he often interviewed those that we today call "career criminals" himself to learn their operating methods—led to his interest in a more formalized system of cooperation between police agencies, at first across the state and then across the nation.[7]

IDENTIFICATION ADVOCACY

Vollmer's interest in identification dated from 1905 when one of his deputies shot and killed a man in a gun fight. The dead man had no identification, so Marshal Vollmer sent the deceased's photograph to the Pinkerton private detective agency in Chicago. The Pinkertons identified him as "The Kid," head of a gang of bank robbers wanted in three countries.[8]

Vollmer established a police records system in the Berkeley Police Department in 1906, when few departments kept any records, but it was not until 1915 that the city council provided for appointment of a police superintendent of records. But the council did allow the purchase of fingerprint equipment in 1909, just five years after the introduction of the new technique in St. Louis. Through the California Police Chiefs Association, Vollmer pushed for a state-wide central bureau of identification.

The California Bureau of Criminal Identification had been started in 1905, but it was designed to serve state agencies, primarily with records from San Quentin prison. There was only limited and awkward sharing of information among chiefs of police and no centralized repository for this data. Vollmer's aim was to expand this bureau to serve all law enforcement agencies in the state.[9] The State Bureau of Identification and Investigation was finally approved in 1917, after previous vetoes of the bill establishing the expanded role. The Governor had been pressured by labor groups who feared creation of another anti-labor state police organization. A sergeant from the Berkeley Police Department was put in charge of the new bureau.[10]

Vollmer, as President of the International Association of Chiefs of Police (see below), called for a "workable plan" for establishing "a national bureau of criminal records and crime statistics." As set out in Chapter 5, some police leaders were suspicious of the national government taking on this function, fearing they would lose control of the IACP Bureau of

Identification or that a future national administration should decide to withhold necessary funding to support a new national bureau.

But, as Vollmer's biographers noted:

> ... In 1925 the IACP records became part of the Federal Bureau of Investigation, an agency that combined record keeping with the responsibility for investigation of federal offenses.
>
> Vollmer was clearly in favor of this dual function and considered it appropriate that the agency be more than just a repository for fingerprints, photographs, and other criminal data. When the California records agency had been formed in 1917, he had attempted to have it enacted as a Bureau of Identification and Investigation, but the move had been blocked by state labor interests. The FBI, as it developed, reflected many of Vollmer's ideas—an efficient system of records, scientific investigative techniques, high personnel standards, and strong leadership. . . . [11]

In the 1930s, when fingerprinting reached a height of popularity under J. Edgar Hoover's encouragement nationally, Vollmer collected some thousands of fingerprints, almost the entire population of Berkeley, on a voluntary basis. He also advocated national compulsory fingerprinting, but opposition from those who believed this would infringe on civil liberties convinced Vollmer to scale back on these proposals. He then advocated that criminals have an identity card to enable police to keep track of their whereabouts. The outbreak of World War II, with the fingerprinting of military personnel and those engaged in war work, ended the national debate on compulsory fingerprinting.

PROFESSIONAL ORGANIZATION LEADERSHIP

In 1906, police chiefs in California organized the California Chiefs of Police Association, and the following year Vollmer was elected president, although Vollmer's title was still Town Marshal. Vollmer began working toward a central records bureau in California. As noted in Chapter 3, August Vollmer, in spite of heading a small California department, was elected President of the International Association of Chiefs of Police (IACP) in 1921. At this time, of course, the IACP had no professional staff to lend continuity to the organization's activities, so the president's leadership was much more important than today. In 1922, the group's annual convention was held in San Francisco and the chiefs could visit Berkeley and see the programs being tried there. More important was Vollmer's visionary address to the assembled chiefs.

Vollmer urged the chiefs, in his "Aims and Ideals of the Police" speech, to adopt numerous important reforms. In discussing recruitment methods, he urged what we call today "civilianization" of policing, the hiring of civilians to handle specialized positions in laboratory and identification work. He called for the increased use of policewomen, especially in the "vast field of pre-delinquency" (crime prevention) and greater emphasis on crime prevention, in Vollmer's words policing's "principal function."

He urged improved police records: "A bureau of records, if properly organized, is the hub of the police wheel." And he followed this recommendation with one for the uniform classification of crimes, which was accomplished by the IACP over the next eight years. And, finally, he called for the petitioning of universities to devote more study to "human behavior, its bearing upon political and social problems, and for the training of practical criminologists, jurists, prosecutors, policemen, and policewomen."[12]

As Vollmer's philosophical successor, Patrick V. Murphy, former New York City Police patrolman who later rose to be Commissioner, and then innovative president of the Police Foundation, described the nexus of policing: despite all the technological advances in police work since Vollmer's time, "the art of police work is still basically human relations."[13]

Part of Vollmer's rise to leadership in the police community was his conduct of surveys of various police departments across the country, culminating in his review of policing nationwide for the Wickersham Commission. Although Vollmer began his surveys with the reorganization of San Diego Police Department in 1917, the Los Angeles survey of 1923–1924 set forth his philosophy of policing, in addition to corrective measures in recruiting, training, allocation of resources, records, and supervision. The Los Angeles survey was followed by Detroit (1925), Havana, Cuba (1926), Chicago and Kansas City (1929), Minneapolis (1930), Santa Barbara (1934), Piedmont (1936), Syracuse (1943), Dallas (1944), and Portland, Oregon (1947). Today, these surveys would appear perhaps simplistic, but considering the state of policing in that era they had tremendous impact.[14]

EDUCATION OF POLICE

Vollmer's most significant contribution toward police professionalism was the recognition of the need for education for police officers. At a time when the educational level of police, even of Vollmer himself and most of the rest of American society, was only that of grade school or slightly beyond, Vollmer sought college-educated police officers and brought college level education to officers already in service.

In 1908, Vollmer began a school for his deputies. Although not the first police training school in America, as Parker (1972) and Carte (1975) called it (St. Louis, as noted in Chapter 2, preceded Berkeley by 38 years in starting a police training school), this school was the first to teach scientific approaches to crime detection. Two of the first instructors were University of California professors William B. Herms of the Parasitology Department, who lectured on the enforcement of sanitation laws, important because of a recent bubonic plague scare, and A. M. Kidd of the Law School, who handled law and evidence. More university faculty members were added in succeeding years.[15]

Education formed a major part of Vollmer's concept of law enforcement professionalism, possibly in part because of his own lack of formal education, but certainly because the University of California campus was in Berkeley. His philosophy, and his admiration for the scientist and the educated man, was set out in an 1937 article in the *FBI Law Enforcement Bulletin*, "The Police Ideal of Service:"

> The service ideal aspires to the personal attainment of knowledge. ... This motivates the policeman to delve profoundly into the theory and practice of dealing with human beings, as individuals and as groups. His search into natural biological and social sciences is an eternal quest for that clue which, if found, will aid the policeman in dealing more intelligently with his fellow men.[16]

Toward this end Vollmer, after beginning a police academy in Berkeley with a university faculty, made what James Q. Wilson called Vollmer's "best-known contribution" to the improvement of police personnel, his "recruiting of college men from Berkeley to serve on the local force."[17] Author Alfred E. Parker, who knew Vollmer, says that the idea of recruiting college men to become policemen began in 1918; the genesis of this idea was Vollmer's recollection of the *Maxims of Confucius:* "The successful administration of any government depends entirely upon the selection of proper men."

One of the best known of these recruits was O. W. Wilson, who became a chief of police, a college teacher, and a writer on police administration. Another college-educated recruit was Walter Gordon, who served ten years on the Berkeley force while attending law school after playing

football and gaining his undergraduate degree. Gordon, later a successful lawyer, was the first black policeman in Berkeley. He had received
threats when first assigned to an all-white beat, but asked Vollmer to let
him work it out. After a few years, when Vollmer considered Gordon's
transfer to another beat, the strongest protest to the possible move came
from the man who had threatened Gordon at first![18]

But Vollmer did not stop with recruiting college students and forming
a police in-service curriculum that in many respects was of college level;
he was instrumental in establishing criminology education at colleges in
California and Chicago. In 1914, Vollmer wrote:

> Every trade or profession demands apprenticeship or schooling, ade-
> quately to prepare a man for his work. . . . Effort is being made to
> educate our officers who are now receiving instruction in the various
> subjects considered essential for the better performance of their duties.[19]

Vollmer recognized the distinction between a trade and a profession,
and between apprenticeship and schooling, and he pursued both goals —
training for officers already in service and education for potential officers.

Under Vollmer's stimulation, the university at Berkeley awarded a
degree with a minor in criminology to a Berkeley officer in 1923, which
appears to be the first academic recognition of police courses in gaining
a degree. In 1924, while acting as police chief in Los Angeles, Vollmer
persuaded the University of Southern California to sponsor lectures for
his command officers. This developed into a full academic curriculum
by 1928, with experienced law enforcement practitioners forming an
advisory panel on the curriculum.

Vollmer taught two courses in police administration, one a seminar, at
the University of Chicago the next year and in 1930 began a law enforce-
ment program at the San Jose State College in California. Together with
San Jose's president and Earl Warren, then District Attorney of Alameda
County, and later Chief Justice of the Supreme Court of the United
States, Vollmer planned a complete program in police science.[20]

Just before his retirement as Chief of Police in Berkeley in 1932,
Vollmer became a professor of Police Administration at the University of
California. By 1935, his reputation was such that the FBI sought him out
to arrange for an FBI Agent to survey his course. Special Agent W.L.
Listerman was selected for this survey and then to teach at the FBI's new
police training school, which became the National Academy. Vollmer,

himself, lectured at the second session of the FBI's police training school, held from January through March of 1936 in Washington, D.C.[21]

The tentative eleven-page outline for the course at the University of California, "Administration of Criminal Justice, Political Science 275a–b," is particularly interesting in its reading list, which includes such works as Raymond Fosdick's *American Police Systems,* Leonhard Fuld's pioneering study, *Police Administration,* Hans Gross's *Criminal Investigation,* Bruce Smith's works and the Wickersham Report. Assignment 2 was on the federal agencies, "with special attention to the recent developments in the Division of Investigation, Department of Justice." This assignment included review of issues of *Fugitives Wanted by Police,* "available in Prof. Vollmer's office." (In 1935, this publication was renamed the *FBI Law Enforcement Bulletin,* but even before the name was changed this publication carried articles on law enforcement, beyond just fugitive information.)

This course covered research procedure, methods, and presentation of results; the state police, federal agencies; sheriffs; private police; the coroner; the head of the police department; selection of police personnel; training programs; distribution of a police force; records; salaries, discipline, promotions and pensions; and a detailed examination of the prosecution of criminal offenses, including those by juveniles.[22]

Pioneers in Policing notes that Vollmer:

> ... projected his educated police officer as an 'all-arounder' who made use of his college courses in science, in sociology and psychology, in government, literature ... as fundamental preparation for doing a better job as a uniformed patrol officer ... [23]

Vollmer's concept of education for police extended beyond the classroom; he encouraged men who trained under him at the Berkeley Police Department to advance to responsible positions with other law enforcement agencies and to teach and write on their own. Acting in this mentor role, Vollmer recommended and encouraged O. W. Wilson to accept the position of Chief of Police of Wichita, Kansas. Wilson was one of the first of Vollmer's "college cops." His reputation gained at Wichita later led to his appointment as head of the School of Criminology at the University of California. Later still, when the Chicago Police Department was wracked by scandal, Wilson was brought in to clean up the department.

Another of the first of Vollmer's men to move up was Sergeant Clarence S. Morrill, who was made superintendent of the newly established California State Bureau of Criminal Identification in 1918. He headed this bureau for 16 years. V. A. Leonard gained a Ph.D. degree after nine years on the Berkeley department and became the head of the new Department of Police Science and Administration at Washington State University and an author in the new field of police texts. O. W. Wilson, in his foreword to Parker's history of the Berkeley Police Department, tells how Charles C Thomas, a publisher of medical texts, visited Berkeley and became friendly with Vollmer and Wilson. This led to this publishing firm entering the police text field. Vollmer's influence on police education was wide-ranging and exceptional overall.[24]

USE OF SCIENCE

The use of science in police work by the Berkeley Police Department under August Vollmer involved three primary areas. First, there was the establishment of one of this country's first forensic laboratories in 1916. Vollmer cited a 1907 death by poisoning case as the genesis of his interest in the use of science in investigation. Ruled a suicide by a coroner's jury, biology professor Jacques Leob of the University of California, a friend of Vollmer's, then showed that the victim could not have administered the poison himself. Professor Leob also introduced Vollmer to the works of Austrian criminologist Hans Gross (see Chapter 4) on scientific criminal investigation.

Vollmer realized the assistance science could render in criminal investigation, as explained by Gross. This led to lectures at the Berkeley police school by a professor at the university's school of pharmacy, Dr. Albert Schneider, who had been doing work in forensic medicine. He joined the Berkeley Police Department in 1916 as a full-time criminologist.[25]

The second use of science in law enforcement by Vollmer involved his encouragement of the development of an instrument for detecting the physiological changes that are associated with lying, known today as the polygraph. After seeing an article on blood pressure variations that accompany deception, Vollmer went to John A. Larson, who was operating a crime laboratory part-time as one of Vollmer's "college cops." Larson was able to build an instrument with the basic features of today's polygraph: the means of recording changes in blood pressure, pulse rate, and rate of respiration on a continuous graph. It was successful in detecting changes associated with lying and these indications could be used in interrogation of the suspect to induce confessions. Polygraph results are today still not admissible as evidence in most courts.

Parenthetically, it also led to Larson's marriage; he met his wife, who had been the victim of a jewelry theft, and he was able to identify a suspect, and get a confession, with his new device! The polygraph was so named by a young man, Leonard Keeler, the son of a friend of Vollmer who had been allowed to help out in the Berkeley Police Department laboratory. Keeler was able to improve Larson's device and later obtained a patent on it, calling it the polygraph (meaning multiple graphs), which is today the most used form of "lie detector."[26]

The third use of science in law enforcement was unrelated to forensic science; it involved August Vollmer's elementary research into the causes of crime, the first such experimentation by a law enforcement practitioner. One of his earliest experiments in this area, the first of its kind in this country, involved the possibility of predicting criminality. Some 220 children in a Berkeley elementary school were given physical and mental examinations, and their home backgrounds were studied. This was under Vollmer's supervision and that of a local psychiatrist, Dr. Jou Don Ball. Of these 220 children, some 22, or 10%, were determined as the most likely to become future criminals. The case histories were locked up at the Berkeley Police Department and not opened for 16 years.

Tracing the 22 children as adults in 1935 was not easy, but was accomplished, and it was found that 20 had been imprisoned or had police records; 2 had been confined to mental institutions. Unfortunately, there is no record of a control group being maintained of the other 200 originally studied to verify these results by today's standards. But the experiment was convincing to Vollmer and others to change their attitudes toward crime prevention. Vollmer learned that a maladjusted child could be discovered from a large group of children and efforts could be made to correct the problems before the child became a delinquent and later an adult criminal.

This type of work by Vollmer led to the formation in 1924 of a Crime Prevention Bureau in the Berkeley Police Department with Mrs. Elizabeth Lossing, a trained social worker, in charge. This bureau concentrated on help for pre-delinquent children, with the help of a coordinating council composed of representatives of local social service agencies and physicians. For a police department to do this kind of preventive work towards crime prevention was a remarkable departure in its day. This work also accompanied and supplemented Vollmer's work in determining the role of the police officer and police department in those days.[27]

THE POLICE ROLE AND PROFESSIONALISM

The first attempts to define the role of police by Vollmer were also very significant to the long-range effect of professionalism as advocated by Vollmer. The problem of professionalism and policing has always been, and continues to be, that the American body politic has never defined what the role of police *should be* in our society. Beginning with Vollmer, to a large extent it has been up to police practitioners themselves, with the often begrudged assistance of the academic community, to define the role of the police. The attitude of the great body politic has been, historically, that the police should do their job with a low profile, but the voters have never spoken with a clear voice as to what the police job is. And so, Vollmer was one of the first articulate police executives to attempt to define the police role for our society.

Police scholar James Q. Wilson, in an introduction to a 1971 reprinting of this most significant of Vollmer's writings, *The Police Role in Modern Society,* wrote that:

Vollmer's most important writings were not those done for the Wickersham Commission, but his own books, chiefly *The Police and Modern Society.* Published in 1936, four years after Vollmer joined the Berkeley faculty, this is a wise, humane, and sophisticated analysis of the limits of the police power in a heterogeneous society laboring under the remnants of a puritanical tradition and lacking any sure knowledge of how crime might be prevented . . . [28]

Wilson quotes Vollmer's conclusion that explains a central dilemma of policing in America:

. . . how can Americans expect police efficiency when, at every step in the apprehension and prosecution of criminals, political influence interferes, and soon a truly vicious circle is started: legislators pass laws prohibiting activities for which a demand persists; illegal means for meeting the demand are devised and the support of the people makes them profitable; political influence, with its inevitable accompaniment of corruption and inefficiency, prevents enforcement of the law and engenders disrespect both for law and for the agents of law enforcement; reformers are aroused; more laws are passed in the vain hope of effecting a remedy, and the circle starts again.[29]

This conclusion, of course, was reached just after the repeal of America's Constitutional experiment with Prohibition and while that legislative and enforcement failure undoubtedly formed the impetus of Vollmer's rationale, this dilemma had been addressed earlier by the police leader. He began his law enforcement career by raiding a Chinese gambling den in Berkeley with disastrous results in the following court case. The gamblers were found not guilty by reason of lack of evidence. A second, better planned, raid produced the evidence needed to convict.[30]

Vollmer distilled his quarter century of experience as a police chief into this book. His complaint was with what he saw as "bad" political influence; he kept his job through "good" political influence, that which developed as a result of his record as seen by the voters and their elected representatives: efficiency and deliverance of necessary services, just as chiefs do today. Vollmer explained the "bad" thusly:

> Political influence, or "pull" is a heavy handicap upon police departments. Yet no American citizen would dream of denying its existence or its power. A former commissioner of police in Chicago has said that, if it were not for the politician in America, and particularly the "fixer" type, the racketeers would be put out of business in a month. The "big shot" in a criminal gang is often in a position to "swing" the vote of a district, and, as a result, gambling and vice promoters dominate the political machines of many communities.[31]

Political influence of the negative type was the most pressing issue affecting policing in Vollmer's time; Vollmer and J. Edgar Hoover followed the lead of the progressive movement in campaigning against the partisan political forces that they saw handicapping police professionalism. But Vollmer also addressed the role of the police officer in terms of community service and crime fighting, the dual role that particularly affects today's analysis of American policing.

Today's increased emphasis on the new strategies of neighborhood policing, citizen involvement in crime prevention, and control of police use of force, especially deadly force, to better relations with the community, is a decided change from the professional model of policing with an emphasis on crime fighting as developed originally by Vollmer, advanced by Hoover, systematized by O.W. Wilson, and adopted by most law enforcement practitioners. But Vollmer did not view police as crime fighters exclusively, or originally; he initially saw police also as social workers, addressing a wide range of social problems.

In a 1919 address to the IACP entitled, "The Policeman as a Social Worker," Vollmer urged police to cooperate with, and make use of, social service agencies to help prevent crime and delinquency. He continued to urge the social dimensions of police work in the 1920s and 1930s. In *The Police and Modern Society,* Vollmer said that "police organizations constitute . . . the logical agencies for the coordination of the resources of the community in a concentrated effort toward crime prevention."[32]

Police historian Samuel Walker (1977) notes that in the 1920s "there was no more articulate advocate of the idea that police should function as social workers than August Vollmer." Walker believes that Vollmer asked that " . . . the police intervene in peoples' lives before they entered lives of crime." Walker raises the issue that in making a referral to a social agency, was the policeman making a suggestion or was he implicitly ordering treatment as an alternative to arrest. This raises a civil liberties issue if you ignore the fact that Vollmer's suggestion applied to "pre-delinquents," children who in recent years have been treated differently in terms of civil liberties. Of course, this question is a product of later decades when the courts had expanded concepts of civil liberties.

Vollmer's biographer, Carte, notes that while Vollmer had a lifelong interest in crime prevention through working with social agencies in handling juveniles, still Vollmer was fixed on the policeman as a detached crime fighter. He believed that the professional must be detached to prevent seizure of police power by partisan interests, the case of most police departments in America at that time. Vollmer even advocated consolidation of police agencies into state-wide organizations for efficiency and advancement of professionalism through detachment from the local community. In some respects, this is a non sequitur, as a detached crime fighter cannot achieve the level of community involvement that Vollmer envisioned, especially from a patrol car.[33]

The police community did not adopt all of Vollmer's progressive social views, as police officers saw the police role as more concrete than theoretical. Plus, social work had advanced to a professional level by this time and, naturally enough, had its own ideas about the prevention of criminality, its own detached professionalism that did not want the advice of the cop on the beat, or his chief.

But Vollmer was, in effect, asking that the police play a more active role in the political (but not partisan) life of the community, which also seemed to be a contradiction. " . . . The major thrust of police professionalism had been to insulate the police from politics."[34] This was useful in building professional autonomy to deflect suggestions that the public have a voice in police policy decisions. James Q. Wilson wrote, professional policing as it developed " . . . in principle at least, devalues citizen opinion *as manifested in personal relations;* professionalism, in this sense, means *impersonalization.*" (Emphasis in original.)[35]

The thrust of police professionalism from the 1930s until the 1970s was managerial; after Vollmer's time professionalism was more concerned with the agency than with the individual police officer. Carte noted that Vollmer constructed a crime fighter who was also a crime preventer, but:

> His most enduring legacy to policing has been his understanding of police administration and of the efficient use of police resources. His larger understanding of the policeman as a professional who is competent to deal with social problems has failed, in part, because he expected too much from education and, correspondingly, from the policeman who would acquire it.[36]

In the decade since Vollmer's biographer wrote this, the cyclical nature of policing in America has caused a revision of this view. Vollmer's view of police involvement in community life has returned to policing. "The policeman's ability to overcome his orientation as a crime fighter," and especially the police chief's ability to lead this re-orientation, is becoming a fact today.

Notes to Chapter 7

1. Eldefonso, 1974, 75–78.
2. Parker, 1972, 5–6. Carte, 1975, 17–20.
3. Eldefonso, 1974, 76.
4. Parker, 1972, 9–10, 36.
5. Eldefonso, 1974, 76.
6. Wilson, 1972, 383.
7. Deutsch, 1955, 215.
8. Parker, 1972, 8.
9. Ibid, 8–12.
10. Carte, 1975, 30.
11. Ibid, 55.
12. Ibid, 56–57.
13. Murphy, 1986.
14. Stead, 1977, 184.
15. Carte, 1975, 26.
16. Vollmer, 1937.
17. Vollmer, 1936b, xii.
18. Parker, 1972, 22–24.
19. Eastman, 1981, 123–124.

20. Ibid.
21. Cotter, 1986, 10.
22. Clegg, 1925.
23. Stead, 1977, 179.
24. Parker, 1972, vii, 30–31.
25. Carte, 1975, 27, 30.
26. Deutsch, 1955, 152.
27. Parker, 1972, 84–89.
28. Vollmer, 1936b, vi.
29. Ibid, 237.
30. Parker, 1972, 7.
31. Vollmer, 1936b, 6.
32. Douthit, 1975, 343–344. Vollmer, 1936b, 235.
33. Carte, 1977, 92–94.
34. Walker, 1977, 83.
35. Wilson, 1967, 160.
36. Carte, 1975, 96.

Chapter 8

THE CRIME COMMISSION ERA

The general failure of the police to detect and arrest criminals guilty of the many murders, spectacular bank, pay-roll, and other hold-ups, and sensational robberies with guns, frequently resulting in the death of the robbed victim, has caused a loss of public confidence in the police of our country.[1]

This was the conclusion—"general failure of the police"—of the National Commission on Law Observance and Enforcement, transmitted to the President in June, 1931, in one of the commission's two reports on police. The chairman of the commission, who gave the group its popular name, George W. Wickersham, former Attorney General of the United States, was joined in the report's opening statement by his fellow commissioners, including Newton D. Baker, Secretary of War during the first World War, and eminent legal scholar, Roscoe Pound.

The Wickersham report was the culmination of a decade of social changes that significantly impacted policing. It was a period marked by changing social values, including a national experiment in sumptuary law (Prohibition), and changes in the nature of crime and public perception of the police role. And, as in the 1960s, this period was marred by racial violence. It was also characterized by the coming of age of the crime commission.

But the most important change in American life, and in policing, was technological: the widespread adoption of the automobile. The automobile altered the physical structure of American cities and changed patterns of daily life; it also profoundly changed police work. Faced with geographically expanding urban areas, police departments had to mobilize their patrol forces. Police leadership encapsulated officers in patrol cars that could be summoned by citizens with the telephone and dispatched by police superiors using newly developed radio communications. This revolution in the nature of police work took place without any thought as to its long-term effect. Not until the late 1960s would its impact begin to be analyzed.[2]

CRIME COMMISSIONS

The crime commission method was the primary means of criminal justice reform in the decade of the 1920s. These commissions were logical outgrowths of the Progressive Movement, but they also were a reaction to the crime-wave scare of the period. Changes in social values following World War I, new population mobility based on the widespread adoption of the automobile, and nation-wide Prohibition of the production, importation, and consumption of alcoholic beverages changed the nature of crime from primarily a local, unorganized affair to a more organized business with the beginnings of interstate ramifications.

The business community and the progressive elite reacted to the public perception of a crime wave. As this period was before adoption of the nationwide crime reporting system that became the Uniform Crime Reporting system, it is hard today to judge whether there was, in fact, an increase in crime. But, the survey of "Crime and Punishment," reported in 1933 by the President's Commission on Social Trends, reported criminal justice developments in the first three decades of the century and "effectively debunked the growing myth of a national crime wave."[3]

There was, however, an increase in the amount of violence associated with crime as reported in the press, and there was a substantial increase in insurance premiums for crime protection. Insurance losses rose from $508,000 in 1914 to $11,812,000 in 1924. Besides crime commissions, action against crime by business included vigilantism. Bankers' councils in Illinois and Iowa, for example, armed and deputized 3,200 men in Illinois and more than 4,000 in Iowa. These efforts were successful in cutting the number of, and the losses from, bank robberies.[4]

These two factors, increased violence and increased costs, motivated the progressive elite and the business community toward the establishment of crime commissions in urban areas. Vigilantism could not be the answer, of course, where there was already an urban police presence. The crime commissions were established on a less partisan basis than those of the 19th century, when the purpose of these investigations was to "throw the rascals (the opposing party) out" so that the progressives could wrest control of the city away from the political machines.

The 1920s could be called the decade of the crime commission; by 1931 there had been 7 local, 16 state, and 2 national crime commissions. The crime commissions represented fulfillment of the ideals of the Progressive Movement—the belief that social problems required the attention of professional experts in various fields working together in some type of bureaucratic organization. In the main, these commissions reinforced ideas for police professionalism that had already been advanced, rather than introducing new ideas. But they were advances themselves in that they viewed law enforcement within the context of the whole criminal justice system.[5]

Aroused by a spectacular daylight payroll robbery in 1917, the Chicago Association of Commerce appointed a Committee on Prevalence and Prevention of Crime which recommended the establishment of a permanent crime commission. The Chicago Crime Commission, still in existence today, was originally composed of over 100 leading citizens in banking, business, and the professions, mainly law, and these volunteers then hired a staff of investigators and statisticians. Initially, the commission was most concerned with the crimes of burglary, larceny, and robbery; Chicago burglary insurance rates were the highest in the country. The commission estimated that crimes of these types cost the business community in excess of $12 million a year at that time.

As a first step, the commission recommended setting up a State Bureau of Criminal Records; this was rejected, so the commission began its own records file. This was the only way the commission could check on the performance of the police with any accuracy and counter police arguments that they lacked a method to positively identify offenders. The Chicago Crime Commission and other commissions, including the Committee on Law Enforcement of the American Bar Association, generally supported, too, the attack on rehabilitation in prisons that marked the 1920s. The commissions tried to limit the courts and correctional administrations in the use of indeterminate sentences, probation, and parole. This reaction came after two decades of expansion in rehabilitation programs; only 12 states had parole laws before 1900, by 1920 some 40 states had parole provisions in their criminal statutes.[6]

While the Chicago Crime Commission became a permanent body, most of the commissions created at this time were short-lived; some were created only for the limited purpose of revising state criminal codes. The crime commissions also represented different interest groups; the Chicago and Los Angeles commissions were created by business interests, while the Kansas City Law Enforcement Association was more politically partisan.

The Cleveland commission (named the Cleveland Survey) had a more sophisticated approach. Created in response to a local judge's involvement in "a particularly sordid crime," the Cleveland Survey involved the bar association and a number of scholars from Western Reserve University in an investigation of the entire criminal justice system in Cleveland. Funded by a private philanthropic organization, which had already backed a survey of the local schools, the Cleveland Survey had a staff of 35 and issued a final report in less than 6 months. The report was authored by Felix Frankfurter and Roscoe Pound, two of America's most eminent legal scholars. Academic and non-partisan in approach, the Cleveland Survey, according to Felix Frankfurter, "marked the introduction of the research method into the field of practical administration of our system of dealing with crime.... "

August Vollmer's research in the area of delinquency and in other facets of policing may not have been known to Frankfurter, but more important, the Cleveland Survey's pretensions toward scientific objectivity overlaid an important assumption of long-term impact. According to police historian Samuel Walker, the Cleveland Survey:

> viewed the police in terms of effective crime suppression. This represented the beginnings of a subtle but extremely important redefinition of the police role in society. Gradually, in the 1920s and more openly in the 1930s, police experts emphasized the crime-fighting image of the police at the expense of the social service aspects.[7]

Whether this law enforcement survey in Cleveland represented the *beginnings* of such a shift, there is no question that this shift gained emphasis in this period. The study of the Cleveland Police Department was conducted by Raymond Fosdick, author of *American Police Systems*. His concern was with administrative efficiency, as the Cleveland Police Department was relatively free of corruption. In his report, Fosdick examined the rational and "efficient" deployment of the patrol force, recommending greater use of motorized patrol and less use of foot patrol. He also recommended greater centralization of control in the department by the closing of many station houses.

Efficiency in crime control was a prime goal of one branch of police reform in this period. As the Chicago Crime Commission reported in 1919:

> The business of crime is being more expertly conducted. Modern crime, like modern business, is tending towards centralization, organization and commercialization.

Echoing President Coolidge's remark that "the business of America is business," the Crime Commission continued: "Ours is a business nation. Our criminals apply business methods."[8]

Business interests were more successful in police reform efforts at this time than the moral reformers, who were more concerned with police corruption and ties to organized vice. Many police departments adopted techniques of modern management at the instigation of crime commissions, while the moral reformers concentrated more on Prohibition enactment and enforcement.

SOCIAL CHANGES

In addition to the crime commissions of the period, three broad social changes in the "Roaring Twenties" had an impact on policing and a long term effect on police professionalism. These were nationwide Prohibition, the "noble experiment" in sumptuary law, racial violence with long lasting effects in our cities, and the failure of police unionism at the opening of the decade.

Nationwide Prohibition had a long-term effect on the nature of crime in the United States which, in turn, had an impact on police professionalism. Prohibition caused widespread changes in American life: millions of people became law breakers by continuing to drink; police and federal Prohibition agents, to a large extent, became law breakers themselves through bribed alliances with gangsters who sought to control distribution of alcoholic beverages. Crime became more organized in this effort to control the liquor trade and violence occurred as gang wars broke out between competing criminal groups.

Prohibition had a long history in this country. Beginning in the early 1800s as a campaign for temperance, by 1855 some 13 states had adopted prohibition. Support of prohibition declined during and after the Civil War and by 1900 only 5 states had prohibition, in spite of efforts by women's temperance groups (women had no other political outlet at this time). After the U.S. entered World War I, the "drys" argued that the use of grain for alcohol production was unpatriotic; grain was needed for food for the army. This argument convinced enough traditionally "wet" urban dwellers to support an 18th Amendment to the Constitution, which took effect in 1920 (after the war was over!) prohibiting the import, manufacture, sale, and transportation of alcoholic beverages in the United States and its territories.

Prohibition caused the rise of underworld gangs engaged in providing alcoholic beverages to much of the urban population determined to avoid this sumptuary law. The demand for liquor was far greater than the demand for control at the local and even on the national level. Violent gang wars, that saw the first criminal usage of the submachine gun, broke out among these competing gangs, sometimes injuring innocent bystanders and fueling the public perception of a crime wave. Even the traditionally "dry" middle class Midwest was affected. This author remembers stories by his father, a small town Midwesterner who worked his way through medical school during the First World War. When Prohibition took effect, he was a resident in pathology in a St. Louis hospital. Having access to the hospital's alcohol supply, he made "bathtub gin" and, although his own father had lost a leg to a gunshot in a hunting accident, the pathologist/bootlegger carried a loaded .45 caliber pistol to make his deliveries of illicit alcohol!

While the Prohibition Era increased the amount of police corruption that had always existed in connection with the enforcement of vice laws, Prohibition also brought the creation of a federal law enforcement presence that impacted on a large segment of American society for the first time. Corruption of much of this law enforcement on the federal level helped bring about national attention to the crime issue and had long-term effects on federal law enforcement.

Preceding the Prohibition experiment, the racial violence which marked the first two decades of the 20th century culminated in over 20 major race riots in 1919, including the Chicago riot in the summer of that year when 38 people died, over 500 were seriously injured, and several hundred were left homeless. This also affected the public's perception of police lawlessness, later documented by the Wickersham Commission. These riots were a response to the Great Migration, the first massive movement of black Americans to northern cities. The influx of black migrants resulted in competition for jobs, housing, and recreation areas. After initial violence from 1900 to 1919, the races settled into an uneasy truce represented by the establishment of the modern black ghetto in American cities.

In many cases the police themselves were either participants in these riots or, by their conduct, condoned the violence by whites against blacks. The 1900 New York City riot was triggered by a black man killing a police officer; as one newspaper reported, "the police virtually led the hoodlums" who rioted. In other cities, the police were passive in response to white violence, even refusing to arrest whites who attacked blacks. In

East St. Louis, the 1917 riot was the subject of a Congressional investigation as it affected rail transportation in interstate commerce. There, after whites in a car randomly shot up a black neighborhood, blacks retaliated by opening fire on a police car, killing one officer. The next day newspapers published inflammatory accounts of the incidents, while the police put the bullet-riddled police car on display at police headquarters! Congressional investigators found that 39 blacks died in the violence that followed.

But the racial violence of this period had little immediate effect on American police. At the annual conventions of the IACP in 1919 and 1920, the problem of race relations was not mentioned. Police administration experts such as Raymond Fosdick, August Vollmer, and Bruce Smith only mentioned blacks with reference to their allegedly high rate of criminal behavior. The pattern of the black ghetto in Northern cities established a surface peace in these cities, but the decades of a different kind of policing that developed in these ghettos—an adversary style—had a long term impact on policing. The country, in general, and the police in particular, were not ready for racial equality. When racial equality did come, it profoundly changed this country, and police professionalism.[9]

Professionalism at this point had come to policing from the outside or from above its ranks. It was first suggested by progressive, elitist reformers for their own political purposes, then professionalism was imposed from the top by progressive police chiefs like August Vollmer. The patrol officers, the bulk of all police departments, had little voice in professionalism until the period of the 1970s, the time of Renaissance II in policing. This came about partially because of the first failure of police unionism, marked by the Boston police strike in 1919.

There have been two significant periods of police unionism, in 1917–1919, and from the late 1960s to the present. The first resulted from the wartime inflation of World War I; there was also an abortive attempt to organize police after the World War II inflationary period. The second period, which began in 1966, also resulted from economic demands, but was more complex in that this period was accompanied by strong feelings of social and political isolation on the part of police. In one sense, the first phase of police unionism was a result of the movement for professionalism. Early reformers wanted to establish police work as a career service; they viewed the constant turnover of police personnel as a mark of the political influence over policing by the machines which they opposed.

In the 1890s police associations could be found in most large cities. These had begun promoting their own interests in city government, political activity to a degree. Police magazines aimed at rank and file patrolmen also appeared as the patrolmen's voice. Police reformers concentrated on administrative improvements and training, not on police pay, which the patrolmen concentrated on out of necessity. The reformers were primarily interested in promoting the concept of a strong, independent police executive and some were critical even of civil service, which they believed interfered with the police executive's independence.

But the direct cause of the initial phase of police union organizing was the inflation resulting from America entering World War I. The cost of living had risen by 25% between 1900 and 1915, while the wages of factory workers more than kept pace. Factory wages had risen as a result of union organizing and during the war, union organizing in industry was encouraged by a federal government vitally interested in maintaining war production. American Federation of Labor (AFL) membership almost doubled during World War I, but police salaries, less dependent on economics than on local government, remained the same during this whole period.

Police saw their economic status declining vis-a-vis the blue collar worker who had union status, but were restrained from union activity by the widespread belief that public service jobs were a privilege and those holding jobs in the public sector gave up some rights for the privilege, including the right of political activity by police officers. This belief was strongly supported by the law; Oliver Wendell Holmes, while a justice on the Massachusetts Supreme Court, declared in the case where a policeman had been dismissed for political activity: "The petitioner may have a constitutional right to talk politics, but he has no constitutional right to be a policeman."[10]

Police were also confronted with organized labor's reluctance to accept them into their ranks. In 1897, the AFL executive council refused to issue a charter to a private police group, arguing that private police generally served management and were "too often controlled by forces inimical to the labor movement." While the AFL did not rule out the possibility of organizing municipal police, nevertheless, it never initiated an organizing campaign.

Two police strikes, in 1918 and in 1919, illustrate the course that police unionism might have taken, and did take. The first, in Cincinnati, was a spontaneous 3-day walkout solely over demands for a wage increase. Although there were opportunities for disorder, quick mobilization of the Cincinnati Home Guard (a World War I volunteer group) put another 600 men on patrol to join the 48 members of the police force who did not strike. A patriotic parade for Selective Service the next day, potentially violent because of Cincinnati's large immigrant German population, was policed by this group and a force of Boy Scouts! The mayor compromised on the third day and the striking patrolmen returned to work, with only the strike leaders subject to charges of insubordination.

The next year, the famous Boston police strike was dramatically different. A police group already had been organized as the Boston Social Club and was considering affiliation with the AFL. After months of agitation for a pay raise (pay had not changed since 1898), the patrolmen faced a new and inflexible Police Commissioner and Rule 35, which specifically forbade membership in any organization with ties to any group outside the police department.

By this time the AFL had changed its position on police membership; at its 1919 convention, the AFL went " ... on record as favoring the organization of the city policemen. ... " Some 33 charters were granted to police groups, including the Boston Social Club. But, by 1919, public hysteria had developed over real and imagined radicalism, believed to be inspired by foreigners and immigrants, and over "foreign" labor tactics, such as the Seattle general strike in 1919. The Boston police commissioner held to his opposition to outside labor group affiliation by a local police union and was supported by a special Citizens Committee appointed by the mayor. Some 19 newly elected officers of the police union were charged under Boston Police Department Rule 35. Some 1,117 Boston patrolmen went out on strike, leaving only 427 officers on duty on September 9, 1919.

Newspapers across the country described Boston as being in a state of anarchy, although the resulting violence was later estimated at only 8 dead, 21 seriously injured, and some $300,000 in property damage. In comparison with the racial violence in other cities at this time, this was relatively minor. But statements by politicians reinforced the image of anarchy; then Governor Coolidge built a national political reputation on his statement, "There is no right to strike against the public safety by anybody, anywhere, at any time." President Wilson, faced with Washington,

D.C., police union organizing at the same time, called police strikes "a crime against civilization."

Similar police organizing in England at this time resulted in passage of the Police Act, which established the Police Federation, a government-sponsored company union that all policemen were required to join. This gave patrolmen at least some voice in their affairs, but in Boston the striking policemen were said by the commissioner to have deserted their posts and were fired. Virtually an entirely new police force had to be recruited and the city provided benefits that exceeded those that the strikers had demanded. Police historian Samuel Walker noted that the failure of police unionism at this time resulted in "the development of a police subculture, isolated from the public and without any formal means of making its voice heard."[11]

THE WICKERSHAM COMMISSION

President Coolidge appointed the first National Crime Commission in 1925, thereby acknowledging that crime control had become a national issue. Members of the commission included Charles Evans Hughes, former Chief Justice of the Supreme Court, Newton D. Baker, former Secretary of War, and Franklin D. Roosevelt, former Assistant Secretary of the Navy—later the first President to significantly expand the federal role in crime control. But the commission was the brainchild of businessmen such as the president of U.S. Steel, and, dominated by business interests, the commission evidenced primary interest in property crimes.

It first proposed legislation aimed at elimination of receivers of stolen goods. Among the commission's many reports, two concerned auto thefts. During its four years of existence, the commission held national crime conferences in 1926 and 1927. After the first conference, the commission was criticized by the dean of the Northwestern University School of Law for not working through the states and not working with professionals in the fields of sociology, psychiatry, social work, corrections, statistics, and criminal justice administration. The criticism had effect, as the 1927 conference included representatives of 26 state and local crime commissions plus another 50 organizations in the crime field.[12]

Probably the most far-reaching impact of this first federal sanction to the anti-crime movement, until then believed to be the responsibility solely of the states and their subordinate jurisdictions, was the slogan coined by one of the organizers of the commission, Mark O. Prentiss. He described the objective of the commission as a "war on crime," according to history professor Nathan Douthit, who attributes the slogan to an article by Prentiss that appeared in the October, 1925, issue of *Current Opinion*. But J. Edgar Hoover used the phrase "war against crime" in his first speech to the IACP on July 14, 1925:

> You gentlemen of the International Association of Chiefs of Police who are enlisted in the endless war against crime . . . who may never hope for an Armistice Day this side of the grave. . . . [13]

Coming just after America's successful involvement in the "war to end all wars," the idea of a war on crime, no matter who birthed it, was adopted by the public, which had been accustomed to propaganda slogans by the war. Political leaders and law enforcement professionals also jumped on the "war on crime" concept; it fit the military model of police professionalism.[14]

Coolidge's successor, President Herbert Hoover, concerned about the lack of enforcement of Prohibition, replaced the National Crime Commission with the National Commission on Law Observance and Enforcement. This commission became known as the Wickersham Commission, after its chairman, George W. Wickersham, former Attorney General of the United States. To fulfill its responsibility to investigate the enforcement of the prohibition laws, the commission conducted the first broad study of crime and criminal justice in America. The Wickersham Commission issued 14 detailed and complete reports, two of which concerned policing: the "Report on Lawlessness in Law Enforcement" and the "Report on Police." The latter was effectively a blueprint for police professionalism by the national government, but without any proposed legislation to carry out its recommendations.

The "Report on Police" was authored by David G. Monroe and Earle W. Garrett, research assistants at the University of Chicago's Department of Political Science, under the direction of August Vollmer, then the university's Professor of Police Administration. Vollmer actually authored the first two chapters of the report which concerned the police executive, but his influence on the rest of the report is very evident. This report was Vollmer's philosophy of policing, developed in his many years as Chief of the Berkeley Police, coupled with the influence of the academic and progressive communities on Vollmer.

But the Report on Lawlessness in Law Enforcement, detailing a widespread pattern of police misconduct (especially the use of the third degree) received the most public attention. According to Walker, this report (# 11), "reflected the heightened public concern about the police. At the same time, however, it represented a dramatic shift in public expectations about the quality of law enforcement." A popular account taken from the report, *Our Lawless Police,* concluded that "The third degree—the inflicting of pain, physical or mental, to extract confessions or statements—is widespread throughout the country." This reportage put the police on the defensive so that the second "Report on the Police" by Vollmer was almost overlooked at first.[15]

This second report, number 14 in the commission's series, had more of a long term effect on police professionalism than the report on lawlessness by police. *Report #14 outlined and charted the path of professionalism for policing for the next two generations.*[16] All 10 of its specific recommendations were adopted on a voluntary basis by most states, cities, and police departments in this country over the years. As shown in Part III, many of these recommendations, which were designed to professionalize American policing, were implemented on the national level by the Federal Bureau of Investigation in the development of that agency as the national service arm of law enforcement. The decentralized police agencies of this country adopted these measures voluntarily with the FBI's encouragement; they were not imposed by the central government as a condition of funding the local police departments, as happened in England.

The ten recommendations of the Wickersham Commission were set out in the report's conclusions:

1. The corrupting influence of politics should be removed from the police organization.
2. The head of the department should be selected at large for competence, a leader, preferably a man of considerable experience, and removable from office only after preferment of charges and a public hearing.
3. Patrolmen should be able to rate a 'B' on the Alpha test, be able-bodied and of good character, weigh 150 pounds, measure 5 feet 9 inches tall, and be between 21 and 31 years of age. These requirements may be disregarded by the chief for good and sufficient reasons.
4. Salaries should permit decent living standards, housing should be adequate, eight hours of work, one day off weekly, annual vacation, fair sick leave with pay, just accident and death benefits when in performance of duty, reasonable pension provisions on an actuarial basis.
5. Adequate training for recruits, officers, and those already on the roll is imperative.
6. The communication system should provide for call boxes, telephones, recall system, and (in appropriate circumstances) teletype and radio.

7. Records should be complete, adequate, but as simple as possible. They should be used to secure administrative control of investigations and of department units in the interest of efficiency.
8. A crime-prevention unit should be established if circumstances warrant this action and qualified women police should be engaged to handle juvenile delinquents' and women's cases.
9. State police forces should be established in States where rural protection of this character is required.
10. State bureaus of criminal investigation and information should be established in every State.[17]

These recommendations were a summary of what needed to be done in American policing in 1930 and represent what the Progressive Movement had advocated over the past forty years, as adapted and adopted by August Vollmer and other progressive police officials. It took time, however, for various local governmental units to adopt these recommendations as Herbert Hoover and the Republicans were not ready to do other than report and recommend. Funds and leadership on the national level had to wait for Franklin Roosevelt's administration.

This report did not specifically recommend that police departments should replace foot patrol with motorized patrol. This took place over the years as an economic necessity and as public expectations of the police role changed. When the widespread adoption of the telephone enabled the public to summon a police officer by telephone and have him quickly respond in a radio-equipped police car, this became the public expectation of the police role—rapid service in response to the public's summons. The public was told by police leaders that this was crime control. Forty years later the thinking public and police leadership began to learn otherwise.

Notes to Chapter 8

1. Report on Police, 1.
2. Walker, 1977, 109.
3. Ibid, 132.
4. Mosse, 1975, 321–322.
5. Walker, 1977, 125.
6. Mosse, 1975, 321–322.
7. Walker, 1977, 127.
8. Ibid, 128.
9. Ibid, 120–125.

10. McAuliffe v. Mayor and Board of Aldermen of New Bedford, 155 Mass. 216 at 220 (1892).
11. Walker, 1977, 119.
12. Mosse, 1975, 323–324. Walker, 1977, 130–131.
13. Hoover, 1925.
14. Douthit, 1975, 337.
15. Walker, 1977, 132–134.
16. Bopp, 1972, 109.
17. Report on Police, 140.

Chapter 9

HOOVER'S NEW FBI

A critical analysis of the FBI concluded that "Organizationally and bureaucratically, [J. Edgar] Hoover was a genius." This was by a journalist who was given access to FBI files just three years after the death of the man who served nearly half a century as Director of the FBI.[1]

While reporting Hoover's failings, which another police authority summarized in 1977 as "attempting to repress political dissent during the nation's involvement in Vietnam," both the journalist and the police official, and other police historians, credit Hoover with building a professional law enforcement agency that had tremendous influence on American policing.[2]

According to the author of *A Short History of American Law Enforcement:*

> In many ways the FBI provided local law enforcement with direction, for the Bureau had dramatically illustrated what a police component could do if it was staffed by competent, well-educated personnel who were provided with advanced training . . . and who were allowed to ply their trade relatively free from the influence of politicians.[3]

This is the essence of the FBI's success after Hoover took over: appointing personnel with legal education, training them in investigative work, and protecting them from political influence. This chapter examines how this came about at a time when other American police agencies were staffed with high school graduates at best, had only rudimentary training, and were still under the worst political influence.

In the years preceding the age of television, J. Edgar Hoover, after he had refashioned the FBI in the image he sought, and General Douglas MacArthur, another 20th century American legend, were also the premier public relations practitioners of their day. "We come not to praise" Hoover, in Shakespeare's words, but to examine his impact on the FBI and on law enforcement, both positive and negative. Part III of this volume, the Renaissance of Professionalism, will detail the law enforcement and policing service role that developed in the FBI in the 1920s and

1930s: nationwide fingerprint identification, Uniform Crime Reporting, the FBI's forensic science laboratory, the FBI National Academy, and other police training, including the *FBI Law Enforcement Bulletin.*

But this chapter will look at Hoover's leadership of the FBI which led to these steps toward law enforcement professionalism: educational requirements for investigators, professional training, and elimination of political influence in appointment of investigators. Despite a recent analysis by social scientist Richard Powers crediting (and blaming) Roosevelt's New Deal with changing the nation's perception of the criminal problem and how it should be met, Hoover's ideas preceded the Roosevelt administration by a decade in proclaiming a "war on crime."

J. Edgar Hoover has been credited by every authority on police administration with changing the FBI from an agency of political hacks, tarred with the brush of scandal, to a professional law enforcement agency of the national government that became as efficient in enforcing laws against certain specified Federal crimes as the Pinkerton Agency had been in the detection of often interstate crime just after the Civil War. In many ways, the FBI is the government's successor to the Pinkerton Agency, within the FBI's jurisdictional limits.

But Hoover was a lawyer, not a police officer; the thrust of Hoover's advancement of the FBI was in the field of law enforcement and investigation, not what is considered today the broader area of policing. In fact, Hoover was criticized by a Congressman in the 1930s for not having police experience—for never having made an arrest! Hoover, quick to answer any criticism, flew to New Orleans to personally arrest Alvin Karpis, one of the most wanted criminals of the 1930s.

ORIGINS OF THE FBI

The FBI dates from July 26, 1908, when then Attorney General Charles J. Bonaparte, at the direction of President Theodore Roosevelt, created a corps of 35 investigators within the Department of Justice. Before 1870, federal investigations were handled by regional United States Attorneys; only in 1871 was $50,000 appropriated for the detection and prosecution of federal crimes. This money was used to hire outside investigators, usually from the Pinkerton Detective Agency, until Congress banned this practice in 1892.[4]

After the Congressional action regarding the Pinkertons, the Department of Justice used investigators borrowed from other government agencies, such as the Treasury Department's Secret Service. While the Justice Department did have a small group of "examiners," these men only handled examinations of court records. Attorney General Bonaparte, grandnephew of the French emperor Napoleon, complained in 1907 that "a Department of Justice with no force of permanent police . . . is assuredly not fully equipped for its work." He appealed to Congress to create such a force; instead, Congress again reacted by prohibiting the Department from using Secret Service personnel for such work—apparently because Secret Service agents' investigations in a land fraud case led to the convictions of several Congressmen. The Attorney General's response has been interpreted, depending on your viewpoint, either as a proper exercise of discretion or a possibly illegal act in defiance of Congress. He issued an order July 26, 1908, organizing a small corps of investigators under Chief Examiner Stanley W. Finch. Early the next year, the new Attorney General, George W. Wickersham, who more than twenty years later gave his name to the first national government commission on crime, designated the new force the Bureau of Investigation, with jurisdiction over matters not specifically assigned to other agencies.[5]

Bonaparte's use of the word "police" instead of law enforcement shows that no differentiation was made at this time between police and law enforcement. The distinction that law enforcement is a *part* of policing, not a synonym, is a more recent development. This distinction, that only came to be articulated in the 1970s, had a very important influence on police professionalism in the 1930s as policing began to adopt a crime-fighting orientation over its initial fledging community service role.

In the beginning, the Bureau of Investigation had only very limited jurisdiction: bankruptcy frauds, antitrust crime, peonage (compulsory servitude), offenses against government property and on government reservations, impersonation of government officials with intent to defraud, and violations of the neutrality laws. Congress passed the White Slave Traffic Act in 1910, which became known as the Mann Act after its author, Congressman James Robert Mann of Illinois. The Mann Act prohibited interstate transportation of women "for the purpose of prostitution" and the Supreme Court's broad interpretation of this statute led to some cases of federal law enforcement monitoring the private moral behavior of citizens, beyond what Congress intended.

It also meant an expansion in personnel for the Bureau of Investigation, as did the beginning of World War I in 1914 when the Bureau enforced the neutrality laws before America entered the war three years later. As

Don Whitehead, author of an authorized 1956 book on the FBI (the foreword was by J. Edgar Hoover) noted, "the Bureau was far from being prepared for the test. . . . " of World War I.[6]

No one agency had clear jurisdiction over sabotage, as shown by the failure to identify those who caused the explosion of two million tons of dynamite on Black Tom Island in New York Harbor in 1916. The Bureau of Investigation, expanded to 400 agents, was given jurisdiction over the new conscription law when America entered the war, in addition to watching the activities of enemy aliens thought to be potentially harmful to the war effort. Unfortunately, the Bureau and the Justice Department joined forces with vigilante organizations, especially the American Protective League, whose members were even issued badges proclaiming them "auxiliaries" to the U.S. Department of Justice.

One use of the American Protective League was to help the Bureau in May 1918 conduct the "slacker raids," dragnets of young men who had supposedly failed to register for the draft. Thousands were arrested for not having draft registration cards on their persons, but only one half of one percent were found to be genuine draft-evaders. Despite the Attorney General's disavowal of using outsiders to conduct such raids, the abuse was repeated in September. The Bureau, in its enthusiasm, was out of the Attorney General's control.

A postwar fear of radicalism in America, highlighted by a series of bombings, including one that damaged the new Attorney General's house, caused the appointment of William J. Flynn, formerly the director of the Secret Service, to head the Bureau of Investigation, with instructions to involve the Bureau more actively in the fight against subversion. A new General Intelligence Division was created in the Department of Justice under Assistant Attorney General Frances P. Garvan, whose immediate assistant was a young lawyer named J. Edgar Hoover. Hoover had attended George Washington University at night while working during the day at the Library of Congress, which probably influenced the development of the FBI's meticulous filing system, resembling as it does libraries' book cataloging systems. Hoover received a law degree with honors in 1916 and a Masters in law a year later.[7]

A native of the District of Columbia, John Edgar Hoover was born on New Year's Day in 1895, the last of the three children of Dickerson and Annie Hoover. His father was head of the printing division of the U.S. Coast and Geodetic Survey, and his older brother became Inspector General of the Steamboat Inspection Service. J. E., as he was known as a young man, attended Central High School in the District, where he was involved in debate and was captain of a company in the school's Cadet Corps. Proud of this, young Hoover even wore his cadet uniform to church each week. His later nickname was "Speed," from an early job delivering groceries. According to Hoover's niece, who lived in the same house for a time, Hoover's mother was of Swiss descent and was the disciplinarian of the family. Like August Vollmer, the main influence in Hoover's early life was his strict mother. Hoover lived with his mother until her death in 1938; he never married.[8]

On July 26, 1917, Hoover became a law clerk with the Department of Justice and was assigned to war work in the Department.[9] At the end of the war, Hoover's immediate superior in the Department, John Lord O'Brien, said that Hoover told him he wanted to remain in the Department. According to O'Brien, he took this up with the new Attorney General, A. Mitchell Palmer, who had Hoover transferred to the Department's Bureau of Investigation. Hoover prepared a brief for the Bureau of Investigation's General Intelligence Division (formerly a division of the Department of Justice) charging a Communist conspiracy to overthrow all non-Communist governments. Today, we know that the Soviet Communist Party's international arm, the Comintern, did have this aim, confirming Hoover's early view of this conspiracy. This view influenced Hoover's thinking to his death.[10]

Under Attorney General Palmer, the Bureau of Investigation led "Red raids" in 1919 and 1920 against the separate Communist and Communist Labor parties. The second of these raids, later known as the "Palmer Raids," was a roundup of an estimated 10,000 people in 33 cities, many of whom were new immigrants who barely spoke English. Later investigations revealed that few of those arrested could be proved guilty of any crime and most had to be released. A few well-known anarchists were deported by the Labor Department, which had authority in these cases, but the Secretary of Labor threw out most of the charges. Palmer said that Secretary of Labor Louis R. Post had "utterly nullified the purpose of Congress in passing the deportation statute...." There was an attempt to impeach Post; Palmer vigorously defended the Bureau of Investigation's tactics, although President Woodrow Wilson childed the Attorney General at a cabinet meeting, "Palmer, don't let this country see red."[11]

These raids brought the Bureau of Investigation into disrepute with many, but it was the corrupt administration of President Warren G.

Harding that added a partisan bias to an already ideological politicized agency. Harding's Attorney General, Harry M. Daugherty, brought in another new director of the Bureau of Investigation, William J. Burns. Like the previous director, William E. Flynn, Burns was a former member of the Secret Service. Burns had retired in 1909 and started the William J. Burns National Detective Agency, which was known to engage in many questionable investigative practices. With this new Director, it became widely assumed that the Bureau of Investigation wiretapped, broke into offices, and kept tabs on Senators and others who criticized the Department of Justice. When Harding's "Ohio gang" took office in 1921, J. Edgar Hoover was promoted to Assistant Director of the Bureau.

During this period, the Bureau of Investigation infiltrated the ranks of railroad strikers to enforce a sweeping Federal court injunction the Attorney General had obtained against a nationwide railway strike. The Bureau also led an attack against the newly revitalized Ku Klux Klan at the request of the Governor of Louisiana, substantially weakening the Klan after various prosecutions under local laws. Both of these campaigns were coordinated by Assistant Director Hoover.

When Vice President Coolidge succeeded to the Presidency after Harding's death, he named a distinguished New England lawyer, Harlan Fiske Stone, as Attorney General to replace Daugherty, who had been tainted by the Teapot Dome scandal. Stone sought a new director for the Bureau of Investigation. When Stone "failed in his search for an outsider with broad law enforcement experience and a good reputation" to take over the bureau, he offered the job to young Hoover, on the recommendation of then Secretary of Commerce Herbert Hoover. The Secretary of Commerce had been advised by his assistant, Larry Richey, of J. Edgar Hoover's qualifications.[12]

HOOVER TAKES CHARGE

In an interview on May 10, 1924, with Attorney General Stone, Hoover is reported to have accepted only on certain conditions, that:

> The Bureau must be divorced from politics and not be a catch-all for political hacks. Appointments must be based on merit. Second, promotions will be made on proved ability and the Bureau will be responsible only to the Attorney General.
>
> The new Attorney General reportedly replied, "I wouldn't give it to you under any other conditions. That's all. Good day."[13]

With Attorney General Stone's backing, J. Edgar Hoover began to clean house; he fired agents with criminal records, including one who had been convicted of murder, and got rid of those with no qualifications other than political connections, such as Gaston B. Means, a swindler who had bilked scores of people out of hundreds of thousands of dollars. Hoover also dropped those on the rolls as "honorary" agents—a New York producer who had brought a burlesque show to Washington and a drunk who performed a lunchtime sideshow outside the headquarters of the Justice Department.[14]

Not long before he died in 1972, Hoover listed what he felt were his most important accomplishments as Director of the FBI in their order of importance; first listed was his reorganization of the Bureau in 1924.[15] Hoover established qualifications for agents for the first time, hiring those with legal or accounting training to replace those unqualified or corrupt that he fired. In 1931, Hoover explained to the Cincinnati Lawyers Club, the first group other than the International Association of Chiefs of Police that he addressed, how this came about:

> The United States Department of Justice is the law office of the United States Government, and, in 1924 when I assumed the duties of Director of the Bureau of Investigation, the then Attorney General, Harlan Fiske Stone, was intent upon operating the Department of Justice as one would operate a large law office. In a large law office there is usually an attorney who prepares the brief, another who tries the cases and another who collects and assembles the evidence. In the Department of Justice the Bureau of Investigation should correspond to the latter [sic, last]. It was felt that for the Bureau of Investigation to efficiently and effectively operate, its personnel should be men with legal training.
>
> This theory was a somewhat novel one as it had generally been held that an investigator must be one with numerous disguises and of the so-called sleuthing attitude. He has been dramatized in many of the motion pictures and stage presentations as a gentleman wearing a rather antiquated sort of derby and huge shoes and have the bearing of, to use the vernacular of the underworld, a 'dick.' Such was not the theory, however, upon which we decided to reorganize the Bureau of Investigation in 1924. At that time but 16% of its investigative personnel consisted of men with legal training. . . . Today, 70% of our investigative personnel are lawyers.[16]

However, the qualifications were for males; Hoover eased out the few female agents already on the rolls. One of the females wrote Hoover threatening letters; not until after Hoover's death were females again

appointed as Special Agents. He established a merit system for promotions and an inspection system, which was later much copied throughout
the Federal government. He improved the rudimentary training system
that had been started under Burns. Describing the training system as "an
intensive effort to develop a competent investigator," Hoover told the
lawyers of the four week course:

> ... during which time lectures are delivered by various experts upon
> the subjects covered in the Bureau's investigative activity ... anti-trust
> laws, the bankruptcy laws, the National Banking Act, the National Motor
> Vehicle Theft Act, and other laws. ... The Bureau of Standards has
> cooperated to the extent of having some of its experts deliver lectures
> upon the theory of ballistics and typewriting identification." [Hoover's
> philosophy of investigation included the fact that the investigator:]
>
> ... must approach his investigation with a judicial attitude of mind;
> that his function is that of securing the facts and not that of getting the
> man. ... It is stressed to our investigators that they are to obtain the
> facts irrespective of whether those facts prove the innocence of the man
> or the guilt. ... Another point stressed to the investigator is the fact
> that he is the servant of the people; that his salary is paid by the
> American citizens, and that he must conduct himself at all times so as to
> lend dignity to the United States and to the organization of which he is
> a member.[17]

Attorney General Stone was satisfied with Hoover's early stewardship;
after seven months he made his appointment to Director of the Bureau
of Investigation permanent. Later, after Stone's appointment as Chief
Justice of the Supreme Court, he continued to act as Hoover's mentor.
Stone used to drop by Hoover's office to see how he was doing, and the
Chief Justice later wrote to Felix Frankfurter that Hoover had:

> removed from the Bureau every man as to whose character there was
> any ground for suspicion. He refused to yield to any kind of political
> pressure; he appointed to the Bureau men of intelligence and education,
> and strove to build up a morale such as should control such an orga-
> nization. He ... made it an efficient organization for investigation of
> criminal offenses against the United States.[18]

These were the qualities that the more progressive chiefs of police
were seeking for their departments: (1) educated officers who would
make police work a career, and (2) freedom from political influence in
the operation of their departments. Hoover, with the Attorney General's
support, proved that it could be done, at least on the national level.
Besides setting this important example, Hoover built the national crimi-

nal identification system that the International Association of Chiefs of Police (IACP) had been seeking as a professional goal.

The beginnings of the national criminal identification system, which occurred just a few months before Hoover was appointed Director, are set out in Chapter 5, but Hoover's organizational ability and management brought about the success of the operation. No legislation had been passed to establish an identification service, thus there were no funds to operate. Hoover quickly got the necessary funds from Congress and the enabling legislation. He then made the identification division indispensable to the nation's police. Hoover's first speech as Director of the Bureau of Investigation was to the IACP on July 14, 1925. Hoover was later criticized for giving too many speeches on the crime problem, and later, on internal security matters. But, according to Hoover's nieces, who lived with the family at the time, Hoover had to practice the speech to overcome a stutter he experienced during public speaking.[19]

Hoover told the IACP that he hoped the Identification Division of the Bureau of Investigation would grow "into a service-unit, unique in the history of crime prevention and detection."[20] This speech contains Hoover's initial thoughts on the role of the Bureau of Investigation as a service to law enforcement. At this time, the Bureau was strictly an investigative agency. During the violence of the 1920s, Special Agents of the Bureau of Investigation were not authorized to carry firearms, nor to make arrests— agents had to ask local police or U.S. Marshals to make the arrests in cases the agents had investigated.[21]

THE BUREAU'S SERVICE ROLE

At the beginning of Hoover's term as Director of the Bureau of Investigation, he gave few public statements. Hoover's first speeches were to the IACP at the group's annual meetings in 1925 and 1926. The next two years he did not make any speeches and in 1929 and 1930 he again appeared before the IACP to report on the progress of the identification division. In 1931, Hoover spoke to the Cincinnati Lawyers' Club, as mentioned, and to the American Railway Association on the work of the Bureau and general law enforcement problems. He also spoke to the International Association for Identification on the Bureau's work in this field and, in October, made his fifth appearance before the IACP.[22]

This was the first time before the IACP that Hoover covered more than the work of the identification division. His speech was entitled

"Modern Aids to Police Work" and in his words concerned "the work of the Bureau as a whole." The newly established Uniform Crime Reporting system was detailed to the assembled chiefs and Hoover spoke of the service role that he saw for the FBI. This service role was to become a major part of the renaissance of police professionalism:

> The United States Bureau of Investigation exemplifies what I hope to be one of the most effective aids to police work, *a service agency to law enforcement officers throughout the United States.* Possibly this statement may be deemed egotistical by some persons. I base this claim, however, upon the daily association of our Special Agents with police chiefs, with sheriffs and with law enforcement officials of every kind in all parts of the country, and upon innumerable assurances received to the effect that *the Bureau of Investigation constitutes itself a service agency for the assistance of police officials everywhere. ...* " [Emphasis added.] [Hoover went on to say that Special Agents and officials of the Bureau:]
>
>   ... are instructed that their primary function is a cooperative one; that active cooperation afforded to law enforcement officials is not only proper and due ... but that the Bureau itself could not effectively function without the aid and support of these officials.[23]

At this time only the fingerprint identification division and the Uniform Crime Reporting system had been developed by the IACP and lodged within the Bureau of Investigation. The scientific crime laboratory, the National Academy, and other police training service functions of the Bureau were yet to come. Hoover went on in the 1931 speech to say that the Bureau's success up to then:

>   ... has been due in great part to the enthusiastic and friendly support it has been fortunate enough to secure from law enforcement officials throughout the country. It is my belief that this is the ideal method of securing that unification of law enforcement agencies that exists by statute in other countries. ... There is no national police force nor should there be any, in my opinion.[24]

Hoover's opposition to a national police force continued through the time of Roosevelt's New Deal when there was considerable advocacy for such a national police force, due to the public's perception of a national crime wave during the 1920s and 1930s. But Hoover also addressed this perception during his 1931 appearance before the IACP:

> I have previously commented upon reports of crime waves and the increase of crime, allegedly or otherwise. I think it may be safely assumed that during any period of economic stress crime may be expected to increase and criminals to develop. One would necessarily

look during these times to an increase in crime. . . . I feel, however, that in spite of flaming headlines and despite wide-spread comment relative to specific conditions and cases, the expected degree of increase has not materialized.[25]

When the 1930s brought Roosevelt's New Deal administration, the Department of Justice under the new Attorney General, Homer Stille Cummings, embarked on a "war against crime," another of the New Deal's "wars" on social and economic problems. Hoover was almost replaced, but eventually the leadership of this "war on crime" fell on his shoulders. The Bureau of Investigation's role in law enforcement was greatly expanded and, on July 1, 1935 the organization was renamed the Federal Bureau of Investigation.[26]

President Franklin Roosevelt's first choice as Attorney General was Senator Tom Walsh, a 74-year-old Montana Senator who had served on the Judiciary Committee that had investigated the Palmer Raids in the 1920s and who had been investigated himself by the Bureau of Investigation during the Teapot Dome scandals. He probably would have replaced Hoover, but the Senator, in the company of his new, young bride on his way to the Presidential Inauguration, died of a heart attack. Roosevelt had to designate an immediate replacement, as the new Attorney General had to give the opinion that would allow Roosevelt to open his administration with the dramatic step of a bank holiday. Roosevelt chose a loyal political operative whom he had already named as governor of the Philippines, Homer Cummings. Cummings had some experience in criminal law and interest in criminology; he also had a reputation as a "scrupulous civil libertarian alert to the danger of debasing justice to appease public hysteria."[27]

Beginning with Roosevelt's inaugural address, with its call to the nation to "move as a trained and loyal army willing to sacrifice for the good of a common discipline," the New Deal was heavy with military metaphor. Roosevelt would ask the Congress for "broad Executive power to wage war against the emergency [of the Depression], as great as the power that would be given to me if we were in fact invaded by a foreign foe." Government departments used military analogies to persuade public support, especially the National Recovery Administration, which was "marching" against low prices and destructive competition. The NRA was headed by General Hugh Johnson, a West Point graduate and former cavalry officer. Attorney General Cummings soon caught the cabinet's "war" fever, announcing that gold hoarders were "slackers," the World War I term for draft evaders.[28]

Cummings asserted federal leadership of the public movement against crime that led to an October, 1933, conference with former Secretary of War Patrick Hurley as chairman, announcing:

> a civic war on crime, in which the general enlistment of the American people will be sought, will be formally declared and a mass offensive will be planned ... [to] unite citizens into a tremendously powerful force against which the scarlet army of crime cannot survive.[29]

Author Richard Gid Powers, in his *G–Men: Hoover's FBI in American Popular Culture,* attributes this "war on crime" to the New Deal, which placed a "seal of credibility on the pop culture myth of a ritual struggle between society and an organized underworld."[30] This thesis, however, neglects Hoover's speech before the IACP eight years earlier that noted that the assembled chiefs were:

> ... representatives of the country's first line of defense, the chieftains of the army of law enforcement ... who are enlisted in the endless war against crime ... [31]

Most police historians attribute the early 1930s' bank robberies and kidnappings to intensifying the "war on crime" outlook, neglecting police pioneer August Vollmer's military service or the reserve service of J. Edgar Hoover, plus the tremendous respect these leaders and the public held for the military just after its victory in World War I.[32] In 1922, before Hoover took over the Bureau of Investigation, he applied for and was granted a reserve commission as a Major in the Army of the United States. In 1926 his assignment for duty with the Assistant Chief of Staff, G-2, expired and the next year he was assigned to Military Intelligence. His appointment in the Officers' Reserve Corps expired in 1927 and he immediately applied for reinstatement and was accepted. In 1935, he was promoted to Lieutenant Colonel.[33]

THE FBI AND THE "WAR AGAINST CRIME"

J. Edgar Hoover reformed and revitalized what was a small federal law enforcement agency, with very limited jurisdiction and virtually no police authority. He envisioned it also as a service agency to local police in this country, beginning with its fingerprint identification facilities. Then, in 1930 the Bureau of Investigation was given the clerical function of collecting and reporting, under the Uniform Crime Reporting system, the first potentially nationwide crime statistics system. But the public perception, shared by the Attorney General and the New Deal administration, of an increase in, or at least a change in the nature of, crime led to a change in the nature of the Bureau of Investigation.

Increased readership of newspapers and increased competition among the press and the new medium of mass communication of radio meant increasingly shrill coverage of gangsterism. Two spectacular crimes helped to solidify a public call for action against crime: the Lindbergh kidnapping and the "Kansas City Massacre." The kidnapping of the child of air hero Charles A. Lindbergh, the first man to fly the Atlantic solo, in March, 1932, led to passage three months later of the Federal Lindbergh kidnap law that, as later amended, provided the death penalty for transporting a kidnapped person across a state line. The "Kansas City Massacre" of June, 1933, involved a gangland attempt to free an escaped convict while he was being transported back to Leavenworth prison. Three gangsters opened fire with machine guns on the escorting Bureau of Investigation agents and police officers in Kansas City, killing three officers and one agent—and the convict.[34]

In July, the administration unveiled its program against crime: the Bureau of Investigation was to be renamed the Division of Investigation, an amalgamation of the Bureau of Investigation and the Bureau of Identification (which was already a part of the Bureau of Investigation, but under separate Congressional authority) and the Prohibition Bureau, which had been transferred to the Justice Department in 1930 and was to be disbanded with the end of Prohibition. One problem that Hoover recognized was the size of the Prohibition Bureau, four times the size of the Bureau of Investigation, and the corruption that existed within it that might overwhelm his Bureau. He took control of the Prohibition agents, but insisted they operate separately from his Bureau of Investigation.[35]

The next April (1934), Attorney General Cummings announced his Twelve Point Crime Program, the result of his promise to the country to develop new laws to "arm the Federal government against the underworld for battle in what he called the 'twilight zone' between Federal and local jurisdiction."[36] These included measures against interstate transportation of stolen goods, interstate flight to avoid prosecution, robbery of Federally insured banks, restrictions on the sale of machine guns, assaulting Federal officers, and authority for Bureau of Investigation agents to make arrests and carry weapons. Congress passed these measures against the background of bank robberies and other crimes by John Dillinger and other bandits that terrorized the Midwest. In Don Whitehead's words, "And then it was that the FBI, literally, went to war against the underworld."[37]

In December, 1934, the Attorney General held a Conference on Crime, addressed by the President of the United States, to build a permanent, unified national law enforcement alliance. Attending were over 600 delegates, representing state attorneys general, U.S. Attorneys and Marshals, police chiefs, bar associations, labor unions, churches, educational associations, and the entertainment industry. Among the recommendations of this conference was that law enforcement officials should publicize themselves and their work so that the public would identify with the law. The delegates heard the Attorney General reject a monolithic national police force—the spirit of the New Deal was to rely on a sense of common purpose and high morale. But he did propose, and the conference recommended, the establishment of a "West Point of Law Enforcement," which was to be a "national scientific and educational center" in Washington for training police officers. This was the genesis of the FBI National Academy, which began in 1935 as an advanced training school for local police officers (see Chapter 12), but took more than 35 years to develop into a truly "national scientific and educational center" as the Attorney General and the conference envisioned.[38]

J. Edgar Hoover reorganized the Bureau of Investigation along law enforcement professionalism lines, no small accomplishment as historians have recognized. This was before the advent of the New Deal, but considering Hoover's quiet first years as Director there is no doubt that he learned some of his latter expertise in public relations from the New Deal's Attorney General, Homer Cummings. But, by 1937 Cummings was Roosevelt's principal architect for the Supreme Court "packing plan" and when this plan was defeated, Cummings lost his political influence. Hoover then by default became the principal national spokesman for law enforcement.

And Hoover's vision for the FBI was for two roles, one that of a police service agency. In the next decade this police service role was to bring about what Hoover later termed a "renaissance" in policing. To an extent, Hoover's early career was as cyclical in development as that of law enforcement as a whole. In the mid-1920s, he was the creature of Attorney General Harlan Fiske Stone. In the last part of the decade, with his successful administration of the Bureau of Investigation and its initial service functions, fingerprint collection and uniform crime reportage, Hoover began to develop as his own man. His close relationship with the IACP also built his leadership role in the law enforcement community. When the Roosevelt administration swept into office with its "wars" against the country's economic and social problems, Hoover again became the "loyal soldier" of an administration, but retained sufficient influence on his own to subtly shape the direction of the "war" on crime, as Chapter 12 shows.

This "war" approach had major impact on policing for the next three decades; only in the 1970s did this approach begin to face re-examination by social scientists and then police professionals themselves. As important as the FBI's influence was to police professionalism in the 1930s and beyond, the "war" on crime approach and its corrolary, the military model of policing, are today being re-evaluated. But historian Richard Gid Powers summarized "Hoover's real significance in American life" as "leadership he furnished the Bureau [and] the law enforcement profession." In his monumental analysis of Hoover's career, Powers said that the FBI today is "striving to embody what was permanently valuable in Hoover's dream of professional, scientific law enforcement."[39]

Notes to Chapter 9

1. Ungar, 1975, 57.
2. Stead, 1977, 263.
3. Bopp, 1972, 123.
4. FBI, 1983, 1.
5. Ungar, 1975, 39–40.
6. Whitehead, 1956, 25.
7. Ungar, 1975, 41–43.
8. Demaris, 1975, 3, 38.
9. Stead, 1977, 264.
10. Demaris, 1975, 53–54. Powers, 1987, 491.
11. Ungar, 1975, 44.
12. Whitehead, 1956, 66. Unger, 1975, 43–48.
13. Whitehead, 1956, 67. (Based on interviews with Hoover.)
14. Ungar, 1975, 46–54.
15. Eldefonso, 1982, 302.
16. Hoover, 1931a. 3–4.
17. Ibid. 6–7.
18. Ungar, 1975. 54.
19. Demaris, 1975, 7.

20. Hoover, 1925, 1.
21. Demaris, 1975, 55.
22. "List of Speeches and Public Statements by Director, 1925–1971. n.d.
23. Hoover, 1931b, 2–3.
24. Ibid, 3.
25. Ibid, 18.
26. FBI, 1983, 10.
27. Powers, 1983, 35–36.
28. Ibid, 36–38.
29. Ibid, 39.
30. Ibid.
31. Hoover, 1925, 1–2.
32. Douthit, 1975, 338.
33. "John Edgar Hoover, Officers' Reserve Corps, United States Army Military Intelligence Reserve." n.d.
34. Whitehead, 1956, 92–98.
35. Whitehead, 1956, 91. Powers, 1983, 41.
36. Powers, 1983, 45.
37. Whitehead, 1956, 102–103.
38. Powers, 1983, 47–49.
39. Powers, 1987. 492.

PART III

RENAISSANCE OF PROFESSIONALISM—1930s

Looking back on the first half of the 20th century at the midpoint, J. Edgar Hoover labeled the decade of the 1930s a "renaissance" in law enforcement professionalism. The services that the FBI was furnishing the decentralized police agencies of this country—nationwide fingerprint identification, Uniform Crime Reporting, scientific crime detection, police training through the FBI National Academy and a journal for police, the *FBI Law Enforcement Bulletin,* —all contributed to this advance of professionalism.

The contribution of these services to police professionalism in America is sometimes not fully credited by today's historians, many of whom were graduate students in the 1970s. They show more concern for the internal security excesses of the FBI in the 1960s. But today's law enforcement practitioners know the value of positive identification through fingerprints, especially of fugitives, the worth of nationwide crime reporting for planning purposes, the usefulness of forensic science for evidentiary purposes, and the necessity of police training to move toward professionalism. The purpose of Part III, then, is to show how these accomplishments in police professionalism occurred, in large measure through the efforts of police themselves organized into the International Association of Chiefs of Police, with the supportive and innovative organizational ability of the most professional law enforcement agency this country has yet seen, J. Edgar Hoover's FBI.

Chapter 10

UNIFORM CRIME REPORTING

Only today are elected municipal officials, the news media, and the public beginning to comprehend the limited impact that police can have on crime rates. The effect of demographics on the total amount of crime committed, and other factors that affect crime which are beyond police control, are just beginning to be understood outside the criminal justice community. The measurable quantification of the total crime affecting this country, the Uniform Crime Reporting system, which was developed by the police of this country as a management tool, unfortunately become an informal rating standard for police by the media and partisan political forces.

Since the late 1920s, when the Uniform Crime Reporting system was proposed by the International Association of Chiefs of Police and then assigned in 1930 to the branch of the Department of Justice then called the Bureau of Investigation, this program grew "from a specialized guide of law enforcement activity to one of the most widely quoted social indices of our time."[1]

Development of this system of crime reporting took considerably longer than the adoption of fingerprint identification. The advantages of relatively easy and speedy identification were more easily grasped by police than the concept of a nationwide crime reporting system. In addition, development of such a reporting system meant that the varied criminal laws of each state either had to be changed to be made more uniform, an obviously impractical endeavor, or the crime reporting system had to have enough leeway built in to accommodate the legal variances between states. This was not an easy accomplishment.

The laws of each state today still vary enough that lawyers trained in one state cannot practice in another until, usually, they pass a bar exam in the other. The American Bar Association is still attempting to have uniform statutes passed in each state in various areas of criminal law. The American system of government decentralization, a basic part of our democracy, poses some practical problems unforeseen as decentralization developed. Yet, the International Association of Chiefs of Police, better known today as the IACP, was able to write a 464-page manual for Uniform Crime Reporting, with the help of one lawyer who had never practiced, that has been the basic guideline for this system for half a century.

As the UCR, as Uniform Crime Reporting is now known to police, developed and the national crime rate was determined, comparison of individual cities' rates of crime also became possible. An unfavorable comparison of an individual city, in the period when police were thought solely responsible for crime control, might lead to a change in police leadership by political leaders. As a natural effect, the new and perhaps less professional chief of police could insure that the crime rate then went down under his new administration by the simple expedient of not reporting all complaints received.

This problem was foreseen by the IACP, as noted in the organization's manual, *Uniform Crime Reporting:*

> the reluctance of some police forces to compile and publish reports showing the number of crimes committed . . . is derived from the tendency to charge the crime rate *against the police* rather than *against the community.* . . . [Emphasis in original] and thus to draw broad generalizations concerning the efficiency of various police forces.[2]

The IACP contrasted this with the reporting of epidemic disease by the U.S. Public Health Service which does not reflect on the efficiency of local health departments.

Another factor that could skew these statistics, based as they are on crimes reported to the police, is the degree of trust that the citizenry holds in their police department. If citizens do not trust the police, they will not report crime. This problem was especially evident during the period of racial unrest in the late 1960s, when the lack of trust for police by the minority community was one of the factors that caused the ghettos to burst into mass violence. Similarly, a new police chief who makes his department more professional, and thus increases community trust of the police, will be faced with an increase of reported crime. Thus, Uniform Crime Reporting had some built-in defects, but it was an improvement over no system at all.

A three-year study of the Uniform Crime Reporting system was completed in 1985. Aware of increased police record-producing capability due to the computer revolution and the needs of new users of this system, the IACP and the National Sheriffs' Association suggested that the FBI form a task force which contracted with a private research firm to undertake the broadest review in history of the system. Far-reaching changes were recommended, which the FBI is now in the process of implementing, which will, in totality, provide a crime information system for the next century.

HISTORICAL IACP LANDMARK

America's first police convention, called by St. Louis Chief of Police James McDonough in 1871, adopted a resolution "to procure and digest statistics for the use of police departments." Convention organizers called for information on crime statistics from many jurisdictions, including some foreign ones, but as this convention was a false start for the IACP nothing came of it except the concept of the principle of uniformity in the reportage of crime information.

Congress also saw the need for crime statistics at this time (1870) and made it the duty of the Attorney General to collect statistics on crime in the several states, as well as the United States. This project had to be abandoned for two reasons: first, a lack of support by police departments in reporting statistics of any kind (by law the federal government could not compel the states to submit the required information) and, second, the Department of Justice could not develop a uniform method of tabulating the data.[3]

When the second call for a police executive convention came in 1894 and the IACP grew out of this second and succeeding meetings, hardly a year passed that a convention delegate did not call for support for standardization and collection of crime statistics, as well as criminal records. The IACP started its National Bureau of Criminal Identification in 1897, but it took another 27 years to get the federal government to adopt it.[4] In 1905, when Major Richard Sylvester, Chief of Police in Washington, D.C., took on the presidency of the IACP, he called for the collection of uniform crime figures. He prepared a "schedule of interrogatories for the consideration and adoption by the Census Bureau." This apparently failed, for in 1908 he urged the IACP to assume the responsibility for the collection of crime statistics in his annual report:

> I have to refer you to the want of uniformity in the preparation of annual reports and statistics. It is especially important that the members of this association should adopt as a criterion some form of a statistical arrangement of their reports which should include population,

social conditions and other facts whereby students and other officials may aggregate, compare and deduce information that may have some degree of reliability. Comparisons purporting to be authentic are too often misleading and to the injustice of the police generally.[5]

Despite Major Sylvester's urgings of either a system operated by the Bureau of the Census or one on the order of the IACP's own National Bureau of Criminal Identification, it took the next generation of IACP members, under the leadership of Chief August Vollmer, to begin the process of standardizing definitions of the various crimes necessary to inaugurate a national system of crime reporting. At the 1922 IACP convention Vollmer divided the business sessions into six sections which met for two days each. All the sections were able to report extensive findings except the one on crime reporting.

This section did report a system of tabulating complaints where money was obtained by theft, fraud, trickery, or violence. This served as a guide for a few departments from 1922 to 1930, when the Uniform Crime Reporting system was adopted, but it never became widely used. The IACP did make contact with the American Bar Association on the crime reporting issue. The Attorney General spoke on the issue of crime reports at the bar group's 1924 meeting. Then, in 1926 the Bureau of the Census published a booklet entitled, "Instructions for Compiling Criminal Statistics." This was largely the work of Professor Sam B. Warner, Director of the Committee on Records and Statistics for the American Institute of Criminal Law and Criminology, and while it suggested a "few of the more essential statistical tables which each police department would find desirable to publish annually . . . it received only token adoption by authorities."[6]

By the time of the 1927 IACP convention, held in Windsor, Canada, the public and even some of the police leaders, were convinced that crime was out of control during the 1920s. But Chief Vollmer, ever a voice of reason, addressed the convention and indicated that the Census Bureau's procedure on crime reporting was a false index to crime, as it was based on criminal commitments rather than on complaints to the police of crime. Vollmer told the convention:

How can we ever know the extent or the nature and distribution of crime or discuss the problem intelligently at our conferences or conduct a successful campaign to prevent crime until police statistics are accurately, adequately and uniformly compiled? We have delayed this matter too long; let us take immediate action.[7]

Immediate impetus for formation of a committee on uniform crime reporting methods came from Commissioner William P. (Silver Bill) Rutledge, the first police commissioner in Detroit to have risen from the ranks. He had served as President of the IACP in 1923–1924 and reported to the 1927 convention that he had requested crime statistics recently from 300 police departments. Only 100 replied, but he told the convention that the statistics were virtually worthless because of their lack of uniformity. Commissioner Rutledge told the convention: "We are in the absurd position of endeavoring to diagnose and cure a social disease with little knowledge of its causes, nature or prevalence." He urged immediate formation of a committee on uniform crime statistics; the convention approved and appointed Rutledge as chairman.

He was joined on the committee by chiefs from Cleveland, Buffalo, Chicago, Boston, New Orleans, Baltimore, Portland, and August Vollmer of Berkeley, plus, later, chiefs from New York, San Francisco, and St. Louis. Realizing that there was great interest in this project beyond just the membership of the IACP, an advisory committee was formed of leading criminologists, representatives of government administration groups, and public officials, including J. Edgar Hoover, Director of the Bureau of Investigation, U.S. Department of Justice. The committee was given unsolicited financial support by the Laura Spelman Rockefeller Fund and was able to hire a staff led by Bruce Smith of the National Institute of Public Administration in New York, who had wide experience with police surveys.[8]

> Bruce Smith enjoyed the distinction of being considered one of the foremost experts in police administration from the 1920s to the 1950s, without ever serving as a policeman.... he was not really a pioneer, although by his work on the development of FBI Uniform Crime Reports he could certainly lay claim to the title.[9]

Smith was the last of the eastern civilian progressive police reformers, a product of Columbia University with degrees in political science and law. He never practiced law, however, becoming instead an assistant to the famous professor Charles Beard, director of the New York Bureau of Municipal Research, later called the Institute of Public Administration, which Smith also headed intermittently thereafter. Smith became a specialist in police surveys, beginning with Harrisburg, Pennsylvania, in 1916. After service in World War I, he surveyed the New Orleans police in 1923. Between 1923 and his death in 1950, Smith was involved in some 50 surveys of American police departments. In 1925, he wrote his first book, *The State Police: Organization and Administration;* the next year he authored "The Metropolitan Police Systems," in *The Missouri Crime Survey* and in 1929, "Rural Police Protection," in *The Illinois Crime Survey.* Thus, Smith brought considerable knowledge of police administration to his study of collecting crime statistics for the IACP.[10]

Bruce Smith, his assistant, Donald C. Stone of the Cincinnati Bureau of Municipal Research, and the police Committee on Uniform Crime Records (now joined by police executives from St. Louis, San Francisco, and New York City) plus the Advisory Committee, with additions of the Director of the Census and a representative of the International City Managers' Association, prepared IACP tentative drafts on crime records, classification of major offenses, and *A Guide For Preparing Annual Police Reports.* In June, 1929, the draft of *Uniform Crime Reporting* appeared and was adopted by the 1929 IACP annual convention. Four thousand copies were distributed to police administrators throughout the country. IACP representatives appeared before Congress for legislation to put into effect the IACP's 1929 convention invitation to the Bureau of Investigation's Division of Identification and Information to operate the system Bruce Smith had developed.[11]

The foreword to *Uniform Crime Reporting* noted that:

> The urgent need for national crime statistics in the United States is so well recognized as to require no debate. . . . It may contribute somewhat to an understanding of the realities of the subject, if the true and necessary relation between criminal statistics and the police is clearly set forth. Compilation of the number of persons tried, convicted and imprisoned do not, and cannot, provide an index of crime and criminality. Only a police record of known offenses will do this. . . . crime statistics must originate with the police and without police support there can be no crime statistics.[12]

This manual set forth the reasons why the Department of Justice's Bureau of Investigation had been selected by the IACP to operate the Uniform Crime Reporting system: (1) the Division of Identification of the Bureau of Investigation already operated a national system of criminal fingerprint identification, (2) it took five years for this division to obtain the full cooperation of the police in forwarding fingerprints and this good will would be necessary in the new endeavor, (3) the Bureau's corps of field agents could render advice to police, unlike any other federal agency, (4) while the Bureau of the Census controls superior statistical techniques it lacks the intimate police contacts of the Bureau,

(5) such statistics are collected in Europe and England by ministries of justice, and (6) "Since the police of this country may either grant or withhold crime returns, it is clear that without police cooperation there can be no crime statistics."[13]

Congress agreed and passed the necessary legislation in 1930 to enable the Bureau of Investigation's Division of Identification and Information to begin collecting the statistics that the IACP had begun to assemble. After President Herbert Hoover signed the legislation into law on June 11, Attorney General William D. Mitchell approved the work of the committee:

> I feel that a very definite step has been taken toward providing peace officers of the United States with an accurate index to the volume, distribution and fluctuation of crime and that the material collected as a result of the plan devised will prove of invaluable assistance to peace officers in their efforts to combat crime.[14]

But the National Commission on Law Observance and Enforcement, better known as the Wickersham Commission, raised objections in a letter to the Attorney General. The Commission said that Sam B. Warner of Harvard "recommended instead that the statistics in each State be collected by a central authority of that State, and by it transmitted to the Bureau of the Census of the United States."[15]

Inspector Clyde Tolson, later the FBI's Associate Director, wrote a lengthy memo on his conference with Bruce Smith regarding the Uniform Crime Reports. When the Wickersham letter was received by the Attorney General, Hoover had to note on Tolson's memo that "By order of the Attorney General, no further action is to be taken in this matter & all arrangements effected are to be temporarily suspended until the Crime Commission can be heard. . . ." Hoover met with Wickersham on June 16 explaining that the Bureau had already begun printing the forms necessary for crime reporting, legislated by Congress and signed by the President, to begin July 1, but that he would hold this in abeyance until he had met with Professor Sam B. Warner. Hoover told Wickersham that Warner was opposed to a system that was already in use by some 600 police departments. Warner could not come to Washington, so Hoover sent one of his executives to meet with him at Harvard.[16]

Warner's objections did not prevail, as in September the Bureau of Investigation printed and mailed a 22-page manual of instructions for police departments which capsulized the 400-page book prepared by Bruce Smith. Thus, the Uniform Crime Reporting program was transferred from the IACP, which had operated it since January, to the Bureau of Investigation on September 1, 1930.[17]

THE SYSTEM

The system developed by Smith was not based on the number of persons arrested, as was the case with most European criminal statistic systems and even the few American ones that existed. The IACP pointed out that this type of system is useful for showing (1) the social characteristics of persons arrested, prosecuted, convicted or imprisoned and (2) the manner in which the machinery of criminal justice functions. But such a system does not tell how much crime has been committed:

> Lack of any constant relation between the number of arrests, convictions, and prisoners, on the one hand, and criminal acts on the other, must always prevent measurement of the extent of crime. . . . Frequent efforts to draw such comparisons and conclusions have yielded conflicting results and done the cause of criminal statistics incalculable harm. . . . The national system of criminal statistics here presented therefore takes the number of "offenses known to police" as a point of departure.[18]

The system used the approach of minimizing the statistical effect of differences between the varying definitions of offenses in the states' crime laws, rather than the impractical approach of seeking uniform laws in the various states, because the first approach promised much earlier results. Also, the uniform classification was based directly on that used by the Bureau of the Census in compiling statistics on prisoners. The IACP also recognized that not all crimes are immediately reported to the police; some "remain concealed owing to the ignorance or indifference of the victims." To minimize the statistical effects of those crimes:

> . . . a careful distinction has been drawn between those offenses which naturally and almost inevitably are reported to public agencies, and those which are less certain of becoming a matter of record.[19]

The offenses, which the IACP believed were "almost inevitably," reported to police, were:

1. Felonious homicide (murder and manslaughter)
2. Rape
3. Robbery
4. Aggravated assault
5. Burglary—Breaking or entering

6.   Larceny—Theft
7.   Auto theft

The first form, "Return A," sent to police departments around the country asked simply for the figures on the number of cases in these categories, plus a listing of the number of police department employees (including civilians).

The Bureau of Investigation issued a publication, *Uniform Crime Reporting: A Booklet Published for the Information of Law Enforcement Officials and Agencies,* when the Bureau began operating the UCR. The Bureau's booklet was just 20 pages long, but noted that the manual, *Uniform Crime Reporting,* would be "gladly furnished police officials on request." The booklet noted that all complaints brought to the attention of police through citizen complaints, reports of police officers, as a result of "on view" arrests, or coming to the police via other officials should be reported. It then went on to define the uniform classifications listed above.

"Homicide is the killing of one human being by another," unless excusable and justifiable under the law, and is divided by state statutes into murder and manslaughter. The differences in the various states between murder and manslaughter caused the system's designers to combine the two into one class of felonious homicide. Rape was the only sexual offense included, because of its aggravated nature and in spite of the differences among the states with respect to age and the ability to consent. Robbery was defined "as the taking or attempted taking of property from the person ... through the use or threat of force or by putting in fear."

Aggravated assault was confined to serious offenses, "most likely to result in severe bodily injury or death," such as assault with intent to kill, poisoning, assault with a dangerous weapon, maiming, and assault with explosives. The uniform crime of burglary, defined at common law as the breaking or entering a dwelling house in the night time with intent to commit a felony, followed the statutory amplifications of entering all structures defined in the various state statutes with intent to commit any felony or larceny. Larceny was defined as stealing the personal property of another, but not including embezzlement or fraudulent conversion. To this definition was added the distinction between grand and petty larceny, grand larceny being the stealing of property worth

$50 or more. Auto theft was defined simply as the stealing of any type of motor vehicle.

Attempts to commit any of these crimes were to be included in the crime category itself, with the exception of homicide. An attempt to commit homicide was to be recorded as an aggravated assault, as the category homicide was to be limited to offenses that actually resulted in death. Rules for scoring the offenses were also given in this booklet; basically, the number of offenses, rather than the number of persons arrested, governed. Also, the seriousness of the crime governed: one robbery would be recorded in a case of robbery and assault, as robbery is the more serious crime, thus was listed before assault in the Uniform Crime list. This came to be called the hierarchial rule of UCR, later criticized for causing omission of some crimes from the total crime count. The booklet ended with comment on the voluntary nature of this program and an offer of assistance by the Bureau in effecting this system of obtaining crime statistics on a national scale.[20]

Both the IACP and the Bureau of Investigation postponed the collection of other data that could be provided by this system: "Lest such additions might prove to be burdensome and perhaps cause the project to fall from its own weight..." But four supplementary return forms were set out in the IACP manual and these were gradually introduced as the system grew. These included Return C, a record of persons charged. At first, statistics in this category were collected by the FBI in the 1940s from fingerprint records received in the Identification Division.[21] Noting that "if crime statistics are ever to be complete for the entire nation... state governments must lend a hand," the IACP manual explained that New York State had recently begun to collect this information from every jurisdiction, urban and rural, in the state and California recently took similar action. The manual urged each state to follow suit, setting forth a model act for each state to follow, if desired.[22]

J. Edgar Hoover echoed this idea of state collection of the data for forwarding to the Bureau:

One of the satisfactory methods of handling work of this kind is through State Bureaus. Should this plan continue, I believe it would be highly desirable to develop this phase of uniform crime reporting. I am strongly in favor and have always expressed myself as advocating the establishment of State Bureaus throughout the country... but I differ with those gentlemen who have urged that we defer the assembling of crime statistics until the establishment of State Bureaus for I am convinced that to do so would result in complete inaction in this field of endeavor.[23]

Hoover's conviction was based on his experience with the Identification Division; after 7 years of operation of the division there were but 23 state bureaus of identification, in spite of constant advocacy by the IACP and the Bureau of Investigation. Half of Hoover's 1931 speech to the IACP was on the UCR. He pointed out that in the year that the Bureau had operated UCR there had been a great increase in the number of cities reporting, from 895 to 1,386. In 1930, the cities reporting had represented a population of almost 34 million people; a year later the cities reporting had a combined population of almost 50 million. The progress of UCR in the decade of the 1930s is illustrated by the Attorney General's report for 1940: by that time a grand total of 4,367 municipal, county, state, and territorial entities representing over 68 million people were submitting reports.[24]

In his 1931 speech to the IACP, Hoover emphasized the necessity of personal contact with UCR contributors, "under the supervision of International Association of Chiefs of Police, the sponsor of the project of uniform crime reporting." He detailed the statutory and budgetary limits on Bureau agents to do this kind of work, and the question of policy in federal agents advising on matters of exclusive state and local jurisdiction. But the IACP had no budget to form an advisory staff such as Hoover suggested, although the IACP's committee on Uniform Crime Reports stayed in existence, urging the creation of state bureaus of identification and information along with modeling local police reporting on the uniform system.[25]

TODAY AND TOMORROW

For half a century, the UCR Program remained based on the IACP's initial concept as set forth in *Uniform Crime Reporting: A Complete Manual for Police*. In 1957, a consultant committee established by the FBI recommended changes in the program in three areas: (1) the population basis for the computation of crime rates, (2) reporting crimes for rural population areas, and (3) the composition of the Part I offense classification. As a result of the committee's report the use of population estimates between 10-year census periods was introduced; the frequency of publication of *Uniform Crime Reports* was changed from semi-annual to annual;

the term "crime index" was introduced; and a procedure for estimating total known crime in the United States was developed.[26]

These changes still left the UCR very close to its original design, while by the mid-1970s the number of contributors had grown to over 15,000 law enforcement agencies, covering 97% of the population. At that time, the IACP and the National Sheriffs Association, now the UCR Program law enforcement advisory groups, proposed a thorough evaluation of the program's effectiveness:

> Their proposal grew from concerns that the national Program itself had remained virtually unchanged in terms of the data collected and disseminated, while an expansion had occurred with respect to the capabilities of law enforcement to supply the crime information, the number and diversity of users of UCR statistics, and the utility of the data.[27]

The FBI contracted with a private research firm in 1982 to conduct this evaluation. The Bureau of Justice Statistics had begun citizen surveys in the 1970s to determine the amount of crime unreported to law enforcement. The news media, among others, began to compare the two sets of statistics from UCR and from Justice Statistics and had difficulty resolving differences between crime reported to police and unreported crime as developed by the originally misnamed "victimization" surveys of the Bureau of Justice Statistics.[28]

Using information gathered from law enforcement, criminal justice practitioners, and academic researchers, the consulting firm, working closely with the FBI, produced a *Blueprint for the Future of the Uniform Crime Reporting Program.* This report provides for significant improvements in the UCR program: unit-record reporting, a two-component system, and quality assurance.[29] The recommendations of the "blueprint" resulted from a consensus of the contributors, users, and operators of the UCR, noting:

> The recommended system reflects the vastly increased capacity of modern police information and data processing systems. It would immediately increase the depth and scope of the UCR program, providing substantially more accurate and useful information about crime in the United States and detailing law enforcement agencies' responses to crime problems in ways never before possible.[30]

As opposed to the current monthly summary reporting system, a unit-record procedure would involve law enforcement reporting information on *each* offense and arrest individually, as is done today only in homicide cases. The sub-data elements, the reportorial "who, what, when, where, why, and how" of each offense, would then be available to law enforcement and to other researchers. The proposed two component system, consisting of Levels I and II, would comprise about 95% of law enforcement agencies, reporting much the same information as today in Level I. But in Level II, which would be composed of the country's largest police agencies, plus a representative sample of smaller ones, reports would cover more data encompassing many more offense categories. The latter can be used to project statistically valid crime projections.

However, as the revolution in data processing hastens the computerization of police records systems, law enforcement is finding that it takes little more resources to program for information required at Level II over Level I, so there may be a re-examination of the two component recommendation. Quality assurance recommendations include audit procedures, agency self-certification of minimum reporting-system standards, increased feedback to local agencies, and strengthening of state UCR Program quality assurance.[31]

The "blueprint" also addressed the possibility of potential integration of UCR data with the survey information developed by the National Crime Survey of the Justice Department's Bureau of Justice Statistics, but the FBI determined that the National Crime Survey must be vastly expanded to allow any useful integration. In addition, UCR publications were analyzed and several recommendations made, such as including more textual and interpretive material. Issuing more information aimed at researchers is the recommended goal.

Now being implemented by the FBI, the *Blueprint for the Future of the UCR Program* is another step in law enforcement professionalism. A milestone of policing's second renaissance (see Part V), it will provide for the "gathering of crime information and statistics for the 21st century."[32]

Notes to Chapter 10

1. Zolbe, 1980. 2.
2. Committee, 1929. 2.
3. Thompson, 1968. 23.
4. Dilworth, 1977. 18.
5. Proceedings, 1908. 25.
6. Thompson, 1968. 26–27.
7. Proceedings, 1927. 76.
8. Thompson, 1968. 28–30.

9. Stead, 1977. 191.
10. Ibid, 191–204.
11. Thompson, 1968. 30.
12. Committee, 1929. vii.
13. Ibid. 12–13.
14. Thompson, 1968. 32.
15. Wickersham, 1930.
16. Tolson, 1930. Hoover, 1930.
17. Zolbe, 1980. 2.
18. Committee, 1929. 3–4.
19. Ibid, 6.
20. Bureau of Investigation, 1930. 5–20.
21. Zolbe, 1986.
22. Committee, 1929. 7–15.
23. Hoover, 1931b. 11.
24. Annual Report of the Attorney General, 1940. 37.
25. Thompson, 1968. 32–34.
26. Committee, 1958. 1–3.
27. FBI, 1981. 4.
28. New York Times, 1986, 15.
29. Zolbe, 1985. 10.
30. Poggio et al, 1985. 22.
31. Zolbe, 1986.
32. Ibid.

Chapter 11

LIBRARY TO LABORATORY

S now softly dusted the northside streets, perhaps in nature's attempt to cover their grime. Inside a cartage firm, the headquarters of mobster "Bugs" Moran, machine gun fire reverberated with the thunder of eternity— seven men died in a hail of .45 caliber slugs. It was February 14 (Valentine's Day), 1929.

The bloodiest massacre of Chicago's prohibition wars provoked a public outcry and led to the founding of what was to become this country's greatest crime laboratory. The FBI Laboratory began in 1932, three years after the St. Valentine's Day Massacre. The FBI Agent who set up the laboratory had attended a scientific crime investigation course at the Northwestern University laboratory. The scientific facility at Northwestern had been founded as a result of the famous gangland mass execution.

Fifty-three years later, in 1985, the FBI Laboratory conducted over one million scientific examinations of evidence; more than a third of these examinations were for state and local law enforcement agencies. Since 1981, the FBI Laboratory has operated the largest scientific crime detection training and research facility in the country. Over the last half century the FBI Laboratory has led the way in the use of forensic science in this country. Most important to police professionalism, since its founding the FBI Laboratory has developed a tradition of protection of the innocent through scientific investigation.

SAINT VALENTINE'S DAY MASSACRE

At the close of the "Roaring Twenties," during the gang wars that plagued Chicago and other large cities, the Al Capone mob attacked George "Bugs" Moran's crime organization. In an attempt to "eliminate" Moran, Capone's gang set up a phony delivery of contraband liquor to Moran's headquarters, a cartage firm at 2122 North Clark St. Six of Moran's followers (and a local dentist, a mobster "groupie") were at the

151

hauling company waiting for Bugs the morning of February 14, 1929.
Moran was late. As he rounded the corner with two more of his men he
saw a black Cadillac, similar to cars used by Chicago police detectives.
Five men, three in police uniforms, entered the Clark Street address.

Moran waited in a nearby coffee shop, planning which men to send
with bail money after what he supposed was a raid. His gang was lined
up facing a brick wall as if for a police search. Neighbors later said they
heard what they thought were were "pneumatic drills" as the gangsters
were machine gunned. Even the real officers of the Chicago police, when
they arrived at the scene, recoiled in shock at the carnage. The gunman
had left leisurely. Police found the victims with their "rolls"—$1,135,
$1,250, $1,200, etc.—still intact.[1]

In response to the public outrage over the executions, a coroner's jury
of specially selected citizens was called by the Coroner of Chicago,
Herman N. Bundesen, to investigate the "massacre." Part of the evidence
that police collected and presented to the jury was the large number of
bullets fired in the attack. Two jurors, Walter E. Olson, President of the
Olson Rug Company, and Bert A. Massee, Vice President of the Colgate-
Palmolive-Peet Company, inquired into the value these bullets might
have. They were told by police that a firearms expert might be able to
determine whether the bullets had been fired from a certain gun. But
while the Chicago police were aware of the science of firearms identification (sometimes called ballistics) in 1929, they had no such expert, nor
even a scientific crime laboratory. As foreman of the jury, Massee contacted
a New York firearms identification specialist, Dr. Calvin Goddard of the
Bureau of Forensic Ballistics, to come to Chicago for the necessary
examinations.

Olson and Massee also agreed to finance a crime lab for the Chicago
coroner and police. Bundesen urged that the laboratory not be connected with the coroner's office or the police department so that it would
be free of political influence. The jurors contacted Northwestern University and in June, 1929, the Laboratory Corporation was organized and
affiliated with the university; it became known as the Northwestern
Crime Detection Laboratory. Calvin H. Goddard was hired as the managing director and was sent to thirteen European countries to study their
police laboratories.[2]

NORTHWESTERN CRIME DETECTION LABORATORY

Colonel Calvin H. Goddard had received a medical doctorate from Johns Hopkins University in 1915, but developed a consuming interest in ballistics during Army service in World War I. In 1926, Goddard presented a paper on ballistics developments at the annual convention of the International Association of Chiefs of Police (IACP):
He described the Bureau of Forensics Ballistics as:

> ... an organization of four individuals who have been trying to collect, correlate, tabulate and disseminate to duly constituted authorities information dealing with the broad subject of arms and ammunition as they figure in legal and particularly criminal cases.[3]

Goddard went on to describe the state of ballistic science at that time, starting with the work of Charles E. Waite, begun in 1915 when Waite was assigned to a special inquiry by a governor in a murder case. Waite determined that the murder bullets could not have been fired by the gun owned by the accused, who had already been convicted. The governor pardoned the man and the real killers were then apprehended.

This caused Waite to look into ways to make firearms evidence infallible, which led to the collection of data on all firearms made in this country and then on those made abroad. This data indicated that no two firearms manufacturers cut the spiral grooves inside the barrel with the same specifications. This process is called rifling which imparts the spinning motion to the bullet thereby improving accuracy. Each gun maker cut the grooves with a different pitch (the rate the grooves turn within the barrel), different widths of grooves, different numbers of grooves, and different depths of grooves. By precise measurement of these different factors it was possible to determine exactly which type of gun fired the bullet in question.

Goddard then explained how irregularities of wear inside each barrel leave distinctive marks on each bullet fired from the individual gun. Irregularities of manufacture of each barrel in the cutting of the barrel grooves also leave tool marks which are imparted to each bullet that passes through the barrel and may later be identified on the bullet. By 1926 Waite had died, but his associate Philip O. Gravelle, who had recently been awarded a medal by the British Royal Microscopic Society, was able to develop the comparison microscope. This instrument allowed viewing the images of two bullets side by side as a composite image and allowed forensic ballistics to become a reliable science.

Goddard, after he perfected his technique with Gravelle's comparison microscope in 1927, offered to examine the bullets involved in the Sacco-Vanzetti case, in which two Italian-born anarchists had been convicted of a holdup-murder in Massachusetts. Goddard's careful examination caused two defense firearms witnesses to withdraw and Sacco and Vanzetti's guilt was confirmed.[4]

The year after Goddard became managing director of the Northwestern Crime Detection Laboratory, he described the laboratory's functions to the 1930 IACP convention. Noting that the average American city had only a fingerprint bureau, a photographic department, and a coroner's office and chemist, Goddard said that this was the beginning stage for European cities. European police then added experts in chemistry, in the use of ultra violet rays, in the use of microscopes, in blood analysis, in tire, foot and finger prints, and in moulage (casting). The Northwestern laboratory was modeled after the best overseas laboratories Goddard could find.[5]

The Northwestern facility had a director who handled firearms examinations, an assistant who was a chemist and toxicologist, a third examiner imported from Vienna who was expert in fingerprints, handwriting, typewriting, and moulage. In addition, the laboratory had a consulting staff of pathologists, bacteriologists, an arson specialist, an anatomist, and others.

Additionally, the laboratory had embarked on a training program for state's attorneys, police officials and detectives. Goddard reported that assistance was given officers from other jurisdictions who wanted to set up laboratories. Goddard left the Northwestern laboratory in 1934 during the Depression, after working a year without pay because of funding difficulties. The Chicago Police Department purchased the Northwestern University Crime Laboratory in May, 1938. Goddard's dream of a central crime and forensic ballistic laboratory in Washington, D.C., to serve the whole Nation, as the IACP's identification bureau did, was then on the point of being realized with the establishment of the FBI Laboratory.[6]

"WHERE IS THE SMOCK?"

With just a very few police crime laboratories in existence in the U.S., along with the private Northwestern Crime Detection Laboratory, developments in this country in forensic science, particularly ballistics, dictated the expansion of scientific crime detection to all of law enforcement in the 1930s. The "crime wave" after World War I and the new Roosevelt administration's "war on crime" set the stage for the federal government to move in this direction. But the Bureau of Investigation had already taken the first steps. Recalling the early abuses of forensic science by self-appointed "experts," J. Edgar Hoover, Director of the Federal Bureau of Investigation, declared in 1936:

> ... we look forward to the time when the unethical itinerant 'so-called' expert willing to testify for whichever side offers the most money, the prosecution or the defense, will become a thing of the past.... An expert must be highly trained in a specialized field. The man who pretends to qualify upon a multiplicity of subjects and through a combination of chicanery with a mumbo jumbo of scientific terms to confuse the prosecution, the defense, and the jury, all looking toward the acquittal of a guilty man, has been allowed too much freedom in criminal cases. Before the trial of accused persons can be made thoroughly fair, this type of unethical expert must become a figure of the past. In only one way can this be accomplished and that is by thoroughly impartial adjudication of the scientific aspects of evidence by experts who are swayed solely by their findings, based upon the solid foundation of scientific fact.[7]

This was Hoover's justification for the FBI Laboratory; he sought facilities staffed by impartial examiners who based their findings on scientific fact. But it took some years to achieve this.

"Impartial adjudication ... based upon the solid foundation of scientific fact" in Hoover's words brought another element of professionalism to law enforcement—the protection of the innocent. In 1931, a woman was found shot to death in Detroit with a suicide note and a gun by her side. Other circumstances suggested, however, that she had been murdered by her husband. He was arrested and at the ensuing trial a private handwriting "expert" testified that the suicide note was a forgery. The husband was convicted. After nine years imprisonment, the suicide note and samples of the woman's handwriting were sent to the FBI Laboratory, where the suicide note was found to be genuine. The husband was freed, "based upon the solid foundation of scientific fact."[8]

The earliest reference to scientific crime detection in FBI files relates to document examination, a field important to the Bureau of Investigation because of the type of cases the Bureau handled. A 1922 letter signed by then Director William J. Burns, but dictated by J. Edgar Hoover, requested a field office to determine the names of "dependable hand writing experts" in its territory.[9] Perhaps the difficulty in finding "dependable" handwriting experts over the next few years led Special Agent Samuel W. Hardy of the Washington Field Office to recommend to Hoover that the Bureau of Investigation:

> ...should broaden its scope of criminal investigation by maintaining laboratories equipped to handle bullet identification, handwriting and typewriting identification, and testing drugs, hair, blood, etc. Such laboratories could be incorporated in the National Division of Identification and Information and if similar identification facilities along these lines were afforded to local peace officers as are now given them on fingerprint exchange it might lead to still closer cooperation between the Bureau of Investigation and other law enforcement agencies.[10]

Agent Hardy had set out the duties of the FBI Laboratory as they were to develop and the reason that the lab should be supported by the FBI—to develop closer cooperation with local police. Hoover replied to Hardy that a library of criminology had been established at Bureau headquarters and some means of extending this facility was being considered. The Research Division of the FBI functioned to study and develop scientific information by a "review of books and publications containing articles on criminological subjects [and in 1932] by undertaking experiments" at the suggestion of "law enforcement officials and the Bureau's own Special Agents."

In August, 1930, Director Hoover sent two Bureau Inspectors, Hugh H. Clegg and J. M. Keith, to attend a symposium on scientific crime detection at Goddard's Northwestern University Crime Detection Laboratory. The next year, Clyde Tolson, later Hoover's second in command, talked with Special Agent Charles A. Appel about the desirability of having an employee of the Bureau attend a course of instruction in scientific crime detection at Northwestern. Tolson noted in a memo to Hoover that the tuition for this course was $100 and suggested that Inspector Clegg or SA Appel attend—at their own expense. The Depression was then making itself felt on the Bureau's budget.[11]

Appel was chosen and his attendance at the Northwestern University in April, 1931, was the real beginning of the FBI Laboratory. Special Agent Appel wrote, in a 1932 memorandum for Hoover, "...the Bureau should be the central clearing house for all information which may be needed in the criminological work...all police departments in the future will look to the Bureau for information of this kind as a routine thing." Appel was the laboratory's first examiner; he remained as an examiner until he retired in 1948, and he organized the laboratory from the beginning.[12]

Appel was a Washington, D.C., native and a law school graduate like Hoover (and born in the same year, 1895). He entered on duty in 1924, the year Hoover was appointed Director. Appel's name is on the July 21, 1932, purchase order, the earliest still extant, for the lab—a microscope for bullet comparison purposes.[13]

A 1933 article by Rex Collier, who wrote extensively about the Bureau of Investigation at that time, described the new laboratory's beginnings:

> Aroused by the ever-increasing menace of the scientific minded criminal-... the United States Bureau of Investigation has established a novel research laboratory where Government criminologists will match wits with underworld cunning.[14]

Apparently in a reference to laboratory coats already purchased, Hoover noted on a picture of Appel in a business suit that accompanied the article, "Where is the smock?"

In 1932, the Research Division had begun a rudimentary laboratory to evaluate "scientific methods and apparatus used in criminal investigative work." Initially, one function of the scientific laboratory was the dissemination of information to law enforcement regarding "improvements in scientific methods." A display of scientific apparatus was being arranged to demonstrate forensic science techniques to visiting law enforcement officials.

The Research Division developed from demands by local law enforcement officials, as well as from the Bureau's own investigative divisions, to provide the service of "studying, developing and disseminating information ... purely research work" to law enforcement. According to a report furnished a Chicago journalist, this research work was for general use, as distinguished from work on a particular case. "Indeed, while work is performed at times upon some particular case, this is for the purpose of experiment only, and the results may not be used in that case, except through the means of outside experts. . . . "[15]

Thus, the FBI Laboratory began as a strictly research facility, really an adjunct to the Bureau's library. The dissemination of information gained was accomplished through publication in the monthly *Fugitives Wanted by Police* (which became the *FBI Law Enforcement Bulletin* in 1935) and through pamphlets on particular subjects.[16]

A 1933 report to the Attorney General summarized some of the cases that the new laboratory had worked on. The sheriff at Cody, Wyoming, forwarded specimens of hair in a rape case to be compared with samples obtained from suspects. In a Kansas City murder case, a note sent to the Governor of Oklahoma was compared to specimens from a typewriter found in a house used by the Brady bank robbery gang and was found identical. In the Lindbergh kidnaping case, a note purporting to be in the handwriting of the kidnaper was found to be a forgery, a tracing of a published photograph of the original note. The ransom notes in the Urschel kidnaping case were found to be prepared on a Remington typewriter, but not one that was found in the course of the investigation.

Sixteen other handwriting or typewriting examinations were summarized for the Attorney General. One state murder and motor vehicle theft case was reported in which fragments of two bullets taken from a corpse were examined and found to be .38 calibre from a revolver, probably a Colt because the barrel grooves, which left marks on the bullets, slanted to the left. Several of the twenty cases reported were local in nature; a high percentage of the laboratory's work in its first months was for state or local authorities.[17]

To help in setting up this laboratory, the Bureau of Investigation contacted experts in forensic science in government, industry, and academia. Foremost among these was Dr. Wilmer Souder, a Bureau of Standards expert "recognized throughout the country as one of the foremost scientists in ballistics and document identification." A 1934 memo requested that Dr. Souder be permitted to assist the Bureau in an official advisory capacity in keeping the "technical laboratory . . . abreast at all times of developments in this field."[18]

A 1934 six-page report on the "Establishment of a Technical Laboratory" noted that previously it had been customary for the Division of Investigation to use "technical experts from outside its organization to make scientific analyses." But the importance and growth of the scientific work necessitated the establishment of a laboratory with "the assistance and advice" of Dr. Souder, an 18-year veteran of the Bureau of Standards. Dr. Souder had spent much of his time at the Bureau of Standards working on "handwriting, typewriting and ballistics identification."

This report also listed the areas of examinations that the new laboratory was capable of performing: ballistics, document examinations (handwriting and typewriting), moulage (castings), micro-analyses of hairs and fibers, and chemical analyses of stains, including blood tests. Also, collections of watermarks, tire tread patterns, bullets, cartridges and powders, along with typewriting specimens, were being gathered and it was noted that these would be made available to all law enforcement officials desiring to use them.

Use of the reference collections maintained by the laboratory was offered immediately, as was examination of physical evidence in state and local crimes, but limited personnel in the laboratory precluded testimony being offered in state cases at that time. Service to the entire U.S. law enforcement community through testimony in local cases by FBI laboratory experts came in 1939 after the laboratory had become established.

GROWTH OF THE FBI LABORATORY

The influence of the FBI Laboratory on police professionalism was due to the Bureau offering its services to state and local law enforcement. This can be viewed from two different perspectives. Some local crime lab officials saw this as an attempt by the FBI to completely dominate the field of forensic science. Social historians today view this, and other developments in law enforcement at the time, as an attempt to deflect the public clamor for a national police force by helping the development of local police professionalism.

In May, 1934, American law enforcement was formally notified of "The Establishment of a Technical Laboratory in the Division of Investigation" by an article in *Fugitives Wanted by Police.* The next issue noted that copies of this article would be furnished any law enforcement agency that requested it; there were 25 requests from agencies in 18 states, from New York to California, and Canada. The notice said that the laboratory was to assist the Bureau with its investigations, but previously it was the practice "to have technical experts outside its organization to make scientific analyses."[19]

The assistance of Dr. Souder was acknowledged in the article, which then described the equipment available in the new lab and the examinations performed. The physical setup in Room 802 of the Old Southern Railway Building (the Justice Building, where the FBI was headquartered for the next forty years, had not yet been completed) involved a borrowed microscope (bids for a comparison microscope had been approved) and a large drawing board, along with an instrument for enlarging and comparing fingerprints. The new Technical Laboratory (Hoover approved the name change from Criminological Laboratory, which implied a study of the causes of crime, on August 3, 1933) did not begin active examinations in current cases until August, 1933. That month it handled 20 cases; 30 were handled in September and 35 in October. These totals grew to 53 in November and 64 in December.[20]

Cooperation with local law enforcement authorities was part of the early mission of the Bureau of Investigation Technical Laboratory. The 1934 report to the Attorney General began with a Wyoming rape case where hairs from the victim and suspect had been sent for comparison. In March, 1933, Hoover replied in detail to a letter from a Texas sheriff inquiring about the examination of blood stains. The exact status of blood stain tests, human or animal and what blood groupings might prove was set out for the sheriff.[21]

Agent Edmund P. Coffey, now in charge of the Bureau laboratory, visited the new Technical Research Laboratory of the New York City Police Department in June, 1934. He met Dr. Harry Soderman, Director of the Police Laboratory at Stockholm, Sweden, who was temporarily helping the New York department set up this lab, and the three lab employees, Lieutenant W. J. McMahon and detectives Maurice Hartnett and Francis Murphy. They had no technical experience, except for Murphy who had handled handwriting examinations for the department for some years. Agent Coffey was particularly impressed with the library of about a thousand volumes dealing with the various sciences that have criminal investigation applications.[22]

Coffey graduated from Georgetown University School of Law in 1926 and became a Special Agent of the Bureau of Investigation in 1930. He was assigned to headquarters in 1932 where he studied fingerprint work and the sciences in general as they applied to law enforcement. He was designated Administrative Officer of the Technical Laboratory soon after the lab was inaugurated and remained in charge of the laboratory until he resigned to go into private industry in 1945. Hoover sent Coffey on a tour of European crime laboratories in 1937.[23]

In April, 1934, there was an exchange of information between Hoover and Newman F. Baker, the new director of the Scientific Crime Detection Laboratory of Northwestern University. Hoover sent Baker an article on the installation of the Single Fingerprint Section, at first a part of the Bureau's Technical Laboratory, for the *Journal of Criminal Law and Criminology.* Two years later there was a report of antagonism on the part of officials at the Northwestern Crime Detection Laboratory who felt that the Bureau was trying to dominate the scientific crime detection field.

Hoover noted on this report that while this was apparently caused by jealousy, "on the other hand our Laboratory is not functioning properly and too loose a system has prevailed."[24]

One innovation of Coffey's was in the training of laboratory personnel. While some European police agencies were training detectives to be laboratory staff, Coffey suggested instead that Bureau lab personnel with scientific background be then trained for the three months as regular Agents of the FBI, which would help them in preparing their reports. In later years, this was expanded to require laboratory agent examiners serve some years on investigative assignments so that they would know some of the complexities of investigations. The more lengthy scientific training first and then investigative training was, and is, the FBI's practice.[25]

The question of the expense of an FBI expert traveling to testify in a distant case when a local expert could testify at less expense came up in 1936. Tolson, Hoover's assistant, felt the Bureau could be criticized by Congress for allowing the higher cost. Hoover reluctantly approved the hiring of local experts when it was at less cost, but thought it "a step backwards. I have wanted to place our lab experts out in front. This new policy will ultimately result in local commercial quacks being given a prestige they don't deserve."[26]

Problems arose in 1938 over document examinations performed by the laboratory. Lack of appropriated funds led to a new policy in April of refusing document examinations in non-Bureau cases. This was to allow research work to improve handwriting analysis and to prevent any "embarrassment" due to erroneous identifications in outside cases. Coffey noted five months later that this policy had resulted in (1) new laboratories being started by other agencies in the federal government and (2) local police had ceased sending all evidence for examination, not just documentary evidence. Coffey suggested that the Bureau reinstitute document examinations for local police, but that examiners not be sent to testify on handwriting examinations ostensibly "because of the pressure of current work on hand," but actually to prevent "embarrassment to the Bureau from a possible error."[27]

The rudimentary status of handwriting analysis at that time, both in the FBI Laboratory and outside, and the hurried training of most of the FBI Laboratory examiners due to rapid expansion of the lab had been mentioned as early as 1936 by Coffey. The lack of qualified instructors to give FBI Laboratory examiners the necessary extensive training was cited as part of the problem by Coffey.[28]

Harold Nathan, then ranking assistant to Hoover, had opposed the employment of outside experts in 1935. Some outside examiners, including staff of the Northwestern Crime Detection Laboratory, complained of FBI domination of the scientific crime detection field—especially the FBI doing the work at no charge to local police. But Hoover replied that the FBI was repaying, in part, the assistance local police had given the FBI in other matters.

The FBI Laboratory continued to expand during the 1930s—the newly developed polygraph or lie detector was used in 112 interviews in 1938. Microchemical techniques and spectography were added to the standard procedures in 1939.[29]

The 1939 Annual Report of the Attorney General was the first one to announce that FBI Laboratory assistance had been given to local, county and state law enforcement agencies in 1,394 instances *without charge* and laboratory experts testified in court in 97 cases. Testimony had been made available in state criminal cases in 24 states and Puerto Rico. This report also stated that "with the development and extension of police training, law enforcement officers in every section of the country have a keener appreciation of the scientific assistance which is available to them."

The Attorney General's report delineated the numbers and types of examinations made in 1939. Examinations of questioned documents continued to account for over half of the 5,559 examinations. Firearms examinations numbered in the hundreds as did microscopic analyses of hairs and fibers and biochemical (bloodstains and spermatozoa) exams. There were almost a hundred microchemical and general chemical analyses and numerous petrographic or geologic exams, plus more than a hundred spectographic and metallurgical exams. Smaller numbers of cryptographic analyses, toxicological exams, explosive analyses, footprint comparisons, glass fracture and photographic exams, tire tread comparisons, lock examinations, castings, and electrical studies were reported.

This growth and expansion of the FBI Laboratory was accompanied by a tradition that when the scientific facts dictated innocence this should be promptly reported. This is true professionalism—experts whose testimony is "based upon the solid foundation of scientific fact'"—and far removed from the "third degree" tactics of policing's early days. Numerous cases of innocence established through scientific examination were chronicled by the Laboratory in this decade.

In 1936 an old prospector was found dead in Alaska, shot through the head. Investigators found the fatal bullet lodged in a window sill. Officers arrested a rival prospector, an old enemy of the victim, who had a rifle of the caliber that had been used in the killing. The arrested man was found to have blood on his socks, which he said came from a reindeer he had killed. Investigators sent the suspect's socks, rifle and the fatal bullet to the FBI laboratory. Scientific fact—the blood stain did test out to be reindeer. Scientific fact—the fatal bullet was not fired from the suspect's rifle. A new suspect was found and new tests showed his guilt.[30]

The contribution of the FBI laboratory to law enforcement professionalism in the 1930s was two-fold: (1) it was available to all law enforcement agencies, and (2) it developed a commitment to the protection of innocence when scientific fact so dictated.

Notes to Chapter 11

1. Nash 1973, 520–522
2. Dilworth 1977a, 76–78.
3. Ibid, 68.
4. Thorwald 1964, 428–453.
5. Dilworth 1977a, 78–82.
6. Ibid, 72.
7. Hoover 1936, 2.
8. Miller 1956, 65.
9. Burns 1922.
10. Hardy 1929.
11. Miller 1956, 35, 38.
12. Appel 1932b.
13. Appel 1932a.
14. Collier 1933.
15. Bureau 1932.
16. Lester 1932.
17. Hoover 1933.
18. Hoover 1934a.
19. Establishment 1934.
20. Miller 1956, 13–14.
21. Appel 1933.
22. Coffey 1934.
23. Hendon 1941, Hoover 1945, Hoover 1937.
24. Baker 1934, Hoover 1934b, Shilder 1936.

25. Tolson 1936a.
26. Tolson 1936b.
27. Coffey 1938.
28. Miller 1956, 51–53.
29. Ibid, 53–57.
30. Hoover 1936, 3.

Chapter 12

FBI NATIONAL ACADEMY

Thirty-five cents a day wasn't much to live on, even in the Great
Depression of the 1930s. But this was what one officer at the National
Police Academy had to do in order to support his family at home while
he attended the 12-week course in Washington, D.C. He graduated, a
stronger, albeit leaner, man. Director J. Edgar Hoover, telling National
Academy graduates in 1939 about this hardship case, said the officer
typified the determination of local police "to increase their knowledge
in scientific crime detection in order that they might be better able to
protect the lives and property of the citizens of their communities."[1]

The thirty-five cents daily living allowance of one student illustrates
the hardships some of the students at the FBI's new police training
school, now called the National Academy, had to undergo to complete
the first national post-graduate course in law enforcement. There was no
tuition, but local officers had to support themselves in Washington, D.C.,
often with little or no backing from their departments. The early accomplishments of the school may be measured by the eagerness of officers to
attend.

The FBI Police Training School was first suggested by Attorney General Homer S. Cummings at his December, 1934, Conference on Crime,
as one of the alternatives to a national police force. Cummings envisioned
a "national scientific and educational center" for police in Washington,
D.C. With the support of the International Association of Chiefs of
Police, and the advice of a committee of IACP members, J. Edgar
Hoover and his assistant director for training, Hugh Clegg, a law graduate and a former professor, put together a police training school that
opened the following July.

Hoover's idea was to train police officers who could return to their
departments and impart their new knowledge to the rest of their
departments. He knew that the federal government could not directly
train all this country's law enforcement officers, nor, under the American
decentralized, federal system of government, should the national govern-

ment attempt this. But, it would be a tremendous step forward in police professionalism if a corps of trained officers were created in police departments across the nation as a cadre to train their fellow officers. From the first class of 23 men, the National Academy grew to 1,000 graduates a year in the 1970s. Graduation from the National Academy became an almost necessary credential for police advancement, so many of its alumni had become chief executives of their agencies.

The change in the nature of crime in the 1920s and 1930s brought a public clamor for a national-wide police force. What might have been viewed as a strictly political device by the activist Roosevelt administration to counter the call for a national police organization, if it had failed, did not. It might have raised questions of how much federal influence on policing was desirable if it had been broader in practice than Hoover made it, but the success of the National Academy and accomplishments of its graduates, as much as any other event, helped to save state and local law enforcement under America's federal system of government. This was no small achievement.

Initially, National Academy graduates found they often needed assistance in training fellow officers. This need led to the gradual development of an FBI field police training program. This extension program grew gradually in the late 1930s, was slowed by World War II in the 1940s, and was the subject of much debate within the FBI early in the 1950s. But, later in that decade and especially in the 1960s, FBI training of police around the country away from the National Academy facility increased tremendously, in what J. Edgar Hoover believed was complementary to college police education, with benefits both for police professionalism and for the FBI.

Today, the training division of the FBI, which handles the training of its own agents in addition to the National Academy, is in the forefront of police training with college and graduate school accreditation in association with the University of Virginia. The National Academy has graduated over 19,000 officers since 1935; of the 13,000 still active in law enforcement, one of seven serves as the executive head of his or her agency.[2] The Training Division also coordinates and directs the FBI's field police training program around the country which, in 1986, reached almost 200,000 police officers, more than a third of this nation's police, through over 5,000 schools.[3]

THE FEDERAL DEBUT IN POLICE TRAINING

Three factors stimulated the federal government's entrance into the local police training field: (1) the overall nationwide lack of police training, (2) the public and news media clamor for a national police organization, and (3) the existence of a federal agency with the only proven training ability in the law enforcement field and the necessary constant contact with local police. This contact with local authorities came about through the Bureau's fingerprint identification service in the decade of 1924–1934 and through the Uniform Crime Reporting system, which the Bureau had to explain to police departments. The newly named Federal Bureau of Investigation had recently expanded its own training program to meet the new law enforcement powers conferred on its agents by Congress.

The transition from a predominantly rural to an urban society which occurred mostly after the turn of the century in this country and the "machine age" which marked this new urbanized America, facilitated the movement of American society, including the criminal element. Even the public perceived the inability of untrained local police, operating primarily in a foot patrol mode, to counter this new criminal mobility and sophistication. The National Commission on Law Observance and Enforcement (the Wickersham Commission) reported on this country's overall lack of police training in one whole chapter, one eighth of the entire 1931 *Report on Police.*

Commission surveys of police training were sent to 225 towns of less than 10,000 population and to all cities with populations of 10,000 to 75,000. Of the 745 questionnaires sent, slightly over half were returned. For towns under 10,000, the commission reported:

> There is absolutely nothing done which by any stretch of the imagination could be considered as police training. Not one of the cities had experience as a requirement of admission to the force; 216 never inquired if the prospective policeman could handle a gun, and 185 sent the man out on duty with no instruction and even without the aid and advice of an experienced man. Forty cities placed the beginner with an older man from periods of a night to one week.[4]

The commission report, supervised by August Vollmer although this chapter (4) of the report is credited to his research assistant David G. Monroe, summarized the results from the returned questionnaires of the cities over 10,000 to 75,000. Some 20 per cent had some method of school training, but of these 78 cities only 15 "gave courses which could be considered to qualify the recruit as the possessor of a proper background for efficient work." Chapter 4 went on to describe four of what it termed "the most elaborate" police schools in the country at that time: Louisville, Kentucky; New York City; Cincinnati, Ohio, and Berkeley, California (where Vollmer was chief). Also detailed were the proposed state supported and controlled schools in New York and California and the initial limited efforts of colleges to start police education programs.[5]

This period of increased public and media awareness of the changing, perceived by the public as growing, crime problem also brought calls for a national police force to meet the crime problem. In 1928, an assistant United States Attorney in Cleveland proposed a unified federal investigative institution and, once this was in operation, joining all municipal and state police agencies within this federal organization. Newspapers in Washington, Kansas City, Boston, and Philadelphia, and civic organizations around the country also endorsed such a national police force in the early 1930s.[6]

Chapter 9 explained how J. Edgar Hoover, appointed Director of the Bureau of Investigation in 1924, reorganized this inefficient and corruption-tainted federal investigative organization and built its contacts with the country's police agencies through the Bureau's Congressionally-mandated fingerprint identification service. In 1930, Uniform Crime Reporting responsibilities were added to the Bureau's responsibilities, again by Act of Congress, and again through IACP lobbying efforts; these led to even more contact with local police. Then, in 1932, Congress passed the federal kidnap law, expanding the Bureau's jurisdiction, this time in what had been a matter of state jurisdiction. This helped move the Bureau into the area of scientific crime detection (see Chapter 11).

In 1933, the Roosevelt Administration through Attorney General Cummings, put the Bureau in the forefront of the federal effort to meet the crime problem and in April, 1934 the Attorney General recommended extensive expansion of the Bureau's jurisdiction and police powers, which Congress enacted. Later that year, at the Attorney General's Conference on Crime, Homer Cummings rejected the concept of a national police force, but did recommend some type of federal training for the nation's police in his December 10 speech to the more than 600 delegates to the conference:

> ... we need methods for better selection and training of personnel, laboratory facilities for work in detection and apprehension, opportunities for scientific research. ... we must have a great national scientific

and educational center for work in this field. Whether this should be called an Institute of Criminology or a Federal School for Training in Law Administration; whether it should include, at its inception, a degree granting Academy for those who may be selected and trained for professional careers; or whether it should begin with the coordination of already existing units of instruction and research and develop gradually—these are less important questions than that we should declare ourselves clearly upon the underlying proposition, there is a need for training and research of this type and that it can be done.[7]

The next day, the Attorney General's subordinate, the re-named Division of Investigation's Director J. Edgar Hoover told the Crime Conference:

I believe also that a National Training School for law enforcement officers is a wholesome and necessary venture. Such a school properly organized and operated along practical lines would fill a long felt want of many police departments who earnestly seek but have inadequate means of obtaining that knowledge of technique with which to properly combat the criminal forces. The value of adequate training has already been proven in the training schools maintained by our Division for its personnel. Thus the plan is no longer an untried theory but a proven and practical fact. With but slight readjustment of operations, these training facilities already established could be extended to the local law enforcement agencies of the country.[8]

Already a practical bureaucrat, Hoover subtly adopted Cummings second concept of a "Federal School for Training" local police using "already existing units of instruction," rather than the "degree granting Academy" that Cummings proposed as a second idea the day before. But, even before Roosevelt's New Deal Administration took office, Hoover recognized the need for police training. He told the Cincinnati Lawyers Club in 1931 (the first group other than the IACP that he addressed as Director of the Bureau of Investigation) that "Police Schools should be established for the training of police officers in all communities."[9] Hoover's adoption of the Attorney General's first proposal was endorsed by Cummings in a radio address the next month:

There is no reason why our existing School of Instruction should not be amplified so that intelligent and serious minded representatives from the various state and municipal law enforcement agencies may have an opportunity to come to Washington, at certain intervals, to study with us. . . . Plans for this development are being formulated. The recent Crime Conference endorsed this idea.[10]

THE FBI NATIONAL ACADEMY BEGINS

As the FBI's new Police Training School was to be based on the Bureau's own training school for its new Special Agents, the logical person to design the new program was the FBI assistant director for training, Hugh H. Clegg. Like Hoover, Clegg was a graduate of George Washington University School of Law. He, too, had worked in the Library of Congress while going to law school, and was even in the U.S. Army Reserves as a Major in intelligence. He became a Special Agent in 1926 and, after being in charge of three different offices, he was made an assistant director at headquarters for training in 1932. Clegg had also taught Latin, physics, and chemistry at different colleges and preparatory schools before he went to law school. Hoover referred to him as "Dean Clegg" in a 1939 speech before a National Academy group.[11]

Noting that while the new school was to be based on the Bureau's own training program for Special Agents, Clegg wrote that as the new course was to assist local law enforcement it would include other subjects for their benefit, including: police records and reports, patrol work, traffic investigations, public health liaison work, police organization and administration, arson investigations, and psychology. Also a member of the IACP, Clegg worked with the IACP Advisory Committee on Police Training, the group that Hoover had asked to help advise on the new school. It was composed of the then President of the IACP, Andrew J. Kavanaugh, Director of Public Safety in Miami, and chaired by Peter J. Siccardi, Chief of the Bergen County, New Jersey, Police Department. Other members were Edward J. Kelly, Superintendent of the Rhode Island State Police, and John L. Sullivan, Chief of Police at Pittsfield, Massachusetts.[12]

One of the first questions that had to be resolved was whether the IACP committee or the Bureau was to have the responsibility for selection of the departments to be invited to the new school. (Invitations were later made to individual officers, rather than departments.) The Bureau's Executive Committee, composed of all the Assistant Directors and chaired by Associate Director Clyde Tolson, recommended that the IACP have the responsibility. One Assistant Director disagreed; Quinn Tamm thought the Bureau should have the selection responsibility since some large police departments were antagonistic toward the Bureau and should not be selected. J. Edgar Hoover agreed with Tamm, noting on the Executive Committee memo, "We will assume the responsibility." This decision led to some later criticism of the Bureau when a few police departments were excluded from attendance at the National Academy because of their relationships with the FBI.[13]

On July 25, 1935, Attorney General Cummings explained what he called "one of the most significant developments in the national program of the Department of Justice for the prevention, detection and punishment of crime." The Attorney General noted how the growth of crime in interstate aspects had led to the Department of Justice stepping into the gap between Federal and state jurisdiction that then existed, but not "with the objectionable idea of creating a national police force." The Attorney General said the previous December's Crime Conference had recommended:

> ... establishment at Washington, D.C. of a scientific and educational center, permanent in form and structure, to provide national leadership in the broad field of criminal law administration. ... the Federal Bureau of Investigation ... will initiate courses offering the most comprehensive and intensive training ever afforded local law enforcement officers in the United States. ... the same course of training that is now given to Special Agents of that Bureau, with the addition of studies designed for the especial benefit of those engaged in State and local police work.[14]

Hugh Clegg's recollection, forty years later, was that Hoover met with the IACP training committee in July, 1935, and they urged the FBI to provide training for local police. According to Clegg, this request, from a law enforcement source, rather than the Attorney General's proposal, prompted Hoover to request Clegg to organize the police school, including a visiting faculty. He was able to enlist visiting lecturers for the new school, experienced police administrators and criminologists, by first seeing Bruce Smith, then the Director of the Institute of Public Administration in New York City.[15]

As the Bureau's journal for police, *Fugitives Wanted By Police* (renamed the *FBI Law Enforcement Bulletin* in October, 1935) noted in the September issue, some 41 authorities had agreed to lecture before the new school. These included the superintendent of St. Elizabeth's mental hospital, who was also a professor of psychiatry, a Major in the Ordinance Department of the U.S. Army who knew the ballistics of police firearms, and a staff member of the Public Administration Service who had installed communication systems for police. A Yale University professor of psychology agreed to lecture on "Crime Motivation" and Professor of Criminal Law Albert Coates, of the University of North Carolina, was to handle criminal law. The chief of police in Milwaukee was slated to lecture on racketeering and the Superintendent of the West Virginia State Police agreed to discuss ethics in law enforcement. The founder of the Harvard Law Review, a practicing attorney, had the subject of evidence; the Suffolk County, Massachusetts, medical examiner, in charge of legal medicine at Harvard, took this subject at the police school. The Bureau of Standards was represented by Dr. Wilmer Souder, who had helped set up the FBI Laboratory, on the subject of firearms identification; and the Assistant Surgeon General of the U.S. taught advanced first aid.

There were professors from Northwestern University, Columbia University, Johns Hopkins, the University of California, and Georgetown on the list, in addition to police officials from Pennsylvania, Chicago, New York, Miami, Portland, Oregon, Berkeley, California, and Evanston, Illinois. Well-known educators and pioneers in the law enforcement field such as August Vollmer, Bruce Smith, and Frank Kreml, Director of Northwestern's Traffic Officers Training School, were also enlisted as was Raymond Moley, Professor of Public Law at Columbia and a member of Franklin Roosevelt's "brain trust." Only law professor Felix Frankfurter had to cancel his appearance, due to his appointment to the Supreme Court. All in all, Clegg recruited a very distinguished and able visiting faculty.[16]

At the same time as he was contacting recognized and competent lecturers in fields impacting on law enforcement, Clegg was designing a detailed curriculum covering the areas of scientific and/or technical subjects, crime records topics, firearms training, investigation, and police administration/organization, as listed in the FBI's police journal the month before the list of visiting faculty appeared. There were more than 200 individual topics in the six general areas listed, covering everything from glass fractures, for which window frames were built and replacement panes obtained, to investigation of arson, aliens, bank robberies, gambling, larcenies, manslaughter and murder, narcotics, prostitution, rape, robberies, and traffic accidents. For the last, $16 worth of miniature scenic material was purchased from the Lionel electric train company.[17]

Practical experience was given in taking and classifying fingerprints, recording crime scenes, and handwriting identification. The Uniform Crime Reporting system was explained, along with overall police records, and the course included various firearms qualifications. This was basically a general police course, but included a survey of police administration and organization to help attendees advance in their own departments. This included police communications; discipline and morale; a survey of foreign and federal law enforcement organizations; law enforcement as a profession; personnel standards, selection and problems; the role of the police executive; policing and politics; social problems and changes relating to law; and public relations. In today's terms, these are still the issues that face police management.[18]

A list of police agencies that had applied for this new school had been started and attending departments for the first class were selected by the Bureau's Executive Conference from this list. The organizations selected included large city departments (New York City, Chicago, Boston, Miami, Baltimore, Dallas, San Francisco, and Cincinnati); five state police agencies (Connecticut, Delaware, Ohio, Pennsylvania, and Rhode Island); and eight smaller departments to total 23. Three FBI Special Agents were also assigned to attend the school, the first "counselors" of what came to be called the FBI National Academy.[19]

Clegg prepared a summary of the educational and police experience backgrounds of the attending officers: three had law degrees and one other was a college graduate. These officers had been chosen by their departments to attend and most sent their best representatives. Six more had some college. Of the rest, more representative of the police population as a whole in this country at that time, four had completed high school, three more had some high school, four had completed grammar school, but two had not even finished grammar school. Two were chiefs of police, twelve were police captains, lieutenants or sergeants, five had special ranks such as investigator, and three were patrolmen. A majority of the class had 10 to 14 years service, four had more than that, seven had less.[20]

The school lasted twelve weeks, which was the same period as new Agents trained at that time, expanded from four weeks in 1931. Attorney General Cummings was the principal speaker at the first closing ceremony and Bureau Director Hoover outlined plans for future schools. Assistant Director Clegg and the members of the IACP Advisory Board, who helped plan the school and its curriculum, also spoke. The valedictory, by Captain James T. Sheehan, Boston Police Department, who had been elected President of the National Police Training School Associates, the new school's "alumni association," stressed "the need for unity and cooperation" in the law enforcement community.[21]

Attorney General Cummings, in his January, 1935, radio address, had said in outlining this training program that it was "the merest beginning." Hoover maintained the beginning's momentum, directing Clegg on October 21, just two days after the completion of the first school, to schedule another to begin on January 6, 1936. He wanted the class enlarged from 23 to 25 students and specifically asked that three departments be included: Newark, Des Moines, and Providence, Rhode Island. Clegg had already requested the FBI Laboratory to prepare a list of reading assignments on forensic matters. The Executive Conference submitted a list of 25 departments to be invited to the second school, but Hoover disapproved four departments, including the Alameda County, California, District Attorney's office which was then headed by Earl Warren, later the Chief Justice of the Supreme Court. Hoover added two California departments and three others, to bring the class up to 26. On the same date, November 7, Clegg ordered more than 100 articles on police training, mentioned in the *Bibliography of Crime and Criminal Justice,* for study by police school attendees.[22]

By 1937, five sessions of the FBI National Police Academy had been held, with 115 graduates from 45 states, representing departments that served a population of over 73 million. By the next year all 48 states, plus the Royal Canadian Mounted Police, police from the Panama Canal zone and Puerto Rico, and New Scotland Yard, had attended.[23] While in later years Hoover defended the supremacy of FBI training, in 1939 at a National Academy retraining session, he noted:

> If we can keep before us the maxim that no one has a corner on the brain market, we can better reach our objectives in maintaining law enforcement on an ethical and professional basis.

Hoover went on to outline his philosophy on training, saying:

> Men should be trained to know their job before entering into a duty status. This training should continue throughout their careers in law enforcement work.[24]

On March 30, 1940, at the graduation of the 13th session of this school, which now had a total of 442 graduates, Mayor Fiorello LaGuardia of New York City, speaking as President of the U.S. Conference of Mayors, called law enforcement "more than a job. It is a profession. The detection of crime is no longer guess work. It is a real science." LaGuardia argued for lateral transfer and promotion of police executives, a concept of professionalism that is only today being practiced on a very limited scale in law enforcement:

In the smaller city the outlook for future promotion isn't as hopeful, and sometimes it becomes discouraging.... There, Mr. Director, is where the National Police Academy might serve a greater purpose than it does now. The National Academy ought to be developed into a West Point for police officers, so that the men coming out of this Academy will have received uniform training and education. It should give a much longer course than that given now. It is now more of a post-graduate school, and it should be made into a real college.[25]

LaGuardia went on to explain that smaller communities could then draw from the entire country for new police chiefs. Hoover did not respond to LaGuardia's recommendation at this ceremony, but did outline his views on law enforcement. He reiterated his stand against a national police force as "unworkable and impractical,...wholly and thoroughly inadvisable." He told the graduates of "such perversions of justice as the third degree" and urged dedication to the protection of civil rights by the "law enforcement profession." His view of the nature of policing was summarized as:

... let us never lose sight for a moment of the standards which must be set and observed if law enforcement is to be an exemplification of honor, integrity, and decency. For, as I have always held, the task of an ideal law enforcement officer is to defend the right, to protect the weak, to aid the distressed, to uphold the law, and to prevent crime.[26]

From 1935 to 1940, National Academy classes were held in various classrooms (one, long and narrow, was nicknamed the wind tunnel) of the then new Justice Building, with firearms training at the Marine base at Quantico, Virginia. In 1940, construction was completed on a brick building at Quantico to house National Academy and other FBI training, which was used until the new FBI Academy was built in 1972.[27] The 1938 Annual Report of the Attorney General noted:

Many graduates of the FBI National Police Academy have returned to their homes and established training schools for the personnel of their own forces. The FBI has assisted them in establishing these schools, and wherever possible has supplied them with instructors in various phases of scientific crime detection and apprehension.[28]

This was the first public notice of what the FBI called the National Academy's extension program.

EXTENSION PROGRAM—FIELD TRAINING

The next year, the Attorney General's report had a section on "Co-operation with Training Schools for Local Police Organizations" which explained that upon invitation the FBI would assist local police in determination of training needs, in the preparation of a program to meet these needs, in the assignment of FBI and other instructors, and in "providing an advisory and consultant service to the local police in connection with their training activities." Thus, the FBI:

> serves as a national clearing house for information, services and assistance in the conduct of police training. During the fiscal year, the Federal Bureau of Investigation cooperated in the inauguration or operation of 183 police training schools located in every section of the country.[29]

This program developed from a recommendation by Hugh Clegg in 1937, in response to an FBI Executive Conference discussion on "the possibility of the Bureau participating, to a greater extent, in training schools for local, county, and state law enforcement officers." Clegg wrote that "it is my frank opinion that the Bureau should do everything possible to dominate the training school situation throughout the United States." J. Edgar Hoover noted on Clegg's memo that: "There is much merit in this. Discuss it at [the next] Executives' Conference."

Clegg went on to recommend that field employees be brought in for training and experience in teaching at the National Academy in order to relieve agent supervisors at headquarters from this assignment. He also was of the opinion that although the FBI should not "openly solicit invitations to teach in police training schools," the Agent in charge of each FBI field division should be aware of all police training schools in his territory and the departments holding schools "should be informed that the Bureau will be pleased to cooperate." But Clegg did qualify this to say that "first consideration and favoritism be shown to those departments which have been represented in the FBI National Police Academy, for to those graduates the Bureau has promised the fullest extent of its cooperation in organizing and conducting training schools." Just eleven days later, Hoover instructed Clegg to list those Agents who should be brought to Washington "for special training and experience in police training methods." He also told Clegg to "discuss before the Special Agents in Charge school the question of the extent to which the Bureau is willing to go to cooperate with local, county, and state law enforcement agencies in their courses of training. . . . "[30]

The previous year Hoover had disapproved an Executive Conference recommendation "that Special Agents of this Bureau be placed in schools and colleges giving courses in police work" saying "it would be better for us to continue to concentrate upon the perfection of our training course through the medium of obtaining information direct from any source which might be able to aid or assist in our project." Hoover thought that the Bureau was "many lengths ahead of any other police training school in the country" and remembered "the experience which we had in sending Special Agent Appel to the school at the Northwestern University in Chicago. . . . Colonel Goddard claimed the credit then for having set up the Crime Laboratory of the FBI, solely because one of our representatives happened to attend his school."[31]

World War II brought new internal security and counterespionage responsibilities to the FBI; police training, as an extension of the National Academy, was directed at ways local police could help in these security areas. Statistics on the number of police schools were not maintained during the war years until 1945 when some 682 schools were recorded. In the next decade, these increased to 2,606 by 1954.[32] Over the next fifteen years, more than 8,000 police training schools were held, reaching almost a quarter million officers in more than 75,000 hours of instruction. These included schools on auto theft, bank robbery, burglary, investigations, arrests, sex crimes, juvenile delinquency, and traffic. Specialized schools on command, supervision, administration, records, photography, defensive tactics, fingerprints, and firearms were also held. In 1956, some 460 schools were held on civil rights; legal matters schools began at the same time and over 600 were held in 1969; riot control schools began in 1965, with some 731 schools that year, declining to 219 in 1968.[33]

The civil rights schools began in 1949 as lectures by Special Agents in Charge under the title "Ethics in Law Enforcement," but in 1953 at a Special Agents conference on civil rights it was recommended that "the Bureau should face the problem squarely and give the lectures before the police departments under the heading of 'Civil Rights'." Then, qualified police instructors, rather than Special Agents in Charge, should handle these classes. The Executive Conference unanimously agreed and Hoover approved this suggestion. The Attorney General was advised of this program, and, in 1956, the Chief Justice of the Supreme Court, Earl Warren, was furnished the FBI training document, "Civil Rights and The Law Enforcement Officer." In a "Dear Earl" letter, signed "Edgar," Hoover told Warren that "we felt it necessary to initiate these schools in view of the racial tensions which have manifested themselves in various sections of the country, particularly in the South."[34]

In the decade 1936 to 1946, FBI police training achieved a professional level beyond most police departments' own training programs and for the smaller agencies was the only training program available. But, in some states such as California, police training and pre-entry on duty college education was also beginning in colleges. The FBI, under Hoover and Clegg, had to re-examine its commitment to professional police training in relation to college education in criminal justice.

In 1936, the FBI's Executive Conference had recommended that the Bureau continue its policy of cooperation with State Municipal Leagues holding police training schools, but by 1947 Hoover believed that FBI police training schools in connection with colleges were found to have "inadequate control by the Bureau." By 1949, the FBI established a policy of non-cooperation with college programs for law enforcement students (rather than for serving officers), where the college was charging attendees tuition. The only exception was for courses attended only by serving officers, where the Bureau would furnish lecturers on the jurisdiction and functions of the Bureau.[35]

Hoover's position on police training was spelled out in a long letter to all field offices and police instructors in 1949:

> For several years the FBI has given leadership to law enforcement in the field of police training. The result has been to stimulate interest, harmonize divergent views, and provide uniformity of training. Initially, because of the under-developed conditions of police education, opportunities for exploitation were available to those who would seek personal profit and advantage. The Bureau has always opposed the penetration of the field of police education and instruction by theorists, disrupters, and the selfishly ambitious.[36]

This letter went on to laud programs in four states where the local FBI office had exhibited "the proper measure of foresight and aggressiveness" in providing "the greatest degree of cohesiveness among law enforcement agencies in order that leadership in police instruction will continue to reside in law enforcement" by joint sponsorship with the state police chiefs' and sheriff's associations in connection with the FBI. The Bureau's "policy of opposition to pre-entry training" was set out "to discourage that type of training."[37]

The debate within the FBI over the police training issue continued into the 1950s, when the American Municipal Association attempted to set up its own program of police training. Some FBI executives recommended that the Bureau stop trying to "dominate" police training efforts and work out a plan of cooperation with colleges. Others, including Clegg, recommended that the FBI withdraw from the police training area, as the National Academy graduates should handle this field. In 1947, Hoover had recommended that Tolson study this area with a view toward possibly eliminating the police training program,[38] but the study resulted only in cessation of "solicitation" of police schools. Hoover noted, "We are not going to get out of the training field nor make any announcement re this curtailment. The only difference is that we will not inspire or solicit requests for training."[39]

The history of the development of pre-entry police education, Vollmer's dream of college education for police officers, along with FBI in-service training of police, continues in chapter 20. Chapter 20 shows how the FBI finally came to terms with, and began to develop, in association with the University of Virginia, its own program of university education for serving police. Today, the FBI uses its own Special Agents, with advanced degrees, rather than a large visiting faculty for this university.

Notes to Chapter 12

1. Hendon, 1939. 8.
2. Webster, 1985. 3.
3. Baker, 1985. 31.
4. Vollmer, 1931. 70.
5. Ibid. 73–85.
6. Whitehead, 1955. 17:2–6.
7. Cummings, 1934.2–6.
8. Hoover, 1934c. 8.
9. Hoover, 1931a. 24.
10. Whitehead, 1955. 17:26–27.
11. Hendon, 1939. 9.
12. Clegg, 1935a.
13. Tolson, 1935a.
14. Suydam, 1935.
15. Clegg, 1976.
16. Bureau, 1934. 4:9.
17. Bureau of Investigation, 1934. 4:8; Coffey, 1935a; Whitely, 1935.
18. Bureau of Investigation, 1934. 4:8.

19. Tolson, 1935b; Clegg, 1935c.
20. Clegg, 1935d.
21. "Exercises," 1935.
22. Hoover, 1935a; Coffey, 1935b; Tolson, 1935c; Clegg, 1935e.
23. Annual Report, 1938.
24. Hendon, 1939. 18–19.
25. "Graduation Exercises," 1940.
26. Ibid.
27. Cotter, 1986. 8, 21, 121–127.
28. Annual Report, 1938. 4–5.
29. Annual Report, 1939. 8.
30. Clegg, 1937; Hoover, 1937b.
31. Hoover, 1936b.
32. Whitehead, 1955. 17:80.
33. Joseph, 1970. 70–72.
34. Tolson, 1950; Clegg, 1953; Hoover, 1956a;b;c.
35. Tolson, 1936c; Hoover, 1947b.
36. Hoover, 1949a. 4.
37. Ibid, 5.
38. Hoover, 1947b.
39. Tolson, 1947.

Chapter 13

THE *FBI LAW ENFORCEMENT BULLETIN*

The Bureau of Investigation official in charge of fingerprints was "unalterably, definitely and unequivocally opposed" to the idea of publishing for nationwide distribution a list of fugitives wanted by police around the country. But Assistant Director Harold Nathan, who proposed this idea, said the opponent of the idea had a "disposition to be senilely obdurate" (colorful phraseology for a government memorandum) and Director Hoover was "very much impressed with the suggestion." Hoover wrote on the suggestion: "We must continue to grow else we cannot justify our present existence." This instance of Hoover's "bureaucratic genius" led to the publication of what eventually became the most widely read professional journal of law enforcement practitioners, the *FBI Law Enforcement Bulletin.*[1]

This journal began in 1932 as *Fugitives: Wanted By Police* to foster "the exchange of criminal identification data among . . . law enforcement officials."[2] Harold "Pop" Nathan, the first Assistant Director under Hoover of the then Bureau of Investigation, wrote the memorandum suggesting publishing a list of fugitives' names, fingerprint classifications, and "other brief pertinent data." Listing fugitives in a publication for law officers was not a new idea; the Texas Rangers had done it a half century before. But a nationwide list, with fingerprint classifications of the fugitives for identification, was one of the first contributions to police professionalism that the FBI had developed without the inspiration of the IACP.[3]

Just three years after the inauguration of the list, the Bureau's Executive Committee recommended to Hoover that the name of the publication be changed to "FBI Police Bulletin" because of the number of articles that had appeared in it of interest to police, in addition to the listings of fugitives. Next to this suggestion, Hoover wrote "Just a thought, instead of using police, how about 'law enforcement.'" And so, the *FBI Law Enforcement Bulletin* appeared in October, 1935—for all law enforcement, instead of just police. Hoover had recognized that police and law enforcement were different parts of the whole, but not that policing does not have to be law enforcement oriented.[4]

Director Hoover then wrote the Attorney General that:

> The Bureau gradually added to the bulletin articles of a scientific nature, information relative to police tactics and treatises concerning the more recent developments in law enforcement technique, until it became, in fact, a journal of a scientific and informative character for peace officials, thus necessitating a change in its name.... it is hoped the Bulletin will prove to be truly a national periodical of interest and value in the field of law enforcement.[5]

It has. This journal has been a history of law enforcement's first renaissance in professionalism, as the FBI trained police in the developing scientific investigative, training, and identification fields, some of this era's hallmarks of police professionalism. It then developed into a cooperative venture, with contributors to the journal representing the scientific, academic, and police communities. These contributions to the journal mirrored the progress in police professionalism in the roughly thirty years between 1940 and 1970 until a second renaissance began to develop in policing. Since 1970, the *FBI Law Enforcement Bulletin* has become more professional, as policing itself has.

FUGITIVES WANTED BY POLICE

By 1932, transportation by rail or road in America had developed sufficiently to enhance population mobility, including the criminal element. Criminal activities no longer were confined to one locale; a criminal could commit a crime in one jurisdiction and have breakfast the next day in another city or state. There was no formal means for law enforcement authorities to trace wanted criminals from one jurisdiction to another. There were few state police agencies and even these were limited by state boundaries. Informal networks between large city chiefs of police had developed to exchange criminal identification information, primarily through the International Association of Chiefs of Police. Wardens of large prisons formed other networks to trace escaped prisoners and in the West, postcards between sheriffs, along with wanted posters, helped track fugitives. The Pinkerton private detective agency had fulfilled the need for interstate exchange of criminal identification information in the last half of the 19th century, but it was a private agency and was hampered in this regard by the anti-labor reputation it acquired late in the century.[6]

The publication of *Fugitives Wanted By Police* by the Bureau of Investigation in 1932 helped close this gap in nationwide law enforcement, although it was really begun to assist and expand the Bureau's fingerprint collection efforts. Fugitive notices were published from fingerprint card notices received by the Bureau in its Division of Identification and, by the second year of publication, one fingerprint of each fugitive was printed with his description, facilitating quick, positive identification. Early issues carried notifications on the arrest of particularly important fugitives in order to generate further participation by local police.

Beginning with the third issue, articles of interest to police also appeared, along with the fugitive information. In the first three years, several articles on fingerprints appeared, including techniques of developing latent fingerprints, the use of fingerprints for civil identification, the standardization of wanted notices, the story of the Bureau's Identification Division, and one on the history of fingerprinting by Dr. Valentine Sava, a criminologist in Bucharest.[7]

While fingerprint-oriented at first, the publication also ran an article on explosives from a St. Louis Police Department special bulletin, a piece on the deciphering of charred records and other articles by scientists at the U.S. Bureau of Standards, a report on testing for blood stains from the District of Columbia Police Department, and a photo illustrated story on bombs by the New York City Police Department. Material from three outstanding local police agencies, from government scientists, and from the Bureau of Investigation established that this journal was to be a cooperative venture between law enforcement agencies and the scientific community.

This journal began after the country had experienced the "Roaring Twenties" with their attendant postwar crime problems, as reported by the Wickersham Commission, and law enforcement began to undergo what Hoover called a "Renaissance." The new FBI publication detailed what the FBI was doing to meet the Commission's challenges to law enforcement: new developments in the nationwide identification of fugitives through fingerprints, the gathering of the first picture of the overall crime problem through Uniform Crime Reporting, and the scientific examination of evidence in the FBI's new Technical Laboratory. The 1930's were the decade of this "Renaissance" and the FBI became the national exemplar to American law enforcement—and this journal, now to be called the *FBI Law Enforcement Bulletin* — became the voice of the FBI at that time.

THE NAME—AND PURPOSE—CHANGE

Hoover declared in the first issue of the newly named Bulletin that:

> ... this publication should provide a clearing house for police officials regarding successful police methods, a medium for the dissemination of important police information, and a comprehensive literature pertaining to the scientific methods in crime detection and criminal apprehension.[8]

Later, Hoover himself described what led to policing's renaissance after World War I:

> Protection could, at times, be bought. Tommy-gun rule was law in some cities—with the guns in the hands of the lawless. Nevertheless, in the ensuing conflict, the balance tipped in favor of the forces of decency and order. The reign of public enemies ended; a period which might be termed the Renaissance of law enforcement followed.[9]

That was Hoover's "war on crime" phrased conclusion written two decades after the 1930s, but it was also a prelude to Richard Gid Powers' social reaction theories on the gangster era and the public's reaction:

> There are positive indications that applause for the criminal, who has been built up by fiction to the character of a hero, has begun to subside; the advancements in scientific crime detection and criminal apprehension methods are well known ... [20]

But scientific crime detection was not well known to local police at that time, thus it became the subject of a number of articles in early Bulletins; articles on blood stains, ballistics, bombs, and firearms examinations contributed by the FBI's new Technical Laboratory were featured. The value of post mortem examinations in the solution of crime, the use of applied physics in crime detection, and spectrography were other subjects covered in early issues. The diverse nature of American law enforcement, with the majority of officers coming from very small departments, made classroom training a logistical problem in the 1930s, but this publication was viewed by the FBI at that time as one way to bring modern training to them.

Contributions by outstanding police chiefs, such as August Vollmer, were indications that the Bulletin was in the vanguard of law enforcement pioneering. Vollmer (see Chapter 7) wrote a long piece on the ideals of police service. In a prelude to developments in the behavioral sciences in the 1970s, Vollmer said that the "policeman must intimately know the factors underlying human behavior if he hopes to succeed in his chosen profession."[11]

Vollmer, like Hoover, advocated freedom from political influence for police. This was an early and continuing theme in the Bulletin's introductions, called "messages to all law enforcement officials from the Director," after World War II. As American police departments were historically involved in local politics at this time, and crime was becoming an issue of national public concern, Hoover wrote in the Bulletin:

> ... the public is demanding efficiency in its law enforcement agencies. This can be effected by raising the level of law enforcement work above the encroachments of political influence.[12]

Hoover went on to call for the training of police executives, which the FBI had begun with its new Police Training School. Eliminating political influence in policing was also a central tenet of police professionalism reformers of the Progressive Movement. It only began to be recognized in the 1970s as partisan political influence, not politics per se, that reformers sought to eliminate.

Both these leaders in law enforcement also advocated rigid discipline imposed by the agency's leadership. This might have been based on both men's military experience, but their rejection of civil service in policing was only vindicated in theory by police professionals many years later. Cooperation between law enforcement agencies was stressed by both. Hoover in an early introduction to the *Bulletin,* compared law enforcement to "a great army moving against a common [criminal] enemy ... " with the *FBI Law Enforcement Bulletin* as the "medium of making information available to all units engaged in the eradication of crime." This advocacy of cooperation, however, was marked by the military model and "war on crime" rhetoric that dominated police professionalism for many years.[13]

In July, 1938, the list of fugitives published each month became a separate insert to the *Bulletin,* which lasted until 1967, when the computerized National Crime Information Center obviated the need for publicizing fugitives in this way. 1939 saw the end of a decade of criminal activity that finally moved Americans and leaders of law enforcement to take action. But, in September of that year, a statement by President

Roosevelt, printed in the October *Bulletin*, directed that the FBI take charge of espionage and sabotage investigations. World War II had begun in Europe. And the editorial direction of the *FBI Law Enforcement Bulletin* altered to meet the national emergency.

BEYOND THE RENAISSANCE

Five months before the war involved the United States, the topic heading "National Defense" was added to the *Bulletin* (topic headings were begun with the first issue of 1940) with an article on the "Duties of Police in National Emergencies." "Prevention of Sabotage" followed in January, 1942. In May, the *Bulletin* began publishing every other month because of the paper shortage in World War II; this lasted until July, 1945.

The topic headings in the table of contents lasted until 1965; they reflected needs for police training that the FBI had featured in the *Bulletin's* first five years: "Scientific Aids", "Police Training", "Police Records" (especially the Uniform Crime Reports) and "Identification." Other headings highlighted areas of increasing police interest: "Traffic" and "Police Communications."

The January, 1940, issue of the *Bulletin* carried an article under "Police Communications" by Bruce Smith, a lawyer beginning to be known for his management surveys of American police departments. The IACP called Smith one of four men in the U.S. who were an "influence for good in American law enforcement."[14]

Introduction topics during the beginning of the war in Europe covered national defense matters, including how to order revolvers earmarked for police use, but police training, fingerprints, and police records were still emphasized during these years. In April, 1940, Hoover reported that some 1,127 agencies participating in the Uniform Crime Reporting system in 1930, when Congress authorized the FBI to collect these statistics, had grown to over 4,300 in 1939.

Just before the *Bulletin* completed its first decade, J. Edgar Hoover wrote about progress in law enforcement and urged:

> ... careful selection of personnel; high educational requirements; thorough training of personnel; rigid discipline; promotions based on merit; freedom from the chains of political interference; detailed investigations; appreciation of evidence; protection of the innocent; complete elimination of any slight semblance of third degree tactics; unbiased testimony in courts of law and protection of civil liberties.[15]

This statement embodied Hoover's philosophy of law enforcement *at this time:* educational requirements and training of personnel, freedom from political influence, and appreciation of the legal necessities. This is how Hoover built the FBI, and he believed local law enforcement should be constructed on the same foundations.

Immediately after the war, in March 1946, Hoover again emphasized the training of police through the "pages of this *Bulletin.*" He stressed that all officers should have access to the *Bulletin.* In November, 1947, Special Agent Edward C. Kemper was named editor of the *Bulletin.* He succeeded Bernard M. Suttler, who had been assigned to FBI Headquarters in 1938, less than two years after appointment as a Special Agent, and SA George L. Carroll, the first full-time editor, who served as such from 1943 to 1947. Kemper, later an FBI Inspector, arranged for the printing of the *Bulletin* at the Government Printing Office in 1947 to give the periodical a more professional appearance. Until then it had been printed in small facilities at the FBI.

Director Hoover noted the printing change in his December introduction, writing that:

> The objective of the *Bulletin,* like that of the other cooperative functions of the FBI, is to advance the profession of law enforcement. It is the desire of the Federal Bureau of Investigation that this publication continue to be developed in such a manner that the greatest degree of service may be afforded to law enforcement generally.[16]

THE QUIET DECADE

By comparison with other periods in the 20th century, the 1950s can be characterized as a quiet period. The greatest war of modern times was over and the mood of the American people was to get back to "normal times." The civil rights revolution had barely started. The late 1950s brought an increase in the juvenile population of the U.S. and a tremendous increase in, or awareness of, juvenile delinquency. The *Bulletin* carried numerous articles on police programs to cut juvenile delinquency; these were supported by Hoover in *Bulletin* introductions, more on this subject than any other.

This period, with the Korean War, saw an increase in alerts to local police on internal security and communism. Professionalism in law enforcement, cooperation between law enforcement agencies in identification and other matters, Hoover's support for the International Association of Chiefs of Police (IACP), as well as his opposition to any national police agency, were also covered in introductions. Reports on uniform crime statistics, on the National Academy, on traffic problems, and on seasonal crime trends, police pay, and on honesty in law enforcement were other topics. In September, 1954, Hoover wrote about child abductions and kidnappings and recommended that children be fingerprinted so they could be later identified. He anticipated by thirty years the 1980s' problem of missing children and the public surge of interest in child fingerprinting for identification.

One of the new law enforcement techniques in this period was the use of police dogs. The St. Louis, Missouri, Police Department was one of the first large American departments to adopt a canine program, a feature that the unit commander felt was instrumental in preventing rioting that afflicted other cities in the 1960s! This new program was initiated by the then President of the Board of Police Commissioners in St. Louis, probably as a result of an article in a 1955 *Bulletin* on the London, England, use of dogs in police work. St. Louis contacted the London police and sent an officer over there to train. The first dog St. Louis acquired in 1958 was from the London police, according to former Sgt. Eugene Broders, the first commander of the unit. In March, 1961, the *Bulletin* ran an article on the operational St. Louis program.[17]

The 1950s also saw articles by doctors from the University of Nebraska, a Smithsonian anthropologist, and a doctor from St. Elizabeth's Hospital on police treatment of the mentally deranged. Technology was addressed in articles on FM radios, then beginning to be used in police work, and the first use of police helicopters, by the New York City Police Department.

In September, 1957 the *Bulletin* addressed the lag in the social sciences in "Some Modern Horizons in Police Training," from the New York City Police Department. The preceding May had seen "FBI Training Assistance for Local Police" covered, which noted that "The *FBI Law Enforcement Bulletin* is published as a means of providing up-to-date law enforcement techniques . . . for reference material . . ." or use in classroom instruction. This noted the initiation of statewide schools in latent fingerprint work (the *Bulletin* had run articles on the subject contributed by the Syracuse, New York, and Columbus, Ohio, police departments). This article also described the 542 schools on civil rights during 1956, attended by 27,194 officers.[18]

An article on the use of seat belts appeared in 1956, when auto manufacturers began installing belts. A California sheriff wrote about the role of an alcohol clinic and articles about policewomen in Philadelphia and Cincinnati showed that the *Bulletin* was ahead of its time in this decade. 1955 saw the appointment of a new editor of the *FBI Law Enforcement Bulletin,* Special Agent Lawrence J. Heim, who served for four years, followed by Agent Charles E. Moore for two years.

THE TURBULENT 1960S

A *Bulletin* article from Baltimore on civilian review boards, a controversial topic in the sixties, appeared in 1960. Various treatments on riot control (from New York City police, the Pennsylvania State Police, the U.S. Army, Hong Kong Police, and a university), and on civil rights from the FBI were also timely in this riotous decade. Ten articles on various foreign police agencies gave an international flavor to the *Bulletin.* IACP views on professionalism, followed by articles on data processing, the National Crime Information Center (NCIC), video identification in Florida, and a 1968 California story on computer applications in law enforcement, were indicative of the *Bulletin's* currency.

Timely articles on pursuit driving training, psychedelic drugs, and a management professor's piece on the budget process also showed the *Bulletin's* view of modern policing. This period saw the appointment of Special Agent C. Benjamin Fulton, editor of the *Bulletin* from 1961 to 1972. Director Hoover's Messages in the *Bulletin,* which were written by the editor but signed by the Director, concerned various facets of the crime problem, civil disobedience, and riots during this period. Organized crime, civil rights, and communism were also addressed. In 1964, Hoover called professionalism a "cooperative effort" between universities, local governments, and law enforcement:

> More states should be making available essential police training. More universities and colleges should be initiating and increasing courses of study oriented toward the development of a career police profession. Law enforcement must raise its sights, broaden its outlook, and insist on a higher caliber of performance.[19]

There had been a policy difference between August Vollmer, the early advocate of police professionalism, and J. Edgar Hoover over legal training in the field of law enforcement. Hoover, a lawyer, wanted his agents to be lawyers and urged at least some legal training for all police officers. Vollmer felt a more general college education was sufficient. The FBI has long emphasized legal training for its Agents, and through the National Academy and local police training schools has extended this instruction to local police.

Hoover oversaw the "Legal Digest," so named in February, 1971, and since then the most popular feature of the *Bulletin.* It is written by FBI Agents, who are law graduates and teach law courses at the National Academy to police officers so they understand police needs in the field of legal education. The Legal Digest began with a memorandum by former *Bulletin* editor ('52–'55), Special Agent Dwight J. Dalbey (who later became the FBI's first Assistant Director of the Legal Counsel Division), after various legal articles by judges and district attorneys were well received by police readership. Dalbey wrote in 1967 that a way for the FBI to meet "the deep and broad demand for legal training in the police field" was "through publication of legal articles in the *FBI Law Enforcement Bulletin.*" Director Hoover, conscious of the sweeping changes in the criminal law then being made by the Supreme Court, noted on this memo, the "More the better."[20]

FBI Director William H. Webster, a Federal judge before his 1978 appointment as head of the FBI, supported Hoover's view of legal training for police. In the November, 1984, *Bulletin,* he announced a new FBI National Law Institute established by the FBI's Legal Counsel Division for local police legal advisors:

> ...the complexity of legal issues encountered by law enforcement officers, managers, and administrators in recent years highlights the need for each law enforcement agency to have ready and continuous access to a qualified legal expert.[21]

RENAISSANCE II

J. Edgar Hoover died in 1972; another rebirth of thinking in policing began about this time. Hoover's final messages to the law enforcement community included ones related to professionalism—his opposition to police strikes and the newest expansion of the FBI's service to law enforcement role: the National Crime Information Center (NCIC).

Clarence M. Kelley succeeded Hoover as Director of the FBI, after L. Patrick Gray served a year as Acting Director. Kelley was a career FBI Agent who retired, after advancing in the FBI to Special Agent in Charge, and became Chief of Police in Kansas City, Missouri. Director Kelley's June, 1974, message in the *Bulletin* gave his definition of professionalism in police work: it required the qualities of intelligence,

dedication, courage, humaneness, and the knowledge generated by cooperation and training, but it especially required integrity. "No law enforcement officer can be a professional without being honest."[22]

He saw to it that the *Bulletin* carried articles by other law enforcement
professionals, along with academics, on this subject. One, by Professor
James Q. Wilson of Harvard, noted:

> In the 1950's the dominant police issue in this country was that of
> professionalism and integrity. Police chiefs spent most of their time
> dealing with the problem of integrity. In the 1960's, without losing
> sight of integrity, the dominant concern for the progressive police
> administrations became police-community relations. It seems to me
> that in the 1970's the dominant issue is the need to redesign police
> organizations and operations so they can better serve crime-control and
> community-service objectives. . . . [23]

Another article that illustrated the problems of the 1970s was "A
Professor's 'Street Lessons' " by a criminology professor who became a
working police officer as a "means of establishing . . . the accuracy of
what I and other criminologists had been saying about the police for so
long." Instead, at a time when police were so much under attack on
campuses and in the academic community, he learned that " . . . lawful
authority . . . is the only thing which stands between civilization and the
jungle of lawlessness." This became the most widely reprinted of any
article that had appeared in the *Bulletin.*[24]

New issues in law enforcement, such as team policing, in California
and elsewhere, the handling of victims, and physical fitness for law
enforcement officers were covered; an article on crime control teams
appeared by Thomas J. Sardino, Chief of Police in Syracuse, New York,
and later President of the IACP. Director Kelley, as chief in Kansas City,
developed a concern with police management which led to numerous
articles on this subject, including one in 1976 on the FBI's new National
Executive Institute.[25]

Director Kelley's tenure saw the appointment of new *FBI Law Enforcement Bulletin* editors: Special Agents John H. Campbell in 1972; Thomas
D. Haddock in 1976; and in 1977 the author of this book became editor.
The *Bulletin* has always been made available at no cost to all federal,
state, and local law enforcement agencies, and is also furnished to other
criminal justice professionals, including educators, who request it. It is
available on microfilm and at depository libraries nationwide which
receive government publications. Theme issues of the *Bulletin* on topics

of importance to police were introduced in 1981; the first concerned collective bargaining in police work. The second was on pedophilia and child pornography, just as public concern over this topic developed. For the first time, the *Bulletin* had to reprint 10,000 extra copies of an issue due to criminal justice community demand. FBI Director Webster introduced the next theme issue, on deadly force, saying that "no court can correct a deadly mistake once it has been made."[26]

Today, the *FBI Law Enforcement Bulletin* is alert to the changes taking place in the progress toward professionalism by the police community. Articles on the Commission for the Accreditation of law enforcement agencies and on the Police Foundation have appeared; Director Webster noted on the *Bulletin's* 50th anniversary:

> Over the years, the Bulletin took on a new direction and emphasis . . . as law enforcement gained the hallmarks of a professional service. Readers can now benefit from articles on management techniques, personnel matters, special operations, legal developments, and computer management, as well as training, investigative techniques, current crime problems, [and] forensic science developments.[27]

From an historical viewpoint, of course, it will take time to judge whether the *Bulletin* is now fulfilling its commitment to the advancement of police professionalism.

Notes to Chapter 13

1. Nathan, 1932.
2. Hoover, 1932.
3. Rigler, 1985.
4. Tolson, 1935d.
5. Hoover, 1935b.
6. Stead, 1977. 114.
7. Fugitives Wanted By Police, 1–3.
8. Hoover, 1935. 4:10.
9. Hoover, 1950. 19:1.
10. Hoover, 1936. "Introduction" FBI LEB 5:2:1. (The *FBI Law Enforcement Bulletin* is known by its initials, LEB, among law enforcement practitioners.)
11. Vollmer, 1937.
12. Hoover, 1936. LEB 5:6.
13. Hoover, 1944. LEB 6:4.
14. McLaren, 1973.
15. Hoover, 1944. LEB 13:6.
16. Hoover, 1947. LEB 16:12.

17. Broders, 1985. Dorn, 1961.
18. LEB 26:5.
19. Hoover, 1964. LEB 33:5.
20. Casper, 1967.
21. Webster, 1984. LEB 53:11.
22. Kelley, 1974.
23. Wilson, 1975.
24. Kirkham, 1974.
25. FBI, 1976.
26. LEB 53:4.
27. LEB 51:10.

PART IV

BEYOND THE RENAISSANCE—1940-1970

College education for police began in California under the impetus of practitioners such as August Vollmer, and later, in the 1950s for returning veterans, under his protege, O. W. Wilson. World War II brought profound alterations to America's way of living. It marked the change from urban to suburban lifestyles for a large segment of the population, with concurrent dependence on the automobile. After the war, expansion of the junior college movement saw further growth in beginning police science curricula; eventually this meant that many police executives were college educated, and rose from the ranks, rather than European-style lateral entry of ranking officers.

The war brought a quantum leap in technological changes, viewed as progress at the time. Policing also changed. It became more impersonal; "efficiency" became the goal and the military model increased in influence. Emphasis was put on the professionalism of the police department, on improving the efficiency of the department, rather than professionalizing the individual officer, as Vollmer had sought. As in American society as a whole, technology reigned. "Stranger" policing developed, characterized by widespread adoption of the patrol car, a necessity in the suburban environment, rather than use of the foot patrol officer. This was especially the case in California, where so many innovations in policing had begun.

The Los Angeles Police Department, under Chief William Parker in the 1950s, became the exemplar of "efficient" professional policing that suited suburban, middle-class America. But, reliance on a philosophy of "deterring" crime through aggressive preventive patrol, rather than preventing it, eventually proved that policing in America had to be supported by all elements of a city's population, not just the suburban middle-class.

Meanwhile, the FBI had raised fingerprint identification to a science, an element of police professionalism and instituted a national central fingerprint file. The civil section of this file had humanitarian uses.

Then, in 1967, the FBI, in connection with the Uniform Crime Record committee of the IACP, began a cooperative federal-state computerized system of crime information, the National Crime Information Center (NCIC), which became the "life blood" of the patrol officer. ·

Chapter 14

ACADEMIC BEGINNINGS

American police college education, as opposed to recruit or in-service training of officers already employed, began in California in the late 1920s at the instigation of Berkeley police chief August Vollmer. This serving police chief, who had only a grade school education himself, in association with academics at the Berkeley campus of the University of California, had a profound effect on police education. Over half a century, Vollmer's pioneering led to police executives of larger departments in this country who are, in the main, college graduates, many with advanced degrees.

American admiration and respect for education, together with an awareness of the rewards of education, brought about this advance in police professionalism. The whole movement toward police education was due to police leaders like Vollmer, rather than academics. And, unlike Europe, the requirement of advanced education for police executives resulted not from government decree but voluntarily, by efforts of police leaders seeking professionalism. This movement for educational advancement for officers up through the ranks also obviated the European practice of lateral entry of ranking officers. In accordance with American democratic practice, this is having the effect of professionalizing the whole police service instead of just the commanding ranks.

Police education, like police training, is one element of professionalism. Control of the educational/training process can dictate trends in the future of policing. While police leaders generally control the direction of their own police training academies, the control of pre-employment education of potential police officers has, at times, provoked conflict between police leadership and the academic community. This potential for conflict was present at the beginning of police education in California and is still seen today in continuing debate over the content of police education and particularly over who educates the police, academics or practitioners.

The rebirth of police professionalism, beginning in the 1970s, follows

American society's emphasis today on legality, civil liberties, and human, rather than property, rights. As one writer put it, American policing is a "barometer of community values," which are in a state of change.

VOLLMER'S INFLUENCE

In 1967, A. F. Brandstatter, then the Director of Michigan State's School of Police Administration (one of the first college programs in the country), traced the history of police education in this country back to criminal law academics. In 1909 the first National Conference on Criminal Law and Criminology was convened in Chicago by the law faculty of Northwestern University, and this brought together "selected educators and practitioners from every branch of the American criminal justice system." This conference resulted in the establishment of the American Institute of Criminal Law and Criminology and the founding, the next year, of the *Journal of Criminal Law and Criminology.* It also brought the translation into English of some of the most important and significant books on criminology, such as Hans Gross's *Criminal Psychology.*[1]

But Brandstatter did not analyze the impact on police professionalism of legal scholars' interest in criminology. Most important to police education was this conference's influence on police pioneer August Vollmer. Vollmer, Chief of Police in Berkeley, California, became a contributor to the *Journal of Criminal Law and Criminology* in 1916 and two years later served as the vice president of the institute and on the editorial board of the journal.[2] Vollmer had already begun an in-service school for Berkeley officers with the assistance of lecturers from the University at Berkeley. This early association with the university's faculty, along with Vollmer's reputation as the most progressive police administrator in the country, led to his teaching summer courses in policing beginning in 1916. As noted in Chapter 7, the University of California at Berkeley awarded a bachelor's degree with a minor in criminology to a Berkeley police officer in 1923, the first academic recognition of police courses for fulfillment of the requirements toward a degree.[3]

Vollmer had the vision of a minimum requirement of a B.A. degree for police recruits and began its reality by hiring college students for police service in Berkeley. He believed that police service "would be measurably improved" if there were a degree requirement for each officer, according to Vollmer's correspondence with Bruce Smith.[4] In

Vollmer's 1935 article "The Police Ideal of Service," his broadly idealistic view of the value of education is set forth:

> The service ideal aspires to the personal attainment of knowledge, —the guiding principle being joy and pleasure in learning. This motivates the policeman to delve profoundly into the theory and practice of dealing with human beings, as individuals and as groups. His search into natural, biological and social sciences is an eternal quest for that clue which, if found, will aid the policeman in dealing more intelligently with his fellow man.[5]

Later that year, J. Edgar Hoover gave the commencement address at Kalamazoo College and spoke of police education:

> I hope the time will come when every educational institution will include a course in law enforcement as part of its curriculum.

But Hoover envisioned not only training for officers:

> . . . the greatest day for our nation will be when all of law enforcement is placed upon a career basis, with merit and ability and integrity and ambition as the prime requisites for an officer's appointment . . .

but also for citizen support of the police:

> . . . a knowledge on the part of every citizen of what good law enforcement consists . . . and of what criminality consists, of what goes to cause crime . . . [6]

During Vollmer's one-year tenure as Chief of Police in Los Angeles, he set up a series of lectures for his command officers by professors at the University of Southern California. By 1928, this lecture series had developed into a full academic curriculum available both to serving officers and students interested in law enforcement as a career. The program had an advisory committee of experienced practitioners in law enforcement. In 1929, Vollmer taught a course, "Police Administration and Police Procedure," and a research seminar at the University of Chicago while on a leave of absence from Berkeley. (Vollmer had surveyed the Chicago Police Department in 1927.) This program was discontinued after Vollmer accepted a position as professor of police administration at Berkeley, but was significant in two ways. It was part of the regular daytime curriculum rather than a summer or night school offering, and it was the first police course established in a political science department.[7]

Another California law enforcement program, rather than a single course, grew out of Vollmer's 1930 meeting with President T. W. MacQuarrie of San Jose State Teacher's College. Earl Warren, then a

California District Attorney, and later Governor of the state and then Chief Justice of the U.S. Supreme Court, consulted with Vollmer and MacQuarrie on this program, which began as a two-year "technical training" course for pre- and in-service police officers. In the junior college segment of San Jose State, a student completing the course was awarded an associate of arts diploma. By 1935, an optional program allowed the student to continue on to earn a bachelor's degree from the four-year college by taking a further two years. This is still the way most police science degree programs work today: junior colleges in association with four-year colleges.

The police science program at San Jose State was headed by George H. Brereton, a University of California graduate and former police officer in Berkeley. In an economic appeal, an advertisement for the San Jose State College program told police officials: "It is cheaper to train your men here than in your own department." In 1935, this program became the San Jose State College Police School. The year before, a similar program had been established at the Los Angeles Junior College.[8]

Vollmer later acknowledged the "seemingly insurmountable obstacles and academic prejudices" that had to be overcome at the beginning of the San Jose program. MacQuarrie recognized that "we were pioneering," so discussions were held with other police officials on program development. MacQuarrie believed the program would provide education that would substitute for the "aimless experience" acquired between high school graduation and age 21, the usual minimum recruitment age for police officers in this country. He also believed that both students and police officials had to be convinced of the "practical nature" of this college training, and so he advocated a "teacher training" model be adopted that included six divisions: (1) selection of the candidate, (2) background education (3) professional training (4) practice in "real world" situations (5) job placement and (6) follow-up.

Since many California police departments were beginning to adopt physical, personality, and mental requirements, students were advised of these requirements before entering the program. Only males with evident physical disabilities were prohibited, but for females, MacQuarrie reported:

> A good many young women wished to take the work but most of them seemed to see in it a dramatic situation, and they were advised to make other plans.... There may be a field someday for policewomen, but at present the demand does not seem to be great....[9]

This restriction was ended in the 1938–39 academic year.

The San Jose program was to prepare students for the "first rung" of the police ladder, patrolmen, and not to " . . . turn out chiefs, captains or experts of any kind." MacQuarrie also emphasized the technical training aspect of the program, to secure student and police acceptance:

> In a four-year course there can be a rounding out of general education, but if the program is limited to two years, most of the time must be spent in courses that appeal to the student and to the field as practical. [Each class should] . . . present and consider situations that come up in the daily work of the policeman. The stress is always on the solution of the problem, and a recommendation for action under similar circumstances.[10]

Beginning in 1935, until the mid-1960s, students were required to purchase, and wear on a periodic basis, police school uniforms. That year, a six-unit "Police Field Work" course was developed that was "organized and conducted as a platoon in the patrol division of a police department." Courses in basic and advanced military training were added in 1937, and during World War II the program was closed for the duration of the war.

In 1932, Vollmer retired as Chief of Police in Berkeley to devote full-time to teaching as a research professor at the University of California. This position resulted from a Rockefeller Foundation grant for a project in administration of criminal justice, to be conducted by the Bureau of Public Administration and the university's Department of Political Science. A new major in criminology was being offered by 1933; Vollmer taught courses in police administration, in addition to his research. The criminal justice curriculum was intended to give the student a general education in academic subjects relevant to law enforcement, not technical training in policing techniques. In a letter, Vollmer explained that the program would be feasible "at every university, providing that the courses were assembled and passed on by people who have knowledge of the police problem. . . . "[11]

In early 1935, when the FBI was designing its national police training school (which became the National Academy), J. Edgar Hoover instructed the San Francisco FBI office to contact Vollmer regarding having an FBI Agent attend his course. Vollmer told the FBI that since the Agent would have undergraduate and law degrees, a concentrated two-week analysis of his course would be sufficient rather than attendance at the whole course. The head of the Bureau's training division, Hugh Clegg, recom-

mended that agent W. L. Listerman proceed to California to confer with
Vollmer and thereafter be assigned to the training division. A preliminary outline of Vollmer's course, "Administration of Criminal Justice,"
(Political Science 275a–b) reveals the comprehensive nature of Vollmer's
undertaking.[12]

The outline for this course begins with an introduction on the historical development of the administration of criminal justice together with a
survey of the literature in the field. Underlying concepts on the nature
of crime, including the differentiation of crime from "mores, customs,
sins" and a review of the historical theories of crime, beginning with
Beccacia, follows, along with a look at criminal offenders. Methods of
research in the field, including social science research, research procedures and methods, and finally, presentation of results, are covered.

Police Administration then covers specific criminal justice agencies:
the state police, federal police agencies ("with special attention to the
recent developments in the Division of Investigation"), sheriffs, private
police, and the coroner. Next is a section on police departments, which
begins with the head of the department, and includes the selection,
training, and distribution of the force, in addition to their salaries and
welfare, plus the department's records and reports. There is a detailed
treatment of the prosecution of criminal offenses, beginning with the
reasons for proving guilt and the historical development of prosecution
in America (as opposed to the Continental system). Details on the
prosecutive process from complaint through trial and appeal, plus problems in the process, including political pressures, and an overall survey
on the criminal court system are included. An equally detailed summary
of punishment, including prison, parole, and probation, follows along
with a special section on the juvenile offender. Overall, this was a most
ambitious course of study, one that covers the whole of criminal justice
education today.

In this period of slow growth of police education, at least by comparison with the explosion of this type of schooling in the 1970s, by 1949
there were at least ten colleges and universities in California offering
courses in law enforcement. This early police education progress in one
state and its proponents were to have a lasting effect on the nature of
policing in America. FBI executives judged at this time that "colleges
and universities are becoming increasingly interested in police training"
and the FBI "should adopt a more liberal attitude toward cooperation
with colleges and universities" in police training. However, as the FBI's

mandate was to train police, not students of policing, the Bureau opted not to furnish instructors to classes involving "pre-entry students" instead of serving officers.[13]

PROGRESS EASTWARD

Vollmer's influence caused California to lead all the other states in education available to police and students in law enforcement, but in the mid-1930s college education for police began to move eastward, first to Michigan State College which formed the School of Police Administration and Public Safety in 1935. Through the efforts of Dr. LeMoyne Snyder and Oscar Olander, then commissioner of the Michigan State Police, the Michigan Crime Commission became interested in the concept of college-level police education. Dr. Snyder approached Michigan State College (now a university), and the School of Police Administration was established.

The original bachelor of science program at Michigan State required three years of course work and a final year of study and practical experience with the Michigan State Police. Course work included English, chemistry, physics, anatomy, physiology, psychology, sociology, economics, bacteriology, hygiene, physical training, and four years of military training. During two months of training with the Michigan State Police, courses in criminal law, evidence, traffic, scientific crime detection, and other police-related studies received college credit. The students were commissioned as Michigan State Police, but also spent some of this final year with local departments. A former motorcycle officer, who had a law degree, was the first, and only, faculty member when the program began; he was succeeded by another attorney. In 1947, A. F. Brandstatter, one of the first three graduates of the program, became head of the program. The faculty was gradually expanded until today it numbers 17 full-time members.[14]

1936 saw the establishment of a four-year course leading to a bachelor of arts degree with a certificate in police science at Indiana University. This program was headed by a criminologist, Dr. Edwin Sutherland, who was also active in the Institute of Criminal Law and Criminology established in 1935 on the Indiana campus.[15] Also in 1936, the Traffic Institute was established at Northwestern University outside Chicago. Headed by Franklin Kreml, an Evanston, Illinois, police lieutenant and a law graduate, the institute "has exerted a profound influence in all aspects of traffic safety." It was funded in part by a grant from the newly formed Automotive Safety Foundation and now has expanded its original purpose to include education in police operations and management.[16]

World War II marked the discontinuance of some police education, but it also saw the beginning of another program on the west coast. September, 1941, marked the start of the police science program at the University of Washington under Dr. V. A. (Vivian Anderson) Leonard, who began his law enforcement career as a Berkeley policeman under August Vollmer. Leonard became the superintendent of records and identification at Ft. Worth, Texas, after eight years at Berkeley. As founder of the University of Washington program, he taught there for seventeen years and authored many books and articles on the criminal investigation process, in addition to earlier works on the polygraph. Only three years after its founding, this program was one of the first to offer a master's degree in police science.[17]

The Southern Police Institute at the University of Louisville, established in 1951 and modeled after the FBI's National Academy police training school, owes its genesis to Swedish economist Gunnar Myrdal who wrote, in his 1944 classic, *An American Dilemma:*

> It is my conviction that one of the most potent strategic measures to improve the Southern interracial situation would be the opening of a pioneering modern police college in the South, which would give a thorough social and pedagogical training as well as a technical police training.[18]

David A. McCandless, the first Director of the Southern Police Institute, had been the Louisville, Kentucky, Director of Public Safety in 1949 when Joseph D. Lohman suggested organizing the institute. Lohman, previously Cook County, Illinois, sheriff, was then Dean of the School of Criminology at the University of California. McCandless visited FBI Headquarters in Washington, D.C., in 1950 to explain the new program and seek FBI assistance in furnishing lecturers.[19]

Initially funded by grants from an affiliate of the Rockefeller Foundation established to aid education in the South and by the Carnegie Foundation and then the Ford Foundation, support from the City of Louisville and the university provided revenues through 1970, when the institute became supported by general university funds. The first faculty member came from the University of Washington, with McCandless as Dean. Within the first 10 years, the institute attracted officers from 167 municipalities in 38 states and 22 foreign countries, to courses in police administration in addition to its seminars in police responsibility in racial harmony.

In 1961, a reassessment of the program was suggested by Associate Director of the institute John C. Klotter, who had previously served with the FBI. This resulted in a re-emphasis on police administration, plus instruction on personnel management, the social and behavioral sciences, and criminal and constitutional law. This expanded course offering earned approval of the university's curriculum committee for 12 semester hours credit from the College of Arts and Sciences in 1962; thus the Southern Police Institute became the first institution of its type to offer college credit for in-service police education, a precedent for other specialized police schools. In 1969, the University Assembly approved the formation of a degree-granting School of Police Administration, with David McCandless as Dean, which he held in addition to his position as Director of the Southern Police Institute. His death in 1971 resulted in the succession of Professor Klotter to both positions.[20]

New York City took a different approach; in 1954 the City College of New York established a police science program jointly with the Bernard Baruch School of Business and Public Administration and the New York City Police Department. At first, this was a two-year program offering an associate degree in police science, with an option to continue on for a bachelor's degree. A Master of Public Administration degree, with a major in police science, was soon offered. The unique aspect of this program was that at first it was only available to those already engaged in law enforcement and it was jointly administered by the police department and the college. The commanding officer of the police academy was made the assistant dean of the college and a joint police department/college committee on curriculum and personnel was established. From this, the John Jay College of Criminal Justice evolved, which is the fifth senior college of the New York City University system with faculty drawn both from the police department and the academic community. Although John Jay primarily serves the New York City Police Department, today general students are admitted.[21]

EDUCATION VS. TRAINING DICHOTOMY

Education toward professionalism began with training by various police departments and then expanded, beginning in California, to college education. College education was marked at first by an emphasis on practical instruction, although Vollmer had a wider view of college preparation for police officers. College education in some respects was modeled after the FBI's National Academy, and this academy and the Southern Police Institute today give college credit for their training.

An early trend in college education for police included an advisory board of police practitioners, to gain more acceptance for this concept in the police community. Generally, these programs were associated with the political science department of colleges, a precursor to today's realization that policing does involve political realities, however non-partisan. Initial two-year programs were more technically oriented than the four-year liberal arts course envisioned by Vollmer. As in police agencies overall, these early programs had considerable military orientation and were usually limited to male students. Colleges depended on police practitioners, with advanced, usually law, degrees for faculty, a trend that has continued over growing opposition from the academic community.

MacQuarrie at San Jose State emphasized practical aspects of law enforcement education, especially in the two-year program, and other early college programs were heavily training oriented to overcome police and academic prejudice against college education for police. But as law enforcement college education became more accepted and as police recruit training grew among departments, competition between college programs and police training academies developed in the form of a distinction between training and education, which still has significance today. Administrators of college law enforcement programs began to state that they were "educating" police officers and potential officers as to the "why" of law enforcement; they also reasoned that the "how" of policing was a training or vocational aspect of police learning which should remain with the various police departments.[22]

Some in the academic community took exception to what they believed was an artificial distinction between the "how" and "why" of police education. Leonard E. Reisman, president of John Jay College, wrote:

> When people ask me "How do you educate policemen?" I have two answers. One is "Like anyone else." But the other is "Teach them the practices, techniques, needs, and the milieu of police work." This point is aptly expressed by Alfred North Whitehead's frequently quoted "There can be no adequate technical education which is not liberal and no liberal education which is not technical; that is, no education which does not impart both technique and vision."[23]

Alfred North Whitehead, an English mathematician and philosopher who was as influential on education as America's John Dewey, was writing about British technical education in the 1920s. The Whitehead material quoted by Reisman begins:

> "The antithesis between a technical and a liberal education is fallacious." Whitehead continues: "In simpler language, education should turn out the pupil with something he knows well and something he can do well. This intimate union of practice and theory aids both. The intellect does not work best in a vacuum."[24]

But the disagreement continued. In an article for *The Journal of Criminal Law, Criminology and Police Science,* Robert S. Prout, holder of a law degree and a master's degree in education, also a former police officer, made the point:

> ... law enforcement at the university level is unique—unique because of the concealed belief that law enforcement education is in competition with the police department responsibility for training.[25]

He makes the argument that universities actually began in Italy and England to train doctors and "clerks for the King's service," not as centers of abstract learning. Further, the classics were not taught originally because they "shaped the mind," but because they were vocationally useful. Prout concluded:

> Their artificial wall of "why" and "how," which is in essence an "education" versus "training" philosophy, is educationally unsound.[26]

In this he echoes Whitehead:

> In estimating the importance of technical education we must rise above the exclusive association of learning with book-learning. First-hand knowledge is the ultimate basis of intellectual life.[27]

While this dichotomy was idealistic in nature, in practical terms it was also the result of economic competition. When a public consensus was reached that police needed training or education, and the public did not differentiate between training and education, police officials, of course, argued that this was their responsibility—it broadened their case for more tax dollars. Universities, and junior colleges, saw a potential market for increasing their share of tax revenues, or grant funds, by adding a whole new class of students.

GROWTH OF POLICE EDUCATION

"1930–1945 represented a period of gradual expansion of law enforcement education." By 1949, some 26 institutions were offering degree programs in criminal justice, but only 11 had programs concentrating on law enforcement. In the next 10 years these programs grew to some 77 criminal justice programs among 56 institutions in 19 states, but in the 1960s there was "a tremendous growth acceleration" that brought the total of such programs, including associate degree ones, to some 125.[28]

J. Edgar Hoover reiterated his belief in education as a mark of professionalism, writing in the *FBI Law Enforcement Bulletin:*

> Inadequate emphasis on the professionalization of law enforcement is one of our Nation's critical shortcomings in the fight against crime . . . More universities and colleges should be initiating and increasing courses of study oriented toward the development of a career police profession.[29]

Then, in 1967, the President's National Crime Commission recommended that "The ultimate aim of all police departments should be that all personnel with general enforcement powers have baccalaureate degrees."[30] These recommendations by the most respected leaders in law enforcement contributed to the next expansion in police education. By 1970, the International Association of Chiefs of Police (IACP) reported the existence of 250 community college programs, 55 bachelor degree programs, some 21 masters and 7 doctorate programs. This expansion was also due to a 1964 Ford Foundation grant to the IACP to encourage "greater interest in law enforcement education on the part of community colleges and universities."[31]

Dividing criminal justice programs into three types, A. C. Germann, professor of criminology at Long Beach, California, State College, defined the three as: vocational, philosophical, and a combination of the two. He favored the last as:

> . . . the graduate of this type of training is able to assume, immediately, the mechanical and procedural demands of an agency, while at the same time retaining, and expanding, those abilities and knowledges useful to his future assumption of supervisory or administrative roles.[32]

A study by Prout in 1972 showed that over half of the law enforcement programs agreed with the combination approach.[33]

Germann, who previously served as an officer with the Los Angeles

Police Department, told a police training group at Memphis State University in 1966 that:

> The American policeman is a barometer of community values, and community values are under change. Emphasis is shifting from property rights to human rights, and most Americans intuitively accept the legitimacy of such shift. Decrying the emphasis for many years in policing on: "results," managerial efficiency, and production, rather than also on legality, morality, and compassion. . . . The modern professional officer is not committed to the interests of any one area or segment of the community and indifferent to the rest; he does not regard policing as a ruthless and mechanical method of protecting the "haves" from the "have nots."[34]

Germann goes on to quote Quinn Tamm, the Executive Director of the IACP, when Tamm was an Assistant Director of the FBI, in what was a reflection of the FBI's emphasis on law. This emphasis can be attributed to J. Edgar Hoover's legal training (and, despite Tamm's and Hoover's falling out after Tamm retired from the FBI and took over the leadership of the IACP, is a reflection of the FBI's continuing grounding of law enforcement professionalism in the law).

The quotation of Tamm's that Germann used in 1967 presages the development of police professionalism today, a generation later:

> The greatest evidence that law enforcement can offer to the community that it has come of age as a profession is a rock-ribbed, unwavering preoccupation with and regard for personal rights and liberties. . . . We must never fail to continually stress in our police schools the need for ever greater familiarity with the rule of law and observance of civil rights. The theme that must run beneath every police training program is that the rule of law is the very heart and soul of American police action. . . . No matter how carefully we teach our young officers and no matter how skilled they become at such techniques as interviewing, patrol, sketching, plaster casting, photographing, and the like, they will not be real officers until the conviction has become part of their very being that everything they do must be done in a reasonable and constitutional manner. This is the true mark of the professional officer.[35]

Notes to Chapter 14

1. Brandstatter, 1967. 9–11.
2. Carte, 1975. 126. Los Angeles, 1956.
3. Ibid 27.

4. Ibid 69.
5. LEB 1937 2:3.
6. Hoover, 1937c. 6.
7. Eastman, 1981. 124.
8. Kuykendall, 1975. 112. Eastman, 1981. 124. Brandstatter, 1967. 13. Kenney, 1964. 99.
9. Kuykendall, 1975. 112.
10. Ibid, 112–113.
11. Carte, 1975. 69–70.
12. Clegg, 1935f.
13. Clegg, 1949.
14. Trojanowicz, 1985. 70.
15. Brandstatter, 1967. 15.
16. Eastman, 1981. 127. Traffic Institute 13.
17. American Polygraph Association Newsletter, 1985. 18–20. Prout, 1972. 586–7.
18. Pomrenke, 1987.
19. Clegg, 1950.
20. Pomrenke, 1987.
21. Brandstatter, 1967. 9–19.
22. Prout, 1972. 587.
23. Reisman, 1967.
24. Whitehead, 1929. 48.
25. Prout, 1972. 587.
26. Ibid, 588.
27. Whitehead, 1929. 51.
28. LEAA, 1975. 45–46.
29. Hoover, 1964.
30. U.S. Commission on Law Enforcement, 1967.
31. IACP, 1970. 2.
32. Germann, 1959.
33. Prout, 1972. 591.
34. Germann, 1967. 603.
35. Ibid, 606–607.

Chapter 15

THE EFFICIENCY ERA

The mayor of Wichita, Kansas, once described O. W. Wilson, his chief of police, as "too damned efficient." Orlando Winfield Wilson, protege and successor of August Vollmer, personified efficiency in policing. Wilson authored *the* text on police administration in the 1950s while a professor of police science at the University of California. Wilson, as chief of police in Wichita, had already established his reputation as a practitioner, and re-established it in Chicago after university service. Wilson believed that "the affairs of a police department should be handled neatly, systematically, and with precision." He was convinced of the need for police organization—"along semimilitary lines."[1]

While the origins of police professionalism were rooted in the Progressive Movement's attempt to "reform" the cities and wrest power from the "bosses," pioneer police and law enforcement leaders August Vollmer and J. Edgar Hoover captured the initiative in the 1920s and 1930s to make the movement toward police professionalism their own. Vollmer, especially, foresaw the "new policeman" who would have "more opportunities to do good, solid, constructive social service. . . ."[2] He had a disciple, Wilson, who adopted and adapted pioneering ideas to make professionalism more efficient, in terms of police services, selection and training of personnel, executive tenure, organization, police records and communications, and especially use of the automobile in patrol work.[3]

Efficiency was the watchword for American business after Henry Ford inaugurated the assembly line for building automobiles in 1913; the era of the time and motion study for all kinds of enterprise bloomed in America. As one police historian put it:

> The standard of efficiency, then, assumed for its realization the application of time measurement to work and human activity, higher degrees of organization and clearer lines of administrative responsibility, better training and education, and the exclusion of personal or political considerations in decision-making.[4]

211

Efficiency in government also became a goal of the Progressive Movement. Municipal government until then had been operated by political machines as a means to assist immigrants in assimilating themselves into American society. Progressives believed that the purpose of municipal government should be to provide efficient services to the middle and upper classes, who paid the taxes necessary to support municipal government. When the mode of efficiency was applied to policing, after the ward bosses had been defeated, it radically altered the concept of American policing.

Changes in American society, the growth of cities, and especially the advent of widespread automobile ownership, dictated changes in the nature of policing, which now had to cope with both urban and suburban populations. The growth of the suburbs in the 1920s and again after World War II, with suburban dependence on the automobile, also created a new class of law breaker—the motorist. Instead of only an underclass of criminal to be policed, policing had to, by default, deal with virtually the whole population, not as its protector from the underclass, but as the enforcer of traffic laws.

Vollmer's theories of police professionalism were directed toward the improvement of the individual officer, the "new policeman," through training and education. Hoover proved that the detection of crime could be enhanced through scientific investigative aids and education and training of the investigator. Both deplored the influence of partisan politics on policing, but that was as far as their pioneering efforts took them. It remained for a second generation of reformers to carry on the task of professionalizing policing, although Hoover saw that "the public is demanding efficiency in its law enforcement agencies" as early as 1936.[5] This second generation relied more on technology than on human relations and concentrated on the professionalization of the department rather than the individual officer. The goal became an efficient department.

As police historian Gene E. Carte noted:

Ultimately the drive for new efficiency and technology became dominant over the search for a "new policeman."[6]

More than anyone else, O. W. Wilson advocated efficiency in policing. His leadership as a practitioner and later in the field of criminal justice education, plus his authorship of the best organized text on police administration, assured wide acceptance of his ideas. The successful prosecution of World War II by the military led to an acceptance by the public of military modes of organization, too, which generated public support of Wilson's theories on policing. The number of veterans of the war who entered policing also ensured acceptance of Wilson's concepts by practitioners.

O. W. WILSON

Wilson was born in 1900 in Veblen, South Dakota, one of six children of Ole Vraalson, an American-born lawyer of Norwegian parentage, who changed the family name to Wilson when Orlando was a boy. The family moved to California; Wilson completed high school and attended the University of California at Berkeley as a mining engineer student. A financial reverse ended family support of Wilson's education, so he had to take a job to continue his schooling. Wilson became one of August Vollmer's "college cops," with a resulting change in his college major to criminology. He graduated in 1924, a protege of August Vollmer, who helped Wilson get an appointment as chief of police of Fullerton, California, in 1925. But the Fullerton community was not ready for a progressive innovator; Wilson's appointment only lasted a year.[7]

In 1928, Wilson was appointed, again on Vollmer's recommendation, as chief of police in Wichita, Kansas. Wyatt Earp had policed Wichita less than fifty years previously, but the town had increased to 100,000 residents and the "cow town" image was past. The police department had not kept pace with the changed community; officers were hired on the basis of a recommendation from a politician or a businessman, issued a revolver, and assigned a beat. There were no entry standards, no formal training, and no code of conduct for officers. Violent crime was rampant and vice flourished; incompetence was the rule for the police, along with brutality.

Wilson, with the backing of Wichita's city manager, was able to build a reputation as an innovative, progressive chief of police, one with a strict sense of law enforcement and personal honesty. His first responsibility, however, was to "clean up" the police department, which he did by firing six officers and forcing the resignation of 15 others in his first year, a fifth of the 100-man force. Wilson's tenure in Wichita brought an in-service training program, which began as Saturday classes for off-duty officers, where they were exposed to Wilson's ideas on policing. Open press policy matters and public relations lectures were included as Wilson thought this kind of training would help the image of the department; officers were also lectured by a professor of municipal administration from a local university. Eventually, Wilson proposed a state-wide training program to the League of Municipalities; Wilson designed the curriculum and recruited the faculty for this program.

Wilson also initiated a code of ethics for the department, which later became the International Association of Chiefs of Police's (IACP) code for police nationwide. He established, for reasons of efficiency and cost factors, one-man patrol cars, a policy that was controversial among police officers across the country for years to come. He also adopted easily recognizable marked police cars and a host of other technological innovations to the police service there.[8]

Wilson's inauguration of personnel policies for recruitment eliminated partisan political influence on the department, but also made him enemies among local politicians and businessmen. Wilson's strict enforcement of vice laws eventually led to his replacement as chief in 1939, but by then Wilson's reputation as a progressive police administrator on the Vollmer model had been made. His interest in police training led to a position on the University of California faculty, but World War II interrupted.

THE MILITARY MODEL

American police departments have been organized from the beginning along the military rank structure and have even drilled in military fashion. Witness the New York City turn of the century annual police parade with its long lines of marching men; St. Louis and many other cities had drillmasters in their police training programs in this early period of policing. This was not organization along military lines in the European style, where police agencies were recruited from, or were part of, the military; Britain and America had determinedly resisted this European practice. But surface similarities to the military did give rise to the concept that police agencies were "paramilitary," although this was a misuse of the term which actually means "standing in stead of the military." But World War II and its aftermath did "alter the basic structure of police service in America." As Edward Farris, a veteran of the Berkeley Police Department and a graduate of the University of California criminal justice program, wrote in a history of policing for *Police Chief* magazine:

> New models of management, organization, operational techniques, and personnel utilization, drawn from military experience, were quickly adapted to policing in the last half of the 1940s.... Knowledge gained

from military experience began to influence the administration and organization of local agencies.[9]

The military metaphor of a "war against crime" had been common both in popular and progressive writings from the turn of the century through the New Deal. As we have seen, J. Edgar Hoover used this metaphor from 1925 onwards:

> Our active police officers are the first lines of offense and defense. They are the ones who actively meet the enemy upon the field of battle . . . [10]

But it was O. W. Wilson's experience in World War II which reinforced his inclination toward respect for authority in any chain of command, together with his writing the most popular text on police administration in 1950, that had the greatest impact on American policing. After Wichita, Wilson went to Chicago to survey police departments for the Public Administration Service. But, after three months, the University of California learned of his ouster as chief in Wichita and offered him a position as a full-time professor of police administration, the first in America.

At about this time, Wilson began work on his first books, *Municipal Police Administration* and *Distribution of Police Patrol Force,* published in 1938 and 1941, respectively. The first work sold 100,000 copies in its various editions and the second was described as "the first thorough-going analysis of the problem and represented a significant step forward in efficient utilization of police manpower resources."[11] Wilson presented the first system for weighing various factors, such as complaints, arrests, accidents, number of businesses, and property losses, to determine how many officers would be required to patrol a given area at a given time of day:

> If one area or shift had twice as many crimes, offenses, accidents, miscellaneous complaints, and arrests as another area or shift, it would be assumed that it had approximately twice the amount of hazards resulting in the need for police service.[12]

During World War II Wilson took a leave of absence from the university and enlisted. He served as a lieutenant colonel assigned to the School of Military Government and became the Director of Public Safety in allied-occupied Italy and then in Germany. In the latter country, Wilson found much that he admired in the police, including their "penchant for organization." As Wilson's biographer, William Bopp, notes:

O. W. had long been convinced of the need for police departments to be precisely organized according to some logical plan. The military system of organization and administration strongly appealed to him. He adopted and adapted many army organizational concepts.... A rigid chain of command was essential to exercise organizational control. Top commanders should unilaterally articulate policy, and rule by fiat. ... In his view, law enforcement should be organized along semimilitary lines.[13]

Bopp also comments that these semimilitary concepts gained wide acceptance in the police community because of Wilson's writings, teaching and example. Wilson, in Bopp's view:

was convinced that a nation of police departments, organized and administered along Wilsonian lines, would ultimately lead to police professionalization. In effect, the dominant organizational strategy of the Wilsonian school of police administration was to organize an agency according to the military model, then place in command a scrupulously honest martinet.... [14]

"BIBLE OF PROFESSIONALISM"

After the war, Wilson spent an additional year in Germany as a civilian employee of the army, with the same duties. He then returned to the University of California where he wrote *Police Administration*, "almost universally regarded as a landmark." From 1950 to 1972, when the book was in its third edition, it had outsold every other text offered by McGraw-Hill's college division. Translated into five languages, *Police Administration* sold some 200,000 copies. Based on the scientific management principles of Frederick Winslow Taylor, Wilson's book stressed "efficiency, hierarchy, and bureaucratic regularity as the key to police reform."[15]

Police Administration begins with ranking four interrelated issues that Wilson believed were as potentially dangerous as the threat of war, as then known, to civilization: "crime, overpopulation, environmental pollution, and social intolerance." Wilson then lists the long-term solutions to the problem of street crime; his solutions incidentally reflect the social concerns of this era: "improved education, elimination of poverty and unemployment, and amelioration of poor family relationships, rather than through the action of any single component of the justice system." But Wilson follows these "long-term solutions" with recommendations for the:

greatest impact on crime *right now* [emphasis in original] . . . "Improved, vigorous, and conspicuous preventive patrol by greater numbers of police in the locations where crime is prevalent.[16]

In Wilson's view, this type of patrol would "deter" crime. This was a new, limited goal for police, replacing Vollmer's broader ideas for "preventing" crime through various social work type of activities. A narrower, "more efficient," definition of the goal for police, deterrence rather than prevention, reflects what was thought at the time as a more realistic view of what the police could do. It also relieved police of crime prevention activities that had gained popularity in the 1930s and 1940s in connection with juvenile delinquency, such as police athletic leagues and boys clubs.

Three other recommendations follow in Wilson's *Police Administration:* more prosecutions, increased court capacity (including elimination of senseless postponements), and education and enforcement against narcotics traffic. In Chicago, where Wilson was chosen in 1960 to reform a department regarded as corrupt, he implemented his first recommendation with the formation of a 500-man task force to practice "aggressive patrolling." This type of vigorous, or aggressive, patrolling when practiced in minority communities, or against minority populations, was cited as one of the causes of the rioting in this country in the late 1960s, because of its perception in the ghetto as harassment. This illustration of policing's need for community support from all major elements of the population, in turn, led to the second renaissance of police professionalism.[17]

Academics and practitioners, who have analyzed Wilson's considerable contributions to police professionalism, criticize his emphasis on the internal environment of policing in terms of today's theories of policing. Carte makes the point that:

> One consequence of this internal focus is a serious weakening of police/citizen contacts, whether with reformers or with the political struggles of racial and ethnic groups who are seeking greater influence in police policymaking.[18]

The civil rights revolution, which so changed American life, had not yet begun when Wilson was writing. It had barely gotten underway when he took over in Chicago, yet his response there, in terms of opportunities for black officers and protection of civil rights advocates, was more "in tune with the troubled times" than that of any other law enforcement leader. It was reported in 1965 that the Chicago Police Department was the best-integrated in the nation at that time, with 11% blacks, many in supervisory ranks, compared to 4% in Los Angeles.

Wilson's thoughts on the internal environment of police administration concentrated on three broad areas: organizational theory, personnel administration, and technology. On organizational theory, Wilson was heavily influenced by the military model. In personnel administration, Wilson followed Vollmer's lead in stressing the need to seek intelligent and honest officers, though by today's standards he went overboard in imposing his own strict ethical standards on his men. Wilson defined the limits of police discretion narrowly, as he believed that if departmental policy was restrictive enough, misconduct on the part of patrol officers would be reduced and, in time, eliminated entirely. His reliance on technology is best illustrated by Wilson's reliance on the radio patrol car (with abandonment of the beat patrolman), a new radio system in Chicago, and the newest computer methods of record-keeping.[19]

Another academic, Lawrence W. Sherman, commented in 1974 that *Police Administration* had:

> become the source of much police change as the bible of 'professionalism'. ... Wilson's book stressed efficiency, hierarchy, and bureaucratic regularity as the key to police reform.... While academics ignored the police for the rest of the decade ... the Wilson-inspired trend in police reform was to abolish footbeats and motorize patrols, close station houses, and centralize both radio dispatching and command decisionmaking.[20]

COOPERATION

And this was what Wilson did in Chicago. He abolished foot beats and increased motorized patrols. He closed station houses and centralized both radio dispatching and command decision-making. When Chicago Mayor Richard Daley, last of the big city political "bosses," appointed O. W. Wilson to be Superintendent of Police in "his" city in 1960, Wilson knew that one of his problems in Chicago would be to deal with organized crime. According to an interview with a former Berkeley, California, chief, Wilson tried to contact J. Edgar Hoover, whom Wilson had not been able to talk to for years, to enlist the FBI's support in the investigation of the "mob." But according to Wilson's biographer, the "viciously dysfunctional ... professional feud" between Hoover and Wilson could not be breached. Bopp devotes a whole chapter of his 1984 work, *Crises in Police Administration,* to this feud.[21]

Three days after Wilson's Chicago appointment, however, the FBI prepared a three-page memorandum for Hoover on Wilson's background, which revealed the beginning of Hoover's antipathy for Wilson: "Wilson toured the Bureau in May, 1937, and evidenced a very cold attitude and was obviously extremely jealous of the Bureau's equipment and efficient personnel." At the same time, the memo continued, an FBI inspector:

> reported in his travels throughout the country he heard indefinite rumors that Wilson was jealous of the Bureau and not particularly friendly. This was evident later that year when Wilson planned [a] police training school and requested Bureau instructors. His request was declined and we subsequently learned Wilson complained that the Bureau was not cooperating with him and that he was going to take the matter to the floor of the next IACP Convention. Wilson was unsuccessful in presenting his complaint to the IACP.[22]

Clyde Tolson, Hoover's Associate Director, wrote on the 1960 memo that "SAC [Special Agent in Charge], Chicago, should be told to give Wilson cold treatment." Hoover noted, "Right."[23]

Wilson's discomfort with strangers, the product of his shy personality, was noted by his biographer.[24] It apparently clashed with the personality of the young clerical employee, working as a messenger for the FBI, who took Wilson on the 1937 tour. The messenger's own personality was later judged lacking; he never became an FBI Agent as other tour leaders did at that time. But Hoover's perception of Wilson as jealous never changed, although based on the opinion not of an Agent but of a messenger. Proud of the FBI, Hoover even in 1937 could not abide criticism of the organization he had built. He even denied Wilson access to the FBI's professional journal for police, the *FBI Law Enforcement Bulletin*, despite Wilson's repeated requests for a subscription.[25]

"The most effective weapon against crime is cooperation. . . . J. Edgar Hoover," reads the quotation on the courtyard wall of FBI Headquarters, the J. Edgar Hoover FBI Building in Washington, D.C. A pamphlet on FBI jurisdiction published by the FBI, originally put out when Hoover was Director, is titled "Cooperation: The Backbone of Effective Law Enforcement." Especially in Hoover's later years, this cooperation had to be on Hoover's terms, perceived most often as leadership of law enforcement agencies on a completely honest basis and recognizing Hoover's view of the FBI's leadership role in law enforcement. Hoover's cooperation did not extend to those prominent law enforcement leaders that

Hoover perceived as threats to his own pre-eminence in law enforcement because they criticized or conflicted with Hoover's FBI.

There *is* competition among law enforcement agencies, just as there is within the military community or any group of similar businesses. This competition can be stimulating to each agency to perform at maximum effectiveness; some larger law enforcement agencies strive to be better than the FBI, in view of the FBI's reputation for effectiveness and professionalism, and some take pride in cooperation with the FBI. Whether this competition or cooperation advances the cause of professionalism depends on a number of factors, as Bopp points out:

> Police Administration is a field which seems to attract into executive positions aggressive, highly competitive men, whose longevity at the top often depends on their ability to assume a crime fighter's mantle. In a professional community as small as law enforcement, populated as it is by such men, in-house conflict will arise naturally, as an inevitable conflict of leadership. Indeed, some rivalries may even be desirable if they lead to a creative, resourceful brand of one-upmanship. Contrari-wise, some professional feuds are not only undesirable, they are dysfunctional and counter-productive, especially if they are grounded on petty jealousy, and pursued as a vendetta with all the attendant blood-letting, viciousness and treachery. Such was the nature of Hoover vs. Wilson.[26]

In fairness to Hoover, however, it should be noted that Bopp does not make a case for any treachery in the relationship between Wilson and Hoover on the part of either leader. Hoover did have other vendettas against chief executives of police departments in other large cities at this time: Patrick Murphy, New York City Police Commissioner; William Parker, Chief of Police in Los Angeles, and even Quinn Tamm, the Executive Director of the IACP, who had been an Assistant Director under Hoover until his retirement from the FBI. Although Hoover had written to Tamm on his retirement that "very few men have served the Bureau and the overall interests of law enforcement with the devotion and the talent that have characterized your efforts," Hoover soon described Tamm as an "empire builder," but did not "believe in a public brawl because this sort of thing hurts law enforcement."[27]

Although Tamm was an FBI executive, he cannot be considered Hoover's protege in the sense that O. W. Wilson was Vollmer's. Tamm, a geologist from the University of Virginia, had come into the FBI in 1934 on the recommendation of his older brother, E. A. Tamm, a former assistant to Hoover, later a federal judge. Appointed a Special Agent assigned to the FBI Laboratory in 1936, two years later Quinn Tamm was put in charge of the Identification Division where he served until 1954. There he began the Identification Division's Disaster Squad (see Chapter 17). Tamm became Assistant Director of the Laboratory Division in 1954 and served in the same capacity in the Identification Division and in the Training and Inspection Division, where he had close contact with the IACP. Retiring in 1961, he accepted the position of director of the Field Services Division of the IACP, "a division which he was instrumental in having the IACP establish."[28]

An illness on the part of the then Executive Director of the IACP, Leroy E. Wike, moved Tamm up to that position in which he served for 14 years. This was the basis for initial friction between Tamm and Hoover; Tamm believed that the FBI had opposed him in this move.[29] Tamm's obituary in the *Police Chief* summed up his career with the IACP:

> Mr. Tamm was truly one of the giants of the law enforcement community, steering the IACP and its member chief executives through the turbulent 1960s and early '70s.... During Mr. Tamm's tenure, the IACP grew from a limited service organization with 4,500 members to an internationally recognized professional association of 10,500. A staff of 18 in 1961 expanded to 135, and the Association's annual budget had increased ten-fold by the time of his retirement. If any individual was responsible for IACP's ascension to its current stature as the preeminent police association in the world, it was Quinn Tamm.[30]

Hoover had had a close relationship with the IACP since 1925, when the FBI had taken over the IACP's fingerprint files. By then the presidency of the IACP rotated on an annual basis and Hoover had no trouble in later years in dominating the IACP because of his longevity and position. But Tamm enlarged the IACP staff, and Hoover believed he was taking authority away from the elected president of the organization. In 1965, a memorandum summarizing the relationship of the IACP to the FBI was prepared by Hoover's Assistant Director for training, a position Tamm had once held. In spite of the assistant director's recommendation that:

> There must be a distinction made between Tamm, IACP staff and its officers if we are to be successful in guiding the activities of this organization," Hoover noted, "Tamm is now the IACP & in view of his hostility I do not intend to placate him.[31]

Tamm, like Hoover, reflected the FBI's view of law enforcement professionalism as being grounded in the law. At the end of the last chapter

Tamm was quoted as saying officers "will not be real officers" until they are convinced "that everything they do must be done in a reasonable and constitutional manner. This is the true mark of the professional officer." Since at least 1937, Hoover had published in the *FBI Law Enforcement Bulletin* the "FBI Pledge for Law Enforcement Officers" which FBI Agents signed. This pledge sets out Hoover's philosophy on law enforcement professionalism:

> ... I shall always consider the high calling of law enforcement to be an honorable profession, the duties of which are recognized by me as both an art and a science. I recognize fully my responsibilities to defend the right, to protect the weak, ... and to uphold the law in public duty and private living. ... To the responsibilities ... of seeking to prevent crime, of finding the facts of law violations and of apprehending fugitives and criminals ... I shall always be equally alert in striving to acquit the innocent and to convict the guilty.[32]

Hoover basically had a legalistic view of law enforcement. For policing overall, he had a perhaps surprising devotion to Constitutional rights; the FBI, for example, gave the Miranda warning long before the Supreme Court's decision in that case. Hoover also reflected Vollmer's views on juvenile delinquency with his advocacy of police athletic clubs for juveniles and other "social work" approaches to this problem in the 1950s. Hoover also believed in efficiency for police agencies; he had built the FBI's reputation, in part, on efficiency. But Hoover's reactions to the disorders of the late 1960s was a law and order approach—training police in the handling of riots—in part because of Hoover's preoccupation with the possibility of communist influence on civil rights leaders.

J. Edgar Hoover's contributions to police professionalism in the efficiency era reflect the complexities of his personality. While he had the legalistic style, it had a few of the elements of the social work style of policing. But Hoover could not cooperate with a powerful executive director of the primary police organization in this country, nor could he with police executives in the Nation's largest cities, for fear one of them might replace him at the FBI. At this time, of course, Hoover and his FBI were mainly interested in this country's internal security, so the progress of police professionalism was left to others, such as O. W. Wilson. Writing about this period in the history of policing in 1975 for the *Journal of Police Science and Administration,* Nathan Douthit said:

> ... the primary emphasis of police professionals centered on ideas for the improvement of the efficiency of police department. ...[33]

Notes to Chapter 15

1. Bopp, 1977. 4–5, 72.
2. Vollmer, 1919.
3. Douthit, 1975. 339.
4. Ibid.
5. Hoover, 1936a.
6. Carte, 1976. 285.
7. Eldefonso, 1982. 303.
8. Bopp, 1977. 37–49.
9. Farris, 1982. 31–32.
10. Hoover, 1936b. 7.
11. Douthit, 1975. 341.
12. Wilson, 1941. 6.
13. Bopp, 1977. 72.
14. Ibid, 72–73.
15. Gazell, 1974. 365. Carte, 1976. 292. Bopp, 1977. 75.
16. Wilson, 1972. 3–5.
17. Gazell, 1974. 371.
18. Carte, 1976. 294.
19. Gazell, 1974. 366–369. Bopp, 1977. 107.
20. Sherman, 1974. 256.
21. Bopp, 1984. 106.
22. Jones, 1960.
23. Ibid.
24. Bopp, 1977. 18.
25. Jones, 1960.
26. Bopp, 1984. 114–115.
27. FBI LEB, 1961. 10. Casper, 1966. 8.
28. FBI LEB, 1961. 10.
29. Jones, 1972.
30. IACP, 1986. 10.
31. Casper, 1964.
32. FBI LEB, 1937.
33. Douthit, 1975. 345.

Chapter 16

THE CALIFORNIA STYLE OF POLICING

O. W. Wilson's style of efficiency in policing, with its military mode of management, was exemplified in California, where Wilson taught. Professionalism had taken hold in California under the early leadership of August Vollmer, especially in the area of police education. William H. Parker, Chief of the Los Angeles Police Department for sixteen years from 1950 to 1966, became the acknowledged leader of the "California-style" of municipal law enforcement. Parker had served as a captain in military government under Colonel Wilson in World War II.

Americans' view of California-style policing was partially due to the new medium of television, particularly the influence of Jack Webb's "Dragnet" program, based on the Los Angeles Police Department. The first popular television police series of the 1950s, Dragnet's trademark was Sgt. Friday's (Webb's) "Just the facts, Ma'am," which symbolized the de-personalization that became known colloquially in police circles as "stranger policing." This was a formal management philosophy that embodied a "properly distant posture between patrol officers and citizens."[1]

Policing had become less corrupt and less lawless by World War II. "Good government" reformers had fostered professionalism in municipal government overall and had wrested control of many cities from political machines. This movement toward professionalism in municipal government began with police departments, many of which became almost autonomous after World War II. Control by the chief had been increased; both internal control of the department and the chief's ability to resist outside political influences had been strengthened. Departments were being re-organized along functional, as opposed to territorial, lines, diminishing the power of the precinct captains and the ward bosses.

As one police historian explained:

Dedicated administrators replaced venal politicians as the new bosses in policing. They made important improvements in the recruitment, training, and management of their officers.... Efficient, uniform law enforcement suited the needs and attitudes of a predominantly middle-class suburban society.[2]

Responsibilities were being transferred away from patrolmen to special squads, especially enforcement of vice laws. "Policing the police" became the formal responsibility of internal affairs divisions, rather than the informal task of crime commissions. Prohibitions against "non-professional" conduct, such as outside employment, political and union activities, were popular among the professional police administrators. Increased educational standards for recruits, increased training, and higher salaries also fostered the professional image. Another police historian noted that "as a result self-policing became the norm virtually everywhere in urban America."[3]

As a result of this autonomy, there was freedom to develop new theories on dealing with crime and order maintenance by police leaders without control by, or even consultation with, political forces. One new theory was that police could not prevent crime—they could only "deter criminal activity," by preventive patrol which became the chief crime control weapon of these new "efficient" police agencies. Eventually it was found that preventive patrol only relocates criminal activity to less policed areas or jurisdictions, if even that. But even more significant, when preventive patrol was applied in an aggressive manner in ghetto areas, it resulted in the police being viewed by the ghetto community as an "army of occupation."[4]

As the Report of the National Advisory Commission on Civil Disorders (the Kerner Commission) noted, among the basic causes of the rioting in the 1960s was the fact that the police had come "to symbolize white power, white racism, and white repression." Specifically, this report singled out "aggressive preventive patrol" and motor patrol as two of the symbols of police repression in black ghetto areas.[5]

THE LOS ANGELES POLICE

August Vollmer was invited to be Chief of Police in Los Angeles by civic leaders in 1923; he gave up in frustration after one year. Many of Vollmer's recommendations for changes in the Los Angeles force were not adopted for twenty years because of political opposition, but a 1949 study found that Vollmer's recommendations had all been adopted by that year. In 1950, after a scandal, William H. Parker became chief of police, having worked his way up from the ranks since 1927. He held that post until his death in 1966, the longest serving chief in Los Angeles until that time.[6]

William H. Parker, born in Lead, South Dakota, in 1902, was the grandson of a lawyer, who had been a leader in driving the lawless out of the Black Hills area of that state. Young Parker's first job was that of hotel detective and janitor in Deadwood and, like J. Edgar Hoover, he was a successful debater in high school. The Parker family moved to Los Angeles in the 1920s; Parker enrolled at the Los Angeles College of Law in 1926 and received an appointment as a patrolman with the Los Angeles Police Department in 1927. Three years later he received his law degree, but remained with the police department for 39 years, except for service during the war. During World War II, Parker served as a captain in the military government branch of the army, specializing in police administration under Colonel O. W. Wilson. After his military service, he returned to the police department and, as assistant chief, he developed and commanded the Bureau of Internal Affairs.[7]

One means of strengthening the police chief, which was adopted under Parker in Los Angeles, was reducing the chief's span of control to a more manageable number of officials who reported to him. Originally advocated by Vollmer, the limited span of control concept had been developed for corporate use. In policing, this concept was then advanced by police pioneers Bruce Smith and O. W. Wilson. The reformers argued that this would untangle involved chains of command; under this scheme, police commissioners or chiefs reduced the number of officials who reported to them, for example, from nineteen to eight in New York City. This change emphasized an hierarchical view of big city policing rather than a collegial view, which was in line with the military chain of command. This, of course, contradicted the position that police officers at the lowest ranks were professionals, another diversion from Vollmer's concepts.[8]

Parker's innovations for the Los Angeles Police Department were administrative: Parker simplified the command structure by lessening his span of control; he freed men for patrol duty (preventive patrol was becoming *the* answer to deterring crime) by getting the sheriff's department to guard prisoners and the California Highway Patrol to take over freeway traffic enforcement. He formed the Bureau of Internal Affairs to investigate police misconduct; developed a procedure to separate police discipline from partisan politics; created an administrative bureau which included intelligence and planning divisions; established an intensive community relations program; and enacted a strict firearms use policy that included internal review of all firearms discharges.[9]

Parker stood for "effective, efficient and professional law enforcement," according to a speech of his in 1962, in which he decried the "appalling lack of demonstrated organized support" for this type of policing. To accomplish the goal of professionalism, Parker called for the raising of police standards, advanced formal education for police, the removal of improper political control of police agencies, and "continued community-wide support and recognition of police performance and accomplishment."[10]

The new generation of reformers, O. W. Wilson and William Parker, police executives themselves, favored replacement of two-man patrol cars with one-man cars. They argued that one-man cars would not only save money by making more effective use of available manpower, but would also ensure wider coverage and quicker response time. But patrolmen's groups opposed this, arguing that by forcing officers to drive and patrol at the same time reduced efficiency and increased hazards of policing. The rank-and-file groups forced postponement of adoption of one-man cars in Boston and New York City for a time, but police executives favoring one-man cars eventually won. The practice of one-man patrol cars increased between 1947 and 1964 to 16 out of 20 large cities, and even more in medium-sized cities. Among those adopting one-man patrol cars were Parker in Los Angeles in the early 1950s and Wilson in Chicago in the next decade.[11]

> In many respects, Parker was the J. Edgar Hoover of municipal policing. He adopted Hoover's ruthlessly authoritarian administrative style and mastered the art of public relations."[12]

Hoover had little interest in patrol strategies, having no experience in municipal policing, so he couldn't fault Parker on one-man patrol cars or preventive patrol. But Parker had made such significant contributions to police administration, in a department that in the past had been widely viewed as one of the most corrupt in the country, that he became a rumored contender for J. Edgar Hoover's directorship of the FBI. This was something the FBI Director couldn't, or wouldn't, ignore because by this time the FBI had become Hoover's life and he had determined never to step down if he could avoid it. In 1955, the Los Angeles office of the FBI reported the rumor that Parker might replace Hoover when the latter retired.[13] This prompted Bureau executives, who spent an inordinate amount time catering to Hoover then, to examine Parker's criticism of the FBI and its Director more closely. A memorandum prepared by the Bureau's Crime Records Division noted Parker's "agitation" for a national clearinghouse to gather information on organized crime and his criticism of the International Association of Chiefs of Police (IACP) for awarding Hoover a plaque in 1953. More important was Parker's criticism of FBI civil rights investigations; while the FBI had civil rights jurisdiction which covered police brutality against citizens, Parker felt that his own Bureau of Internal Affairs should be allowed to handle all complaints against the Los Angeles police. After Parker's criticism of the FBI's civil rights investigations against the Los Angeles police, Hoover noted that he had "no use for this fellow Parker and we should keep our guard up in all dealings with him."[14]

Another memorandum from the then assistant director of the FBI's training division criticized Parker's 1955 speech on the exclusionary rule at an IACP meeting, noting:

> his principal complaint was that the courts are throwing out cases in California because of certain activities taken by police officers . . . What Parker actually is advocating (perhaps unknowingly) is that the so-called 'police state' be established; that police be above the law; that the end justifies the means.[15]

This kind of reportage was calculated to infuriate Hoover, who believed in the supremacy of the law. Parker never did achieve the professional, national stature he sought through leadership of the International Association of Chiefs of Police (IACP); his way was blocked again and again by fellow chiefs. Although he blamed the FBI for his defeat in the IACP, there is no evidence in FBI files to support Parker's claim. And, of course, Parker never replaced Hoover; the political genius was at the helm of the FBI until his death.

Most significant to the Los Angeles police and to departments around the country, Chief William H. Parker "made rigorous personnel selection and training a major characteristic of the L.A.P.D." Less than 10% of the applicants who passed the Civil Service exam were selected for appointment, after higher standards for scholastic achievement, physical fitness, intelligence, and a psychiatric exam were enforced. Then, the recruits attended a thirteen-week training program which emphasized rigid discipline:

Parker thus molded an image of a tough, competent, polite, and effective officer by controlling recruitment. During the 1950s this image had made the L.A.P.D. the model for reform across the nation.[16]

This was a continuation of the professionalism process that had begun in California years before, and was marked by progress in education for police. By the end of the 1950s, some 43 California colleges had police science programs, of which 35 were low-cost junior colleges. Over three quarters of the nation's two-year law enforcement programs were in California, which raised the educational level of municipal officers significantly.[17] One author noted that the Peace Officer's Association of California, organized in 1921, was "primarily responsible for the police developments in the State . . . " and that the California Plan for Peace Officer Training, established in 1936, made available through the State Department of Education a comprehensive in-service training program. By 1964, some 50 colleges had programs in police science or administration.[18]

THE LEGALISTIC STYLE

In 1968, Harvard political scientist James Q. Wilson produced a thought-provoking analysis of police department styles, in which he characterized the three broad types of policing that he saw then in existence: watchman style, legalistic style, and service style. These, of course, were not mutually exclusive, and each department studied had elements of each, but could be generally characterized as being mainly of one style. The first, watchman type, deals with "non-serious" crime "as if order maintenance rather then law enforcement" was the department's principal function. The administrator influences the department to ignore minor violations, especially traffic, juvenile, vice, and gambling so as:

> . . . to use the law more as a means of maintaining order than of regulating conduct, and to judge the requirements of order differently depending on the character of the group in which the infraction occurs.[19]

Another type of policing that Wilson defines is the "service style," where:

> . . . the police take seriously all requests for either law enforcement or order maintenance. . . . but are less likely to respond by making an arrest or otherwise imposing formal sanctions (unlike police with a legalistic style).[20]

The next type, which Wilson called the legalistic style, marked the Los Angeles police under Chief Parker, a career police officer who had obtained a law degree when he began policing. As Professor Wilson defined this type of policing:

> The police will act, on the whole, as if there were a single standard of community conduct — that which the law prescribes — rather that different standards for juveniles, Negroes, drunks, and the like. Indeed, because such persons are more likely than certain others to commit crimes, the law will fall heavily on them and be experienced as "harassment."[21]

Legalistic style policing is, of course, a political scientist's definition of one broad style of policing, but it also also came to include, under Parker and Wilson, aggressive, preventive patrol activity, which implies enforcement of a single standard of community conduct. This is the type of patrol that characterized the Los Angeles police, performed by middle-class, mainly white, patrol officers who were recent veterans of the armed forces, as three-fourths of the Los Angeles officers were in 1953.[22]

New York City Police Commissioner Patrick Murphy, where police had dealt with minority immigrants for many years, described "stranger" policing as:

> ... not so much a community police service as the occupation of conquered territory by an alien army. Under stranger policing, for instance, it is permissable for officers to hide in their radio cars with windows rolled up, communicating not with the community but only with each other, the dispatchers at headquarters, and their own private thoughts. In this "philosophy" of policing, the community — the law *abiders* — hardly get a wave from a passing car. I remember once, many years removed from being a beat cop, meeting with Mayor Tom Bradley of Los Angeles in his office. Others in the room included some of the top brass of the L.A.P.D. Bradley, a former L.A.P.D. lieutenant, had just returned from a trip to New York and had noticed, he was telling us, how friendly New York cops seemed to be, at least by comparison to the aloof, Kaiser-like L.A. police. "Do you think," he asked with the police brass in the room, with a twinkle in his eye, "that at the academy we could begin to teach our police officers how to smile?" [Emphasis in original.][23]

Police professionalism in this era, indeed local government as a whole, operated on three basic assumptions. First, that public service was not a means to encourage social mobility. Municipal government, especially the police, was supposed to provide the best possible service at the lowest possible cost. Service came to be defined as answering citizen complaints by radio-dispatched patrol cars, rather than crime control or order maintenance. Second, local control was not a source of political legitimacy. No matter how great a majority at the polls, the winning party had no right to interfere in department affairs. And, third, "immigrant life-styles were not an expression of American culture." The great middle class of the American public came to include among immigrants the later residents of urban ghettos, black Americans.

Thus, the police imposed a conventional morality on newcomers, in effect enforcing the mythic idea of the melting pot. Other municipal agencies—fire departments, schools, public works, transit, welfare, even sanitation—also enjoyed freedom from legislative, executive, and judicial oversight as a result of municipal professionalization. These agencies aroused less animosity than police as they imposed middle-class, conventional morality, although police historian Fogelson concluded "it is hard to see why." Perhaps, because police are the most visible, in terms of 24-hour availability, uniforms, and only they have the power, and means, to arrest, of all the municipal authorities.[24]

Advances in professionalism such as higher educational requirements, recruit testing, and background investigations, plus loosening of residency requirements to secure a larger applicant pool, also worked to the disadvantage of new minority groups. These minorities were, in effect, the latter-day immigrants in American larger cities. The new basic assumptions of big-city policing, that municipal government as a whole, and policing in particular, were not agents of social mobility, as they had been before the turn of the century, and immigrant (or different) life-styles were not to be tolerated, caused the new urban "immigrant" population to view the police in a different way than the earlier Irish or German immigrants had. Over the years, the Irish and the Germans had made many police departments their own, but new immigrants, faced with professionalism requirements, could not do this, as yet.

By the 1950s, police reformers, and a large majority of the American people, believed that police effectiveness "was essentially a function of their capacity to prevent criminal activity. . . . " O. W. Wilson and Chief Parker developed a theory of crime prevention that argued, in effect, that police could not alleviate the social problems that were believed, at that time, to cause crime, such as poverty and prejudice, but could deal with "effects" of crime, as Parker described them. The police:

> . . . could contain but not convert criminals, repress but not prevent crime. As the so-called 'thin blue line' that separated the lawless from

the law abiding, the police could deter criminal activity by increasing the likelihood of intervention, apprehension, and punishment.[25]

Especially in California, police departments adopted this theory of crime prevention developed by Wilson and Parker: reducing the opportunities to commit crime by preventive patrol. This patrol had to be aggressive, embodying tactics such as "field interrogations," which worked in middle-class, white communities, but caused problems in the black and Chicano ghettoes. There young people spent much of their time on the streets, especially those out of work. How could patrol officers who did not know black or Chicano life styles, since they did not know these minorities personally, distinguish between law-abiding blacks and Chicanos and those who were criminals? How could officers determine which of the many young men who hung out on the streets to stop for field interrogation and search? The field interrogation in the ghetto challenged the life style of many ghetto residents. Thus:

> ... the tactic of preventive patrol, even if employed in a dispassionate way, also tended to discriminate against the blacks, Mexicans, and Puerto Ricans.[26]

In the 1960s, police were the victims of the professionalism advanced by their leaders—J. Edgar Hoover, O. W. Wilson and Chief William H. Parker, et al—who had preached professional law enforcement as the goal of police, rather than order maintenance. And these leaders had advocated professional law enforcement from the new, suburbanite mindset of middle-class values. With this new orientation, minimizing order maintenance, police had forgotten the underlying violent nature of America, reflected in the disorders that police in America had been created to control. The violent reaction against civil rights workers in the South should have alerted police officials, and the American public, to society's powder keg that the police were sitting on. But the public, even academics, and police officials did not foresee what was coming and the Los Angeles ghetto, Watts, boiled over in 1965 with a rapidity and violence that terrified police and public alike.

RIOTING—AGAIN

The 1960s, as in other periods in America's history, brought large scale urban rioting; there were 43 riots or large-scale disturbances in 1966 alone. In response to black America's perception of despair over their lack of civil rights and, overall, their position in American life, black

Americans in the ghettos fought back with urban violence. The National Advisory Commission on Civil Disorders (the Kerner Commission), created by President Lyndon Johnson in the summer of 1967, reported as its basic conclusion that the "nation is moving toward two societies, one black, one white—separate and unequal." For law enforcement, the problem focused on how to police the ghettos:

> What white Americans have never fully understood—but what the Negro can never forget—is that white society is deeply implicated in the ghetto. White institutions created it, white institutions maintain it [including the police], and white society condones it.[27]

All of America's big cities were eventually affected, but two cities, Los Angeles and Chicago, had riots in their ghettos in 1965 that underscored the failures of "efficient" policing. Author Joseph Wambaugh, a Los Angeles police sergeant at the time, devoted more than 40 pages to the Los Angeles riot in his first novel, telling how the disorder affected police:

> "Good thing they're too ... dumb to make fire bombs out of wine bottles," said [patrol officer] Silverson and Gus [another officer] cringed as a rock skidded over the already dented deck lid and slammed against the already cracked rear window. A glass fragment struck the Negro policeman whose name Gus had already forgotten, or perhaps it was buried there among the ruins of his rational mind which had been annihilated by terror.... "Friday the thirteenth," muttered Silverson, slowing down now that they had run the gauntlet on Eightysixth Street where a mob of fifty young Negroes appeared from nowhere and a cocktail had bounced off the door but failed to burst.[28]

The Kerner Commission report described the orgy of violence that long, hot summer as "the worst since the Detroit riot of 1943." In four days, and nights, 34 persons were killed, 864 injured, 4,000 were arrested, and over $35 million worth of property was destroyed or damaged.[29] *Time* magazine cataloged the hysterical crazy quilt of calls on the police radio during the riot:

> Manchester and Broadway, a mob of 1,000 ... Shots at Avalon and Imperial ... Vernon and Central, looting ... Yellow cab overturned ... Man pulled from car on Imperial Highway ... 88th and Broadway, gun battle ... Officer in trouble.[30]

Only on the third day of the riot did the Mayor approve Chief Parker's request, made the previous day, to call out the California National Guard. By Friday, 2,000 guardsmen rolled into the riot zone in convoys led by jeeps mounting machine guns. By Sunday night, there were 10,000 troops in the city, including an 840-man Marine Reserve unit equipped with 40,000 rounds of ammunition ordered in by the Pentagon.

The Los Angeles riot had been touched off by the arrest of a Watts resident for drunken driving by a California Highway Patrol team, another "efficient" agency noted for California-style policing. The next week saw a riot begin in Chicago when a speeding hook and ladder fire truck, answering a false alarm in a ghetto area, struck and killed a black woman. Only a month before, the particular fire company had been picketed by a militant civil rights group demanding that the all-white fire company hire blacks. O. W. Wilson's Chicago Police Department, in spite of being more heavily integrated than the Los Angeles police, also relied on preventive patrol to deter crime to the neglect of order mainte-nance and could not cope with the racial disorder. Chicago also had to request National Guard troops. There was another, more serious, riot in Chicago the next year.[31]

The federal government ordered the army and the FBI, through its National Academy, to institute riot control training for municipal police. In 1977, one police historian described California policing as:

A highly trained, well-educated, and higher-paid class of policemen that made good use of advanced technology and management tech-niques.... The public and government had committed themselves to the idea of honest, efficient, and professional law enforcement, free from the domineering influence of corrupt politicians.[32]

Other police administrators and academic students of policing who saw the handwriting, or grafitti, on the ghetto walls, judged that it was time to re-examine the tactic of aggressive preventive patrol, and the strategy of California-style policing. The Kerner Commission had ana-lyzed police conduct and patrol practices historically, noting that in an earlier era the third-degree, arrests on suspicion, and "justice" dispensed from a nightstick were common. But the 1960s riots "took place in cities whose police are among the best led, best organized, best trained and most professional in the country." Yet, some of the patrol practices of the "most professional police departments may heighten tension and enhance the potential for civil disorder."

The commission was not attacking police professionalism per se, only the practice of aggressive preventive patrol aimed at Negroes, especially Negro youth living in ghettos, either by roving task forces (as in O. W.

Wilson's Chicago Police Department) or the entire patrol force, "expected to participate and to file a minimum number of 'stop-and-frisk' or field interrogation reports . . . " (as in Parker's Los Angeles Police Department). The Kerner report also criticized the "motorization of police" as affecting law enforcement in the ghetto:

> The patrolman comes to see the city through a windshield and hear about it over a police radio. To him, the area increasingly comes to consist only of lawbreakers. To the ghetto resident, the policeman comes increasingly to be only an enforcer.
>
> Loss of contact between the police officer and the community he serves adversely affects law enforcement. If an officer has never met, does not know and cannot understand the language and habits of the people in the area he patrols, he cannot do an effective police job. His ability to detect truly suspicious behavior is impaired. He deprives himself of important sources of information. He fails to know those persons with an "equity" in the community—home-owners, small businessmen, professional men, persons who are anxious to support proper law enforcement—and thus sacrifices the contributions they can make to maintaining community order.[33]

Police historian Samuel Walker summarized and critiqued Chief William H. Parker's military orientation for policing and patrol policies:

> Parker immediately proceeded to clean house by establishing the most authoritarian and militaristic administration in the country. . . . The military ethos of professionalism in Los Angeles served two purposes. First, it gave officers a clearly defined sense of purpose: that they were engaged in an unending "war on crime." Second, it supported the rigid internal discipline. Even the department's harshest critics admitted that Parker had eliminated corruption.[34]

Even O. W. Wilson could not shape the Chicago Police Department as completely as Parker had in Los Angeles; in 1960, Wilson did not have a pool of World War II veterans from which to chose recruits. Nor did he have broad public support for his new "efficient" department, or the commitment to "good government" that pervaded California. But to continue Walker's critique:

> Parker's accomplishments, however, illustrated the hazards of the new style of police professionalism. While it uprooted corruption and instilled the department with a sense of mission, the militaristic approach aggravated relations with some segments of the community. The major- ity of the public, the white middle and upper classes, were highly impressed by Parker's reforms (and he carefully cultivated their sup- port through sophisticated public relations). The lower classes, and

particularly members of the growing black and Chicano ghettos in Los Angeles, found themselves the targets of the "war on crime." The department developed the technique of aggressive preventive patrol, designed to stop, question, and frisk large numbers of suspicious persons. Minorities came to view this as systematic harassment. Los Angeles police officers, meanwhile, developed a shorthand for "suspicious" persons which inevitably emphasized young blacks as potential criminals. ... leaders in the black community voiced criticisms of the police department. Parker's "war on crime" ideology, however, had a built-in defense mechanism. The police represented the "thin blue line" between civilization and savagery. ... [35]

In the 1950s' McCarthy era, when militant anticommunism was popular among the great majority of Americans, Parker, like J. Edgar Hoover, attacked critics as communists or those who unwittingly, perhaps, served the purposes of international communism. Walker continues:

> The military style of police professionalism aggravated race relations. It increased tension-filled contacts between police and minorities.... Thus, the accomplishments of police reform through the 1950s set the stage for the police-community-relations crisis of the 1960s.[36]

The Kerner Commission and Fogelson label the police tactic of preventive patrol as the culprit in the police-community-relations crisis of the 1960s. Walker adds to preventive patrol the Los Angeles "militaristic" approach, but these two elements of the 1950s policy that Chief Parker and O. W. Wilson thought would "deter" crime were products of their times. They were eventually discarded—at the point of a hurled Molotov cocktail.

Notes to Chapter 16

1. Murphy, 1977, 39.
2. Johnson, 1981, 197.
3. Fogelson, 1977, 184.
4. Ibid, 189, 240, 259.
5. National Advisory Commission on Civil Disorders, 1970, 5.
6. Carte, 1975, 126. Eldefonso, 1974, 78. Johnson, 1981, 120.
7. Eldefonso, 1982, 307–308.
8. Fogelson, 1977, 179–180.
9. Bopp, 1972, 128. Johnson, 1981, 120.
10. Parker, 1962, 7, 14.
11. Fogelson, 1977, 186.
12. Walker, 1980, 211.

13. Los Angeles, 1955.
14. Jones, 1960a.
15. Mason, 1955.
16. Johnson, 1981, 121.
17. Bopp, 1972, 129.
18. Kenny, 1964, x.
19. Wilson, 1968, 140.
20. Ibid, 200.
21. Ibid, 172.
22. Wilson, 1957, 5–7.
23. Murphy, 1977, 39–40.
24. Fogelson, 1977, 262.
25. Ibid, 231, 187.
26. Ibid, 231, 259.
27. Nat'l Advisory Comm. on Civil Disorders, 1968, 1, 21.
28. Wambaugh, 1970, 328.
29. Nat'l Advisory Comm. on Civil Disorders, 1968, 20.
30. *Time*, 1965, 13–18.
31. Ibid.
32. Bopp, 1977, 130.
33. Nat'l Advisory Comm. on Civil Disorders, 1968, 158–160.
34. Walker, 1980, 211.
35. Ibid, 211–212.
36. Ibid.

Chapter 17

GROWTH OF FBI SERVICE ROLE

After the introduction of fingerprinting, and its acceptance as an identification system superior to Bertillon's anthropometrical method of body measurements, the police community, as represented by the International Association of Chiefs of Police (IACP), urged establishment of a central bureau of identification in the United States. Raymond Fosdick, in his pioneering 1920 work *American Police Systems,* also called for such a national system. The result was, finally, as set out in Chapter 5, the Bureau of Investigation's Division of Identification and Information. This development prompted the European author of *The Century of the Detective* to note, in some awe, that:

> There came into being an identification service of vast proportions which functioned with a precision European observers of American police developments would have thought unattainable. The United States became the greatest arena for experimentation in dactyloscopy (fingerprinting)—in that arena the method received the kind of confirmation which the pioneers in the field could not have hoped for in their boldest dreams.[1]

The development of the National Crime Information Center (NCIC) added the information dimension, through computerization, to the search for wanted persons, stolen property and automobiles, missing persons, and, finally, to the whole criminal record process through the Interstate Identification Index. This last was a synthesis between identification based on fingerprints and the latest development in technology: the ability of the computer to digest and manipulate huge amounts of data instantaneously.

NATIONWIDE FINGERPRINT IDENTIFICATION

The Bureau of Investigation's Identification Division, first known as the National Division of Identification and Information, began on July 1, 1924, with the consolidation of two fingerprint collections: those main-

239

tained by the IACP in its Bureau of Identification and those in the Leavenworth Penitentiary collected by the Department of Justice. Until that year, there was no one central repository for fingerprint records in the United States. Some cities had their own fingerprint bureaus— St. Louis was the first, in 1904—but there was little exchange of records between jurisdictions.[2]

The Bureau of Criminal Identification was located in the building of the U.S. Penitentiary at Leavenworth, Kansas. It employed 40 people, some of them inmates, to handle about 400,000 fingerprint records and just under a hundred thousand Bertillon records sumitted by some 630 law enforcement and penal agencies, including six state bureaus of identification in California, Florida, Iowa, Massachusetts, Ohio, and Washington State.[3] In 1922, C. S. Morill, Superintendent of the California Identification Bureau, told the IACP "that the sooner they do away with the Bureau at Leavenworth, where it is handled by convicts, the better. . . . " The California Identification Bureau had been set up in 1917, at the urging of August Vollmer and his fellow California chiefs, and included not only identification records, but a stolen, lost, and pawned property division. This wasn't matched on the national level until the establishment, in 1967, of the National Crime Information Center (NCIC) by the FBI.[4]

The IACP fingerprint collection was roughly the same size as the Leavenworth accumulation, so that, combined, the two collections totaled 810,188 fingerprint cards and some 200,000 Bertillon files. The Leavenworth fingerprint cards were transferred to the Bureau of Investigation on October 23, 1923, but because of a delay in Congressional authorization and appropriation until July 1 of the next year, there was "some confusion and delay" in setting up the division.[5]

J. Edgar Hoover, the new Director of the Bureau of Investigation, lost no time in putting the two fingerprint files together, and discarded use of the Bertillon records as "practically worthless," in the words of an employee of the new division. In 1927, Hoover extended the services of the new Division of Identification nationwide to "all the correspondents of the Bureau regardless of the population of the city. . . . " The Bureau's annual report for 1929 commended the cooperation of law enforcement agencies, particularly the association of chief executives, the IACP, and showed an increase in fingerprints on record to almost one and a half million in just under five years.[6]

Just over half a century later, in 1986, total fingerprint cards reached 176,930,370 in the FBI collection, of which roughly two-thirds were arrest records and one-third were for government, including military, service. These represented over 56 million people (because many criminals had multiple arrests and even civilians might be represented more than once). From a beginning staff in 1927 of 47 employees, the Identification Division employed 3,600 people to handle this tremendous volume of records in the 1980s.[7]

The potential of fingerprint identification in the investigation of crime was quickly grasped by the criminal justice community; 1,200 regular contributors in 1924 grew to over 7,200 agencies in 1935 and to 62,000 contributors in 1986. As Hoover explained in 1935, this was:

> One of the most easily demonstrable examples of cooperation in this Bureau's Identification Division. More than 7,200 law enforcement agencies in the United States and in 65 foreign countries submit fingerprints of persons under arrest for search in the Bureau's files. Within 36 hours after their receipt, replies to these fingerprints are sent out, and in more than 47% of all cases the Bureau is able to report an identification, indicating that the person had been fingerprinted on at least one previous occasion. This policy, which is now so well established that it is almost mechanical with most departments, is of untold assistance in their work. It brings about the apprehension [should be identification rather than apprehension] of more than 365 fugitives from justice each month. It offers the court a positive record of the subject's previous history in order that his sentence may be fixed.[8]

In 1933, the U.S. Civil Service Commission turned over the fingerprint records of more than 140,000 government employees and applicants and the FBI initiated a Civil Identification Section of the division. This section grew with the addition of armed forces personnel fingerprint records, with 12 million under arms in World War II, plus aliens and civilian employees in the defense industry. A peak was reached in 1943, when over 28 million fingerprint cards were received, an average of over 93,000 records per working day. Hoover and the FBI already had spearheaded a campaign to collect fingerprints for non-criminal use. Publicity about amnesia and accident victims being identified through fingerprints convinced most of the public of the value, and lack of stigma, to being fingerprinted for later identification purposes. For a time, even sightseers visiting FBI Headquarters for the public tour were invited to be fingerprinted, and numerous celebrities, including motion picture stars, were fingerprinted. Civic groups were invited to be fingerprinted, usually by local police. As Hoover told the IACP in 1935:

There is also much work to be done in the field of civil fingerprinting. Already many good citizens of America have evinced interest in the efforts of forward-looking citizens to establish as large a civilian noncriminal file as possible. It is a task of education in which I feel we should join for the good of society—certainly there could be no more interesting program for local civic organizations than a talk by your fingerprint expert upon fingerprinting in general and the advantages of contributing to the civilian file.[10]

Hoover went on to cite the number of people who disappear each year and cannot be identified, thus are committed to institutions. He gave as an example Los Angeles County, which had 100 such victims in 1934, and he cited the number of "unknown" dead in the country who are consigned to potter's fields, claiming that "unknown" is a misnomer because:

> . . . somewhere someone knows them, someone searches for them, some- one loves them. They are unidentified dead, often condemned to pauper burial merely because the marks of their fingers are not upon a pasteboard card. The criminal can be identified; the honest man cannot, thus thousands annually wander about the country afflicted by loss of memory; children disappear and are lost forever . . . [a prelude to the 1980s concern about missing children]. Much of this can be prevented by civil fingerprinting . . . [as the public learned in the 1980s]. Let us point out the benefits to humanity of a central identification bureau where the deposition of fingerprints is the mark of an honest man. Let us show the benefits in business, in safety of travel, in rescue during time of illness or loss of memory. I believe the public will welcome it—and every effort exerted along this line means a lessening in the tremendous task which enforcement agencies must shoulder in the daily hunt for thousands upon thousands of missing persons.[11]

Hoover was helped in this campaign by military use of fingerprints and the advent of World War II with its massive conscription. Huge numbers of fingerprint cards of servicemen were added to the FBI's civil file, as were those of the growing army of defense workers in that war. Public sentiment outweighed the anti-fingerprinting arguments of civil libertarians such as Max Lowenthal, an attorney who authored an attack on Hoover in 1950. Lowenthal objected to the FBI collecting non-criminal fingerprints, which he thought might be used in some way as part of the "police state" he believed Hoover wanted to implement. Lowenthal quoted Hoover when he told Congress that he, Hoover, had "never advocated compulsory fingerprinting on a national basis." Some did advocate compulsory fingerprinting, but Hoover better understood the public's sentiment that tolerated voluntary collection of fingerprints, but not the regimentation that would be required in compulsory finger-printing. Also, Hoover and the FBI used the civil fingerprint files for the humanitarian purposes only, not any ulterior purpose.

On January 31, 1949, the FBI's Identification Division recorded its 100 millionth fingerprint card, that of young movie star Margaret O'Brien. Then, in 1979, a Special Agent assigned to the Technical Section of this division, recorded the 200 millionth card, that of baseball star Stan Musial. The civil fingerprinting campaign also helped prove its humani-tarian value by the formation of the FBI Disaster Squad in the division's Latent Fingerprint Section just before World War II.[12]

LATENT FINGERPRINTS

The two primary uses of fingerprints, (1) positive identification of individuals, and (2) identification and prosecution of perpetrators of crimes by fingerprints left at the scene, are represented in the FBI's Identification Division. Dr. Henry Faulds, the Scots missionary in Japan, had first linked culprits to crime scenes by patent (visible) finger marks left at crime scenes. But most finger marks left at crime scenes are latent (invisible until developed), caused by perspiration and body oils on the fingers. These took special expertise to develop, and once developed, the size of the Bureau of Investigation identification files even in 1924 precluded searching for a single fingerprint.

A 1928 Colorado bank robbery involved the bank president wounding one of the bandits before the banker and his son were shot. Hostages were taken, and one was killed, along with a doctor who had been lured into treating the wounded criminal. The doctor's car was examined by an investigating officer for fingerprints, and although the car had been wiped clean, a fragmentary latent fingerprint was found on a window. The latent print was sent to the Bureau of Investigation, but the Bureau was not able to search it as the Bureau's fingerprints were classified and filed on the Henry system, which involved all ten fingers. Because of the viciousness of the particular crime, all the supervisors in the new Identi-fication Division memorized the latent print in the hopes of spotting it someday. More than a year later, a set of fingerprints were received from California; they turned out to have been submitted under a false name, but were identified as those of an ex-convict, Jake Fleagle, who had served time for robbery in Oklahoma. The fingerprint supervisor realized he had seen one of the prints before—the fragmentary latent print sent in from the Colorado bank robbery. As a result of this identification, Fleagle was located, and, firing at officers attempting to arrest him, was shot and killed. His accomplices in the bank robbery were also identified; as a result four innocent suspects who had been charged with the Colorado crime were released. This accomplishment could only be repeated some 60 years later, when computer automation of the Identification Division, and some state identification agencies, was about to be completed, as set out in Chapter 20.[13]

By 1932, the criminal fingerprint files were growing at the rate of over 2,000 cards per day and had reached three and a half million. Few actual latent print examinations were conducted—only 21 cases in 1932, with 18 identifications being made. But, knowledge was being gained and skills were being developed on the part of a few fingerprint examiners. In November, 1932, an FBI fingerprint examiner was called to testify in St. Paul, Minnesota, regarding a latent print developed on a gun and the inked fingerprints of a suspect. At this time, three employees of the Identification Division were selected for training in testifying about latent print identifications and J. Edgar Hoover ordered a study be made of various single fingerprint classifying systems for use in identification. By February of the next year, a single fingerprint file was in place, based on a method developed for classifying and filing single fingerprints by Chief Inspector Harry Battley of London's New Scotland Yard.

By July, the first latent print identification had been effected by a search of the single fingerprint file, which was composed of the prints of kidnappers and extortionists, at first. This year, too, saw the inauguration of iodine fume examinations to develop latent fingerprints on some paper evidence. Until then, latent fingerprints had been developed in the field by application of black or gray powder (with a base of lamp-black and charcoal for black, and ground chalk and mercury for the gray), and little evidence had been received by the FBI for processing for fingerprints—only identification of the latents. The small staff of the Single Fingerprint Section worked closely with the scientists of the FBI's new technical laboratory on developing better methods to process latent fingerprints, and for a time the Single Fingerprint Section was a part of the technical laboratory. In 1934, the section processed $5,000 in paper currency recovered in the Lindbergh kidnapping case with a silver nitrate solution process, along with ransom notes in the Hamm kidnapping case in St. Paul, Minnesota. In 1936, the Single Fingerprint Section was made a part of the Identification Division.[14]

Fingerprints are such probative evidence for connecting suspects with crime scenes that the FBI realized it had to fight any fraud in this area, in order to secure judicial acceptance of this type of evidence. In the early years of the Identification Division, the FBI campaigned against forged fingerprints and false testimony about fingerprints by hired "experts." For example, in 1937 the FBI received a letter from Tennessee enclosing a "latent fingerprint" from a crime scene, along with the fingerprint card of a suspect. The alleged latent print was found to be a photograph of part of one impression from the suspect's fingerprint card. Had the fraud not been discovered, the FBI would have linked the "suspect" with the crime.[15]

The most significant humanitarian use of fingerprinting in the positive identification of individuals came about as a result of an airplane crash that caused the death of two FBI employees. In late August, 1940, a regularly scheduled airliner carrying 25 passengers from Washington, D.C., to Pittsburgh crashed in a storm near Lovettsville, Virginia. J. Edgar Hoover sent Quinn Tamm, other FBI Agents, and fingerprint experts from the Latent Fingerprint Section to the scene to identify the FBI employees on board: a new Agent reporting to his first office and a stenographer on vacation. On arrival, the FBI found little identification work being done, because no one knew exactly how to proceed. The FBI personnel offered to take charge of identification efforts and all 25 victims were identified.[16]

Realizing that identification of disaster victims is necessary for insurance purposes, estate settlement, and for the humanitarian aspect of alleviating the anxiety of relatives, the FBI instituted the practice of offering the ranking law enforcement official or transportation official involved in any disaster the services of the Disaster Squad, a small group of FBI Agents and fingerprint specialists assigned to the Latent Fingerprint Section of the Identification Division. This cost-free, humanitarian service is offered pursuant to Federal Regulations today. As of early 1987, the Disaster Squad had assisted in identifying victims of 148 disasters, including the 1978 mass murder-suicide of 913 people in Jonestown, Guyana, the 1980 volcanic eruption of Mount St. Helens in Washington State, the October, 1983, terrorist bombing that killed 241 U.S. Marines in Lebanon, and the Space Shuttle "Challenger" disaster in 1986. On occasion, positive identification has been made by comparison of a portion of a fingerprint no larger than a quarter inch square.[17]

Of course, the success of this humanitarian use of fingerprints is based on the building of the civil section of the FBI's enormous fingerprint file. Without the draft, which led to the largest accumulation of civil prints, and without the vision of J. Edgar Hoover, who spearheaded the drive to collect civilian fingerprints, this file will dwindle in size until it no longer represents the proportion of the population that it did a decade ago. Then, the work of the Disaster Squad will not be as effective in identification by fingerprint. At this date, only dental forensics offers the possibility of replacement in the area of identification, but how can dental records be collected in a central location?

In 1950, the "Battley System" of single fingerprint classification was replaced with a less time-consuming method called the "five-finger" or "strip" (a strip of five fingerprints, or one hand) system. That year the section was enlarged and the name was changed to the Latent Fingerprint Section. Four years later, a new chemical method of developing latent fingerprints on paper was researched and perfected by the Latent Fingerprint Section. This was ninhydrin, which came to the attention of the Identification Division from an article in the March 5, 1954, issue of *Nature,* a publication of the British Association for the Advancement of Science, some three-quarters of a century after Faulds and Herschel published their findings on fingerprinting in the same journal. For the next 30 years, this method was used in almost 90% of the cases where latent prints were developed by chemicals by the FBI. In one case latent prints were found on evidence more than fourteen years after it had been touched.[18]

NATIONAL CRIME INFORMATION CENTER

The FBI's most useful cooperative service to the patrol officer, on a daily basis, is the National Crime Information Center (NCIC). Over half a million daily queries of this computerized system of wanted persons and stolen property, compared to the number of police officers in this country, means one query per day per officer in the U.S. Generally, only detectives use the FBI Laboratory, and the massive fingerprint files are the province of larger departments' identification officers. National Academy training is limited by space and budget to less than a thousand officers a year, of the roughly 500,000 officers in this country. Other police training reaches more officers, but not on a daily basis. But, NCIC enables every police officer to arrest fugitives, recover stolen property, find missing persons, in short, to be a more professional officer, every day, all across the nation.[19]

The National Crime Information Center, known to police officers by its initials NCIC, was conceived in 1966 by the FBI and the Committee on Uniform Crime Records of the IACP. It began operations on January 27, 1967, with 15 law enforcement agencies and 1 FBI field office operating on a test schedule of 2 hours per day. There were 5 computerized files at first: wanted persons, stolen vehicles, license plates, firearms, and other identifiable stolen property, containing 23,000 records, known as "hot" files among law enforcement officials. In 1968, a securities file was added and the vehicle file was expanded to include aircraft and snowmobiles. The next year brought the addition of stolen boats and dune buggies. The network was expanded so that by 1972 the system reached 102 law enforcement agencies, plus every FBI field office, thus providing service to all 50 states and Canada.

Linkage between computers came early in NCIC history; the first computer-to-computer interface was with the California Highway Patrol in April, 1967; an interface with the St. Louis, Missouri, Police Department soon followed. NCIC's first computer was one with only 128K bytes, half the capacity of the home computers available in 1987. Total yearly transactions—entries, inquiries, clears, and others—increased from 7 million in 1968 to over 25 million in 1971—more than 68,000 a day. But the real measurement of the value of the system is the number of "hits" recorded, the number of times a wanted person, or a stolen car or gun, is identified.

In January, 1968, after a year of operation, NCIC was averaging 275 hits a day; by 1972, this had grown to 700 hits a day, on a record base which had increased from 346,000 at the end of 1967 to 3,330,000 four years later. In 1986, the *NCIC Newsletter* reported that Pittsburgh police had made an inquiry on the serial number of a gun that had been pawned. The NCIC hit indicated that the gun had been stolen in the burglary of a house in Newport News, Virginia, a few days earlier. Subsequent investigation resulted in the arrest of an individual who had been involved in as many as 25 rapes in Virginia.[20]

The current size (more than 18 million records in 1986) and variegated nature of the files (where hits might only indicate an individual has a prior record) no longer allow the statistic of number of hits to indicate the value of the system. Instead, detailed surveys are used to measure the overall value of NCIC. For example, does a hit on a wanted person result in more than one arrest, does the hit result in the recovery of weapons or contraband and does it result in additional charges being filed? To avoid overburdening NCIC user agencies, these surveys are limited to a certain percentage of the users during a given month. Then, projections are made for the whole system for a year. The 1984 survey on the wanted person file gave an inference that a mean of 47,628 wanted persons were located (plus or minus 3,492) in the calendar year as a result of NCIC inquiries.[21]

While the apprehension of fugitives or the recovery of stolen property is a tangible benefit of the system, the intangible benefits are also significant. There is the savings of investigative time, accrued through more rapid apprehension of wanted persons. Also, there is the crime prevention element of rapid apprehension, as the wanted person might well have committed more crimes if the person had not been apprehended. And, there is the benefit to the safety of police personnel, when they are able to determine before approaching a suspect vehicle, if the vehicle is stolen or if a wanted person, known to be armed and dangerous, may be driving the vehicle.

In 1968, the NCIC staff and Working Committee (of the NCIC Advisory Policy Board, elected to represent NCIC users) began to discuss implementation of a computerized criminal history (CCH) file, as a logical extension of the system. FBI Director Hoover, in his last testimony before the House Subcommittee on Appropriations, pointed out the desperate need to speed up the criminal justice process, which the CCH was meant to do by furnishing criminal history information to prosecutors and courts virtually instantaneously. But the CCH file was found to be too much of a burden on state identification systems and it had to be abandoned. There were Congressional concerns raised, but the NCIC Advisory Board approved CCH replacement with the Interstate Identification Index in 1983.

This newest file, called III (pronounced triple-eye), today contains arrest records, based on fingerprints, on ten and a half million people, and is accessible not only by police, but by prosecutors, courts, and others comprising the whole criminal justice system. Access to this type of information, in most cases in minutes, has been called one of NCIC's greatest assets since the beginning of the system twenty years ago.

When NCIC receives a request for a record on an individual, the system computer at FBI headquarters in Washington, D.C., automatically sends a message to the state computer where this individual's record originated, or, for states not yet on-line in the system, the FBI Identification Division handles the request through its computerized files. (See Chapter 20 for the story of the huge job of computerizing the millions of FBI identification records). The time required to search the ten and a half million records (more than 20 million names, including aliases) is one-fourth of a second, so a response can be received from the state computer very quickly. Benefits over the CCH file are the cost savings to state identification agencies, due to the automatic update capability for newly assigned FBI numbers and elimination of the costly manual matching and data entry previously required. Also, this decentralizes the FBI's record keeping responsibility by making the states primarily responsible for record maintenance and dissemination.[23]

In the early 1980s there was considerable media attention given to the problem of missing children, with the *New York Times* reporting a million runaways a year and *People Magazine* claiming that 50,000 children are parentally abducted (in divorce cases) each year. Statements were made in the media that a nationwide missing person system was virtually nonexistent, in spite of the establishment of the NCIC missing person file five years before. But, the entry of only 114,000 missing juveniles per year, compared to the estimated million runaways each year, indicated "that full potential of the file is not being utilized," according to the FBI official in charge of the file, writing in the *FBI Law Enforcement Bulletin.*[24]

The NCIC missing person file, which became operational in 1975, and had almost 60,000 records in 1987, includes five categories: (1) disabled missing who are threats to themselves or others, (2) missing who are endangered, (3) missing for involuntary reasons, ie. through abduction or kidnapping, (4) missing juveniles, those who are unemancipated by the laws of the state of their residence, and (5) catastrophe victims. Juveniles made up three-quarters of the more than 56,000 entries in the missing file in 1987. Of the missing juveniles (in 1982), only 3.2% of the entries are for children under 11, and 10% of the records are for children in the age bracket 11 through 13. Juveniles between the ages of 14 and 17 make up more than 85% of the missing juvenile file (age 18 or over account for only 1.2% of the file). Not surprisingly, the spring month of May accounts for the largest number of missing juvenile entries (almost

15,000), and the approach of the holidays in December is the least, under 10,000.[25]

As a result of the public concern, caused by the media attention, Congress passed the Missing Children Act in 1982. It is estimated that the majority of missing juveniles return home within 24 to 48 hours, thus many police departments have policies governing the amount of time that must elapse before a missing juvenile entry is made in the NCIC. The Missing Children Act empowers a parent or legal guardian to inquire directly with the FBI to determine if an NCIC entry has been made and, in those rare instances where local authorities refuse to enter the missing juvenile, the FBI will make the entry at the parent's or guardian's request.[26]

Canadian warrants for wanted persons were added to the NCIC in the U.S. in 1980 because of the amount of travel over the border between the two nations. In 1987, these were merged into the Foreign Fugitive File. In 1983, unidentified remains of persons were added, to correlate unidentified bodies with the descriptions of missing persons on a nation-wide basis. In November, 1985, a white female in "poor mental condition" was reported missing in New York City and an NCIC entry was made. The next day, a report was taken on a white female suicide victim who had jumped in front of a Long Island subway train. This report was entered into the unidentified person file (in New York City as in the country as a whole, these reports are too voluminous to match manually), but the computer provided the possible match, the fourth time unidentified remains had been identified with a missing person file. As the New York State Police Information Network noted:

> Without the file matching capability, the unidentified woman may well have been buried as a 'Jane Doe' and the grief of the family, based upon the uncertainty usually associated with missing persons, would have lasted indefinitely.[27]

The other files in the NCIC system are the U.S. Secret Service protective file, the smallest file with only 61 records in 1986 out of the total of almost 18 million records, and the Originating Agency Identifier file, which identifies the agency which originated the particular entry to an inquiring agency.

In 1986, the SEARCH Group, a non-profit consulting organization, prepared a report for the Bureau of Justice Statistics on the NCIC and its "hot" files, which the group called "the most heavily used type of criminal justice information." The introduction to the 70-page report noted that:

> Police officers in the field rely upon immediate access to these files, by radio or mobile terminal, to determine whether vehicles or other property have been reported stolen and whether individuals they encounter in the course of their duties are wanted for criminal offenses and, more important, whether they may be armed and dangerous. . . . criminal justice officials . . . regard the hot files as "life blood" information for officers on the street, who must rely upon it in making hurried and perhaps irreversible decisions affecting their own safety and the lives and liberty of the persons they deal with . . .
>
> Despite its importance, however, relatively little has been published concerning the hot file system . . . there has been no publication . . . describing in detail the types of information maintained in this federal-state cooperative system and the procedures in place . . . to keep the files accurate, complete and current. . . . [28]

The whole NCIC system is only twenty years old, but it has become the "life blood" of information for officers on the street. This is the new efficiency in policing that Americans expect today, a development by the FBI that exemplifies federal-state cooperation. It is also a cooperative venture with law enforcement professionals across the country, particularly the IACP, that serves the criminal justice community as a whole, but in particular, protects the patrol officer on the street—allowing the officer to perform in an efficient and professional manner.

Notes to Chapter 17

1. Thorwald, 1964. 103.
2. Hoover, 1931a.
3. Jones, 1985.
4. Thompson, 1968. 38–41.
5. Annual Report, 1924. 71. Annual Report, 1939. 16. Whitehead, 1956. 135.
6. A. S. M. 1926. Hoover, 1927. Annual Report, 1929.
7. Division of Identification, 1925. 7/1. FBI, 1986. 25.
8. Hoover, 1935c.
9. Annual Report, 1924. 71. FBI, 1986. 9.
10. Hoover, 1935b. 9–10.
11. Ibid.
12. Lowenthal, 1950. 368–397. Jones, 1985.
13. Hoover, 1973. 13, 29–30.
14. Jones, 1983. 1–3.
15. Whitehead, 1956. 137.

16. FBI, 1976. 27. Hazen, 1987.
17. Hazen, 1987. FBI, 1976. 28–29. Title 28, Code of Federal Regulations, Section 0.85.
18. Jones, 1983. 5–6.
19. FBI, 1986b.
20. FBI, 1986c. 3.
21. FBI, 1984. 7.
22. FBI, 1972.
23. Rathbun, 1985.
24. Bishop, 1982.
25. Ibid.
26. FBI, 1983.
27. FBI, 1986c. 3.
28. Woodward, 1986. 1–2.

PART V

RENAISSANCE II—1970S ONWARD

The riots of the 1960s left a legacy to policing: the concept that police are not alone in their responsibilities to control disorder and defeat crime. This era began a second renaissance of policing in America. Led by police executives Patrick V. Murphy and Clarence M. Kelley, in company with academics such as James Q. Wilson, Renaissance II was sparked by two Presidential commissions on law enforcement and civil disorders. The second generation of police leadership brought experimentation that tested, and rejected, the basic theories of crime deterrence developed by O. W. Wilson.

New methods of policing involving citizens and neighborhoods began to end the encapsulation of the police officer in the patrol car that had developed as the automobile became a part of American life. This re-established the 19th century concept that police were created to serve the community through interaction with the population they policed. Police education was expanded with considerable federal funding. Experiments examining various police strategies by police departments were conducted by the Police Foundation with state of the art academic testing methods (financed by a huge grant from the Ford Foundation). The FBI re-defined its service to law enforcement role with emphasis on education, training, and research.

New giants in policing emerged from practitioners and academia: a career New York City police officer who eventually headed four different urban departments, including New York City, and fostered experimentation at the Police Foundation; a Harvard professor of government who became chairman of the board of the Police Foundation; and a career FBI agent who became chief of a Mid-West police department and then returned to the FBI as J. Edgar Hoover's successor. The new concepts and strategies from these police practitioners, organizations, and academics point the way for police professionalism in the 21st century.

Chapter 18

PROFESSIONALISM REDEFINED

... the ability of the police to act against crime is limited. The police did not create and cannot resolve the social conditions that stimulate crime. They did not start and cannot stop the convulsive social changes that are taking place in America.[1]

These conclusions about policing in the 1960s: the rising crime rate, urban rioting, and the campus anti-war violence of the 1960s—"the convulsive social changes" of the era—signaled the beginning of the second renaissance of police professionalism. This second renaissance was marked by a new willingness to experiment on the part of police executives and a rebirth of the spirit of service to the community, particularly in the return to the concept of order maintenance, instead of solely the function of law enforcement. The beginning of recognition that the whole community, not just the police, was responsible for crime began to redefine Americans' conception of policing.

Renaissance II brought new leaders to policing: a New York City patrolman who advanced to the commissioner's post, commanded three other municipal police departments along the way, and then became head of a new federal law enforcement aid project, and, finally, led the Police Foundation for over a decade; a professor of government at Harvard University who helped the commissioner guide the research-oriented Police Foundation; and a new Director of the FBI, a career FBI Agent who retired to the position of chief of police in a Mid-Western city and then brought his police management experience to revitalize the FBI.

THE COMMISSIONS AND PREVENTIVE PATROL

The 1960s saw two Presidentially appointed commissions examining the direction American society was taking, and, in particular, the role of the police. The first was the President's Commission on Law Enforcement and the Administration of Justice, headed by a former Attorney General, Nicolas Katzenbach. This commission, which issued its general report in 1967, consisted of attorneys and political figures, including two former attorneys general, academics, civil rights leaders, and one police chief executive, Thomas J. Cahill of San Francisco. The commission's consultants and advisors included professors in the criminal justice field, a number of police executives, and FBI officials.[2]

The introduction to this report noted that the police are "the part of the criminal justice system that is in direct daily contact both with crime and with the public," an echo of Leonard Fuld's truism in his 1909 work *Police Administration*.[3] The report also quoted August Vollmer's pessimistic view on the overall futility of law enforcement without intelligent law making:

> The most eminent of modern police administrators, August Vollmer, once said: "I have spent my life enforcing the laws. It is a stupid procedure and has not, nor will it ever solve the problem unless it is supplemented by preventive measures."[4]

This report set forth a number of preventive measure recommendations in social justice terms, but noted that "Americans are a people used to entrusting the solutions of their social ills to specialists, and to expecting results from the institutions those specialists devise." One of those institutions is police patrol, the object of which:

> . . . is to disperse policemen in a way that will eliminate or reduce the opportunity for misconduct and to increase the likelihood that a criminal will be apprehended while he is committing a crime or immediately thereafter.[5]

This was O. W. Wilson's, and most police executives', conventional wisdom on policing: patrol deters crime. Wilson was an advisor to the Commission. This commission did not question the institution the specialists had devised.

But a year later another report, of yet another Presidentially appointed commission, examined one tactic of the patrol strategy, "aggressive preventive patrol," and found it counter-productive:

> The police are faced with demands for increased protection and service in the ghetto. Yet the aggressive preventive patrol practices thought necessary to meet these demands themselves create tension and hostility.[6]

O. W. Wilson was not an advisor to this commission. The 1968 report dealt with a more specific problem facing police, the urban riots, and singled out a cause, aggressive preventive patrol, that police executives could change themselves, without going to the municipal authorities for more money, men, or equipment.

We can date law enforcement's second renaissance from 1968, from the second of these two reports, in effect. A crack in the wall of the conventional wisdom of patrol strategy had been made; the tactic of aggressive preventive patrol had been named "counter-productive," as some few police executives already believed. The Kansas City, Missouri, Police Department/Police Foundation experiment, under Chief Clarence M. Kelley, which tested the overall efficacy of preventive patrol, was the second blow to O. W. Wilson's theory of crime deterrence. As Patrick V. Murphy noted, "The movement away from 'stranger policing' has begun and should continue."[7]

The 1967 commission report made four sets of recommendations regarding policing, in the areas of community relations, personnel, operations and organization, and pooling of resources and services. The largest number of recommendations came in the personnel area, with advisement to encourage lateral entry, to require a bachelor's degree for supervisory positions (and as an eventual goal for all law enforcement positions), for more active recruiting on college campuses and from ghetto areas, and for further training of in-service officers. In operations, the commission advocated including police in community planning, employing legal advisors, and experimenting with team policing. The commission also took a position on the pooling of resources, advocating consolidation of law enforcement in counties or in metropolitan areas.

In the area of community relations the 1967 report recommended that (1) community relations units be established in cities with substantial minority populations, (2) that more minority-group officers be recruited, (3) citizen advisory committees be established in minority-group neighborhoods, (4) that emphasis be put on community relations in training and operations, and (5) that adequate procedures be provided for processing citizen grievances against all public officials.[8]

Then, the second commission report the following year echoed recommendations (2) and (5) regarding hiring more minority officers and establishing grievance procedures. But this report also recommended (1) eliminating "abrasive practices" in the ghetto (aggressive preventive patrol), (2) providing more police protection in the ghetto, (3) development of innovative programs to "insure widespread community support for law enforcement," and (4) hiring "community service officers," ghetto youths between 17 and 21 to perform less than full police duties in ghetto neighborhoods.[9]

The next twenty years brought a wide variety of innovative experiments designed to gain "widespread community support for law enforcement." One of these was the 1973 Safe and Clean Neighborhood Act of the New Jersey state legislature. Basically, this act attempted to develop safe neighborhoods by establishing foot patrol beats in certain high crime areas. The program's philosophy was that:

> ...the uniformed walking patrol officers, by being highly visible on the streets, are not only helping to prevent crime and enforce the laws, but at the same time are helping to restore confidence in citizens and are improving public relations with merchants and residents.[10]

THE COMMISSIONER AND FOOT PATROL

Patrick V. Murphy began his police career as a foot patrolman in New York City. He realized the valuable community contact that foot patrol provided the police. Son of a sergeant in the New York City Police Department, and brother of both another sergeant and a captain, Patrick V. Murphy, a World War II Navy flyer with a wife and one son, needed a job after the war. In his words, he:

> ...needed a good-paying job...by 1973, when I retired from policing at the acme of the industry—the Police Commissionership of the City of New York—I took to the presidency of the Police Foundation (my new job) a reputation as a reformer, as a bit of a maverick, even as something of a radical intellectual on the subject of American policing.[11]

Along the way, Murphy gained the top police administrator posts in Syracuse, New York; Detroit, Michigan; and Washington, D.C.; and became the first administrator of the short-lived Law Enforcement Assistance Administration. He had more practical police experience than any other police administrator in the country, before or since, and:

> ...his long-range impact on American policing will be judged by students of police history as significant as that of August Vollmer or J. Edgar Hoover.[12]

The 1967 commission position advocating consolidation of smaller police departments into county-wide or metropolitan area-wide law enforcement agencies was also advanced by Murphy, who wrote that:

> ...a great many American communities are policed by a farcical little collection of untrained individuals who are really nothing more than guards.[13]

Murphy advocated consolidation of departments into units of not less than 200 officers in order to provide some degree of specialization and expertise. At least, Murphy argued, there might be county-wide overlays of large departments with smaller departments for those communities that could afford them. This line of thought brought Murphy into conflict with the International Association of Chiefs of Police (IACP), which at that time was dominated by chiefs of small departments. Murphy recognized the democratic ideal of small departments accountable to their constituencies:

> In truth, there is a grain of remarkable de Tocqueville-style insight in the *idea* of an elected chief police official ... [14]

But in practice Murphy saw sheriffs' or police departments of under 200 men to be too small to be professionally effective. State enactments requiring a minimum of training for any peace officer in that state answer part of Murphy's complaint about non-professionalism on the part of very small departments, but still do not provide a full solution to this problem. In the FBI of two generations ago, J. Edgar Hoover saw each Agent as a generalist who, theoretically, could investigate any kind of case. Today, the complexity of our society mandates specialization in the investigation of violations of federal laws, thus the FBI has specialized to a degree.

After Murphy retired as Police Commissioner of New York City, he became the president of the Police Foundation, a Ford Foundation-funded research group directed by academics and police executives. After the IACP's dispute with him over consolidation, he caused the formation of the Police Executives' Research Forum (PERF), like the Police Foundation a research-oriented organization but one directed by police executives of larger departments. Another requirement for membership in PERF is a college degree, which was a recommendation of the 1967 commission for police chief executives but today still has been met by only half of the thousands of police chiefs.

Murphy cited professionalism in his argument for larger police agencies, but he recognized one truth that pre-dated modern concepts of professionalism. From his earliest days on the New York City Police Department, he was bored with routine foot patrol until he realized and articulated the truth that officers, before the concept of professionalism developed, had known:

> ... that intimacy between a patrol officer and the residents of the territory under patrol was a necessary part of the social contract which

permitted police officers the substantial authority and responsibility they possessed.[15]

He noted that technological improvements in policing can sometimes have a destructive effect on the "art of policing." Policing, like medicine, may be a science, but they both still have elements of an art. He cited, as the prime examples of this effect, the automobile and the radio, which, as they became available:

> ... the friendly style of policing that existed naturally when officers walked among the people in the commercial zones and shopping streets and other densely peopled sections was gradually replaced by a more mathematical, technological style: the patrolling of America from behind closed doors, on wheels, in communication with the outside world through a windshield and over a radio frequency.

> At the time, no one really knew any better; the use of the car and the radio on the face of it seemed like an unobjectionable idea. What little was written on the subject reassured the police that they were preventing crime by their increased presence (the car covering much greater distance in any period of time). Quality, it seemed, was to be measured in quantity.

> The actual effect of the technology was to increase the distance between the community and the police, and thereby dilute the quality of the police service, even though the intention was otherwise. Being closer and friendlier, the foot officer knew much more about crime, delinquency, criminal associations, and ex-offenders on his relatively confined patrol beat ... [16]

Later, in the Police Foundation's Newark Foot Patrol Experiment, Murphy noted that while foot patrol does not reduce crime, as routine motor patrol doesn't either, "it does measurably and significantly affect citizens' feelings of safety and mobility in their neighborhoods."[17]

In a 1972 essay, "The Criminal Justice System in Crisis," Murphy noted that "the police have limited ability to act against crime:"

> Emphasis on this "catcher of criminals" aspect of police functioning has led to a tendency on the part of both the public and the police to underestimate the range and complexity of police work ... the policeman spends a good deal of time settling disputes, finding missing children, recovering stolen property, directing traffic, providing emergency medical aid and helping little old ladies who have locked themselves out of their apartments.[18]

This essay explains "neighborhood policing," as begun by the New York City police under Murphy's leadership: a police supervisor and a team of police officers is made responsible for policing a part of one precinct continuously—far more responsibility than the officers have had in the past. Prior to the development of the concept of police professionalism (and Murphy claimed "there is no police profession in the United States" in this 1972 essay) police realized that citizen cooperation was a necessary element of order control and law enforcement. The automobile and radio were technological advances that eclipsed citizen cooperation, but, today, the strategy of citizen cooperation is returning to policing, and one tactic of this strategy is foot patrol. Murphy's ideas on foot patrol and his inauguration of "Neighborhood Policing" in New York, expanded in 1972 and 1973, but prematurely ended by 1975's fiscal crisis in New York City, formed a significant part of today's concepts of policing. The social contract aspects of these types of policing became the intellectual basis of the second renaissance in policing. These social contract ideas were expanded on by academics such as Harvard professor James Q. Wilson, and validated by experiments carried out by various departments in cooperation with the Police Foundation.

THE PROFESSOR AND "BROKEN WINDOWS"

A professor of Government at Harvard University, a prolific and thoughtful writer on the theories of policing, and a member of the Police Foundation board of directors since its founding, James Q. Wilson (no relation to O. W. Wilson) seems to agree with Murphy on the status of police professionalism, or, at least, argues that police professionalism will differ from that of other professions. Wilson explains that the medical and legal professions provide a service the quality of which the client is not in a position to judge for himself, but the police officer's role is not to cure or to advise, but to restrain. "Whereas health and counsel are welcomed by the recipients, restraint is not," hence police professionalism will differ in kind from the medical and legal professions.[19]

In 1968, the year that the National Advisory Commission on Civil Disorders condemned aggressive preventive patrol, Wilson published *Varieties of Police Behavior,* in which he differentiated policing into three styles: watchman, legalistic, and service styles. He noted that "the patrolman's role is defined more by his responsibility for *maintaining order* than by his responsibility for enforcing the law," based on his surveys that showed the patrol officer "encounters far more problems of order maintenance than opportunities for law enforcement." Wilson and his research team did some of their research in 1963–1964 in Syracuse,

New York, when Patrick Murphy was the new chief of police in that city, and the two men knew each other.[20]

Professor Wilson and Harvard research fellow George L. Kelling, former director of the Police Foundation evaluation staff, returned to the theme of order maintenance in a brilliant essay entitled "Broken Windows," published in *The Atlantic Monthly* in March, 1982. They saw order maintenance as being enhanced by foot patrol, as shown by the Police Foundation study in Newark, New Jersey, which demonstrated how foot patrol restored confidence in the population of the neighborhoods that received this service.

These authors noted that while state officials were enthusiastic about foot patrol, police chiefs were skeptical. Foot patrol reduced the mobility of police, who then had difficulty responding to citizen calls for service. More significant to police chiefs familiar with New York City Police Department scandals about "cooping" (sleeping on duty), foot patrol also weakened headquarters control over patrol officers, until the technology of the hand-held portable police radio was developed. Officers, themselves, disliked foot patrol because of its working conditions, and because in some departments it was used as a form of punishment. Also,

> Academic experts on policing doubted that foot patrol would have any impact on crime rates; it was . . . little more than a sop to public opinion. But, as the state was paying for it, local authorities were willing to go along.[21]

The authors pointed out that a Police Foundation evaluation, based on a carefully controlled experiment in Newark, showed that foot patrol did *not* reduce crime. Skeptics might say that the citizenry was fooled into thinking themselves safer, but the Police Foundation found that the citizenry *believed* their neighborhoods were safer, in spite of the non-reduction of crime, because the other source of fear—"the fear of being bothered by disorderly people"—had been reduced. Wilson and Kelling described the everyday concern of "reputable" people in our cities as fear of:

> . . . not violent people, nor, necessarily, criminals, but disreputable or obstreperous or unpredictable people: panhandlers, drunks, addicts, rowdy teenagers, prostitutes, loiterers, the mentally disturbed. What foot-patrol officers did was to elevate . . . the level of public order in these neighborhoods.[22]

What this program in Newark, and others in the last twenty years, accomplished was to show the concern of the public about the extent of public order in their cities. Crime might be reported in the news media, but everyday public concern included concern over disorder. People wanted to be left in peace to enjoy their work and recreation, in effect, their lives:

> The people of Newark, to judge from their behavior and their remarks to interviewers, apparently assign a high value to public order, and feel relieved and reassured when the police help them maintain that order.[23]

The authors recounted the psychology experiment where two "abandoned" cars, without license plates, were parked, hoods up, on a street in the Bronx and in Palo Alto, California. The car in the Bronx was attacked by vandals within minutes and in a day everything of value had been removed. The car in the California suburb sat untouched for more than a week, until the psychologist smashed part of it with a sledgehammer, to test the "broken window" theory. In a few hours, the California car was destroyed as completely as the one in the Bronx. Because of the anonymous nature of life in the Bronx, vandalism occurs more rapidly than in staid Palo Alto, but,

> . . . once communal barriers—the sense of mutual regard and the obligations of civility—are lowered by actions that seem to signal that "no one cares" . . .

then vandalism can occur anywhere. These authors suggest that " 'untended' behavior also leads to breakdown of controls."[24]

But, when these authors come to the historical and police behavioral aspects of their argument, their case is not as persuasive. They discount arguments over legalities, decriminalization, and discrimination. Legalities belong to the law enforcement side of policing, not the order maintenance, these authors argue, and decriminalization of "disreputable" behavior, which removes the "ultimate sanction the police can employ to maintain neighborhood order—is, we think, a mistake." For discrimination, the authors can only hope that by selection, training, and supervision "police will be inculcated with a clear sense of the outer limit of their discretionary authority."[25]

THE NEW DIRECTOR AND CRIME RESISTANCE

Clarence M. Kelley was sworn in as the Director of the FBI on July 9, 1973, just over a year after the death of J. Edgar Hoover. (A Justice

Department attorney, L. Patrick Gray, had been named acting Director the day after Hoover died, but withdrew from Senate confirmation after he became implicated in the Watergate scandal.) When appointed, Kelley was a 61-year-old native of Kansas City, Missouri, who had a law degree from the University of Kansas City. He had been a career FBI Special Agent since 1940, with time out for World War II service in the Navy, serving in the FBI as an investigator and a firearms instructor until appointment as a supervisor at FBI Headquarters in 1951. He then served as a field supervisor, an Assistant Special Agent in Charge of a field office, a headquarters Inspector, and a Special Agent in Charge of two FBI field offices until his retirement in 1961, when he became Chief of Police in Kansas City for the next twelve years.[26]

Patrick Murphy said of Kelley:

> He was progressive and willing to innovate. He championed participatory management. . . . By 1971, Chief Clarence M. Kelley said, "Many of us in the department had the feeling we were training, equipping, and deploying men to do a job neither we, nor anyone else, knew much about. . . . " [he] sought assistance from the Police Foundation for developing several experimental projects including the patrol experiment. . . . His unusual willingness to allow experimentation and evaluation provided an opportunity for the Foundation to support the type of pioneering to which it is dedicated. . . . It is not easy for police departments to conduct operational experiments. For one thing, maintaining experimental conditions cannot be permitted to interfere with police responsibility for life and property. . . . [this project] ranks among the few major social experiments ever to be completed.[27]

The patrol experiment was the first to evaluate police operational procedures and had the most impact of any Police Foundation study. Conducted for a year beginning October 1, 1972, it showed that increasing or decreasing the level of routine preventive patrol had no appreciable effect on crime, fear of crime, or citizen satisfaction with police service. The study divided one patrol division's 15 beats into three groups of five beats each, using computer techniques to equalize the groups in terms of crime figures, population, and calls for police service. One group was termed "reactive," where patrol was eliminated and patrol cars entered only in response to calls; a second group of beats was the "control," where the level of preventive patrol was continued as before. The third group became "proactive," with twice the level of preventive patrol.

Victimization surveys before and after the experiment measured the crime rate in the three groups of beats, in addition to the fear of crime and citizen attitudes toward police. The three groups of patrol beats— reactive, proactive, and control—showed no appreciable statistical differences in victimization (crime), fear of crime, or attitude toward delivery of police services. "Even one fear of the experimenters, that traffic accidents would increase in the reactive group of beats, did not occur."[28]

The willingness to experiment was just one of the qualities that Clarence Kelley brought with him to his leadership of the FBI. He also established the policy of "participatory management," which allowed FBI Agents of whatever rank to have a voice in the operation of the organization that they had helped build. Kelley established priorities in FBI investigations, the concept of quality over quantity, to get away from the FBI's emphasis on strictly statistical accomplishments that had grown up under J. Edgar Hoover and had been criticized by modern management experts during Hoover's last years. These priorities recognized that organized crime, white-collar crime, and intelligence investigations had to be the province of the federal government because of their interstate ramifications that could not be addressed adequately by local law enforcement. Kelley's successor, William H. Webster, then refined these priorities, adding terrorism investigations, and recognized that the FBI should have a role in the foremost crime problem facing this country, narcotics abuse. Webster directed the FBI's experience in organized crime investigations to the investigation of narcotics, which Hoover had been reluctant to address.

The concepts Kelley introduced to the FBI were, of course, the new management trends in the 1970s: a willingness to hear and accept ideas from employees, the establishment of priorities in the work of any organization, and a willingness to experiment in an examination of basic concepts. Kelley brought them to law enforcement, which was probably the most tradition-bound career in existence. In getting these management trends accepted in the FBI, and among law enforcement agencies as a whole, Kelley advanced the law enforcement career toward professionalism. Law enforcement began to resemble more closely the medical and legal professions, which recognized the contributions of individual practitioners and, especially in medicine, had been built on a record of willingness to experiment in the last two centuries. In addition, Kelley caused changes in the FBI's approach to its service role in the areas of police training, identification, and forensic science, which are detailed in Chapter 20.

Kelley also advanced professionalism by recognizing the citizen role in combating crime, which he termed "crime resistance." As an article in the *FBI Law Enforcement Bulletin*, prepared under Kelley's direction, described the concept:

> Crime resistance is, in essence, an attitude—an attitude that manifests itself when citizens take measures to avoid becoming victims of crime and when they join with those in law enforcement in reacting to criminal activity.... It means resistance to the idea that everyone must live in isolation and shrink from contact with others. It is resistance to being immobilized by fear.[29]

In July, 1975, four police departments, in conjunction with the FBI and the Police Foundation, initiated four crime resistance projects to demonstrate how citizens, with the help of their police departments, could resist "and thereby reduce targeted crimes through low-cost, self-help measures." The communities and their targeted crimes were Birmingham, Alabama—trafficking in stolen property; De Kalb County, Georgia—crimes against youths; Norfolk, Virginia—crimes against women; and Wilmington, Delaware—crimes against the elderly.[30] In each community, two FBI Agents and two police officers joined to form a crime resistance task force to look at crime from the point of view of the victim. This program "contributed to reductions in targeted crimes in all four of these projects."[31]

As Kelley noted in the introduction to the booklet *Crime Resistance:*

> Helping citizens to resist crime is not another community relations program. It is, instead, a distinct law enforcement function. Educating and alerting people to how they can reduce their vulnerability to the crimes about them is a continuing responsibility of law enforcement, and it is as necessary as a patrol force.
>
> The answer to crime is not more tax money. Our best hope is that citizens will reach the understanding that crime is not a police problem but an American problem—a problem that must be addressed by every citizen acting individually and in concert with neighbors in their own communities. It is the role of law enforcement to be the protagonist in this process.[32]

The crime resistance program was based on a profound understanding of the historical basis of society's efforts against crime through the centuries, that "without citizen involvement, the police are helpless."[33] And as the program report also noted:

> Many police departments have initiated various crime prevention efforts, but quite often these efforts have been spasmodic and pamphlet-oriented.

This is not to say that these programs have had no impact, but only that in most cases they have not been sufficiently sustained.

To make crime resistance a reality among a community's citizens requires a full-time effort by a front-line police unit. This effort must be directed toward generating and guiding citizen involvement in attempting to stop crime before it happens . . . [34]

The program also recognized the impatient nature of American society and that for this program to have its maximum impact it needs to be "sufficiently sustained."

A recent work, edited by a Northwestern University professor, catalogs community crime prevention efforts in four catagories: property identification, security surveys, citizen patrols, and citizen crime reporting. Editor Dennis P. Rosenbaum noted that:

> . . . citizen involvement through community crime prevention programs acknowledged that the success of law enforcement was highly dependent upon the participation and cooperation of the populace in anticrime efforts. . . . it was not until the mid-1970s that community crime prevention fully crystalized as an integral component of widely held criminal justice doctrine.[35]

The National Neighborhood Foot Patrol Center published a 1986 listing of over 200 police departments nationally that have begun community policing programs in the last twenty years, consisting of foot patrol, "park and walk" or motorcycle-scooter and walk (combined foot and motor patrol), team policing, use of special vehicles, auxiliary or reserve volunteer citizen programs, or types of neighborhood response units. These included departments in 43 states (all except Delaware, Kansas, Mississippi, New Mexico, North and South Dakota, and Wyoming) and the departments ranged in size from very small (1 to 5 officers) to the country's largest, 23,000 officers. Most of the largest departments in the country, New York City, Los Angeles, Chicago, Houston, Dallas, Detroit, Boston, Philadelphia, San Francisco, Washington, D.C.; Dade County, Florida; Baltimore, and Cleveland have community policing programs, usually foot patrol or a combination of foot and motor patrol.[36]

In the decade of the 1970s, the new readiness to experiment that exemplified a resurgence of intellectual activity on the part of police administrators resulted in the re-examination and re-evaluation of the basic customs of policing. Robert Peel's original concept that London's "new police," like history's "hue and cry" and its descendants, the constable and the watchman, which had to depend on the citizenry to serve the community, was re-born. Twentieth century Presidential commissions reiterated this dependence on citizen cooperation in crime control, and delineated the failure of O. W. Wilson's theory of crime deterrence through aggressive preventive patrol.

The strategy of experimentation was championed by practitioner Patrick Murphy through the Police Foundation (of which more will be described in the concluding chapter) with the cooperation of Clarence Kelley and other police leaders. The tactic of foot patrol, as a form of community policing, and other strategies involving the community in resisting crime, was championed by practitioners Murphy and Kelley, joined by academics. The academics have been led by James Q. Wilson, who articulated the neglected order maintenance function of policing and its value in reducing fear of crime, especially, again, through foot patrol. Depending on how professionalism is defined, this willingness to question, to experiment, to re-examine previously accepted theories of policing, constituted a rebirth of professionalism, a Renaissance II to use J. Edgar Hoover's word.

Notes to Chapter 18

1. President's Commission, 1967. 1.
2. Ibid, v–vii.
3. "...the police department is the department of the city government with which citizens come into the most intimate contact." Leonard F. Fuld, *Police Administration,* New York, G. P. Putnam's Sons, 1909. Reprint ed. Montclair, New Jersey, Patterson Smith, 1971. 420.
4. President's Commission, 1967. 2.
5. Ibid, 1.
6. National Advisory Commission, 1968. 8.
7. Murphy, 1977. 264.
8. President's Commission, 1967. xi.
9. National Advisory Commission, 1968. 8.
10. Police Foundation, 1981. 22.
11. Murphy, 1977. 19–20.
12. Deakin, 1986. 4.
13. Murphy, 1977. 71.
14. Ibid, 74.
15. Ibid, 39.
16. Ibid, 262–263.
17. Police Foundation, 1981. iii.

18. Curran, et al 1973. 20.
19. Ibid, 4.
20. Wilson, 1968. 16–18.
21. Wilson and Kelling, 1982. 29.
22. Ibid, 30.
23. Ibid, 31.
24. Ibid.
25. Ibid, 33–35.
26. FBI biography, 1986.
27. Police Foundation, 1974. iii–iv.
28. Deakin, 1986. 4.
29. FBI, 1977.
30. LEB, 1977. 44:3. 3–11.
31. Ibid, 1.
32. FBI, 1977. v–vi.
33. LEB, 1977. 44:3. 6.
34. FBI, 1977. 9.
35. Rosenbaum, 1986. 21.
36. Trojanowicz et al, 1986. 49–55.

Chapter 19

EDUCATION FOR A "CAREER POLICE PROFESSION"

A physician is an authority with the power of life and death in situations involving physical disorder. A policeman is a life and death authority in situations of social disorder.[1]

The American Bar Association, the legal professional organization, quoted the above in its 1973 *Standards Relating to the Urban Police Function.* Continuing the comparison of these two "life and death" authorities, the Bar Association went on to note that it takes 11,000 hours of training to educate a physician, but the average policeman receives only 200 hours of training.

In terms of training *beyond a college* education, American law enforcement is professional, at least on the federal level where college is required for investigators, followed by agency training. In terms of education, the FBI is the most professional law enforcement agency in America with its requirement of at least a baccalaureate degree, and a law or accounting degree, prior to another four months of training. A third of FBI agents have a graduate degree in law or another discipline before the FBI's postgraduate training. Of course, FBI agents are investigators, not police officers. Policing, as far as educational requirements, is not yet uniformly professional, but for a decade the federal government attempted to elevate local policing, through funding of education for police, to improve the performance of their order and crime control functions and reduce perceived police authoritarianism, thus moving them towards the status of professionalism.

The Wickersham Commission in the 1930s was the first Presidential commission to recommend further education for police officers. Generally, expanded recruit training in police academies resulted over the next three decades. In June, 1940, as a result of the depression, the New York City Police Department recruited 300 men, of whom more than half had college degrees. But, by 1950, a special Census report indicated the median educational level of all police officers in the United States was 11.7 years of schooling. This report indicated that 53% of America's police had not completed high school, 34% were high school graduates,

271

9% had one to three years of college, and only 3% had graduated from college or beyond.[2]

By 1986, the percentage of police officers who had less than a high school education was less than 1%, according to one survey. Another 21% had completed high school and over 26% had college degrees or beyond, a tremendous increase. A majority of police officers had associate degrees or some college.[3] A survey of chiefs of police from departments with over 75 employees (almost 500 departments) showed that just over 50% had bachelor's degrees and another 18% had graduate degrees in 1982. By the next year this had increased to almost 57% with a bachelors degree and almost 26% with a graduate degree.[4]

In the 1950s, two states, California and New York, had begun to require some basic police training for recruits and advanced in-service training for officers already on duty, but this requirement did not include completion of a certain educational level prior to the training. The New York State training did include college level education to meet some of the requirements necessary for a two-year associate degree.[5] This mandatory training grew out of a long range Police Training Program inaugurated in 1945 by chiefs of police, sheriffs, and the FBI. The Municipal Police Training Council, which exempted the New York City Police Department and the New York State Police, as these two organizations already had established recruit training programs, tripled the number of training hours to 240 for police recruits throughout the state, but, most significant, made the training mandatory rather than voluntary. At the same time, collegiate education oriented toward police was growing in New York State, California and other states, especially with institutions granting two-year or Associate degrees.

The junior college movement, begun in the 1920s, grew tremendously after World War II. These community colleges were, initially, career-oriented, rather than providing a liberal arts education. It seemed as though the United States was aiming toward providing all its citizens with fourteen years of education, instead of the twelve that ended with graduation from high school. In 1967, the International Association of Chiefs of Police (IACP), together with the American Association of Junior Colleges, jointly prepared guidelines for law enforcement programs in junior colleges:

> The courses that are most readily available in any community college curriculum are some of the most desirable from law enforcement's standpoint. Yet, in the past, there has been a failure to take advantage of

such offerings by most police agencies in the country. Courses such as English, sociology, psychology, political science, logic, and history are the very foundation of law enforcement's body of knowledge. To deny this would be to deny an emerging police profession, because all specialized fields of advanced study must be based upon certain academic core subjects. A field of human endeavor such as the police service has a broad base of essential knowledge and must demand of its practitioners certain achievements in terms of initial study.[6]

However, the academic aims of the junior college movement in police science, agreed to by the police leadership and academic communities, were subjected to Congressional pressure in the form of federal funding to provide for college education for police. This was a continuation of the political process, begun in the New Deal administration, of dealing with social problems by providing federal funding, or what has been called the uniquely American solution of "throwing money at the problem."

Higher education alone cannot solve the major problems facing policing in this country, of course. According to one comprehensive study, these problems are caused more by the "structure of our society and polity than they are by the people who do police work." These include inadequate methods for achieving police objectives, conflicting public expectations about what police objectives should be, and poor relations between police and the public. "Blaming the police for failing to prevent crime, of course, is like blaming doctors for failing to control cancer." As this study noted:

> The social conflicts and rising crime of the 1960s threw the police into the national spotlight. Their long-standing problems were rediscovered by several presidential commissions, whose empirical research on policing provided many new insights about the causes of police behavior. The research provided little information about the solutions to police problems, however, and most of the recommendations of the various commissions were old ideas that had yet to be tested. Among these ideas was Vollmer's vision of a college-educated police service.[7]

In 1967, the President's Commission on Law Enforcement and Administration of Justice recommended that police set as a goal the "requirement of [a] baccalaureate degree for general enforcement officers" and "require immediately baccalaureate degrees for supervisory positions." As the commission noted, "Although there is a need for vocational training, it is not and cannot be a substitute for a liberal arts education." The commission went on to quote J. Edgar Hoover's introduction from the May, 1964, *FBI Law Enforcement Bulletin* where he noted that colleges and universities "should be initiating and increasing courses of study oriented toward the development of a career police profession."[8]

But in 1967, there were only 39 baccalaureate and 18 advanced degree criminal justice programs in higher education institutions in the whole of the United States. A decade later these had increased ten-fold to 376 baccalaureate and 140 advanced degree criminal justice programs, in addition to an increase of from 152 associate degree programs in the field to some 729 two-year programs.[9]

LAW ENFORCEMENT EDUCATION PROGRAM (LEEP)

The primary cause of the expansion in police education in the 1970s was the President's Commission on Law Enforcement, which caused the passage of the Omnibus Crime Control and Safe Streets Act of 1968. This act created the Law Enforcement Assistance Administration (LEAA), and, in turn the Law Enforcement Education Program, known to police and educators alike as LEEP, which:

> . . . provided major financial incentives for law enforcement officers to return to schools and for schools to create programs responsive to those students.[10]

LEEP, and its parent LEAA, lasted little more than a decade, but provided a nucleus of college-educated officers, many of whom have advanced today to leadership positions in their police agencies, and a tremendous number of officers with associate degrees or at least some exposure to college. But police practitioners and the academic community as a whole are still debating the purposes, types, and even the value of college education for police. James Q. Wilson, for example, commented positively on the case for college education:

> It selects from the general population men who have certain qualities (motivation, self-discipline, general intelligence) that are possibly quite useful in a police career; second, it inculcates certain characteristics (stability, urbanity, self-control) that might be especially desirable in an officer.[11]

Congress, as part of this 1968 act, replaced the three-year old Office of Law Enforcement Assistance that had used small grants to help develop police science degree programs with the Law Enforcement Assistance Administration (LEAA), which was "embroiled in controversy throughout its history." LEAA was used by police in large measure to secure grants for police hardware thought useful for riot control, often in communities that had not been affected by the massive disorders of the period. To avoid accumulation of power in another Washington bureaucracy, 85% of LEAA grants were distributed to states in the form of "block grants." States had to establish planning agencies to receive these funds. The State Planning Agencies, composed of local criminal justice officials, had to develop plans for using the money. Thus, there were no central priorities achieved through considered thought and/or research to determine significant police needs, and LEAA became, in effect, a funding agency for the police hardware industry.[12]

LEAA was the parent of the Law Enforcement Education Program and in its first seven years of existence LEEP provided almost $200 million in grants and loans for police education; which meant over half a million years of higher education for thousands of officers. In 1976, over the objections of the Ford Administration, Congress directed that this popular program be continued. The establishment of LEEP followed the social and political disruptions of the 1960s, which were viewed as a threat both to social order and to democratic processes. A professor of law and sociology at Cornell observed that police clashes with protestors in the anti-war movement, students at universities, and at the 1968 Democratic Convention in Chicago:

> ...suggested a view of the police as a highly authoritarian group isolated from the rest of society and oriented toward right-wing ideology. This was enough to convince many liberal politicians and reformers that the answer to police violence was higher education. Likewise, the inability to cope with the ghetto riots of the 1960s and the seeming helplessness to check the spiraling crime rate convinced conservative politicians that advanced police training was desirable.[13]

This, of course, neglected the historical basis on which the "new police" had been created in England and this country: to *prevent* disorder, not *control* massive disorder once it had begun. But the emphasis on crime control, not order control, over the past several decades and the new efficiency era in American society that eventually affected the police reduced police emphasis on order control. And, of course, once a mob has taken control of the streets, historically, only a military-type response can regain control.

The Cornell professor went on to note that no "evaluation or serious public debate" had been performed to determine if LEEP had "made a difference in the quality of law enforcement in America." But the next year, 1978, the Police Foundation published its evaluation of LEEP and police education overall:

> The idea that police officers should be college educated has become a cornerstone of the movement to professionalize the police. . . . Yet much police education today is intellectually shallow, conceptually narrow, and provided by a faculty that is far from scholarly. Rather than helping to change the police, police education appears to support the status quo, teaching what the police do now instead of inquiring what they could do differently.[14]

The Police Foundation report had actually been preceded by a number of academic critiques and two LEAA studies that had found faults with LEEP. A professor at a 2-year college defended the community college concept of police education in a 1971 article that quoted the American Association of Junior Colleges (above). This author, a retired FBI Agent, commented on the areas of education that professional educators disagree over, primarily the "value of the humanities in the overall process of education." He noted that academicians had concluded:

> . . . that the goals or objectives of the humanities are most desirable in the preparation for police service. . . . A taste or pinch of pure police science might be thrown in, if available, to add some flavor to the curriculum. . . . [But, he concluded] . . . It will hurt rather than help the status of police science education if an oversell is done on the values of the humanities for police work.[15]

The Cornell professor concluded that the problem with police, as seen by the various national commissions, was not their inability to respond effectively to the rising crime rate, "but the threat the police posed to democratic processes and values." He noted that "many colleges instantly created criminal justice curricula in response to the available funding," but that the original goal of "democratizing the police was displaced in favor of professionalizing the police," by the bureaucracy of LEAA. "Thus, implementing and evaluating the program became problematic."[16]

Some 10 schools, out of 1,000, received more than 10% of LEEP funds. Led by the John Jay College of Criminal Justice in New York City, these included three schools in California, a total of three in New York City, one each in Washington, D.C., Boston, and Kentucky. This analysis showed that:

> While it may be true that each region of the country receives its fair proportion of funds based upon population and criminal justice system personnel, it is not clear that money has filtered down to the

troubled urban departments which were the sources of greatest concern in the late 1960s.[17]

The bottom line is whether this federally funded program of grants for education of police officers had a positive effect on these officers and their police agencies. The Cornell author claimed that various studies found vocationally oriented students relatively impervious to changes in authoritarianism, while four-year liberal arts courses seem far more likely to change authoritarianism than vocational police science courses:

> Education has been widely held to provide the policeman with greater dignity, improve his efficiency, strengthen his image, enable him to recognize and deal more efficiently with social problems, and generally 'professionalize' the law enforcement field. We suspect that much of the support of higher education funding for police has been founded upon a diffuse belief that since the rest of the population has become better educated, the police should enjoy a corresponding increase in their education.[18]

But this article argues that the purpose of this program was to reduce conflict between the police and other social groups and to provide more effective crime control. According to this article, more and better experimentation or surveys are needed to determine whether these goals, rather than the professionalization of police, have been achieved.

Another professor, who had been affiliated with a West Coast police department, asked this question of criminal justice baccalaureate programs: "Have we grown too fast without adequate quality control?" He noted, in 1971, that the question of whether to educate or train is still unresolved, in spite of the statement of the President's Commission on Law Enforcement and Administration of Justice that while there is a need for vocational training, "it is not and can not be a substitute for a liberal arts education." Arguing that nonetheless a balance among criminal justice, behavior science, and communicative courses should be achieved, this professor went on to write that "criminal justice programs must become permanent residents in the total college community . . . rather than programs within existing non-criminal justice departments." This professor also decried the lack of academic tradition among criminal justice instructors, who "do not yet have the academic tradition that have long motivated their arts and science colleagues. They must develop the traditionally recognized academic skills if they are to be truly accepted as serious educators, rather than semi-retired practitioners."[19]

LEAA'S EVALUATION OF LEEP

In 1975, the Law Enforcement Assistance Administration published its own 500-page survey of criminal justice education and training, which covered LEEP college participant programs, management training and education, FBI programs in the police training field, law enforcement training academies, and even legal and corrections education. Federal assistance amounted to some $80 million by LEAA, $16 million by the FBI, and $128 million in veterans' benefits to students enrolled in criminal justice programs, for a total of nearly $225 million in 1975. The LEAA survey concluded that the LEEP program "appears to have contributed significantly to the rapid improvement in educational level of police officers in the period 1970–74, as compared with the trend of the preceding decade." The proportion of officers completing at least one year of college rose from 20% in 1960 to 32% in 1970 and then to 46% in 1974. But:

> The quality of many LEEP-funded criminal justice programs appears to be seriously deficient in a number of respects. . . . [the ten-fold increase in educational programs in the decade 1965 to 1975]. . . . brought substantial problems, associated with the absence in criminal justice higher education of a clearly defined body of knowledge or a *set of goals or perspectives*. . . . Lack of articulation between the goals of community colleges and four-year colleges, and lack of differentiation between training courses and educational programs have been additional major problem areas. (Emphasis added.)[20]

While LEAA guidelines emphasized "education" over specialized skill training as the primary goal of these programs, some 35% of law enforcement courses were found to be training-type offerings, with some 23% of the faculty not having advanced degrees.

An LEAA grant to Michigan State University resulted in a 1975 monograph by Larry T. Hoover that has been widely cited as a summary and critique of LEEP. In examining the rationale for educational upgrading, this author tried to measure the improvement in effectiveness of the police in first, their crime control function, second, their order maintenance function, and third, their discretionary power. Difficulties encountered included the lack of appropriate productivity measures, the influence of agency milieu, the subliminal nature of educational attributes, and "present limitations on the police patrolman's role." Four states, "representative of national characteristics," were studied: California, Michigan, Texas, and New Jersey.

Major findings indicated that some 37% of recruits to police service have been in college for at least one year (California had an atypical 73%) and some 10% had completed at least four years of college. But only 13% of the collegiate police recruits had received direct financial assistance through LEEP. Some large metropolitan agencies had difficulty in attracting collegiate recruits, because 58% of the recruits indicated their choice of agency depended, in part, on the agency system of rewards for completed education. More important, agency reputation and promotional opportunities affected their choice of department. About half of the collegiate police recruits had majored in law enforcement, with the associate degree terminal to a large proportion.[21]

This researcher cited the Presidential Commission on Law Enforcement and Administration of Justice, the Police Foundation, the American Bar Association, and "authorities too numerous to quote as individuals" (Vollmer, Fosdick, Wilson E. Purdy, Donal MacNamara, Allen Gammage, William Parker, Quinn Tamm) for the proposition that education is the key to professionalism. Larry T. Hoover noted that:

> some twenty professional groups, including law, medicine, engineering, architecture, teaching, veterinary medicine, pharmacy, etc. . . . have set minimum academic requirements. . . . to improve the quality and economic status of their practitioners in order to protect the public. . . . genuine professionalism based upon a service ideal is intrinsically related to higher educational standards.[22]

In one chapter devoted to the content of law enforcement curricula, Larry T. Hoover observes that baccalaureate programs tend to "to take the theoretically based criminal justice systemic approach," while programs at community colleges are "focused exclusively upon the police component of the criminal justice system." The monograph concluded that both 2-year and 4-year schools' curricula include "far too many professionally oriented courses" to the exclusion of general education courses more essential to students' development. Further, especially the community college course work offers training in performing operational tasks to the exclusion of courses that explore new concepts. In a word, the curricula are too vocational, and they "reinforce the most parochial concepts prevalent in the police field."[23]

POLICE FOUNDATION REPORT ON EDUCATION

In its 1978 report *The Quality of Police Education,* the Police Foundation prefaced its findings by noting that:

A decade ago the American police were in trouble. Conservatives criticized the police for failing to control crime. Liberals criticized them for brutality, corruption, racism, and failure to provide due process. . . . Today it is police education that is in trouble. The decade of rapid expansion has come to an abrupt halt . . . Higher education for police has been torn by internal strife among police educators and attacked by police administrators, academics, and several national study groups. The central thrust of this criticism is that police education is generally low in quality.[24]

This report was authored by Lawrence W. Sherman, an assistant professor in the Graduate School of Criminal Justice at the State University of New York and executive director of the National Advisory Commission on Higher Education for Police Officers. The commission, assembled by the Police Foundation to examine the question, "How can the quality of police education be improved to make it a more effective force for *changing* the police?" was chaired by Warren Bemis, former president of the University of Cincinnati, and included Tom Bradley, then mayor of Los Angeles and a former police lieutenant there; Lee Brown, then public safety commissioner of Atlanta; Norval Morris, dean of the University of Chicago Law School; Patrick V. Murphy, then president of the Police Foundation; a chief of police from Connecticut; an executive of the American Council on Education; and two other teaching lawyers.

This commission solicited the views of over two hundred state and national organizations representing law enforcement and education and held regional public forums in San Francisco, New York, and Chicago, where faculty members in police programs expressed their views, along with police officers, city administrators, police union leaders, representatives of minority police officers, and college administrators. This was not an experiment to test a policing concept, such as the Kansas City patrol experiment was. This study had a preconceived conclusion—*changing* the police—but also examined the role education has had and can have in professionalizing the police. The report did note that in the three forums held there was:

... a striking lack of consensus on the objectives of higher education for police officers, particularly on the issue of changing the police versus merely making them more efficient.[25]

But, quoting philosopher Alfred North Whitehead, "Education is the acquisition of the art of the utilization of knowledge," or how to use knowledge, the Police Foundation decided that what is needed is police education for change, not teaching basic police skills or increasing the "systems efficiency" of policing as an institution.[26]

This Police Foundation report also had a preconception about the type of education that would foster changes in policing, ie., liberal arts, not technical police science curricula. But it did recommend that the LEAA, or its successor agency or organization should establish:

> A long-term program of research following cohorts of officers through-out their careers... [for] determining the curriculum most effective for changing the police, as well as for answering the more basic question of whether education can make a difference in police behavior.[27]

The political handwriting was already on the wall—public concern about crime was diminishing to the extent that national funding for police education was about to lose Congressional support. This report also noted that higher education cannot provide an applied body of knowledge about police work that is comparable to that offered in medicine, engineering, or even agriculture. Education can prescribe how to repair broken bones, build sound bridges, and grow crops more efficiently, but with the state of knowledge now available education cannot prescribe the proper methods of order control with the same degree of certainty.[28]

The Police Foundation and its commission grouped their recommendations for police education into two general areas: educational quality and fostering change. The first area, educational quality, addressed the curricula content of police education; the college environment; faculty qualifications; and the student experience. The Foundation noted that there were three types of "police education programs" and all are too narrow. One type is the interdisciplinary liberal arts and science curriculum in criminal justice and criminology, which stresses the understanding of crime and social control. The second is a professional education curriculum in criminal justice that explains the complex operations of, and issues affecting, the entire criminal justice system. The third is more vocational in nature, a paraprofessional training in police science. But the Foundation recommended that officers be educated in a wide variety of disciplines:

... including but not limited to the police education programs. Given the great concentration of resources and enrollments in these programs, however, it is most important that their curriculums be changed.[29]

Ten years later, after LEAA was abolished and LEEP ended, this "concentration of resources" has evaporated and another recommendation of the Foundation could be reevaluated. Under the process of change, the Foundation recommended that police departments place less emphasis on educating personnel already recruited to the police service and more emphasis on recruiting the educated. This report notes that college graduates often leave police work early, "possibly out of dislike for the current authoritarian atmosphere of most police departments." This is correlated with another recommendation that police departments conduct "properly evaluated experiments with new organizational designs more appropriate for college-educated personnel." Alternatively, a Canadian study suggested that police adopt a strategy of recruiting nongraduates, subject them to initial training, which this study found does not instill authoritarianism, and then send them to college. This might have been the purpose of LEEP, but funds were too limited to accomplish this goal.[30]

"Tensions and disagreements about curriculum content constitute a normal state of affairs. . . . Faculties of law and medicine continue to hold divergent opinions about what professional education should really accomplish" noted an academic author.[31] And overall objectives or goals of education change within the educational establishment. In the ancient world, mathematics and the natural sciences were not perceived to have any relationship to action; ethics and politics were considered practical wisdom. Today, "the relationship of knowledge to contemplation and practice has been virtually reversed."[32] At the end of the last century, J. H. Newman in his 1873 work *The Idea of a University* proposed the goal of preserving old knowledge and moral values. John Dewey advanced the goal of furthering democracy in 1916.[33] Two years later, Veblen (and 30 years after him, Hutchins) advanced the pursuit of knowledge and truth for their own sakes as objectives of education. In 1930, Oxford's A. Flexner, in *Universities: American, English, German* said that colleges should be for discovering new knowledge and solving problems. Then came the goal of preparing students for careers, until Clark Kerr proposed accomplishing all of these goals at the same time.[34]

Police education in 1978, said the Police Foundation, is like the condition of medical education seventy years before when Abraham Flexner made a detailed examination of every medical school in the U.S. and Canada. The Flexner report (1910), with the help of foundation support and the growing strength of the American Medical Association, integrated medical education into the university community and forced the diploma mills out of business. Later, there were similar reports in engineering and business education. "In hopes of producing a similar impact on police education, the Police Foundation decided . . . to sponsor this report."[35]

The Police Foundation report recommended a broad education, with the number of police science courses not exceeding one-fourth of the total course work required. Police education programs at the undergraduate level should give "less emphasis to issues of police management and supervision" as few police officers become supervisors, and greater emphasis to the major issues of doing police work, including "the value choices and ethical dilemmas." The Foundation also recommended that courses on police work be continually revised to include the "rapidly growing research findings . . . such as the inexpensive research monographs published by the U.S. Law Enforcement Assistance Administration and the Police Foundation."

Other recommendations to colleges with criminal justice programs included offering these programs as a long-term commitment with a core of full-time faculty, libraries facilities comparable to other programs at the college. Classes should take place on campus and academic credit for life experience in police service or for attendance at police agency training programs should be severely limited. Community colleges should phase out their two-year programs. Faculty members should have at least two years of postgraduate education. LEEP, and the Congress, were criticized for requiring course work be "directly related" to law enforcement and criminal justice.[36]

CONCLUSION

Despite the unfocused and associate degree level of the educational advances under LEEP, criticized by the Police Foundation and other academics, there has been over the last 30 years a 23% advance in the collegiate educational level of America's police. Criminal justice has emerged as a nontraditional academic discipline, with a traditional tension in its educational philosophy.[37]

Carroll D. Buraker, writing in 1977, when he was assistant chief of the

Fairfax County, Virginia, Police Department, summarized the three advantages of college-educated police personnel: first, "a liberal education helps insure the proper use of police discretionary powers ... [such as] the decision to arrest or not arrest, to act or not act, and to shoot or not shoot." Second, there is an "expected improvement in the effectiveness of officers in performing their crime control function, through better motivation and a greater ability to apply systems and technology." Society as a whole, and policing in particular, is becoming more technical and more education is needed to cope with it. Third, "college-educated police are more able to perform their 'order maintenance' function more effectively through the more balanced use of social counseling and law enforcement techniques."

One liability is possible boredom with police work. Boredom with police duties is not critical to continued employment according to one LEAA study, but educational level is important to whether the officer intends on staying with the same department. Lateral transfer of personnel is, however, broadening toward professionalism as a whole; thus, this is not a liability except to the chief who loses personnel. Second, there is lack of proof that the college educational standard is valid, which the courts now require for job standards:

> At this point, there is no body of conclusive evidence that college education necessarily makes a better police officer. Until such research is undertaken, we cannot say categorically that education is a prerequisite for law enforcement duties.[38]

Notes to Chapter 19

1. Killinger, 1975. 164.
2. Hoover, 1975. 14.
3. Trautman, 1986. 10.
4. Witham, 1985. xi.
5. Chronister, 1982. 3. LEB, 1961b.
6. Lankes, 1971. 587–589.
7. Sherman, 1978. 34.
8. President's Commission on Law Enforcement, 1967. xi. Killinger, 1975. 141–142.
9. Fike, 1977. 457.
10. Ibid, 458.
11. Wilson, 1975b. 113.
12. LEAA, 1975. 47. Walker, 1980. 237.
13. Jacobs, 1977. 1.
14. Sherman, 1978. 18–19.

15. Lankes, 1971. 591–592.
16. Jacobs, 1977. 3–6.
17. Ibid, 9.
18. Ibid, 17.
19. Tracy, 1971. 577.
20. LEAA, 1975. V 1–6.
21. Hoover, 1975. viii–ix.
22. Ibid, 2.
23. Ibid, 34–35.
24. Sherman, 1978. ix–x.
25. Ibid, xix–xxi, xi–xii, 40.
26. Whitehead (1928) 1967. 4. Sherman, 1978. 59–60.
27. Sherman, 1978. 5.
28. Ibid, 58.
29. Ibid, 3.
30. Sherman, 1978. 13. Dalley, 1975. 468.
31. Broderick, 1980. 38.
32. Fike, 1979. 462.
33. Dewey, 1916.
34. Kerr, 1964.
35. Sherman, 1978. xi.
36. Ibid, 3–13.
37. Adams, 1976. 303.
38. Buraker, 1977. 94.

Chapter 20

FBI SERVICE ROLE REDIRECTION

There is great emphasis today by all major professions to achieve recognition in their respective fields and in furtherance of this to establish appropriate goals, standards, and a code of ethics. Law enforcement is no exception. Academic achievement is one characteristic of such professionalization.[1]

J. Edgar Hoover

To those aware of the criticism of J. Edgar Hoover during the last years of his life for the excesses the FBI was charged with in the internal security field, the advancement in professionalism of law enforcement services inaugurated by the FBI in the decade before his death is all the more remarkable. The process of expansion and accreditation of the FBI Academy curricula with the University of Virginia began under Hoover. Hoover correctly saw no major problems with accreditation of the FBI National Academy. As Director of the FBI for half a century, he had built such a professional law enforcement agency that the organization continued its contributions to law enforcement after his death.

And ideas continued to come from the FBI corps of agents after 1972, helped by the new leadership of the FBI. Clarence M. Kelley, a career FBI agent and manager before he retired who then became chief executive of a large police department, followed Hoover and was responsible for implementation of many innovations, especially the National Executive Institute. As chief of police in Kansas City, he worked with the Police Foundation on the seminal police patrol experiment. As FBI Director, he then encouraged the FBI Laboratory to embark on a research and training program for local crime laboratories. Kelley's advocacy of participatory management and his openness to new ideas enabled him to remake the FBI both as an investigative agency and in its second role as a law enforcement service agency. Federal judge William H. Webster, who followed Kelley, continued to expand the FBI's research program with approval of the National Center for the Analysis of Violent Crime at the FBI Academy. All three directors—Hoover, Kelley, and Webster—recognized the potential of the computer in the identification field.

The decade of the 1970s, with federal funding for police education, including the expansion of FBI training capabilities, the beginning of an active cooperation between academia and police leadership to experiment with policing's practices, fostered by the privately funded Police Foundation led by Patrick Murphy, the maturation of the National Crime Information Center, the computer automation of fingerprint identification, and the growth of the FBI Laboratory in research and training into a leadership position in the forensic science community, amounted to a second renaissance in the professionalism of policing.

NATIONAL ACADEMY

Significant new directions for the National Academy in the 1970s were: first, a huge increase in the FBI's capability to train local police in the National Academy and, second, college accreditation of the program. Chapter 12 outlined the beginning of the National Academy and, in 1970, FBI Special Agent, later Assistant Director, Kenneth E. Joseph prepared "A Study of the Federal Bureau of Investigation's Contribution to Law Enforcement Training and Education in the United States," for his Ph.D. in education from Michigan State University. This study noted the inadequacy of police training in the 1930s, the development of what became the FBI National Academy training program for police, FBI field training schools for local law enforcement authorities as an adjunct to the National Academy, and, most important, the expansion and new priorities of the local police training program by the FBI.[2]

In a 1972 article, just before his death, J. Edgar Hoover noted:

> At present . . . some 200 men are annually attending the FBI's National Academy. . . . With the new facilities, this number will jump to 2,000—a ten-fold increase. . . . At the same time, the FBI is developing, through extensive cooperative studies with the School of General Studies, University of Virginia, academic accreditation for educational phases of the academy program. . . . of importance is the potential impact of this program in helping raise the overall educational level of law enforcement as a profession.[3]

Hoover did not live to see this increase in the educational level of law enforcement as a profession. He had first suggested this expansion a generation before; in a 1951 letter to Rear Admiral Sidney W. Souers, Special Consultant to President Truman, Hoover had enclosed a ten-page proposal for expanding the FBI National Academy to become the "West Point of Law Enforcement," using Mayor LaGuardia's phrase of a decade before. This would include payment of transportation expenses and maintenance costs of local officers attending, which was implemented in the 1972 expansion of the Academy. As a result of President Johnson's 1965 message to Congress calling for improvement of law enforcement, the Congress appropriated funds for the expansion of FBI training facilities at the U.S. Marine Corps base at Quantico, Virginia, through the Omnibus Crime Control Act of 1968. The expanded campus was designed to train some 2,000 officers instead of the 200 the National Academy had been training annually before.[4]

Beginning in 1967, the FBI Training Division selected FBI Agents for advanced education in psychology, sociology, police administration, law, education, educational administration, and educational technology to qualify the National Academy faculty for the accreditation process. Student officers at the National Academy can now earn both undergraduate and graduate college credits from the University of Virginia for their academic work at the Academy. According to a 1954 FBI memorandum, college credit had been awarded some police officers graduating from the National Academy, but this depended on the college the officer applied to for credit.

Additional appropriations in 1968 enabled the FBI for the first time to assign agents as police instructors on a full-time basis in the FBI's nationwide field training program, which had begun as an adjunct of the National Academy. The year before, selected FBI agents received specialized training instruction on police management and human relations work, forming two-man "management" teams to discuss a variety of management topics, including recruitment, selection, and evaluation of personnel, performance rating systems, planning and inspection, organization, human relations in management, and supervisory/management development. In the next two years, over eight thousand law enforcement administrators attended two hundred such schools across the country. Other specialized courses were offered in the FBI's expanded field training program in this period: legal instruction to insure police officers understood and abided by recent Supreme Court decisions, mob and riot control courses to cope with cities' disorders during the late 1960s, community relations courses to defuse the conditions that had led to the disorders. All of this expanded police training occurred under J. Edgar Hoover.[5]

A comparison of National Academy curricula from 1939 to 1969 shows a more than 50 percent increase in criminal law courses, an almost 50 percent increase in administration curricula, and growth of more than 50 percent in behavioral science courses.

> The curriculum that began to emerge in 1972 represented a shift from emphasis on nuts and bolts, how-to-do-it vocational skills courses which dominated in 1935 to an in-depth view of academic disciplines providing insights for the police manager. . . . [6]

Academic work concentrated on the behavioral sciences, adult education, forensic science, law, and management science. In the five years between 1972 and 1979, the proportion of officers with college degrees in each class of 250 students rose from 20 to 80.

Dr. Joseph, then in charge of the FBI Academy, raised some questions about the institution in an 1979 article:

> Will it remain essentially as it is today? Will it evolve into an accredited university for law enforcement? Or, perhaps, will it become a highly specialized training center for law enforcement specialists? This debate will, and should, occur. From the discussions on the Academy's future will come decisions which will help shape the future direction of law enforcement training for many years to come.[7]

NATIONAL EXECUTIVE INSTITUTE

Clarence Kelley's experience as the chief executive of a major police department, before his appointment as Director of the FBI, caused him to direct the FBI to implement a program of advanced training for police chief executives. This was also based on the recommendation of the International Association of Chiefs of Police (IACP) committee on the police executive, chaired by Chief Edward Davis of Los Angeles, which recommended that:

> A national executive program should be established to provide advanced instruction in a wide variety of courses for police chief executives' enrichment and development.[8]

The Management Science unit at the FBI Academy developed a program that was presented to the IACP's Major City Chiefs subgroup, who unanimously endorsed this combination of brief but intensive learning experiences at the FBI Academy with requirements for extensive independent research and study preparatory to each session. Topical areas covered were national political and social trends affecting the local police function, affirmative action, media and labor relations, future structure of police organizations, financing of police operations, and the impact of crime on the police function. The detailed program was approved for college credit by the University of Virginia.[9]

NATIONAL CENTER FOR THE ANALYSIS OF VIOLENT CRIME

One characteristic of professionalism in the police field since 1970 has been the willingness of law enforcement agencies to conduct research, in tandem with the academic community, on police methods and the problems that confront police. The Police Foundation, with the cooperation of more progressive police agencies, brought about this revolution in police management (see final chapter). The FBI, in cooperation with local authorities, has implemented certain research efforts that show great promise in violent-crime control efforts. The National Center for the Analysis of Violent Crime "is a law enforcement oriented behavioral science and computerized resource," which coordinates research, training, and investigative support functions regarding the serial violent offender, particularly murderers.[10]

In 1981, the Attorney General tasked each bureau within the Department of Justice to outline its efforts to reduce violent crime, as the violent crime wave that had begun in 1963 showed no signs of abating. The Behavioral Science unit of the FBI Training Division had been active in crime analysis and criminal profiling for some years with considerable success, and had completed its first law enforcement-oriented research project: in-depth interviews of 36 sexually oriented serial murderers.

> Criminal profiling will never take the place of a thorough and well-planned investigation nor will it ever eliminate the seasoned, highly trained, and skilled detective . . . [but it has become] another investigative weapon . . . in solving a violent crime.[11]

This research project was conducted by FBI agents in cooperation with academic and mental health professionals, under a grant from the National Institute of Justice. In the course of their travels, Behavioral Science unit Agents had exposure to a variety of police programs designed to deal with violent crime, such as former Los Angeles Police Department Commander Pierce R. Brooks' Violent Criminal Apprehension Program (VICAP) and the Arson Information Management System

(AIMS), developed by Dr. David Icove. In 1982, the concept of a National Center for the Analysis of Violent Crime was developed.

The goal of this center has been to reduce the amount of violent crime by serving as a law enforcement clearinghouse for the most difficult to solve violent crimes: serial homicides, forcible rapes, child molestation, and arson. The center collects and analyzes violent crime data and provides assistance to law enforcement agencies to more rapidly apprehend perpetrators of violent crime:

> ... Unlike other disciplines concerned with human violence, law enforcement does not, as a primary objective, seek to explain actions of a violent offender. Instead, its task is to ascertain the identity of the offender based on what is known of his actions ... to prevent further violence.[12]

The Violent Criminal Apprehension Program part of the center operates to link these unsolved crimes together nationwide, providing assistance in the coordination of complex interagency investigations. The center uses the latest computer engineering advances, with promising results for the future.[13]

FBI LABORATORY

The *Crime Laboratory Digest,* a new FBI publication for forensic scientists, noted on the retirement from the FBI of Assistant Director of the Laboratory Dr. Briggs J. White:

> In addition to the important role he played in the formation of the ASCLD [American Association of Crime Laboratory Directors], Dr. White is credited with his innovative leadership and vision in changing the traditional role and outlook of the FBI's Laboratory. Under his guidance, expanded programs in research, communication, and training of state and municipal law enforcement crime laboratory personnel were inaugurated.[14]

Briggs White, a native of Bristol, Colorado, who received a Ph.D. in chemistry in 1940 from the University of Colorado, joined the FBI as a laboratory technician the same year, then completed his Agent's training in April, 1942, and was assigned to the Laboratory until he retired in 1975. He was assigned to the New York and other offices of the FBI for field experience for just a few weeks at a time. In 1961, he was promoted to second in charge of the Laboratory and was put in charge in 1973.

White explained that at the time he entered the FBI, eight years after the FBI Laboratory had been established, the Laboratory had concentrated on document examination work and he was one of the first group of Ph.D.'s hired with expertise in other areas of scientific examination. This expansion of the Laboratory continued through World War II with the demands on the facility for examinations in sabotage cases, where chemistry and metallurgy expertise particularly were needed. At this time, too, Robert Frazier, probably this country's foremost expert in firearms examinations, joined the FBI Laboratory.

Research by the Laboratory was limited at this time to work by practicing examiners when they could fit it into their schedules. White traveled to Boston, for example, to do research in blood chemistry. Hoover permitted this research, when time was available, but not being a scientist himself, Hoover was primarily concerned with the Laboratory completing its regular work and was not fully aware of the necessity for "networking" among forensic scientists to develop this growing field, according to White.

In 1973, when Clarence Kelley was appointed Director of the FBI after J. Edgar Hoover's death, White was promoted to Assistant Director in charge of the FBI Laboratory, the first Ph.D. in science to hold this position. At one of the first meetings Kelley had with the Assistant Directors, he explained that while he had served in the FBI for twenty years under Hoover, some things could and should be changed in the FBI and encouraged the Assistant Directors to present him with ideas for changes. White went to Director Kelley and suggested that the Laboratory embark on a regular research program in forensic science. Kelley agreed and a research center for the Laboratory was established at the FBI Academy at Quantico, VA, in 1981.[15]

Also, at Dr. White's suggestion the American Society of Crime Laboratory Directors also proposed that the FBI Laboratory engage in advanced training of state and local crime laboratory technicians. At that time, an FBI survey of local crime laboratories in the U. S. revealed that there were some 180 local governmental forensic science facilities, staffed by some 3,000 criminalists:

> While a number of the laboratories are of considerable size, the majority are relatively small and our initial survey developed that they have a great need for training to improve their technical proficiency.[16]

As a result of this survey, the FBI hosted a symposium on crime laboratory development, which resulted in the formation of the American Society of Crime Laboratory Directors by virtually all the crime laboratories in the nation. This organization of over a hundred such facilities discussed legislation, management, communication, education, and organization in the forensic science field. The first symposium was funded by the Law Enforcement Assistance Administration and hosted by the FBI at the FBI Academy at Quantico. The second was entirely sponsored by the FBI. The Laboratory had already established, under Dr. White's leadership, a masters degree program at George Washington University in Washington, D.C., that was completely taught by FBI personnel from the Laboratory, but was open to any forensic science graduate students.[17]

The new Forensic Science Research and Training Center houses a permanent instructional staff, the Forensic Science Training unit, which provides expert forensic science instruction to state and local crime laboratory personnel and a group of scientists in the research staff. As the only facility of its kind in the United States, its goals are to develop (1) new and reliable methods that can be applied in forensic science, (2) to study technical problems confronting forensic scientists in order to overcome them and (3) to evaluate current technology and ascertain its application to forensic science. Sometimes research work is done with scientists at the University of Virginia, such as recent work on monoclonal antibodies that can identify human, as opposed to animal, blood.[18] New or improved techniques developed at the center include new techniques for "tagging" petroleum products, a new method of typing red blood cells and a method of determining the sex of an individual from a dried bloodstain. Other research has been in the areas of gunshot residues, explosives, and sex determination of forcibly removed hairs. In 1987, there were 25 separate course offerings for crime laboratory personnel.[19]

Over the years the FBI Laboratory has developed in three areas: document analysis, scientific analysis, research/training, and special projects. The Document section examines physical evidence involving handwriting, ink and paper, alterations of documents, and evidence involving shoe prints and tire treads. This section also handles translation of foreign language material, cryptanalytic examinations of secret communications, and the FBI polygraph program. The Scientific Analysis section handles chemistry, toxicology, arson, firearms, toolmarks, hairs and fibers, blood, metallurgy, mineralogy, number restoration, glass fractures, explosives, paints, plastics, and other related matters. The Forensic Science Research and Training Center provides investigator and examiner training in addition to limited research capability. The Special Projects section provides forensic examination of photographic evidehce, photographic operations and training, and exhibit functions, including those for trials.[20]

By the early 1980s, the FBI Laboratory performed over a million scientific examinations on evidence annually, a third of them at no cost for state and local law enforcement authorities. With the laboratory's new emphasis on training (over 1,000 forensic science students had been trained that year), the increase in the number of examinations for state and local authorities has been stabilized in recent years:

> The present policy is to concentrate on providing sufficient training to state and local crime laboratory examiners of physical evidence to decrease their dependence on the FBI Laboratory. Direct services will continue to be provided when law enforcement agencies do not have access to jurisdictional laboratories and where the jurisdictional laboratory does not have the necessary instrumentation and/or expertise to perform the indicated examination.[21]

IDENTIFICATION SERVICE

As the computer replaces the industrial revolution with a technological/ information age, law enforcement, too, has gained an invaluable tool, especially in the field of identification. The pioneering work done by the FBI in automating fingerprint identification has provided the basis for most of the automated fingerprint systems used today by police departments. Writing about these systems, two Virginia police chiefs called the "automation of fingerprints for classification and matching . . . the most significant technological innovation in law enforcement in decades. . . ."[22]

As early as 1934, the FBI's Identification Division had experimented with automation; only the punch card system was then available, and it was not able to cope with the daily workload in the Identification Division. By 1939, the FBI's fingerprint files had grown to 10 million cards. Today, the FBI's criminal fingerprint file contains over 83 million cards on more than 22 million persons. An average workday brings some 32,000 fingerprint cards to the Identification Division. This volume of work has required the employment and training of over 3,600 employees at times.

FBI progress toward automation by computer was initiated in 1963 in cooperation with the National Bureau of Standards. The automation of the FBI's Identification Division's fingerprint work involved two kinds of information: criminal history records and fingerprints. Electronic data processing could be readily adapted to convert the criminal history records. But computer hardware had to be designed to "read" fingerprints. The FBI and the National Bureau of Standards chose digital image processing as best suited to fingerprint automation. In effect, an entirely new method of classifying fingerprints had to be developed beyond the Henry system, which itself had been extensively expanded by the FBI to cope with the its huge collection of fingerprints.[23]

A fingerprint reader had to be developed which would determine the position and orientation of the locations where the pattern of ridges end or split (bifurcations); this is called the minutiae of the fingerprint. The FBI contracted to build engineering models of fingerprint readers. Concurrently, the NBS developed computer logic and alogorithums (mathematical formulas) to search and match fingerprint data derived by these fingerprint readers. As work on the computer fingerprint reader hardware and software began, the FBI Identification Division also started to computerize the criminal history records and print reports of identified file subjects automatically, the first phase of the Automated Identification Division System. The entire project had to be accomplished in phases, both to take advantage of computer developments and to allow the daily work of the division to continue during implementation.

In 1983, the second phase of this system was connected with the National Crime Information Center (NCIC)'s Interstate Identification Index (see Chapter 17). States that can access the Interstate Identification Index can thus make on-line requests for records from the FBI's Identification Division and receive them back on-line.[24]

The next phase of the Automated Identification Division System provides better service by reducing processing time for fingerprint records for both the criminal justice system and employers/licensing agencies. In 1988, fingerprint work processing will be reduced from the current two to three weeks to less than 18 hours for 95 percent of the requests for fingerprint record checks.

Automation of the FBI's fingerprint work was initially concentrated on the processing of ten-print fingerprint cards, since this was the bulk of the workload most seriously in need of automated support. However, as fingerprint identification began early in this century as a process to identify the criminal for court handling, the use of the new system of identification to solve crimes through latent fingerprints left at the scene of a crime was also developed. So, too, with the progress of automation. In recent years, computer technology has helped solve criminal cases as an aid in latent fingerprint identification. It is more feasible to let the computer perform tasks too labor intensive to be performed manually, and this is possible as more of the FBI Identification Division's data is placed in computerized files.

In the past, an FBI latent fingerprint specialist would attempt every approach humanly possible to try to identify latent prints submitted as evidence in a case. But, after exhausting all possible suspects or leads without making an identification, the case would have to be returned to the contributing agency unsolved. The Fleagle case in 1928, detailed in Chapter 17, illustrates this problem. With the introduction of the computer, it has become feasible to use new techniques to select logical suspects in cases involving crime-scene latent fingerprints in certain cases. The Latent Descriptor Index program uses latent fingerprint pattern types, physical description of the subject information, if available, and case information to conduct a computer search of the Identification Division's automated files. With the introduction of the semiautomatic fingerprint readers—SAR terminals—fingerprint minutiae data can now be used in these searches to further limit potential suspects.

A new automated capability, called the Automated Latent System Model, provides an on-line searching and matching capability against a data base of repeat offenders and individuals known to be associated with special interest groups of major concern to the FBI. This works by entering the personal descriptive information, special interest group designation(s), and fingerprint data into a semiautomatic fingerprint reader terminal. The Automated Latent System Model selects candidates from the data base that match the descriptive information submitted. Then all possible candidates are compared with the latent fingerprint via the matching algorithms. The final step in the fingerprint identification process is the comparison of the incoming fingerprint card or latent print with a candidate fingerprint card selected by the automated search process. This is done by a qualified fingerprint examiner who decides whether the two prints are identical or not. All identifications are verified by a second examiner. In order for these comparisons to be made, the candidate fingerprint card had to be retrieved from the manual fingerprint file and, after the comparison was made, returned to the file.

Work began in 1983 on an Automated Image Retrieval System which displays stored fingerprint images to the examiner, thus eliminating the manual fingerprint card retrieval process. This will also eliminate the problem of misfiled or out-of-file fingerprint cards which happen in a large manual filing system. But the important advantage of this system will be the response time savings. It will also permit the introduction of an on-line identification service through use of electronically transmitted fingerprint search requests from contributors.

This system is also a three-phase program. The first phase is the determination of the rigorous requirements for image quality, image capture, storage, and retrieval. The image-processing requirements for fingerprint images present an unusually complex problem in preserving the necessary detail of the fingerprint impression used by the fingerprint examiner. Again, the second phase will be the testing of a pilot Automated Image Retrieval System and finally the process of implementing production models into the overall automation system.

The requirements of the first generation automated fingerprint reader were to be able to read the minutia characteristics (ridge endings and bifurcations) used by fingerprint examiners to identify an individual's fingerprints. After that reader was developed and tested, the potential for the reader to produce data which might be used to automatically classify a fingerprint was recognized. An attempt was made to add this capacity to the first readers, but it was learned that automatic classification was a much tougher job than minutiae reading.

Although there are some commercially available automated identification systems, which local and state law enforcement agencies are beginning to use to great advantage, these systems have limited classification capabilities. The classifications produced by these systems are not compatible with the Henry-based NCIC classification system. More important to the Identification Division, these systems are incapable at present of handling the extremely large fingerprint file of the FBI.

Also in this project are development of specific fingerprint classification rules for the computer to use; since the major requirement is to be compatible with the live fingerprint examiner, the rules are the same as those used by the examiner. This approach is based on artificial intelligence concepts and use of rule-based systems to mimic the human decision process utilized in classifying a fingerprint. These more diversified services will be provided over existing criminal justice communications networks such as the FBI's NCIC and the National Law Enforcement Telecommunications System (NLETS). Efforts of the Identification Division to provide faster services will be in the direction of nationwide, on-line, automated fingerprint identification searches.[25]

The re-direction of the FBI's service to law enforcement role has added to the progress toward professionalism for police: in education through accreditation of the FBI National Academy, expanded and improved FBI police training nationwide, and the National Executive Institute for police executives; the reorientation of the FBI Laboratory's mission toward training of forensic science laboratory personnel; the new emphasis on research in policing begun by the Police Foundation and mirrored by the FBI in its National Center for the Analysis of Violent Crime and the Forensic Science Research and Training Center; and the automation of identification records using computer technology.

As J. Edgar Hoover said in 1970, after he had led one renaissance in law enforcement and helped begin a second:

> ... Law enforcement will either vigorously progress and thereby increase its professional stature or disappointingly regress and consequently sink into a quagmire of mediocrity. The direction in which the profession goes depends entirely upon the actions of its members. The FBI dedicates itself to providing for the needs of local law enforcement in an effort to assist and encourage further professional development.[26]

Notes to Chapter 20

1. Joseph, 1970. 119–120.
2. Ibid, 7.
3. Hoover, 1972.
4. Hoover, 1951. Joseph, 1970. 94.
5. Joseph, 1970. 101, 111. Gerarty, 1954.
6. Joseph, 1970. 25, 97–100, 131–6, 153–8.
7. Ibid, 27.
8. IACP, 1976. 119.
9. FBI's National Executive Institute, 1976.
10. Webster, 1986. 1.
11. Douglas & Burgess, 1986. 13.
12. Ibid, 9.
13. Depue, 1986. 2–5.
14. FBI, 1975. 1.
15. White, 1986.
16. Kelley, 1973.
17. FBI, 1974.
18. Bishop, 1986. 19.
19. Doran, 1982. 744–5.

20. Annual Reports of the Attorney General, 1983, 1984.
21. Webster, 1985. 79–81.
22. Buracker, 1984. 2.
23. Banner, 1985. 2.
24. Lyford, 1983. 10.
25. Neudorpher, 1986. 3–8.
26. Joseph, 1970. 121.

Chapter 21

THE 21ST CENTURY

S ir Robert Peel, the founder in 1829 of London's police, wanted the English police service to succeed in order control through public approval, rather than through any show of force as the military had used. The police service was to be:

> ... in tune with the people, understanding the people, and drawing its strength from the people.[1]

As American police approach the 21st century, this descendant institution of the English police is approaching this goal, primarily through "community policing," the central feature of which is "encouraging direct cooperation between citizens and the police."[2] This is *not* community *control* of policing, the radical demand of the 1960s, but policing *for* the community, where "police serve, learn from, and are accountable to the community. Behind the new professionalism is a governing notion: that the police and the public are co-producers of crime prevention."[3] The trend toward community policing, marked by a return to some forms of foot patrol, has been fostered by the research first conducted by the Police Foundation in the private sector and then by other organizations in the federal government and police community. In 1979, four police organizations representing 80% of the police community banded together to promote accreditation of police agencies in the U.S., fostering the concept one author developed that professionalism is not so much a matter of quality as a quantitative process.[4]

COMMUNITY POLICING

In Reston, Virginia, where the author has lived for over twenty years, a "new town" was built in the Washington, D.C., suburban community of Fairfax County. This county has the eighth largest county police department in the country, with almost a thousand officers in 1987. The author observed the planned town of Reston (which does not have its own police department) grow from an experiment to a bedroom community, largely populated by upper-middle class "liberals," and then to a high tech-oriented community. In its early years it was one of the first suburbs to actively seek low-cost, subsidized housing. It also heavily supported the arts, and the first little league sport was not baseball, but soccer.

The Fairfax County Police Department was formed in 1940 to perform police and law enforcement duties that had been handled by the county sheriff's department. As the county grew, the department expanded to where it is now the largest police department in the state. In the early 1970s, Reston experienced the explosion of drug use by the "60s generation." It was especially noticeable in the shopping area that was the first town center; youths began to congregate and abuse drugs and alcohol there. Their disorderly conduct attracted the attention not only of the merchants, but of the community as a whole as the center had been designed by the developer to attract strollers (you had to walk into the center; parking was outside of it).

The Fairfax County Police tried a variety of tactics to "clean up" the center, which had attracted the "hippies" of that generation. Undercover operations against the drug users and distributors helped, but the real solution finally was foot patrol by officers permanently assigned to the area. Ostensibly, the officers were there for law enforcement, but the sense of the neighborhood was that the area needed order control. As the "hippie" culture faded, just one patrolman acting as a community service officer patrolled the center on foot. He spends three-quarters of his duty time walking the center, handling what he calls "public relations,"—notifications and public service duties. As with most patrol officers in this country, little time is spent on law enforcement, more is spent on maintaining community standards of order maintenance.

The two huge shopping centers in the county periodically have officers walking, in addition to their own private security guards, but Reston is the only area with one officer permanently assigned primarily to foot patrol. Eminently suited to the neighborhood (this 20-year veteran of police work has a master's degree in divinity and also works as a pastor in drug and alcohol rehabilitation), this officer embodies the best in what the older generation remembers about the "cop on the beat." Miscreants often approach the officer to "turn themselves in" for violations for which there is process outstanding.[5]

This is the essence of community policing. For a suburban police department which must use motor patrol (and even helicopters) to police

Virginia's largest county, both in geographic and population terms, to recognize and effectively solve a particular neighborhood's problem with foot patrol is community policing at its best. Knowing the community, and willingness to experiment to solve particular neighborhood problems, is the direction policing is taking now, and will take into the 21st century.

This type of policing, of course, has historical antecedents: citizen involvement in crime control is deeply rooted in virtually all cultures. In Western culture, it predates formal, governmental police agencies in the form of kin policing and its later forms of tything, "hue and cry," and "watch and ward" (see Chapter 1). The earliest English and American "new police" relied heavily on citizen cooperation, but as police became more professional in terms of efficiency and society and police became more reliant on technology (the automobile), the intimate relationship between the citizen and the police was neglected. "Stranger policing" was the technological response to the polity's demand for efficient law enforcement. But, beginning in 1967 with the Presidential commission condemnation of "stranger policing," police professionals have experimented with a great variety of community policing programs. These programs also represent our society's change in emphasis toward rights of people versus property rights.

Hundreds of these types of programs have been implemented with varying success. The value of the individual programs depend on the neighborhood in which they are implemented. In line with this country's decentralization of government, police agencies, in turn, have learned that different solutions have to be attempted in different neighborhoods within communities, sometimes even within different periods as the neighborhoods change. These programs are grouped generically into four different categories: community-oriented programs, youth-oriented programs (as demographics dictate crime trends), programs targeted at other special groups, and programs targeted at specific problems. According to a recent study, a majority of the largest cities having police departments of over 1,000 officers (31 in this country in 1986) have some form of foot patrol programs: Atlanta, Baltimore, Boston, Chicago, Cleveland, Dallas, Detroit, Denver, Honolulu, Houston, Los Angeles, Milwaukee, Miami, New York, Philadelphia, San Antonio, San Diego, San Francisco, and Washington, D.C. These programs can also include neighborhood storefront police stations, decentralized team policing, crime stoppers, crime resistance programs, neighborhood watches, civilianization, and motorscooter-type patrol, all of which add up to community-oriented policing.[6]

The *FBI Law Enforcement Bulletin* has reported these developments in community policing. In Syracuse, New York, where Patrick Murphy had been chief of police in the 1960s, Chief of Police Thomas J. Sardino, President of the International Association of Chiefs of Police in 1984, outlined the Crime Control Team concept in a 1971 article in the *Bulletin*. Based on a study of the Syracuse Police Department by Dr. James F. Elliott, a physicist with General Electric on a leave of absence to study policing, authored *The "New" Police*, published in 1973. Dr. Elliott had concluded that "new technology alone was not the panacea of police problems . . . that top management of the police department can delegate more responsibility and that the lower-level policeman can accept it." Rejecting the military model of management, Sardino opted for a form of team policing that he believed increased the individual officer's professionalism by giving the officer more responsibility.[7]

Building rapport between police and the populace was the thrust of a neighborhood police unit in Albany, New York, that used storefront police offices, blazer-type uniforms, and foot patrol that "developed and maintained a productive relationship with the community."[8] "National Neighborhood Watch Program" in the January, 1974, issue of the *Bulletin* outlined the origins of this citizen cooperative burglary prevention program that originated with the National Sheriffs' Association. Rochester, New York, was the site of yet another team policing program reported in the *Bulletin*. Experimentation on this concept in Rochester began in 1970. Demonstrating the department's willingness to experiment, and to evaluate the experiment, the program was then implemented city-wide in 1975.[9] "Crime Stoppers," the mass media reward program that has become national in scope, began in Albuquerque, New Mexico, 18 months prior to the article in the August, 1978, issue of the *FBI Law Enforcement Bulletin*. The article explained its operation, and success.[10]

Recent studies have shown that people want a "visible police presence" to improve the quality of life in their communities, and this means at least some police foot patrol. The Kansas City/Police Foundation research project on preventive patrol showed that random motor patrol did not materially affect the crime rate or the community's fear of crime. On-going studies show that the most promising developments for actually having an impact on the crime rate are the programs targeted at removing high-rate repeat offenders from the streets, if problems can be solved in implementation of these experiments.

But, as a young patrolman in New York City after World War II, former Police Foundation president Patrick Murphy learned the value of contact with the citizens he served on foot patrol. In New Jersey, passage of the Safe and Clean Neighborhoods Program in 1973 made state funds available for foot patrol in selected cities (28 in 1975, rising to 32 in 1980) in compliance with state criteria. Two-thirds of the $12 million allocated was available for the "safe" part of the program. As a result of inquiries from state officials to the Police Foundation as to the cost-effectiveness of this program, the Foundation undertook a multi-faceted study of the question of foot patrol.

In Newark, New Jersey, the Foundation worked with the police department and the state to design an experiment with foot patrol to test a number of hypotheses: that (1) foot patrol would improve citizen attitudes toward police, (2) foot patrol would reduce crime, either reported crime or crime victimization, (3) foot patrol would increase the number of arrests, and (4) foot patrol would increase job satisfaction of officers assigned it.

The complexities of conducting the overall New Jersey survey and especially the Newark experiment fill a 130-page report which affords a perception of the difficulties faced by the researchers in such a project. But the findings developed shed new light on foot patrol: (1) residents were aware of foot patrol to a much greater extent than motorized patrol and viewed police more favorably as a result, (2) crime rates, measured by reported crime or by victimization surveys, were *not* affected, (3) residents *perceived* diminishment of crime and disorder problems, and (4) officer job satisfaction did increase.[11]

As Murphy's preface to this report notes:

One of the questions citizens most ask of mayors, council members, and police chiefs is, "Why don't we have foot patrol, like in the good old days?" The good old days were a time of tightly knit urban neighborhoods ... and few patrol cars in which officers could be encapsulated and made remote from the citizens they served.... Citizens associate the officer on the foot beat with a time when crime rates were low and they felt secure in their neighborhoods.

[This] study concludes that, although foot patrol (like routine motor patrol ...) does not appreciably reduce or prevent crime, it does measurably and significantly affect citizens' feeling of safety and mobility in their neighborhoods.[12]

Today, police departments are experimenting with a variety of crime attack strategies, including decoy operations, covert patrol, field interrogations (which the National Advisory Commission on Civil Disorders condemned for its effect on race relations), repeat offender programs, saturation patrol (first tried in New York City in 1954 with some success, but great expense), and repeat complaint address policing. These strategies remain, for the most part, unevaluated, according to Lawrence W. Sherman in *Communities and Crime.* They may work in some areas, particularly those with concentrated high crime rates such as exist in New York City, but these tactics can never, nor are they intended to, gain the widespread public support that community policing engenders.[13]

Professor of law and sociologist Jerome Skolnick noted in *The New Blue Line* that the new strategy of community policing requires a genuine commitment on the part of the police chief executive, plus public support. This innovation also requires the chief to motivate the rest of the police department, as these new ideas run counter to tradition, and can thus encounter police union opposition. But Richard Ayres, an FBI lecturer to the police community on unionism, argues persuasively that unions can contribute to police professionalism by lessening job dissatisfaction. He advances the thesis propounded by Paul Hersey and Kenneth Blanchard in *Management of Organization Behavior*[14] that there are motivation and hygiene factors in any career; the latter include working conditions and salary, which are the conditions that unions address. If the union gains its objectives alleviating these potential dissatisfiers, the motivators—achievement, responsibility and growth—some of the elements of professionalism, are enhanced.

In 1975, when police unionism had crested, Ayres noted:

A professional is motivated by accomplishing an interesting, challenging task and from his feeling of accomplishment alone, not from the salary, working conditions or other environmental factors that are peripheral to the job.[15]

THE POLICE FOUNDATION

The police officers' and the physicians' life and death authority, mentioned at the beginning of chapter 19, is just one of the parallels between these two callings. Education, professional standards and ethics are beginning to be additional parallels. But, most striking, is the acceptance of the necessity of research probative of the value of curative techniques, of the body in medicine, of the community in policing. Research came of age in policing with the establishment of the Police Foundation in 1970.

The Police Foundation was initially best known for its year-long, Kansas City Preventive Patrol Experiment, completed in 1973, which showed that the level of preventive police patrol did not affect the crime rate or citizens' fear of crime. This conclusion caused a re-examination of one of policing's basic tenets, that crime is prevented by random police patrol. More important, the study opened policing's door to experimentation by showing that experiments could be conducted while a police department carried out its responsibilities to life and property. This was one of the goals of the Police Foundation: to overcome natural police objections to experimentation, objections based on fear the process would interfere with normal operations and obligations.

> The mission of the Police Foundation is to foster improvement and innovation in American policing and, thus, to help the police in their mission of reducing crime and disorder in America's cities.[16]

Or, as the concluding chapter of Patrick Murphy's 1977 book, *Commissioner*, summarized the philosophy of the Police Foundation: it "rests not on the proposition that American policing, with minor modifications, is in good shape but on precisely the opposite."[17]

Beyond the basic mission statement, underlying assumptions about police work guide the Foundation; over the last 16 years these assumptions have become guiding standards for much of American policing. The Foundation believes that the control of crime and the maintenance of order depends on the cooperation of citizens, thus police must be close to the citizens they serve. This belief is now a tenet of police practice that has helped to foster today's community-oriented policing programs, designed to bring police and the citizenry closer together.

In 1970, McGeorge Bundy, President of the Ford Foundation, met with then FBI Director J. Edgar Hoover and outlined the Ford Foundation's plan to begin a Police Development Fund, which would have 30 million dollars to spend over the next five years in grants to police departments to bring about major reforms. The foundation was to be guided by a board of directors consisting of members of the legal, academic, and police communities, including Quinn Tamm, Executive Director of the International Association of Chiefs of Police (IACP) and a retired FBI executive.

The social changes of the 1960s were outlined as reasons for this new effort in a statement by Bundy:

> The need for reinforcement and change in police work has become more urgent than ever in the last decade because of rising rates of crime, increased resort to violence, and rising tension, in many communities, between disaffected or angry groups and the police.[18]

This statement was an echo of the Presidential Commission's condemnation of stranger policing, and the rest of the Ford Foundation report on the new organization also showed its Progressive Movement historical background. It observed that a fundamental attack on crime would require a national effort to lessen poverty, slums, ill health, and illiteracy, but noted that remedies to the criminal justice system "cannot wait for action on the full range of our social ills." Noting that federal funds would be available in the 1970s to assist local police for the first time (the Law Enforcement Assistance Administration), the Foundation expressed concern whether our society would end up with more of the same system or with "something new and significantly different" in policing, because:

> We leave to the police many of society's problems, whether or not they are equipped to handle them. We have neither articulated a precise role for them in combatting crime, nor structured their broader role in the community. Nevertheless, whenever the lid blows, we call the police.[19]

The first study to have a major impact on police operational practices was the landmark Kansas City Preventive Patrol Experiment. Conducted from October 1, 1972, to September 30, 1973, when Clarence M. Kelley was chief of the Kansas City department, this study showed that increasing or decreasing the level of routine preventive patrol had no appreciable effect on crime, fear of crime, or citizen satisfaction with police services. The Kansas City preventive patrol evaluation divided one patrol division's 15 beats into an experimental area of 3 groups of 5 beats, using computer-based techniques, with similar crime figures, population characteristics, and calls for police service. One group of beats was designated "reactive," where preventive patrol was eliminated and patrol cars entered only in response to calls for service. A second set of beats was the "control," where the usual level of preventive patrol was maintained. A third "proactive" group of beats, with twice the usual level of preventive patrol, was also established.

Victimization surveys before and after the experiment, reaching a total of 1,200 households, also determined the fear of crime and attitudes of citizens and businessmen toward police. The three sets of experimental patrol conditions—reactive, proactive, and control—appeared not to affect crime, delivery of police services, or the fear of crime, in the way police had often assumed they did. Even one fear of the experimenters, that traffic accidents would increase in the reactive group of beats, did not occur.

As Patrick Murphy's foreword to the report on this experiment noted:

It is not easy for police departments to conduct operational experiments. For one thing, maintaining experimental conditions cannot be permitted to interfere with police responsibility for life and property.... [This] ranks among the very few major social experiments ever to be completed ... never before had there been an attempt to determine through such scientific examination the value of visible police patrol.[20]

The decade of the 1970s brought numerous Police Foundation experiment reports and other studies of law enforcement issues to this country's police community. These experiments were carefully designed by social scientists using the latest methods of statistical analysis and verification, in cooperation with the various police departments that were helping conduct the tests. And the various experiments and reports were on subjects that the law enforcement community recognized as important issues for policing. This was a successful effort to prove the validity of Police Foundation experimental methods that produced valid conclusions. The few earlier analyses of policing had not been accepted by the law enforcement community because the research methods or the data had been found lacking in some aspects.

Some of the issues addressed in 1974, the year of the Kansas City patrol experiment report, included the subject of policewomen on patrol in Washington, D.C. The Police Foundation report concluded that gender is not a legitimate occupational qualification for patrol work. This year also saw publication of *Guidelines and Papers from the National Symposium on Police Labor Relations,* jointly sponsored by the IACP and the Police Foundation. The next year, 1975, brought a study of officer height and its relationship to selected aspects of performance; a study of the cost and impact of police corruption; and an experiment in San Diego, California, that showed the value of field interrogation in deterring certain crimes, particularly those committed by youths in groups.

The remainder of the decade saw a report on an experiment that addressed the peer review approach to modifying the behavior of police officers (*Kansas City Peer Review Panel,* 1976). Another reported on the effectiveness of patrol officers and detectives working in teams in Rochester, NY (*Managing Investigations,* 1976). Then, a study of three intervention approaches—authority, negotiation, and counseling, led a majority of officers in the experiment to decide that negotiation was the most important approach for recruits to learn (*The Police and Interpersonal Conflict,* 1976). The experience of six California cities in police personnel exchanges; *Police Response Time* not strongly affecting citizen satisfaction with police service in Kansas City, MO (1976); and different approaches to criminal apprehension in Kansas City (1976) were other reports. The Foundation also published *Police Chief Selection: A Handbook for Local Government* in 1976.

The next year brought a report on *Patrol Staffing in San Diego* (1977), a most important study of the comparative effectiveness and safety of one- or two-officer units which concluded that one-officer units are more efficient and safer. This year saw the results of studies in Detroit and Kansas City showing the importance of threats as predictors of domestic violence (*Domestic Violence and the Police,* 1977), a critical area to police patrol officers. The hard-to-maintain, but useful, team policing concept as an alternative to traditional patrol methods was detailed (*Cincinnati Team Policing Experiment,* 1977).

Performance Appraisal in Police Departments, Police Personnel Management Information Systems, and *Selection through Assessment Centers: A Tool for Police Departments* were all the subjects of 1977 reports. The next year brought a general administrative survey, *Police Practices,* 1978, which was a continuation of a study begun in 1951 by the Kansas City Police Department, and the history of a failed attempt to bring about radical change in a major American police department (*The Dallas Experience,* 1978).[21]

The quality and quantity of these experiments and reports brought credit to the Police Foundation and to the social scientists who designed and implemented these pioneering studies. In a single decade, the Police Foundation had become a force for change and improvement in American policing. All of the Police Foundation's various experiments are having impact on policing, and will continue to have into the next century. But two, especially, illustrate community-oriented policing: the previously described Newark foot patrol project and a domestic violence experiment in Minneapolis.

Perception of citizen safety on the part of women entered into the

Minneapolis Domestic Violence Experiment, which took place over a year and a half in 1981 and 1982. Under a grant from the National Institute of Justice (NIJ), a cooperative effort on the part of the Minneapolis Police Department and the Police Foundation tested police responses to domestic violence, which is "the staple and bane of every patrol officer's work life," according to former police officer James K. Stewart, now Director of the National Institute of Justice.

As the Police Foundation summary report on this project noted, this "was the first scientifically controlled test of the effects of arrest for any crime." And the experiment showed that of the three standard methods police use in responding to domestic violence: arrest, counseling both parties, or sending assailants away from home for several hours, arrest was the most effective response as it resulted in considerably less recidivism.[22]

The purpose of this experiment was to test the validity and effectiveness of (1) the traditional police response of doing as little as possible in domestic violence cases because the offenders would not be punished by the courts, (2) the psychologists' view that police mediate these disputes, but not make arrests, or (3) the approach recommended by the Police Executive Research Forum (formed by the Police Foundation as a separate organization of major city chief executives with college degrees) and by many women's groups that police treat domestic violence as a criminal offense subject to arrest.

Previous research in this area suggested that arrests take place in less than 10% of the cases, in spite of violence in one- to two-thirds of the incidents. Recently liberalized legislation in Minnesota, allowing police to make arrests for misdemeanor assault without having witnessed the assault, allowed design of a classic lottery-type experiment. The three different responses being tested—arrest, counseling, and separation—were governed by a color-coded set of report forms for officers' use. Alternating colors dictated the response the officers were to follow in each case.

Follow-up interviews by a female staff, plus criminal justice reports on the alleged assailants, were collected for six months after the experiment in the 314 cases studied. Only three of the 136 assailants arrested received formal sanction from a judge, but all spent the night in jail. The Police Foundation Report on this experiment carefully notes all the variables that might have affected the results, but the clear conclusion was that arrest had the best potential of reducing repeat violence in these types of cases.

This has impacted legislative action in other states that has effected police actions in domestic violence cases, thus returning a measure of civility to the marital relationship. New York City, Los Angeles, Washington, D.C., Baltimore County, San Francisco, Seattle, Denver, and Minneapolis have imposed mandatory arrest policies, reflecting that "Society has taken a different view of domestic violence than existed 10 years ago," according to a Washington, D.C., police official.[23]

Complementing the research of the private Police Foundation, is a Department of Justice component, the:

> National Institute of Justice is the primary Federal sponsor of research in criminal justice . . . it serves as a bridge between the capabilities of the research community and the needs of the State and local criminal justice systems—police and judges, prosecutors and defenders, corrections officers, legislators, and city council members.[24]

In 1982, under its first Presidentially appointed Director, James K. Stewart, a former Oakland, California, police official, the National Institute of Justice (NIJ) has funded recent Police Foundation studies, including the Minneapolis domestic violence experiment, and has been involved in community control of crime projects, along with other current goals. These include in the police field reduction of the demand for and supply of illegal drugs; reduction of violent crime through identifying and apprehending the career criminal; the development of non-lethal weaponry (in cooperation with the FBI); reduction of the fear of crime; and assessing the direct and indirect costs of crime.[25]

NIJ maintains the National Criminal Justice Reference Service as a tool of professionalism; containing over 80,000 references today on a computerized base, Director Stewart noted that this reference service " . . . can be one of the foundations to continue building law enforcement's reputation as a profession. . . ."[26]

Another valuable service of the NIJ is the Technology Assessment Program (TAP), which services the law enforcement community on a very practical level. Operated for the past ten years to test law enforcement-related products, through the Law Enforcement Standards Laboratory of the National Bureau of Standards or through private technical laboratories, TAP has an advisory council of federal, state, and local law enforcement officials who assess technological needs and recommends evaluation priorities. Three committees compose this council: weapons and protective equipment, chaired by an FBI supervisory Special Agent assigned to the Firearms Training Unit at the FBI Academy; the deputy commissioner of the New York Division of Criminal Justice heads the communications equipment committee; and the director of the Illinois Police Laboratory chairs the systems committee. Periodic reports and newsletters are issued to inform the entire law enforcement community of test results on various products, recently reports on ballistic vests, pistols, and communications equipment.[27]

ACCREDITATION

Police professionalism in the 21st century will involve the community service mode of policing, tailored to individual communities and neighborhoods, and based on the research conducted in the 1970s and beyond. In addition, there is a movement toward the professionalism of police agencies through accreditation that began in the 1980s by police leadership, including the largest association of police executives, the IACP. By definition, accreditation "is attaining professional stature."[28]

In 1979, the Commission on Accreditation for Law Enforcement Agencies was formed, through the efforts of four police executive organizations which represent some four-fifths of America's police agencies: the IACP, the National Sheriffs' Association (NSA), the National Association of Black Law Enforcement Executives (NOBLE), and the Police Executive Research Forum (PERF). (PERF was formed at the instigation of Patrick Murphy and the Police Foundation for college graduate police chiefs of the country's largest police agencies.) While initially funded by a start-up grant from the Law Enforcement Assistance Administration (LEAA), the Commission is now supported by accreditation fees from police departments and from private sector grants.

Each of the four police organizations developed preliminary accreditation standards in the six major areas that the standards covered: (1) law enforcement role, responsibilities, and relationships with other agencies; (2) organization, management, and administration; (3) personnel administration; (4) law enforcement operations; (5) prisoner and court-related services; and (6) auxiliary and technical services. Almost a thousand standards were developed to help increase police agency capabilities to prevent and control crime, to enhance agency effectiveness and efficiency in the delivery of law enforcement services, to improve cooperation with other law enforcement agencies and other components of the criminal justice system, and, finally, to increase citizen and police employee confidence in the goals, objectives, and practices of the police agency.[29]

The whole commission, composed of 11 members from the law enforcement community and 10 from private and public sectors, after considerable testing in the police community, approved the standards. The commission, appointed after unanimous consent of the president and executive directors of each of the founding law enforcement associations, consists of leaders in local and state government, education, the judiciary, labor, and business, in addition to chiefs of police, sheriffs, and leaders in law enforcement education. The commission's authority for standards-setting is derived from the four law enforcement associations and the accreditation process is completely voluntary.[30]

The commissioners adopted the FBI rule on the use of deadly force:

> . . . an officer may use deadly force only when the officer reasonably believes that the action is in defense of human life, including the officer's own life, or in defense of any person in immediate danger of serious physical injury.[31]

In a Tennessee case, the Supreme Court of the United States recently struck down the old common law rule that an officer may shoot at any fleeing felon, thus this standard brings the professional department in line with the law. More important, this standard brings law enforcement closer to our society's increasingly high regard for human life. This, and the other standards, reflect a need for "written policies in today's litigious society," according to the new executive director of the commission, former police chief Ken Medeiros. In 1985, Mederiros replaced the commission's first executive director, James Cotter, who had been in charge of the FBI's National Academy police training program from 1962 to 1977.[32]

The commission began accepting applications for the accreditation process, which takes 18 to 24 months, in the fall of 1983. Just four years later 51 police agencies had been accredited and another 560 were in the accreditation process.[33] Because the initial start-up funding grant for the accreditation commission came from a federal agency, and because there has been an historic distrust of federal law enforcement among some police chiefs, there has been some initial criticism of the accreditation process, particularly in California and New York. These were the first two states to establish minimum standards for training law enforcement officers, almost thirty years ago, and some chiefs in those states maintain that their state standards are better than the accreditation commission's requirements. One California chief was quoted, in a newspaper article on accreditation, as saying that "We don't need someone back in Washington to tell us how to behave."[34]

As of 1987, no police departments in New York State and only two in California had been accredited, one of which was the San Diego County Sheriff's Department. So far, the Midwest and the South are best represented among states with departments accredited or involved in the accreditation process: Ohio has 55; Illinois with 54; Florida, 53; Massachusetts, 47; Texas has 42; Georgia, 30; and Virginia with 27. As the Tallahassee, Florida, City Manager said:

> Accreditation represents a culmination of a growing professionalism. ... accreditation encourages others to strive for the best.[35]

This is an exciting, innovative, and challenging era in policing. This new Renaissance has parallels to the already established professions in education and use of applied research. Policing has rediscovered its roots in the community. With the help, but not control, of the FBI and other agencies of the federal government, in the 21st century, to paraphrase Gilbert and Sullivan's 19th century "H. M. S. Pinafore:" "When constabulary duty's to be done, the policeman's lot is not a happy one," but it will be a more professional one.

Notes to Chapter 21

1. Critchley, 1967. 52.
2. Trojanowicz, 1986. 56.
3. Skolnick, 1986. 214–215.
4. Moore, 1970. 7.
5. Holsburg, 1987.
6. Trojanowicz, 1986. FBI, 1986d. 250–316.
7. Sardino, 1971. 16–17.
8. McArdle, 1972. 10–11.
9. Knapp, 1975. 3–8.
10. MacAleese, 1978. 6–8.
11. Police Foundation, 1981.
12. Ibid, iii.
13. Reiss, 1986. 367–372.
14. Englewood Cliffs, N.J., Prentise Hall. 1972.
15. Ayres, 1975. 403.
16. Police Foundation, 1985.
17. Murphy, 1977. 256.
18. Ford Foundation, 1970. i.
19. Ibid, 4–5.

20. Kelling, 1974. iii.
21. Deakin, 1986. 4–5.
22. Sherman, 1984. 1.
23. Horwitz, 1987. 1.
24. National Institute of Justice, 1985. 1.
25. Criminal Justice International, 1987. 23.
26. Stewart, 1985. 15.
27. Shubin, 1987. 11–13.
28. Joseph, 1980. 6.
29. Cotter, 1983. 19–21.
30. Commission on Accreditation, 1984.
31. Commission on Accreditation, 1987a. 1–2.
32. McAllister, 1987. A-7.
33. Commission on Accreditation, 1987b.
34. McAllister, 1987. A-7.
35. Medeiros, 1987.

BIBLIOGRAPHY

UNPUBLISHED MATERIAL

Appel, C.A. 1932a. Memorandum for Director 7/21. FBIHQ file 62-22716-8.

—— 1932b. Memorandum for Director 7/26. FBIHQ file 62-22716-6.

—— 1933. Letter to Sheriff Ross Smiley Clarksville, TX, 3/2.

Baker, Newman F. 1934. Letter to J. Edgar Hoover 4/5. FBIHQ file 80-11-402.

Broders, Eugene. 1985. Telephonic interview by author, 6/6.

Bureau of Investigation, 1925. "Outline of the Organization of the Division of Identification, Bureau of Investigation, 7/1/25."

—— 1932. Summary memorandum 10/26. FBIHQ file 62-22716-42x.

Burns, William J., 1922. Letter to Baltimore 9/19. FBIHQ file 66-892-2.

Casper, J.J. 1967. Memorandum to Mr. Mohr, "Police Training: Legal Materials" 2/1. FBIHQ file 94-3-1.

—— 1966. Memorandum, "Quinn Tamm, Executive Director, IACP," 2/21. FBIHQ file 94-1-1531x.

—— 1964. Memorandum to Mr. Mohr, "Quinn Tamm, Executive Director, IACP," 11/2. FBIHQ file 67-37651-467.

Clegg, Hugh H. 1925. Memo to Mr. Tolson 2/4. FBIHQ file 62-28063-14.

—— 1935a. Memorandum for Director 7/12. FBIHQ file 66-5025-2X.

—— 1935b. Memorandum for Director 7/19. FBIHQ file 66-5025-2x1.

—— 1935c. Memorandum for Director 8/5. FBIHQ file 66-5025-25.

—— 1935d. Memorandum for Director 7/31.

—— 1935e. Memorandum for Director 11/7. FBIHQ file 66-5025-111X.

—— 1935f. Memorandum for Mr. Tolson 2/4. FBIHQ file 62-28063-14.

—— 1937. Memorandum for Director 5/17. FBIHQ file 67-80010-22.

—— 1949. Executive conference memorandum for Director, 10/18. FBIHQ file 1:1152-143.

—— 1950. Memorandum for Mr. Tolson 9/18. "Police Training Institute, University of Louisville."

—— 1953. Executive Conference memorandum on Civil Rights for Mr. Tolson 6/29. FBIHQ file 1-1152.

—— 1976. "The Origin of the FBIHQ Academy" 12/16. MS.

Coffey, E.P. 1934. Memorandum for Mr. Tolson 6/9.

—— 1935a. Memorandum for Mr. Edwards 6/27. FBIHQ file 66-5025-2.

—— 1935b. Memorandum "Reading Assignments," for Mr. Edwards 9/26. FBIHQ file 66-5025-44.

_____ 1938. Memorandum for Mr. Nathan. 7/13. FBIHQ file 67-12019-253.

Cummings, Homer. 1934. "Address Delivered at the Attorney General's Conference on Crime" Constitution Hall, Washington, D.C. 12/10. FBIHQ file 62-32578-607X.

FBIHQ, 1986. Office of Congressional and Public Affairs biography of Clarence M. Kelley.

Gearty, G.C. 1954 memo to Mr. Harbo "College Credit and Recognition for Bureau Training Schools," 6/9. FBIHQ file 1-1152-324.

Hardy, Samuel W. 1929. Letter to Director 12/26. FBIHQ file 62-22716-1.

Hazen, Robert, 1987. Latent fingerprint specialist, interview with author 3/17/87, FBIHQ, Washington, D.C.

Hendon, R.C. 1939. Memorandum for Mr. Tolson 9/21.

_____ 1941. Memorandum for Mr. Nichols re E.P. Coffey 10/14. FBIHQ file 67-12019-293.

Holsberg, Karl. 1987. Officer, Fairfax County Police Department, interview with author 5/20. Lake Anne Center, Reston, Virginia.

"Hoover, John Edgar, Officers' Reserve Corps, U.S. Army, Military Intelligence Reserve," Research Unit OCPA document, n.d. FBIHQ.

Hoover, John Edgar. 1925. Untitled speech before the IACP at Indianapolis, IN, 7/14.

_____ 1927. Memorandum for Mr. Maynor, 4/1. FBIHQ file 66-1631-458.

_____ 1930. Memorandum for the Attorney General 6/17.

_____ 1931a. Speech "Bureau of Investigation," Cincinnati, Ohio, Lawyers' Club 2/12.

_____ 1931b. Speech "Modern Aids to Police Work" before IACP at St. Petersburg, FL 10/13.

_____ 1933. Memorandum for Attorney General 9/18.

_____ 1934a. Memorandum for Mr. William Stanley, Assistant to the Attorney General 1/15. FBIHQ file 80-11-300.

_____ 1943b. Letter to Newman F. Baker 4/10/34. FBIHQ file 80-11-402.

_____ 1934c. "Detection and Apprehension" Address before Attorney General's Crime Conference 12/11. FBIHQ file 62-32578-90.

_____ 1935a. Memorandum for Mr. Clegg, 10/21. FBIHQ file 66-5025-74.

_____ 1935b. Memorandum for the Attorney General. 10/21.

_____ 1935c. Letter to S. Lennart Cederborg, 2/16. FBIHQ file 62-28063-17.

_____ 1936a. Memorandum for Mr. Tolson, 7/4.

_____ 1936b. "Science in Law Enforcement," address before the International Association of Identification, Dallas, Texas. 9/29.

_____ 1937a. Memorandum for Mr. Coffey 8/26. FBIHQ file 67-12019-228.

_____ 1937b. Memorandum for Mr. Clegg 5/28. FBIHQ file 67-80006-70.

_____ 1937c. Address "Adventures in Scientific Law Enforcement," Kalamazoo College, Kalamazoo, MI 6/14.

_____ 1938. Address "Law Enforcement—A Profession," before Peace Officers Association of California, San Diego, California 10/6.

_____ 1938a. Address "Soldiers—In Peacetime," before American Legion, Los Angeles, CA 9/19.

_____ 1945. Letter to Mr. Edmund P. Coffey 11/5.

_____ 1947a. SAC letter 35, 3/31. "Police training schools in connection with colleges and universities." FBIHQ file 1-1152.

_____ 1947b. Memorandum for Mr. Tolson, 9/12. FBIHQ file 1-1152-135.

_____ 1949a. SAC letter 83, 9/6. "Police training schools." FBIHQ file 1-1152.

_____ 1949b. SAC letter 104, 11/16. "Police training schools—Colleges and Universities." FBIHQ file 1-1152.

_____ 1951. Letter to Rear Admiral Sidney W. Souers, 10/2. FBIHQ file 1-1152-242.

_____ 1956a. Memorandum to Attorney General, "Civil Rights Matters," 1/9. FBIHQ file 1-1152.

_____ 1956b. Memorandum to Attorney General, "Specialized Civil Rights Schools," 6/5. FBIHQ file 1-1152.

_____ 1956c. Letter to Earl Warren 5/8. FBIHQ file 1-1152.

Jones, J. M. 1983. "Latent Fingerprint Section, Identification Division," 2/15, MS.

_____ 1985. Special Agent-Section Chief, Latent Fingerprint Section, Identification Division. Interview with author 12/16 at FBIHQ, Washington, D.C.

Jones, M. A. 1960. Memorandum to Mr. DeLoach, "Orlando W. Wilson," 2/25. FBIHQ file 62-54900-19x2.

_____ 1960a. Memorandum to Mr. DeLoach, "William H. Parker, Chief of Police, Los Angeles, CA," 12/23. FBIHQ file 62-96042-74.

_____ 1972. Memorandum to Mr. Bishop, "Quinn Tamm, Executive Director, IACP, Meeting with Mr. Gray." 6/5.

Joseph, Kenneth E. 1970. "A Study of the Federal Bureau of Investigation's Contribution to Law Enforcement Training and Education in the United States," thesis, University of Michigan, for Ph. D., College of Education.

Kelley, Clarence M. 1973 "Developments in the Role of the FBIHQ Laboratory" SAC memorandum 11/28, #53-73.

Lester, W.H.D., 1932. Memorandum for the Director 11/25. FBIHQ file 62-22716-73.

"List of Speeches and Public Statements by Director, 1925–1971," Research Unit, Office of Congressional and Public Affairs document, n.d. FBIHQ.

Los Angeles letter 1956, to Director. "August Vollmer Memorial Scholarship Fund." 10/23, FBIHQ file 62-28063-47.

Los Angeles letter 1955, to Director. "William H. Parker, Chief of Police, Los Angeles Police Department," 10/17. FBIHQ file 62-96042-24.

A. S. M. 1926. Memorandum for Mr. Hoover, 3/18. FBIHQ file 66-1631-229.

Mason, E. D. 1955, Memorandum to Mr. Tolson, "William H. Parker, Chief of Police, Los Angeles," 10/17. FBIHQ file 62-96042-26.

Medeiros, Kenneth H. interview with author 8/24/87, Fairfax, VA.

Miller, Fred M. 1956. "A Digest of the Early History of the FBIHQ Laboratory," Washington, D.C., January. FBIHQ, MS.

Murphy, Patrick V. interview with author 6/26/86, Council of Mayors, Washington, D.C.

Nathan, H. 1932. Memorandum for the Director, 7/11. FBIHQ file 94-3-1.

O'Connor, H. T. 1940. Memorandum for Mr. Hince 6/24. FBIHQ file 67-25768-124.

Parker, W. H. 1962. "The Police Service—A Key to Community Quality," speech at Salt Lake City, 9/6. FBIHQ file 62-96042-85.

Schilder, L.C. 1936. Memorandum for the Director 3/20. FBIHQ file 67-443-C-49.

Suydam, Henry. 1935. Memorandum for J. Edgar Hoover 7/25.

Tolson, Clyde. 1930. Memorandum for the Director 6/9.

———— 1935a. Memorandum for the Director "Invitations to attend Bureau's Police Training School" 6/13.

———— 1935b. Memorandum for the Director 6/21. FBIHQ file 66-2554-157X.

———— 1935c. Memorandum for the Director, 11/7. FBIHQ file 1-4-112X.

———— 1935d. Memorandum for the Director 7/25. Re "Suggestion letter #99." FBIHQ file 94-3-1.

———— 1936a. Memorandum for the Director 6/30. FBIHQ file 67-80010-18.

———— 1936b. Memorandum for the Director 7/10. FBIHQ file 66-2554-305x.

———— 1936c. Memorandum for the Director, 6/18. FBIHQ file 66-2554-274X.

———— 1947. Executive Conference memorandum for the Director, 9/19. "Police field training." FBIHQ file 1-1152-44.

———— 1949. Executive Conference memorandum for the Director, 12/20. "Police Training." FBIHQ file 1-1152-159.

———— 1950. Executive Conference memorandum for the Director, "Training—Civil Rights Schools," 5/31. FBIHQ file 1-1152-185.

Wickersham, George. 1930. Letter to Attorney General 6/12.

White, Briggs J. 1986. Interview with author 6/9, Oakton, VA.

Whitehead, Don 1955. Research material from FBIHQ.

Whitely, R. 1935. Letter to Director 9/6. FBIHQ file 66-5025-38.

Zolbe, Paul A. 1986. Interview with author 10/20 at FBIHQ, Washington, D.C.

PUBLISHED MATERIAL

Adams, Reed. 1976. "Criminal Justice: An Emerging Academic Profession and Discipline," *Journal of Criminal Justice*, 4:303–314.

American Polygraph Association Newsletter, 1985. 18:3.

Annual Reports of the Attorney General of the United States, 1924–1984. Washington, D.C., Government Printing Office.

Ayres, Richard M. 1975. "Police Unions: A Step Toward Professionalism?" *Journal of Police Science and Administration*. 3:-4.

Baker, Mark. 1985. *Cops: Their Lives in Their Own Words*. New York, Simon & Schuster.

Banner, Conrad S. & Stock, Robert M. 1985. "The FBI's Approach to Automatic Fingerprint Identification," *FBI Law Enforcement Bulletin*, 54:1. 2.

Bishop, Demery R. & Schuessler, Timothy J. 1982. "The NCIC's Missing Person File," *FBI Law Enforcement Bulletin*, 51:8.

Bishop, Jerry E. 1986. "What's New: Plastic, Blood and More Eggs," *The Wall Street Journal*, December 22. 21.

Bohardt, Paul H. 1982. "Policing, 1950's," *The Police Chief*, 49:11.

Bopp, William J. 1977. *"O.W." O.W. Wilson and the Search for a Police Profession*. Port Washington, New York. Kennikat Press.

_____ 1984. *Crises in Police Administration.* Springfield, Ill., Charles C Thomas.

Bopp, William J. & Schultz, Donald O. 1972. *A Short History of American Law Enforcement.* Springfield, Ill., Charles C Thomas.

Brandstatter, A. F. 1967. "History of Police Education in the United States" *Police Science Degree Programs,* Office of Law Enforcement Assistance, University of Maryland.

Broderick, John J. 1980. "1994: Training and Education in Law Enforcement," *The Police Chief,* September, 37–39.

Buraker, Carroll D. 1977. "The Educated Police Officer: Asset or Liability," *The Police Chief,* August. 90–94.

Buraker, Carroll O. & Stover, William K. 1984. "Automated Fingerprint Identification: Regional Application of Technology," *FBI Law Enforcement Bulletin,* 52:8. 1–5.

Bureau of Investigation, 1930. *Uniform Crime Reporting: A Booklet Published for the Information of Law Enforcement Officials and Agencies.* Washington, D.C.

_____ 1934. *Fugitives Wanted By Police,* 4:8, 4:9.

Carte, Gene E. 1976. "Technology versus Personnel: Notes on the History of Police Professionalism Reform," *Journal of Police Science and Administration,* 4:3.

Carte, Gene E. & Carte, Elaine H. 1975. *Police Reform in the United States: The Era of August Vollmer, 1905-1932,* Berkeley, University of California Press.

Cary, John H. & Weinberg, Julius. 1975. *The Social Fabric: American Life from the Civil War to the Present,* Boston, Little, Brown.

Catton, Bruce, 1961. *The Coming Fury: The Centennial History of the Civil War* Vol. 1, New York, Doubleday.

Chronister, Jay; Gansneder, Bruce M.; LeDoux, John C.; Tully, Edward J. 1982. *A Study of Factors Influencing Continuing Education of Police Officers.* FBI/DOJ, July, n.p.

Chapman, Samuel G. and St. Johnson, T. Eric. 1962. *The Police Heritage in England and America.* East Lansing, Mich., Michigan State University.

Collier, Rex. 1933. "Science Versus Crime," *The Evening Star,* Washington, D.C. 2/13.

Commission on Accreditation for Law Enforcement Agencies, 1984. "Accreditation Program Overview," pamphlet, n.p.

_____ 1987. *Commission Update* XXXV:Summer.

_____ 1987a. *Standards for Law Enforcement Agencies,* n.p.

_____ 1987b. "Information" newsletter, April 8.

Committee on Uniform Crime Records. 1929. International Association of Chiefs of Police, *Uniform Crime Reporting: A Complete Manual for Police.* New York, J.J. Little & Ives.

_____ 1959. *Uniform Crime Reports, Special Issue,* Washington, D.C., Government Printing Office.

Conley, John A. 1977. "Criminal Justice History as a Field of Research: A Review of the Literature 1960–1975," *Journal of Criminal Justice,* 5:

Cotter, James. 1983. "Law Enforcement Accreditation: A Big Step Toward Professionalism," *FBI Law Enforcement Bulletin,* 52:9.

_____ 1986 (ed) *FBI National Academy, 1935-1985,* privately printed.

Criminal Justice International. 1987. "James K. Stewart" 3:1. Jan.–Feb.

Critchley, T.A. 1967. *A History of Police in England and Wales.* Constable & Company Ltd. reprinted 1972 Montclair, N.J. Patterson Smith.

Curran, James T.; Fowler, Austin & Ward, Richard H. (eds.). 1973. *Police and Law Enforcement,* New York, AMS Press.

Dalley, A.F. 1975. "University vs. Non-University Graduated Policemen: A Study of Police Attitudes," *Journal of Police Science and Administration,* 3:4. 458–468.

Davis, Edward M. 1982. "Policing 1960's and 1970's," *The Police Chief,* 49:11.

Deakin, Thomas J. 1978. "Police Organization in the United States," *Policia Espanola,* Madrid, Spain. 16:1.

———— 1986. "The Police Foundation." *FBI Law Enforcement Bulletin,* 55:11. 1–10.

Demaris, Ovid. 1975. *The Director: An Oral Biography of J. Edgar Hoover.* New York, Harper's Magazine Press.

Depue, Roger L. 1986. "An American Response to an Era of Violence," *FBI Law Enforcement Bulletin,* 55:12. 2–5.

Deutsch, Albert. 1955. *The Trouble With Cops.* New York, Crown.

Dewey, John. 1916. *Democracy and Education.* New York, Macmillan.

Dilworth, Donald C. (ed). 1976. *The Blue and the Brass: American Policing 1890–1910,* Gaithersburg, MD, Police Management & Operations Division, International Association of Chiefs of Police.

———— 1977a (ed) *Silent Witness: The Emergence of Scientific Criminal Investigations,* Gaithersburg, MD, Bureau of Operations and Research, International Association of Chiefs of Police.

———— 1977b (ed) *Identification Wanted: Development of the American Criminal Identification System 1893–1943,* Gaithersburg, MD, Police Management & Operations Division, International Association of Chiefs of Police.

Doran, William Y. 1982. "The FBI Laboratory: Fifty Years," *Journal of Forensic Science,* October 743–748.

Dorn, Walter H. 1961. "Man Dog Teams Serve St. Louis Most Effectively," *FBI Law Enforcement Bulletin,* 30 (March) 3–6.

Douglas, John E. & Burgess, Alan E. 1986. "Criminal Profiling," *FBI Law Enforcement Bulletin,* 55:12. 9–12.

Douthhit, Nathan. 1975. "Enforcement and Nonenforcement Roles in Policing: A Historical Inquiry," *Journal of Police Science and Administration,* 3:3.

Eastman, George D. & McCain, James A. 1981. "Education, Professionalism, and Law Enforcement in Historical Perspective, *Journal of Police Science and Administration,* 9:2.

Elliott, J.F. 1973. *The "New" Police.* Springfield, Ill., Charles C Thomas.

Eldefonso, Edward; Coffey, Alan & Grace, Richard C. 1982. *Principles of Law Enforcement.* New York, John Wiley & Sons.

"Establishment of a Technical Laboratory in the Division of Investigation, The," 1934, *Fugitives Wanted By Police,* 3:5.

"Exercises Marking Termination of First FBI Police Training School," 1935. *FBI Law Enforcement Bulletin,* 4:11.

Farris, Edward A. 1982. "Five Decades of American Policing, 1932–1982," *The Police Chief,* 49:11.

Federal Bureau of Investigation, 1937. *FBI Law Enforcement Bulletin,* 5:6. 12.

———— 1957. "FBI Training Assistance For Local Police," *FBI Law Enforcement Bulletin,* 26:5. 16.

———— 1961. "Quinn Tamm, Assistant Director, Retires From FBI" *FBI Law Enforcement Bulletin,* 30:3. 10.

———— 1961b. "Long Range Plan of Police Training Is Called a Success," *FBI Law Enforcement Bulletin,* 30:4. 20–25.

———— 1972. "A Tribute to Cooperative Spirit," *FBI Law Enforcement Bulletin,* 41:2.

———— 1974. *Report: Second Annual Symposium on Crime Laboratory Development,* 9/23–27. Quantico, Virginia.

———— 1975. *Crime Laboratory Digest,* April. 3.

———— 1976. "Ever Ready to Assist: The FBI Disaster Squad," *FBI Law Enforcement Bulletin,* 44:10. 27–31.

———— 1976b. "FBI's National Executive Institute," *FBI Law Enforcement Bulletin,* 47:9. 3–8.

———— 1977. *Crime Resistance,* Washington, D.C. Government Printing Office.

———— 1977b. "Message from the Director," & "Crime Resistance: A Report," *FBI Law Enforcement Bulletin,* 44.3. 1, 3–11.

———— 1981. *Crime in the United States.* Washington, D.C. Government Printing Office.

———— 1983. *The F.B.I.: The First 75 Years.* Washington, D.C., FBI.

———— 1983b. *NCIC Newletter,* Spring.

———— 1984. "NCIC Report on the Wanted Person File Survey, April, 1984," 10/17. Washington, D.C. FBI.

———— 1986. *Fingerprint Identification.* Washington, D.C. U. S. Government Printing Office.

———— 1986b. *National Crime Information Center: The Investigative Tool,* June. Washington, D.C. FBI.

———— 1986c. *NCIC Newsletter,* n.p. 86-2. 3.

———— 1986d. *Crime in U.S.* Washington, D.C. Government Printing Office.

Fike, Louis B.; Harlan, John P. & McDowell, Charles P. 1977. "Criminal Justice Curricula: A Reflective Glance." *Journal of Police Science and Administration* 5:4. 456–464.

Fogelson, Robert M. 1977. *Big City Police.* Cambridge, Mass., Harvard University Press.

Ford Foundation, August 1970. *A More Effective Arm.* n.p.

Fosdick, Raymond D. 1920. *American Police Systems.* The Century Co., reprinted 1969 Montclair, NJ Patterson Smith.

Future of Policing, The: A Panel Report, 1984. William O. Douglas Institute for the Study of Contemporary Social Problems, Seattle, Washington.

Gazell, James A. 1974. "O. W. Wilson's Essential Legacy for Police Administration." *Journal of Police Science and Administration,* 2:4.

Germann, A. C. 1959. "Scientific Training for Cops." *Journal of Criminal Law, Criminology and Police Science,* 50:206.

———— 1967. "Education and Professional Law Enforcement." *Journal of Criminal Law, Criminology and Police Science,* 58:4.

"Graduation Exercises—13th Session, FBI National Police Academy," 1940. *FBI Law Enforcement Bulletin,* 9:5.

Green, James A. & Young, Alfred J. 1976. " 'The Finest'—A Brief History of the New York City Police Department," *FBI Law Enforcement Bulletin,* 44:12.

Hall, James P. 1978. *Peacekeeping in America: A Developmental Study of American Law Enforcement: Philosophy and Systems,* Dubuque, Iowa.

Haller, Mark H. 1976. "Historical Roots of Police Behavior: Chicago, 1890–1925," *Law & Society,* Winter, 1976, 303–323.

Holden, Richard N. 1986. *Modern Police Management.* Englewood Cliffs, N.J., Prentice-Hall.

Hollingsworth, Dan, 1982. "Policing, 1940's," *The Police Chief,* 49:11.

Hoover, John Edgar. 1932. *Fugitives Wanted By Police* 1 (January) 1.

———— 1935a. "Introduction," *FBI Law Enforcement Bulletin,* 4 (October) 1.

———— 1935b. "Modern Problems of Law Enforcement," Address before the IACP convention 7/9. Washington, D.C., Government Printing Office.

———— 1936. "Introduction," *FBI Law Enforcement Bulletin,* 5 (June) 1.

———— 1937. "Introduction," *FBI Law Enforcement Bulletin,* 6 (April) 1.

———— 1944. "Introduction," *FBI Law Enforcement Bulletin,* 13 (June) 1.

———— 1947. "Introduction," *FBI Law Enforcement Bulletin,* 16 (December) 1.

———— 1964. "Message from the Director," *FBI Law Enforcement Bulletin,* 33 (May) 1.

———— 1972. "Professional Training, A Vital Need," *Justice Magazine,* 1:1.

———— 1973. "The Role of Identification in Law Enforcement: An Historical Adventure," *FBI Law Enforcement Bulletin,* 41:3. 3.

Hoover, Larry T. 1975. *Police Educational Characteristics and Curricula,* Law Enforcement Assistance Administration, Washington, D.C. Government Printing Office. July.

Horan, James D. 1967. *The Pinkertons: The Detective Dynasty That Made History.* New York, Crown.

Horwitz, Sari. 1987. "D.C. Police to Make Arrests in Domestic Violence Disputes," *The Washington Post,* 6/3. A-1.

IACP, 1908. "Proceedings of the Annual Conventions," 25.

———— *Proceedings of the Annual IACP Conventions,* 1927.

———— 1964. "International Association of Chiefs of Police: Its History and Purpose," *The Police Chief,* 42:10.

———— 1970. *Law Enforcement Education Directory.* Washington, D.C.

———— 1976. *The Police Chief Executive Report.* Law Enforcement Assistance Administration, Washington, D.C.

———— 1986. "In Memoriam, Quinn Tamm," *The Police Chief,* March, 10.

Jacobs, James B. & Magdovitz, Samuel B. 1977. "At LEEP's End: A Review of the Law Enforcement Education Program," *Journal of Police Science and Administration,* 5:1.

Johnson, David R. 1979. *Policing the Urban Underworld,* Philadelphia, Temple University Press.

——— 1981. *American Law Enforcement: A History.* St. Louis, Mo., Forum Press.

Joseph, Kenneth E. 1980. "Law Enforcement Accreditation: Meeting Tomorrow's Challenges Today." *FBI Law Enforcement Bulletin,* 49:10.

Joseph, Kenneth E. & O'Connor, James A. 1979. "The FBI Academy: 1984 *FBI Law Enforcement Bulletin,* 48:7.

Kelling, George L. et al, 1974. *The Kansas City Preventive Patrol Experiment: A Summary Report.* Washington, D.C. Police Foundation.

Kelley, Clarence M. 1974. "Message from the Director." *FBI Law Enforcement Bulletin,* 43:6. 1.

Kelly, Martin A. 1973. "The First Urban Policeman," *Journal of Police Science and Administration,* 1:1.

Kenney, John P. 1964. *The California Police.* Springfield, Ill., Charles C Thomas.

Kerr, Clark. 1964. *The Uses of the University.* Cambridge, Mass., Harvard University Press.

Killinger, George G.; Cromwell, Paul F., Jr. 1975. *Issues in Law Enforcement.* Boston, Holbrook Press.

Kirkham, George L. 1974. "A Professor's 'Street Lessons' " *FBI Law Enforcement Bulletin,* 42 (March) 14–22.

Knapp, Norman R. 1975. "Coordinated Team Patrol: From Experiment to Implementation" *FBI Law Enforcement Bulletin,* 44:12.

Kreml, Franklin M., 1982. "Policing, 1930's," *The Police Chief,* 49:11.

Kuykendall, Jack L. & Hernandez, Armand P. 1975. "Undergraduate Justice System Education and Training at San Jose State University: An Historical Perspective." *Journal of Criminal Justice,* 3:111.

Lankes, George A. 1971. "How Should We Educate the Police?" *The Journal of Criminal Law, Criminology, and Police Science,* 61:4.

Lathan, Frank Jr. 1984. "A Historical Look at Police Badges," *Law and Order,* 32:8.

Law Enforcement Assistance Administration, 1975. *The National Manpower Survey of the Criminal Justice System.* Vol. 5. "Criminal Justice Education and Training." Washington, D.C. Government Printing Office.

Lee, Edward L. II. 1971. "An Overview of American Police History," *The Police Chief,*" 48:10.

Lowenthal, Max 1950. *The Federal Bureau of Investigation.* New York, William Sloane Associates.

Lyford, George & Wood, Udy. 1983. "National Crime Information Center," *FBI Law Enforcement Bulletin,* 51:3.

McAllister, Bill, 1987. "Spurred by Dramatic Rise in Lawsuits, Police Agencies Warm to Accreditation, *The Washington Post,* 3/17. A-7.

McArdle, Edward C. & Betjemann, William N. 1972. "A Return to Neighborhood Police," *FBI Law Enforcement Bulletin,* 41:7.

MacAleese, Greg. 1978. "Crime Stoppers," *FBI Law Enforcement Bulletin,* 47:8.

McAuliff, 1892, v. Mayor and Board of Aldermen of New Bedford, 155 Mass. 216.

McClure, James. 1984. *Cop World,* New York, Random House.

McLaren, Roy C. 1973. "In Memoriam: Orlando Winfield Wilson," *The Police Chief,* 37:1.

Mayor's Message with Accompanying Documents to the City Council of the City of St. Louis at its April Session, 1868. St. Louis, Mo., Democrat Book and Job Printing House.

Mecum, Richard V. 1979. "Police Professionalism: A New Look At an Old Topic," *The Police Chief,* August, 46–49.

Meltzer, Milton, 1960. *Mark Twain Himself.* New York, Thos. Y. Crowell.

Moore, Mark H. & Kelling, George L. 1983. " 'To Serve and Protect': Learning From Police History," *The Public Interest,* Winter.

Moore, Wilbert E. 1970. *The Professions: Roles and Rules.* New York, Russell Sage Foundation.

More, Harry. W. 1976. (ed.) *The American Police: Text and Readings.* St. Paul, Minn., West.

Morris, Norval. 1986. "Innovations in Policing: A Review of *The New Blue Line. Michigan Law Review,* 84:69.

Mosse, George L. (ed.). 1975. *Police Forces in History.* London, Sage Publications.

Murphy, Patrick V. & Plate, Thomas. 1977. *Commissioner: A View From the Top of American Law Enforcement.* New York, Simon & Schuster.

Nash, J. Robert. 1973. *Bloodletters and Badmen.* New York, M. Evans.

National Advisory Commission on Civil Disorders, 1968. *Report of.* Washington, D.C., U. S. Government Printing Office, 1970.

National Institute of Justice, 1985. *Shaping Criminal Justice Policy.* Washington, D.C. Government Printing Office.

Neudorfer, Charles D. 1986. "Fingerprint Automation," *FBI Law Enforcement Bulletin,* 55:3. 3–8.

The New York Times, 1986. "FBI Says Reported Crimes Rose 8% in First Half of Year." October 15. 15.

Nickell, Joe. 1980. "The Two Will Wests'; A New Verdict," *Journal of Police Science and Administration,* 8:4.

Parker, Alfred E. 1972. *The Berkeley Police Story.* Springfield, Ill., Charles C Thomas.

Pate, Antony M. et al. 1986. *Reducing Fear of Crime in Houston and Newark.* Police Foundation, n.p.

Poggio, Eugene C. et al. 1985. *Blueprint for the Future of the Uniform Crime Reporting Program.* U.S. Department of Justice, Washington, D.C. U.S. Government Printing Office, 1985.

Pogrebin, Mark R. & Regoli, Robert M. 1986. *Police Administrative Issues: Techniques and Functions.* Millwood, N.Y., Associated Faculty Press.

Police Foundation. 1974. *The Kansas City Preventive Patrol Experiment: A Summary Report,* Washington, D.C., Police Foundation.

———— 1981. *The Newark Foot Patrol Experiment,* Washington, D.C., Police Foundation.

———— 1985. Brochure. n.p.

Pomrenke, Norman & Campbell, B. Edward, 1987. "A Tradition of Excellence: The Southern Police Institute," *FBI Law Enforcement Bulletin,* 56:2.

Powers, Richard G. 1983. *G–Men: Hoover's FBI in American Popular Culture.* Carbondale and Edwardsville, Ill., Southern Illinois University Press.

———— 1987. *Secrecy and Power: The Life of J. Edgar Hoover.* New York, The Free Press.

President's Commission on Law Enforcement and the Administration of Justice,

1967. *Task Force Report: The Police,* Washington, D.C., U. S. Government Printing Office.

Prout, Robert S. 1972. "An Analysis of Associate Degree Programs in Law Enforcement," *The Journal of Criminal Law, Criminology, and Police Science,* 64:4.

Rathbun, Emmet A. 1985. "Interstate Identification Index," *FBI Law Enforcement Bulletin,* 54:1.

Reisman, L. E. 1967. "How Do You Educate a Policeman?" *American Association of University Women Journal,* 60:188.

Reiss, Albert J. & Tonry, Michael. 1986. *Communities and Crime.* Chicago, University of Chicago Press.

Reith, Charles. 1952. *The Blind Eye of History.* London, Faber & Faber Ltd., reprinted Montclair, N.J., Patterson Smith.

Reppetto, Thomas A. 1978. *The Blue Parade.* New York, The Free Press.

Richardson, James F. 1974. *Urban Police in the United States.* Port Washington, N.Y., Kennikat Press.

Rigler, Erik. 1985. "Frontier Justice in the Days Before NCIC," *FBI Law Enforcement Bulletin,* 54 (July) 16–22.

Robinson, Cyril D. 1978. "The Deradicalization of the Policeman: A Historical Analysis," *Crime & Delinquency.*

Rohr, John A. 1978. *Ethics for Bureaucrats.* New York, Marcel Dekker.

Rosenbaum, Dennis P. (ed). 1986. *Community Crime Prevention: Does It Work?.* Beverly Hills, Cal., Sage Publications.

Sardino, Thomas J. 1971. "The Crime Control Team," *FBI Law Enforcement Bulletin,* 40:5.

Sherman, Lawrence W. 1974. "The Sociology and the Social Reform of the American Police," *Journal of Police Science and Administration,* 2:256.

Sherman, Lawrence W. and the National Advisory Commission on Higher Education for Police Officers. 1978. *The Quality of Police Education.* San Francisco, Jossey-Bass.

Sherman, Lawrence W. & Berk, Richard A. 1984. *Minneapolis Domestic Violence Experiment,* April, Report #1. Police Foundation, n.p.

Shubin, Lester & Hernon, Jolene, 1987. "Testing Technology for Law Enforcement Agencies," *FBI Law Enforcement Bulletin* 56:1.

Skehan, James J. 1939. *Modern Police Work.* Brooklyn, N.Y., R.V. Basuino.

Skolnick, Jerome H. & Bayley, David H. 1986. *The New Blue Line.* New York, The Free Press.

Smith, Bruce. 1940. *Police Systems in the United States.* New York, Harper.

Smith, Joseph D. 1984. "Police Unions: An Historical Perspective of Causes and Organizations," *The Police Chief,* 51:11.

Stead, Philip John. (ed.). 1977. *Pioneers in Policing.* Montclair, N.J., Patterson Smith.

Stewart, James K. 1985. "National Criminal Justice Reference Service," *FBI Law Enforcement Bulletin,* 54:7.

Tafoya, William L. 1986. "Law Enforcement Beyond the Year 2000," *The Futurist,* Sept.–Oct.

Task Force Report: The Police. 1967. President's Commission on Law Enforcement and Administration of Justice, Washington, D.C.

Thompson, John L. 1968. "Uniform Crime Reporting: Historical IACP Landmark," *The Police Chief.* 46:2.

Thorwald, Jurgen. 1964. *The Century of the Detective* trans Winston, Richard & Clara. New York, Harcourt, Brace & World.

Time, 1965. 86:8 August 20. 13–18.

Tracy, Charles A. 1971. "Survey of Criminal Justice Subject Matter Baccalaureate Programs," *The Journal of Criminal Law, Criminology, and Police Science,* 61:4.

Traffic Institute brochure, n.d. "The 61st Police Administration Training Program."

Trautman, Neil E. 1986. *Law Enforcement Training.* Springfield, Ill., Charles C Thomas.

Trojanowicz, Robert C. 1985. "Michigan State's School of Criminal Justice Celebrates 50th Anniversary," *The Police Chief,* 53:8.

Trojanowicz, Robert C. & Harden, Hazel A. 1985. *The Status of Contemporary Community Policing Programs,* East Lansing, Mich. National Neighborhood Foot Patrol Center, School of Criminal Justice, Michigan State University.

Trojanowicz, Robert C. et al. 1986. *Community Policing Programs: A Twenty-Year View,* East Lansing, Mich. National Neighborhood Foot Patrol Center, School of Criminal Justice, Michigan State University.

Trojanowicz, Robert C. et al 1987. *Community Policing: Community Input Into Police Policy-Making,* East Lansing, Mich. National Neighborhood Foot Patrol Center, School of Criminal Justice, Michigan State University.

Tully, Edward J. 1986. "The Near Future: Implications for Law Enforcement," *FBI Law Enforcement Bulletin:* 55:7.

Two Hundred Years of American Criminal Justice: An LEAA Bicentennial Study. 1976. Law Enforcement Assistance Administration, U.S. Department of Justice, Washington, D.C.

U. S. Commission on Law Enforcement and Administration of Justice, 1967. *The Challenge of Crime in a Free Society.* Washington, D.C., Government Printing Office.

Ungar, Sanford J. 1975. *FBI.* Boston, Atlantic Monthly Press.

Vollmer, August. 1936. *The Police and Modern Society.* Bureau of Public Administration, University of California, reprint ed. Montclair, N.J, Patterson Smith, 1976.

———— 1919. "The Policeman as a Social Worker," *The Policeman's News,* 6:12.

———— 1937. "The Police Ideal of Service," *FBI Law Enforcement Bulletin,* 5:2. 3–6.

Vollmer, August; Monroe, David G. & Garrett, Earle W. 1931. *Police Conditions in the United States: A Report to the National Commission on Law Observance and Enforcement* Washington, D.C., U.S. Government Printing Office.

Walker, Samuel. 1976. "The Urban Police in American History: A Review of the Literature," *Journal of Police Science and Administration,* 4:3.

———— 1977. *A Critical History of Police Reform.* Lexington, Mass., Lexington Books.

———— 1980. *Popular Justice: A History of American Criminal Justice.* New York, Oxford University Press.

Waller, M.H. 1976. "Historical Roots of Police Behavior," *Law and Society Review.* Winter.

Walls, H. J. 1974. *Forensic Science: An Introduction to Scientific Crime Detection,* London, Praeger, 1968, 2 ed.

Wambaugh, Joseph. 1970. *The New Centurions.* New York, Dell.

Watson, Paul J. 1986. "Future Trends in Law Enforcement Training," *Illinois Police Officer,* 17:1.

Webster, William H. 1984a. "Director's Message," *FBI Law Enforcement Bulletin,* 53:4. 1.

_____ 1984b. "Director's Message," *FBI Law Enforcement Bulletin,* 53:11. 1.

_____ 1985. *1986 Appropriation Request: Testimony of Director before the House Subcommittee on Appropriations, April 2, 1985.* U. S. Department of Justice, Federal Bureau of Investigation, Washington, D.C.

_____ 1986. "Director's Message," *FBI Law Enforcement Bulletin,* 55:12. 1.

Weinstein, Allen & Wilson, R. Jackson. 1978. *Freedom and Crisis: An American History.* New York, Random House. V.2.

Whitehead, Alfred North. 1929. *The Aims of Education and Other Essays.* Reprinted 1957. New York, The Free Press.

Whitehead, Don. 1956. *The FBI Story: A Report to the People.* New York, Random House.

Wilson, George R. 1974. "Historic Guardians of Our Nation's Capital," *FBI Law Enforcement Bulletin,* 42:4.

Wilson, James Q. 1967. "Police Morale, Reform, and Citizen Respect: The Chicago Case," in *The Police: Six Sociological Essays,* ed. David J. Bordua, New York, John Wiley.

_____ 1968. *Varieties of Police Behavior,* Cambridge, Mass. Harvard University Press.

_____ 1975a. *Thinking About Crime.* New York, Basic Books.

_____ 1975b. "A Long Look at Crime." *FBI Law Enforcement Bulletin,* 44:2. 2–6.

_____ 1983, ed. *Crime and Public Policy.* San Francisco, ICS Press.

Wilson, James Q. & Kelling, George L., 1982. "Broken Windows," *The Atlantic Monthly.*

Wilson, O.W. 1941. *Distribution of Police Patrol Force,* Chicago, Public Administration Service.

_____ 1957. *Parker on Police.* Springfield, Ill., Charles C Thomas.

Wilson, O. W. & McLaren, Roy Clinton, 1972 (3rd ed.) *Police Administration,* New York, McGraw-Hill.

Witham, Donald C. 1985. *The American Law Enforcement Chief Executive: A Management Profile,* Washington, D.C. Police Executive Research Forum.

Woodward, Paul L. 1986. *Criminal Justice "Hot Files,"* Washington, D.C. U. S. Government Printing Office.

Zolbe, Paul A. 1980. "The Uniform Crime Reporting Program: 50 Years of Progress," *FBI Law Enforcement Bulletin* 49:9.

_____ 1985. "Blueprint for the Future of the UCR Program," *FBI Law Enforcement Bulletin* 54:10.

INDEX